Nasser's Gamble

✷

Nasser's Gamble

HOW INTERVENTION IN YEMEN CAUSED THE SIX-DAY WAR AND THE DECLINE OF EGYPTIAN POWER

Jesse Ferris

PRINCETON UNIVERSITY PRESS
PRINCETON AND OXFORD

Published by Princeton University Press, 41 William Street, Princeton, New Jersey 08540
In the United Kingdom: Princeton University Press, 6 Oxford Street, Woodstock, Oxfordshire OX20 1TW

press.princeton.edu

Jacket Photograph: *Abdul Nasser Meets the Yemeni People.* from *al-Quwwat al-Musallahah,* Egyptian weekly journal, *supplement* to volume 412, May 1, 1964. Courtesy of The Arabic Press Archive, Moshe Dayan Center, Tel Aviv University Israel.

Library of Congress Cataloging-in-Publication Data

Ferris, Jesse, 1972–
Nasser's gamble : how intervention in Yemen caused the Six-Day War and the decline of Egyptian power / Jesse Ferris.
p. cm.
Includes bibliographical references and index.
ISBN 978-0-691-15514-2 (hardcover : alk. paper) 1. Egypt—Foreign relations—1952–1970. 2. Egypt—Military policy—History—20th century. 3. Nasser, Gamal Abdel, 1918–1970. 4. Yemen, North—History—Revolution, 1962—Participation, Egyptian. 5. Yemen (Republic)—History—1962–1972. 6. Israel-Arab War, 1967—Egypt. I. Title.
DT107.83.F47 2013
956.04'6—dc23 2012028784

British Library Cataloging-in-Publication Data is available

This book has been composed in Palatino

Printed on acid-free paper. ∞

Printed in the United States of America

1 3 5 7 9 10 8 6 4 2

✷ Contents ✷

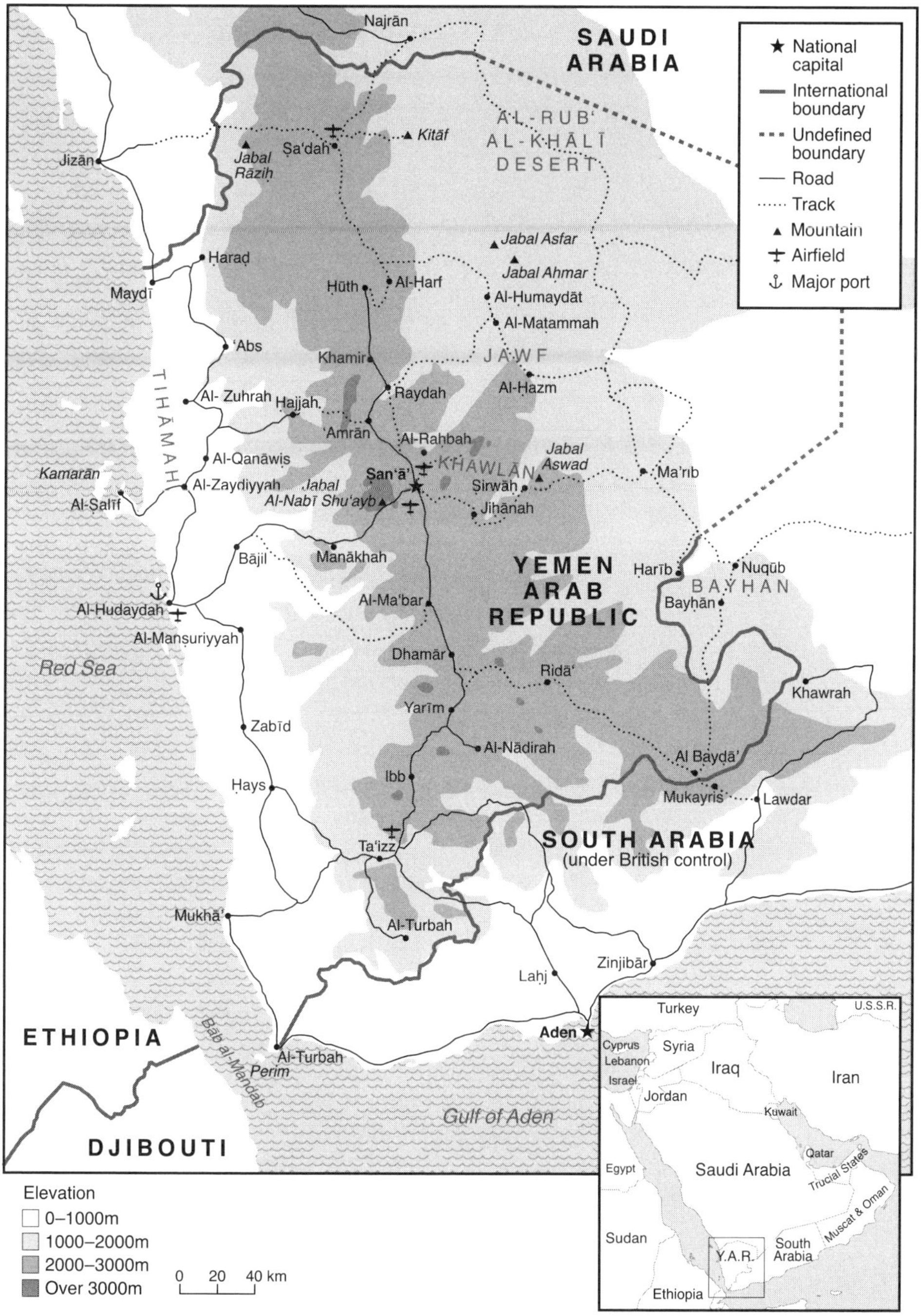

Map of Yemen ca. 1965.

✷ Acknowledgments ✷

THE OPENING LINES of a first book afford a singular opportunity to pay tribute to those who have shaped one's growth as a scholar. My intellectual story begins with Donald Kagan, who taught me all about foxes. The late Bill Odom then tried to get me into hedgehogs. Michael Doran guided me into the labyrinth of Middle Eastern politics—and suggested that I "look at Yemen" and "take Russian." I went to Stephen Kotkin seeking perspective on Russia and came away with a new approach to history.

Many other distinguished colleagues and friends have helped shape this book. Şükrü Hanioğlu, who has been unstinting in his support, read several drafts and provided many helpful comments; so did Bernard Haykel, who shared his private library with me. Elie Podeh contributed expertise in Arab politics and valuable counsel along the way. Bernard Lewis furnished invaluable references and encouragement. L. Carl Brown read through the entire manuscript and provided many insightful comments. Mark Kramer and the editorial staff at the *Journal of Cold War Studies* helped refine the ideas contained in the second and fourth chapters. Michael Oren provided helpful advice and support at key junctures. Oscar Sanchez generously shared the results of his research. David Freedel, the best language instructor I have ever known, taught me Russian. The noble-hearted Musa Odeh transformed my Arabic. Gali Dagan, a true friend, endured many hours of conversation about Yemen. Vladimir Shubin, Alexei Vassiliev, Oleg Peresypkin, Constantine Truevtsev, Zaid al-Wazir, Qassim al-Wazir, and many others shared their reminiscences. Desmond Lachman and Yotam Margalit contributed economic expertise. Rachel Green and Maayan Ravitz-Shalom jealously guarded my time. Ira Bein, Frank Grelka, Shaul Levy, Rami Livni, and Baker al-Majali assisted with research. Shane Kelley designed the maps. David Luljak prepared the index. Hanna Siurua afforded help with transliteration. David Altshuler, Richard Boylan, Gabrielle Chomentowski, Yoav Di-Capua, the late Haim Gal, Yuri Gershtein, Arch Getty, Ami Gluska, Regina Greenwell, Lorenz Luthi, Vitaly Naumkin, Michael Reynolds, Yaacov Ro'i, Eran Shalev, Anita Shapira, Reg Shrader, Uriel Simonsohn, Tawfiq Uthman, Alan Verskin, Tsering Wangyal, and Salim Yaqub all helped in various ways. I am deeply indebted to Daniel Stolz, whose thoughtful diligence made it possible to turn a rough draft into a complete manuscript in relatively short order.

I owe a special thanks to Brigitta van Rheinberg for shepherding this project deftly through to a swift conclusion. Larissa Klein, Leslie Grundfest, Dawn Hall, Dmitri Karetnikov, and the dedicated staff of Princeton University Press helped make the birth of this book a surprisingly painless experience. This project would not have been possible without the generous support of the Israel Democracy Institute, the Andrew W. Mellon Foundation, the American Council of Learned Societies, the Donald and Mary Hyde Fellowship Fund, the Kennan Institute, the Social Science Research Council, the Princeton Institute for International and Regional Studies, and the Departments of Near Eastern and Judaic Studies at Princeton University. I am indebted to the staff of the Arabic Press Archive at the Dayan Center at Tel Aviv University, whence come most of the images. I am especially grateful to Arye Carmon for drawing me into the extraordinary institution he has built and for providing such a stimulating environment for the completion of this project.

I owe so much to my parents—not only for their love but also for their discipline; to my sister, for her understanding; to Noah and Eli, for inspiring love beyond words; and especially to Kathryn, who lured me all the way from Latin class in college to an accidental PhD. This book is dedicated to Susan, whose DNA is inscribed in every line.

Introduction

A LOW-RESOLUTION PHOTOGRAPH of Egypt's international position around 1960 would have looked something like this: For the first time in centuries, perhaps millennia, Egypt was completely free of foreign domination. The great powers of the East and of the West competed against each other to arm Egypt's military, build its industry, and feed its people. Egyptian power extended deep into the Levant, further than at any time since Muhammad Ali. Egypt's charismatic president, Gamal Abdel Nasser, was the undisputed leader of the Arab world. Peace reigned, thanks to an astute leadership's assiduous avoidance of war.

A second snapshot taken a decade later would have revealed a dramatically different picture: Following the secession of Syria in 1961 and Israel's conquest of the Sinai Peninsula in 1967, the territory under Egypt's effective control had shrunk by 20 percent. Nasser's reputation was in tatters, shredded by serial setbacks at home and abroad. Egypt's economy lay in debt-ridden ruin, its future dependent on Saudi largesse. Ties with the United States had disintegrated. And the defense of the realm from Israeli attack relied on a Soviet division in quasi-occupation of the Nile Valley.

The reflexive answer to the question "What happened?" is "June 1967." Looking back nearly half a century later, Israel's crushing victory over Egypt looms so large that it makes other factors appear small and insignificant in comparison. Viewed in retrospect, the Six-Day War is an obvious watershed separating the age of Egyptian ascendance from the following two generations of inglorious stagnation. But a closer look at the gloomy picture of Egypt post-'67 reveals that many of its ingredients were already present on the eve of the Six-Day War. Egypt still possessed the Sinai desert, but its territorial expansion had long since ground to a halt; Nasser was still the most popular Arab leader, but his image was tarnished; Saudi financial aid was not yet a factor, but Egypt's economy hovered on the brink of disaster; diplomatic relations with the United States endured, but they had sunk to their lowest point since 1952; and although the Soviet armed forces were not yet welcome on Egyptian soil, Cairo's dependency on aid from Moscow had never been greater.

In the span of less than a decade, Egypt lost its regional leadership position, its independent posture in the Cold War, and its truce with Israel. How did this happen? What drove the destabilization of Egypt's foreign relations in the 1960s? And, since in tandem with these international developments the Egyptian economy went from sluggishness to the verge of collapse, the state underwent intensified socialization, society became less free, and Nasser's appeal waned considerably, one should also pose the question: To what extent were Egypt's foreign and domestic predicaments related, and how did they figure in the diminution of Egyptian power over the course of the decade and thereafter? Clearly, there can be no monocausal theory of this decline. But some causes are more significant than others. The main argument of this book is that the key to the decline of Egyptian power at the height of the Cold War lies in Egypt's five-year intervention in the Yemeni civil war.

The central axis, around which Middle Eastern politics revolved at the height of the Cold War, was not, as is often assumed, the Arab-Israeli conflict; it was rather the inter-Arab conflict between Egypt and Saudi Arabia. Between 1955 and 1967, the so-called Arab Cold War split the Arab world in two, aligning revolutionary military regimes backed by the Soviet Union against conservative monarchies supported by the United States and Great Britain. The two major contenders in this bitter struggle for power and influence were Moscow-backed Egypt and Washington-supported Saudi Arabia. In its early phases, the Arab Cold War consisted mostly of vociferous propaganda and intelligence intrigue. But in September 1962, the Arab Cold War turned hot. The occasion for this flare-up was a coup d'état in Ṣan'ā', where a coterie of military officers succeeded in overthrowing the Imamate, a dynastic institution of religious rulers belonging to the Zaydi branch of Shiite Islam. Despite the great distance separating Ṣan'ā' from Cairo, the Egyptian government sprang to the aid of the revolutionaries, while the Saudi monarchy, fearing that the revolution would prove contagious, vowed to do everything within its power to restore the Imam. The local civil war that ensued thus became caught up in a regional struggle for power, which was itself embedded in the global Cold War at its peak.

From October 1962 until December 1967, Egypt and Saudi Arabia were locked in a bloody struggle to control the outcome of the Yemeni civil war—and shape the political future of the Middle East. For Egypt, this struggle would prove more costly in lives, treasure, and squandered influence than any of its wars with Israel—with the possible exception of 1967. From a few hundred commandos at the beginning of October 1962, the Egyptian expeditionary force grew to about 70,000 men by the summer of 1965. The force's presence in Yemen threatened both Saudi Arabia and the British position at Aden, producing a near-immediate Saudi-British rapprochement after decades of conflict. The clash between Egypt and two key American allies on the Arabian Peninsula strained US-Egyptian relations to the breaking point. The ensuing suspension of US aid to Egypt exacerbated the burden wartime expenditure placed on the economy, already strained by the radical socialization drive of the 1960s, and drove Egypt deeper into debt to the Soviet Union. As shortages proliferated and casualties mounted, popular discontent soared to a level unknown since the revolution of 1952. All the while the army continued to stagnate in Yemen, increasingly restless and ill prepared for large-scale conventional war. Egypt, in short, was already deep in the throes of political, military, and economic crisis when Israel delivered the coup de grâce in 1967.

Overshadowed by the titanic battle with Israel, which fixed world attention on Sinai and Suez from 1967 onward, Egypt's five-year campaign on behalf of the fledgling republic in Ṣan'ā' was an episode of tremendous significance not only for the states directly involved in the conflict but also for the region as a whole. The decline of Egypt and the rise of Saudi Arabia, the twilight of Arab nationalism and the dawn of political Islam, the end of decolonization and the fate of the Cold War in the Middle East—these were the grander themes at play in the forgotten war in Yemen.

The Golden Age of Nasserism

The revolution of July 1952, which toppled the Egyptian monarchy and brought to power a clique of young nationalist officers, ushered in an era of radical politics to the Arab Middle East. In the years that followed, a revolutionary tidal wave rolled through the Arab world, swallowing Iraq in 1958 and, at its peak, threatening to engulf both the kingdom of Saudi Arabia and the Hashemite monarchy of Jordan. Although instability came in local flavors, most Arab revolutionaries followed, to varying degrees, the nationalist ideology of pan-Arabism, which Stephen Humphreys has defined simply as "that form of Arab Nationalism which seeks to unite all the Arabic-speaking peoples from Morocco to Iraq and Oman within a single country."[1] The doctrine of pan-Arabism

[1] R. Stephen Humphreys, *Between Memory and Desire: The Middle East in a Troubled Age* (Berkeley: University of California Press, 1999), 277n. Adeed Dawisha, however, argues

traced its intellectual roots to Syria and Iraq. But Egypt, as the largest and most powerful Arab state, soon became its most important practitioner. Since both Egypt's trajectory from 1952 to 1970 and the career of pan-Arabism became identified with the memorable leadership of Gamal Abdel Nasser, the term *Nasserism* has come to denote the era as a whole, the policies Nasser introduced during his reign, and the Egyptian brand of pan-Arabism he espoused.

Most attempts to come to terms with Nasser's legacy have rightly highlighted the transnational or more specifically pan-Arab characteristics of Nasserism.[2] It is therefore ironic that the present attempt to locate the source of national decline in a foreign adventure should begin with an emphasis on the essential Egyptianness of the phenomenon. But it is difficult to make sense of the international politics of the Middle East in the period under discussion without recognizing that Nasserism as foreign policy was first and foremost an Egyptian ambition for regional hegemony.

A series of propitious historical circumstances in the late 1950s and early 1960s combined to produce the specific expression of an ancient Egyptian impulse for preeminence. These circumstances included the weak legitimacy of the post-Ottoman system of "nation"-states; the consequent surge in pan-Arab sentiments in the mid-twentieth century; the wave of decolonization coursing through the developing world in the postwar period; the waning of British imperial power; the ensuing power vacuum in the Middle East; the Cold War competition between the Soviet Union, the United States, and their respective allies; and the immense personal charisma of Gamal Abdel Nasser. Although a physical empire was probably never in the cards, the aspiration for predominance in the Arab world—and to a lesser extent, throughout the Middle East and Africa—constituted the most persistent attribute of Egyptian foreign policy under Nasser.[3]

that Arab nationalists did not distinguish between pan-Arabism and Arab nationalism (*Arab Nationalism in the Twentieth Century: From Triumph to Despair* [Princeton, NJ: Princeton University Press, 2003], 1–13).

[2]See, for instance, Shimon Shamir, "The Fall of Nasserist Messianism" (Hebrew), in idem, ed., *The Decline of Nasserism, 1965-1970: The Fall of a Messianic Movement* (Hebrew) (Tel-Aviv: Mif'alim universiṭa'iyim le-hotsa'ah la-or, 1978), 16.

[3]Cf. Dawisha, *Arab Nationalism*, 2. See also Michael Doran, "Egypt: Pan-Arabism in Historical Context," in *Diplomacy in the Middle East: The International Relations of Regional and Outside Powers*, ed. L. Carl Brown (New York: I. B. Tauris, 2001), 97–120; and L. Carl Brown, *International Politics and the Middle East: Old Rules, Dangerous Game* (Princeton, NJ: Princeton University Press, 1984), 169–71.

Transforming Egypt into the preeminent power in the region required a strong military nourished on a steady diet of advanced weaponry; a healthy, independent economy; an ideology of transnational appeal; and a reliable source of leverage on the world stage. The Cold War provided just the constellation of opportunities for the fulfillment of all four conditions. Soviet geostrategic needs supplied the rationale for arming the Egyptian military, US interests demanded the pacification of Egypt through economic aid, decolonization offered a suitable context for the development of a specifically Arab doctrine of national liberation, and the stiff competition between the superpowers afforded ample scope for manipulation and maneuver.

The Cold War environment was crucial. Indeed, the architecture of Nasser's mature policy toward the great powers ultimately rested on a single principle, apparently inculcated by his Yugoslav mentor, Tito: to maximize foreign aid and political clout in the context of the Cold War it was necessary to steer clear of dependence on either of the two competing powers, and instead to play one off against the other. For Nasser everything depended on navigating the tightrope of neutralism. Bereft of oil, short on arable land, and weighed down by a rapidly growing (and mostly illiterate) population, Egypt operated on narrow margins even without the added burden of hegemonic ambitions. Although its rulers had two major cards to play, the first—Egypt's cultural and political centrality—was intangible, while the second—Egypt's strategic real estate—was nonnegotiable. In order to maximize the potential of this mixed hand, considerable dexterity and resourcefulness were required.[4]

Nasser's skillful management of the competition between the superpowers for a seat in the cockpit of Arab nationalism produced the golden age of Nasserism. Assured a steady supply of advanced weapons and cheap development credits from the East, and plentiful economic aid from the West, Egypt in the late 1950s and early '60s seemed to benefit from the best of all possible worlds. Astoundingly, Nasser's regime derived those benefits without any of the limitations associated with membership in either bloc: Egypt belonged to no defense pact, hosted no foreign bases, and professed neither capitalism nor communism in the conduct of its domestic policy. At home, the regime utilized plentiful foreign aid to launch an ambitious development plan designed to industrialize Egypt and double its national income within a decade.

[4]Cf. Dawisha, *Arab Nationalism*, 142–47; Doran, "Pan-Arabism in Historical Context," 97.

Abroad, Nasser used the immunity afforded by superpower favor to conduct an activist, immensely popular foreign policy at the helm of the Arab nationalist movement, the nonaligned movement, and the broader national liberation front in Africa and the rest of the Third World.

With hindsight it is perhaps too easy to conclude that this was a dream that could not last, that sooner or later it would be shattered in an inevitable collision between the regime's stubborn independence and the vital interests of one or more of the great powers. It was not merely that Nasser's tussles with the superpowers betrayed a flair for indignant brinksmanship rarely tempered by a willingness to retreat when the circumstances demanded; there were also limits to Egyptian behavior, beyond which the threat to great power interests overrode their fear of losing Egypt. Even barring some giant conflagration, it seems in retrospect unavoidable that one of the two great powers, disappointed with the escalating costs of—and meager return on—its investment, would eventually tire of the competition and retire.

The crux of the problem, however, was internal. A double contradiction existed at the heart of Nasserism. First was the gap between intent and action. Like most revolutions the Egyptian revolution promised a sweeping transformation of state and society. Yet the revolutionaries who came to power in 1952 did surprisingly little to generate the capacity necessary to realize their grandiose visions of change. Students of the Nasser era have rightly focused on his failure to articulate a comprehensive ideology or a political program and on his unsuccessful (and perhaps half-hearted) attempts to construct a mass organization that would constitute a durable basis for his rule.[5] But it was in the armed forces—the very institution whence the Free Officers emerged, and upon which they staked their claim to power—that the gap between purpose and effort was most glaringly obvious.

Even absent a territorial dimension, the aspiration to pan-Arab unity under Egyptian stewardship demanded a strong army—for reasons of prestige and deterrence alike. Nor was this merely a theoretical requirement. In practice the Egyptian military was called upon repeatedly to deter aggression or hold territory against a hostile power in the first decade after the revolution: against Israel, France, and Great Brit-

[5] See, e.g., Raymond Baker, *Egypt's Uncertain Revolution under Nasser and Sadat* (Cambridge, MA: Harvard University Press, 1978), 13, 50–51, 101, 239; Richard Dekmejian, *Egypt under Nasir: A Study in Political Dynamics* (Albany: State University of New York Press, 1971), 53–55, 64–65, 144–54, and passim.

ain in 1956; Iraq in 1961; Syria in the same year; Morocco in 1963; and Saudi Arabia after 1962. Yet despite the demonstrable need for a strong military—and this is one of the central paradoxes of the Nasser era—the regime seems to have done everything within its power to build an army that was magnificent in parade but impotent in battle.[6] Two features stand out from the damning portraits of Egypt's military painted by students of the 1967 war: rampant incompetence at the highest echelons and an appalling deficit of training at all levels.[7] There was, in other words, a gulf between the regime's soaring rhetoric and its almost flippant approach to implementation. The Free Officers may have spared no effort in the attempt to secure their regime, but they conducted the serious business of revolution in an almost amateur manner that would appear strange to students of Soviet Russia, Nazi Germany, or even Fascist Italy.

The second contradiction involved a gap between aims and means. The incongruence between Egypt's limited resources on the one hand, and the limitless ambitions of its leaders on the other, bred tensions that foreign aid could suppress for only so long. From King Farouk to President Mursī, every ruler of Egypt in the postwar period has faced the same fundamental dilemma: how to support a rapidly growing population on a near-stagnant resource base. As Nasser never tired of telling his interlocutors, his biggest problem was how to feed 600,000 new mouths every year. The solution the Free Officers adopted was, by and large, the Soviet one. Agricultural Egypt was to be transformed from above into an industrial powerhouse, substituting state enterprise for private property and local production for foreign imports. With proper direction this new indigenous industry, it was hoped, would spur economic growth at a pace outstripping the growth rate of the population. Even under optimal conditions, however, the plan launched in 1960—like the giant dam on the Nile that remains its most vivid testament—required at least a decade of stable progress to produce results, and a decade of stability was anything but what Nasser had in store for the 1960s. At home and abroad Egypt's ambitious rulers champed impatiently at the bit of economic reality. Nasser and his colleagues showed

[6] This is a harsh judgment, with which Nasser's private secretary concurs. Sāmī Sharaf, *Sanawāt wa-ayyām ma'a Gamāl 'Abd al-Nāṣir: Shahādat Sāmī Sharaf*, 2 vols. (Cairo: Dār al-Fursān li-l-Nashr, 2005), 1:319.

[7] This is most apparent in the memoirs of the Egyptian chief of staff in 1967, Muḥammad Fawzī, *Ḥarb al-thalāth sanawāt1967/1970: Mudhakkirāt al-farīq awwal Muḥammad Fawzī, wazīr al-ḥarbiyyah al-asbaq* (Cairo: Dār al-Mustaqbal al-'Arabī, 1984–86), 8–67.

little inclination to make the sacrifices necessary to keep the development plan on track by restraining government expenditure or public consumption. Nor did they appear capable of setting priorities. Yet priorities were essential in a situation where exports continued to stagnate while the population grew at a rate consistently surpassing 2.5 percent per annum. From a purely internal perspective, there appears to have been a built-in tendency to overextension and collapse.[8]

At the same time these internal dynamics affected—and could not fail to be affected by—external factors of great consequence. Egyptian policy did not take place in a vacuum; the image of total freedom of action on the international stage was an illusion. In Egypt's situation at the beginning of the 1960s, with no foreign currency reserves left to speak of, and an appallingly low national savings rate, the controlled accumulation of external debt was the only way to finance the import of food, capital, and arms until the industrialization drive bore fruit. Egypt's success hinged on the uninterrupted supply of foreign aid.[9] Yet no single factor contributed more to jeopardizing this crucial supply line than the regime's reluctance to limit its commitments abroad. Nasser's commitment to the export of revolution set him on a collision course with his neighbors. This necessarily brought him into conflict with their great power allies.

Like revolutionary France at the end of the eighteenth century, republican Egypt under Nasser's charismatic rule posed a threat to the teetering legitimist order that predominated in the Arab Middle East, from Morocco to Iraq, and from Yemen to Jordan. Like the new nationalism wielded by Napoleon, the militant nationalism brandished by the Free Officers menaced the weak states of the Arab East with a new form of legitimacy that heralded revolution and regime change. There was, however, an important difference. Unlike Napoleon's Grande Armée, Nasser's army, though the biggest in the Middle East, was still too weak to threaten Arabia, Mesopotamia, and the Levant with outright con-

[8] John Waterbury, *The Egypt of Nasser and Sadat: The Political Economy of Two Regimes* (Princeton, NJ: Princeton University Press, 1983), 41, 83; Khalid Ikram, *Egypt: Economic Management in a Period of Transition* (Baltimore: Johns Hopkins University Press, 1980), 341–42. A crisp summary of the regime's predicament is to be found in a dispatch by the British ambassador to Egypt, Sir George Middleton. Middleton (Cairo) to Walker, no. 49, December 18, 1964, FO 371/178580, PRO.

[9] P. J. Vatikiotis, *Nasser and His Generation* (London: Croom Helm, 1978), 215; Kirk Beattie, *Egypt during the Nasser Years: Ideology, Politics, and Civil Society* (Boulder, CO: Westview Press, 1994), 192–93; Baker, *Egypt's Uncertain Revolution*, 45–46.

quest. The nature of the threat was different. Up to 1962, it was the endless string of coups and conspiracies, funded by Egyptian money, aided by Nasser's agents, and encouraged by the vociferous blare of revolutionary propaganda emanating from Cairo radio, that made the peril palpable.

If Nasser inspired exaltation in the Arab masses, his most pronounced effect on their leaders was fear. Following his successful campaign against the Baghdad Pact—a pro-Western alliance Iraq, Turkey, Iran, Pakistan, and Great Britain established in 1955—Nasser's rising star began to unnerve monarchs from the Maghreb to the Persian Gulf. His political triumph against the British, the French, and the Israelis in the Suez War of 1956 precipitated a historic reconciliation between the rival Saudi and Hashemite royal families.[10] Two years later, when Nasser announced a union between Egypt and Syria, the Hashemite kingdoms of Jordan and Iraq hurried to form a federation of their own. Although the federation dissolved over the summer as Iraq convulsed in revolution, the new nationalist regime in Baghdad soon turned out to be as hostile toward Egypt as the Iraqi monarchy had ever been.[11] Indeed, as Nasser went from strength to strength after 1956, it was not only Arab monarchs who began to shift uneasily on their thrones. If, as some pan-Arab intellectuals proclaimed,[12] Egypt was the latter-day Prussia, and Nasser was its Bismarck, what attitude could the Middle Eastern analogues of Denmark, Austria, and France possibly assume toward the expanding entity other than alarm? This was as true in Amman and Riyadh as it was in Jerusalem and Ankara.

With hindsight it seems a foregone conclusion that sooner or later Egypt's restless rulers were bound to incur the wrath of the principal guarantor of the conservative order in the Middle East, the United States. The relatively harmonious history of relations between Egypt and the United States in the latter quarter of the twentieth century suggests that the logic of geopolitics alone did not foreordain a clash—it was the revolutionary policies of the Nasser regime that made conflict

[10] See Elie Podeh, "Ending an Age-Old Rivalry: The Rapprochement between the Hashemites and the Saudis, 1956–1958," in *The Hashemites in the Modern Arab World: Essays in Honour of the Late Professor Uriel Dann*, ed. Asher Susser and Aryeh Shmuelevitz (London: Frank Cass, 1995), 85–110.

[11] James Jankowski, *Nasser's Egypt, Arab Nationalism, and the United Arab Republic* (Boulder, CO: Lynne Rienner, 2001), 138–39, 151–55.

[12] ʻIzzat Darwazah and Sāṭiʻ al-Ḥuṣrī, cited in Elie Podeh, *The Decline of Arab Unity: The Rise and Fall of the United Arab Republic* (Brighton: Sussex Academic Press, 1999), 29.

all but inevitable.[13] Of course, it was these same policies that made Egypt appealing to Soviet policy makers. Although Nasser and Khrushchev might quarrel over Arab Communists, as they did in 1958, Moscow was far less likely to apply the brakes on Egyptian foreign policy than Washington. The paramount Soviet objective in the Arab Middle East was to minimize US influence in a region close to the southern borders of the Soviet Union. In practice, this boiled down to winning allies and turning foes against the United States. Whether or not Communism flourished among the Arabs—a dubious proposition in any case—was ultimately of secondary importance from the Kremlin's perspective; as long as Nasser was making trouble for the Americans, he was worth the investment. The Americans too sought to block the spread of their rival's influence in the region. But to anti-Communism they added a second, in some ways transcendent, objective: to assure the steady supply of cheap oil to the West. The oil factor translated into a much greater degree of commitment to the region. In practice, protecting the supply of oil meant preserving the regimes that pumped it.

The importance of Middle Eastern oil had three important implications for US policy. First, it meant that the United States had greater stakes in the Arab world than the USSR ever did. From this followed a greater determination to safeguard interests. Second, the centrality of oil meant that US stakes in the Middle East were *not*, for the most part, located in petroleum-starved Egypt. It was easy to lose sight of this basic truth in the heady years of Kennedy's love affair with Nasser: ultimately, US interests in Egypt were derivative and negative. They were derivative because what mattered had less to do with Egypt itself but rather with Egypt's role in the Middle East. And they were negative because the objective of US friendship was to restrain Nasser and avoid worse alternatives to his rule. In fact, the paramount US interest in stability ran exactly counter to the Free Officers' commitment to upending the status quo; the illusion of common interests was a balloon waiting to be punctured.[14] Finally, the oil factor introduced a higher degree of complexity into US policy. Since the Americans had so much to lose, they had perhaps too much to defend. Whereas the Soviet position in the Middle East rested upon one country above all—Egypt under Nasser—the United States had at least one other key Arab ally to consider, the

[13] Cf. Malcolm Kerr, "'Coming to Terms with Nasser': Attempts and Failures," *International Affairs* 43, no. 1 (1967): 67–69.

[14] John Badeau, *The Reminiscences of John Badeau* (New York: Oral History Research Office, Columbia University, 1979), 240.

Kingdom of Saudi Arabia, whose strategic worth, in American eyes, surpassed that of Egypt.[15] This is one reason why, when Egyptian commandos descended upon the Arabian Peninsula in the fall of 1962, much more was at stake than the future of Yemen.

Idealism and Pragmatism in Nasser's Foreign Policy

Perhaps the most significant aspect of Egypt's hegemonic aspirations was that they were disguised by, and at times confused with, the promotion of revolutionary ideals. This was especially true with regard to pan-Arabism. The Arab yearning for unity at midcentury provided fertile ground for the promotion of Egyptian-led solidarity among the weak and divided offspring of the defunct Ottoman mother-state. As is often the case with revolutionary entities, the sincere espousal of transnational ideals by the Free Officers camouflaged the less appealing pursuit of Egyptian state interests, which typically involved a naked struggle for power, and cloaked the subversive attempt to speak to the people over the heads of their leaders in a mantle of legitimacy. Whether by accident or design, the ambiguity of Egypt-as-state and Egypt-as-revolutionary-vanguard served the purpose of bolstering state influence quite well.

Indeed, all of the international causes associated with Nasserism—Neutralism, Pan-Arabism, Anti-Imperialism, Anti-Zionism, Arab Socialism, even Anti-Communism—are best understood both as desirable goals in and of themselves *and* as implements for the pursuit of Egyptian primacy. To take one further example: Egypt's principled opposition to imperialism. Nasser's anti-imperialism was suffused with a similar ambiguity between utility and belief. The adoption of anti-British policies was natural for a junta that rode to power on a promise to rid Egypt of its British overlords. Yet once independence had been achieved, the continued pursuit of a relentless campaign against British influence in the region did not stem merely from an ideological commitment to the founding principles of the revolution: it issued from a pragmatic desire to undercut one of the primary obstacles to the expansion of

[15] On the origins and evolution of the Saudi-American alliance, see Parker Hart, *Saudi Arabia and the United States: Birth of a Security Partnership* (Bloomington: Indiana University Press, 1998). On the primacy of Saudi Arabia in US calculations, see Warren Bass, *Support Any Friend: Kennedy's Middle East and the Making of the U.S.-Israel Alliance* (New York: Oxford University Press, 2003), 99–100.

Egyptian power. As London's influence waned, anti-British speech and action came to serve a more subtle series of objectives as well. Opposition to Great Britain enabled Nasser to undermine the legitimacy of his rivals, which, with few exceptions, relied on the residues of British power. It also allowed him to threaten US interests without attacking America directly. Above all, Nasser's championship of the popular anti-imperialist cause cemented his position as natural leader of the Arabs.

The utilitarian aspects underlying much of Nasserist propaganda do not diminish the significance of ideology in Nasser's foreign policy. Indeed, the imperative of living up to vague revolutionary ideals lent an undisciplined character to an otherwise calculating leadership. Perhaps this was because Nasserism never amounted to an elaborate doctrine on the model of Marxism-Leninism, or because the Free Officers never produced anything approaching a coherent blueprint for the transformation of the state. In any event the underlying commitment to a sharp break with the monarchic and colonial past, to a radical transformation of Egyptian society, and to the uncompromising preservation of national honor made the consistent practice of pragmatism difficult. As students of Nasser have observed, this lent a distinctly messianic quality to Nasserism, which tended to push Egypt into uncompromising positions of principle and fanciful overextension.[16]

And yet the messianic strain coexisted with a strong dose of what Isaiah Berlin famously termed a "sense of reality," which trimmed the excesses of Nasser's ambition at key junctures in his career.[17] In fact, many of Nasser's major decisions bear the stamp of pragmatism: witness his decision to relinquish Egyptian claims to Sudan in 1954, his acquiescence in Britain's right to reoccupy the canal zone in time of war, his acceptance of a UN peacekeeping force on the Sinai Peninsula in 1956, his determination to let Syria go its separate way in 1961, and his resolution to sue for peace with Saudi Arabia in 1965.[18] But the distance from pragmatism to opportunism can be a short one. Indeed, all of the decisions listed above can also be explained as temporary concessions to reality, which did not signify long-term abandonment of a radical goal.[19] And many others came abruptly, bearing the marks of an impulsiveness bordering on recklessness: the surprise announcement

[16] Vatikiotis, *Nasser and His Generation*, 197; Shamir, "Fall of Messianic Nasserism," 10.

[17] Shamir, "Fall of Messianic Nasserism," 13–14.

[18] See also Brown, *International Politics*, 171.

[19] Doran, "Pan-Arabism in Historical Context," 105.

of an arms deal with Czechoslovakia in September 1955, the dramatic nationalization of the Suez Canal in July 1956, the hurried dispatch of Egyptian soldiers to Yemen in September 1962, and the sudden break with a decade of prudence in May 1967 come to mind.

In any event, ideology cannot fully account for the impetuous character of Nasser's foreign policy. There was an undeniable *restlessness* about the regime, reminiscent of Khrushchev's style of government, that lengthened the shadow of unpredictability the revolution cast on the region from 1955 to 1970. One thinks of the rapid shifts between verbal extremes; the sharp twists and turns in policy; the frenetic, periodic reorganizations of government.[20] Nowhere was this more apparent than in the realm of rhetoric. Nasser had a penchant for letting words run wild. To a certain extent the verbal excesses reflected personal character. But they were also the bread and butter of Arab political discourse in an age of uncertain legitimacy. While a conservative king felt compelled to tone down the rhetoric because it was a war he could not win, a populist president had a tendency to escalate the war of words because it was a war he could not lose. Regardless of how seriously it was intended, all the talk about revolution was perceived as a mortal threat by the shaky governments of the surrounding Arab states. And there was a limit to how forgiving sensitive monarchs could be toward a leader who specialized in invective ad hominem.

In large measure the instability of Egypt's foreign policy stemmed from an extreme emphasis on national prestige.[21] Adeed Dawisha is certainly correct in viewing this as a direct consequence of Nasser's obsession with dignity. The identification of the state with the charismatic individual at its head blurred the boundaries between the collective and the personal, creating a volatile situation in which any slight against the president constituted an inexcusable offense against the national honor, and vice versa. As an individual, Nasser was hypersensitive, ever quick to take offense and rarely one to swallow pride. And since the president personified the state, his sensitivities became Egypt's. This made anticipating Egypt a risky business for intelligence agencies the world over. And it made dealing with Egypt on a bilateral basis extremely trying.

[20] See, e.g., Leonard Binder, "Gamal 'Abd al-Nasser: Iconology, Ideology, and Demonology," in *Rethinking Nasserism: Revolution and Historical Memory in Modern Egypt*, ed. Elie Podeh and Onn Winckler (Gainesville: University Press of Forida, 2004), 52.

[21] Adeed Dawisha, *Egypt in the Arab World: The Elements of Foreign Policy* (London: Macmillan, 1976), 136.

The unpredictability of the whole package—by turns messianic or pragmatic, impulsive or calculating, abusive or conciliatory—was enough to unsettle the most steely nerved of neighboring autocrats.

The Nature of Middle Eastern Politics

This book is primarily about local agency. In important respects it elaborates on the thesis Malcolm Kerr introduced in his classic work, *The Arab Cold War*. As Kerr intimated in a preface to its last edition, one of his main concerns had been "to dispel the notion of Arab politics as a projection of decisions made in Washington, London, Moscow, and Jerusalem."[22] In his view, as in mine, Arab politics was first and foremost about Arab agency.

Implicit in this view was a rejection of what the late Elie Kedourie termed the "Chatham House Version" of Middle Eastern history, an interpretation still alive in contemporary analysis of the Middle East.[23] The Chatham House version, more a set of attitudes and assumptions than a school of history, privileges the deeds, and especially the misdeeds, of foreign powers—from the Ottoman Empire to the United States of America—over the actions of locals. According to this reading of history, many of the region's endemic problems, such as sectarianism, political violence, and war, owe ultimately to the malevolent designs and false promises of external actors. At its most extreme, the Chatham House version tends to absolve indigenous governments of responsibility over their own destiny, portraying them as essentially passive—at worst acted upon by, at best reacting to the machinations of colonial powers and their agents. Whatever the merits of great power policies toward the Middle East over the last several centuries—and no one can deny their importance, for both good and evil—an excessive focus on external actors obscures local dynamics that are often far more important for understanding the major developments of regional history.

In this particular drama, set in Yemen of the 1960s, the deeds of external players—be they great powers, like the United States and the Soviet Union, or regional players operating offstage, like Israel or Iran—take a

[22] Malcolm Kerr, *The Arab Cold War: Gamal 'Abd al-Nasir and His Rivals, 1958–1970* (New York: Oxford University Press, 1971), vi.

[23] Elie Kedourie, *The Chatham House Version and Other Middle Eastern Studies* (New York: Praeger, 1970).

back seat to those of the principal actors: Egyptians, Saudis, and Yemenis. While the familiar bogeymen of modern Middle Eastern politics (Americans, British, Zionists, and Communists) all play an important part in this story, their role is ultimately secondary to that of the main protagonists, Arabs whose fate lies largely in their own hands.

This is also a story about the nature of relations that developed among the Ottoman successor states after the Second World War. As was the case elsewhere in the developing world, decolonization provided the crucial backdrop for the practice of international politics. But it is remarkable how swiftly the supposedly common struggle against European domination came under the shadow of fraternal conflict. The myth of pan-Arab unity—a powerful one that continues to exert strong emotional attraction on citizens, policy makers, and scholars alike—tends to obscure the reality of pluralism, division, and conflict that has prevailed in the Middle East throughout the second half of the twentieth century. The Middle East in the postwar period is neither the romantic Eden of pan-Arabist theory nor the postcolonial trauma ward implied by Kedourie's opponents: it is a violent place where weak regimes vie for survival and supremacy using Arab nationalism as a battering ram.

Political weakness was arguably the most important source of regional instability and the driving force behind the disputatious character of inter-Arab politics. This weakness stemmed from one characteristic common to all the Ottoman Empire's Arab successor states: an acute deficit of legitimacy.[24] The legitimacy deficit operated on two planes of meaning simultaneously: first, in the sense of a just and accepted domestic order within each state, and second, in the sense of an agreed framework for the negotiation of change in the international order, without which the practice of diplomacy is impossible.[25] Whether monarchic or republican in form, all the young Arab regimes suffered to varying degrees from shallow political traditions, authoritarian government, minority rule, and a proclivity for political violence. As a consequence a deep sense of insecurity plagued every single member of the Arab League. Although they would not have appreciated the irony, the two principal adversaries in this story—King Faysal of Saudi Arabia, guardian of the holy sites of Islam, and President Nasser of Egypt, champion of secular pan-Arabism—shared a remarkable sense of vulnerability

[24] Michael Hudson, *Arab Politics: The Search for Legitimacy* (New Haven, CT: Yale University Press, 1977).

[25] Henry Kissinger, *A World Restored: Metternich, Castlereagh, and the Problems of Peace, 1812–1822* (Boston: Houghton Mifflin, 1957).

and a similar preoccupation with domestic stability. At home, insecurity produced iron rule. Abroad, it bred aggressive rhetoric, ceaseless subversion, and an emphasis on ideological absolutes rarely susceptible to reasoned compromise. The resultant regional dynamic was one in which fragile regimes, preoccupied with the quest for legitimacy, engaged in a never-ending contest of one-upmanship. The image of an assemblage of despots housed in glass busily pelting one another with stones aptly depicts inter-Arab politics at the height of the Cold War.

The Place of the Intervention in Egyptian Memory

The civil war in Yemen was the single most important foreign policy issue facing Egypt, the Arab world's center of gravity, between October 1962 and May 1967. Yet it has all but disappeared from the history books. Nowhere is this truer than in Egypt itself. An aging Egyptian veteran of the war, driven by a near-death experience in the late 1990s to break his vow never to speak out, titled his memoir *The Embarrassed Silence and the Yemeni Revolution*.[26] What baffled the author was the astonishing lack of scholarly or journalistic writing by Egyptians about the war—especially when compared with the substantial Yemeni literature on the subject—and the ensuing vacuum in public consciousness. To this day there are no good answers to such basic questions as: How many Egyptians died in the war? How much did it cost? What role did the Egyptian government play in the coup d'état that precipitated the intervention? Or even: What took place on the battlefield between 1962 and 1967? To grasp the scope of the omission one need only consider a hypothetical situation in which the Vietnam War—to which the intervention in Yemen is often compared—was virtually excised from American historiography of the twentieth century.

The biggest obstacle remains the closure of the relevant Egyptian archives to researchers of any nationality. As a consequence our position today is little better than it was in the mid-1970s, when Luwīs 'Awaḍ posed the question: "must the Egyptian people wait forty more years before they can read a documented historical study of the Yemen War, [explaining] why it began and why it ended ... how many soldiers did we lose ... and how many guineas did we expend?"[27] The closure

[26] Ṣalāḥ al-Dīn al-Maḥrizī, *Al-Ṣamt al-ḥā'ir wa thawrat al-Yaman* (Cairo, 1998).

[27] Luwīs 'Awaḍ, *Aqni'at al-nāṣiriyyah al-sab'ah: Munāqashat Tawfīq al-Ḥakīm wa-Muḥammad Ḥasanayn Haykal* (Beirut: Dār al-Qaḍāyā, [1975?]), 21–22. All translations are the author's unless stated otherwise.

of the archives has left the historical playing field to the memories and biases of aging participants. Unfortunately for historians, the caution—and pessimism—of one outspoken veteran continues to characterize official attitudes in Egypt: "As for when the story commenced, when Cairo knew about it, what was the position of those responsible concerning it, this I cannot expose or enter into details, for there are state secrets, which it is inappropriate to discuss or publish, and which it is necessary to preserve for a long period, until they lose their value in the course of time. Despite my conviction that only a paltry few know how the story began, and my great doubt that any of them will one day put in writing the entire truth, I will not waver here in refraining from setting down the historical facts, even though I know that the [archives of the] supreme command of the armed forces and the supreme command of the state are empty of documents that would aid the researcher in the future to discover the secrets of the Yemen revolution."[28] Perhaps this explains why only one professional historian in Egypt has been brave enough to tackle the subject thus far. Published in 1981 and based entirely on published sources, Aḥmad Yūsuf Aḥmad's *The Egyptian Role in Yemen* remains the most systematic study of Egyptian decision making during the war.[29]

To a certain extent, the relative silence on Yemen in Egypt over the last forty years reflects inertial perpetuation of the censorship the Nasser regime enforced over the course of the war. The easy shift from intimidating suppression to unconscious repression was accomplished through the sudden and forceful takeover of the national agenda by the *naksah*—the "setback" of June 1967. There was no opportunity to come to terms with the legacy of Egypt's involvement in Yemen because the war was superseded immediately by a crisis of greater urgency, which captivated the attention of the politically conscious for the better part of a decade. This decade, moreover, passed mostly under the sway of Anwar Sadat, an enthusiastic proponent of the intervention in Yemen and one of those most responsible for its consequences. Although Sadat himself wrote quite openly, if briefly, about his role in the Yemen imbroglio, the subject can hardly be said to have gotten a full vetting in public.[30] In any event, the war received something of a free pass in the

[28] Ṣalāḥ al-Dīn al-Ḥadīdī, *Shāhid ʿalā ḥarb 67* (Cairo: Dār al-Shurūq, 1974), 38.

[29] Aḥmad Yūsuf Aḥmad, *Al-Dawr al-miṣrī fī al-Yaman (1962–1967)* (Cairo: Al-Hay'ah al-Miṣriyyah al-ʿĀmmah li-l-Kitāb, 1981).

[30] Anwar el-Sadat, *In Search of Identity: An Autobiography* (New York: Harper and Row, 1977), 162–63.

decade of reckoning with Nasser's legacy following his death in 1970. There were more convenient failures on which to dwell.

More broadly, Egyptian reserve on Yemen appears to stem from deep-seated discomfort with the place of the episode in the country's history. A noble, selfless campaign on behalf of oppressed fellow Arabs on the one hand, it involved undeniable elements of fratricide and occupation on the other. Waged in the name of progressive pan-Arab ideals, the war also served the Egyptian leadership's less savory quest for regional hegemony at the expense of the more popular struggle against Israel and the more important struggle for Egypt's own development. It was hard to reconcile the noble ideals that inspired men to fight and die so far from home with the betrayal of those same ideals by those who sent them. It was, and still is, more convenient to debate the immaculately legitimate conflict with Israel, setbacks and all, than to come to terms with the Saudi-Egyptian war in Arabia.

Nevertheless, a number of Egyptians have broken the silence on Yemen over the years. The first to disturb the peace was journalist Wagīh Abū Dhikrī, in *The Flowers Are Buried in Yemen*, a historical novel published not long after Nasser's death.[31] The former Yemen correspondent for the influential Egyptian weekly *Ākhir Sā'ah*, Abū Dhikrī recounts the history of the war from the vantage point of a commando officer. The narrative comprises the wartime correspondence between the man and his wife and relates the progressive disillusionment that affects each of them as they experience the painful gap between propaganda and reality on the ground in Yemen and in Egypt. No doubt intended as an allegory for the disillusionment of the Egyptian population with the war, the book challenged the official narrative of a just and necessary war. In his attempt to dismantle the triumphalist narrative of official Egypt, Abū Dhikrī ended up tipping the scales too far in the other direction. Moreover, as was the case with Abū Dhikrī's accomplished contemporary Tawfīq al-Ḥakīm, author of the explosive tract *The Return of Consciousness*, there was something sour about the belated effort of a previously committed intellectual to deconstruct Nasserist mythology after the death of its idol.[32] Nonetheless, the attempt was

[31] Wagīh Abū Dhikrī, *Al-Zuhūr tudfanu fī al-Yaman* (The flowers are buried in Yemen) (Cairo: Dār al-Waṭan al-'Arabī, 197?).

[32] Tawfīq al-Ḥakīm, *'Awdat al-wa'ī* (Beirut: Dār al-Shurūq, 1974). As Shim'on Shamir points out, this was a shortcoming common to all the early critics of Nasser in the 1970s ("The Fall of Nasserist Messianism," 49–50). See also Tharwat 'Ukāshah, *Mudhakkirātī fī al-siyāsah wa-l-thaqāfah* (Cairo: Dār al-Hilāl, 1990), 1:16.

revealing; here was an important journalist, who had written dozens of enthusiastic reports from the field over the course of the war, confessing that all along he had been either lying or hopelessly naive. Abū Dhikrī exposed the lie that he and his fellow journalists had helped sustain, day after day, year after year, by means of tendentious reporting from the field delivered in an unfailingly exulting tone.

Another of the war's early critics was, surprisingly, Egypt's former chief of military intelligence and its first commander of operations in Yemen, Ṣalāḥ al-Dīn al-Ḥadīdī. In *Witness to the Yemen War*, published in 1984, Ḥadīdī argued that the intervention had been a disastrous error on the part of the politicians, who let a private vendetta against the Saudi monarchy get in the way of the national interest.[33] Although Ḥadīdī focused his ire on the political echelon, he presented a damning portrait of corruption, insubordination, and incompetence in the armed forces.

Not surprisingly, most other former officials have chosen to exonerate Nasser, mitigate his responsibility, or minimize the costs of the intervention. Thus, for example, journalist and Free Officer Aḥmad Ḥamrūsh concluded in his multivolume study of the Nasser era that the intervention had been just and necessary.[34] Writing soon after Nasser's death, Ḥamrūsh exculpated the political echelon but condemned Egyptian military administrators for squandering, in their myopic militarism, a historic opportunity to transform Yemeni society and eliminate its feudal and tribal characteristics forever. In this Ḥamrūsh followed the tendency of the Egyptian Left to fault Nasser for engaging in halfway measures.[35]

Even officials prepared to grapple seriously with the legacy of the war have labored under a continued reluctance to criticize Nasser, reinforced by lack of archival materials. In 1992, General Maḥmūd ʿĀdil Aḥmad published the most ambitious attempt by a veteran at a scholarly chronicle of the war. His massive *Memoirs of the Yemen War*, which relies on personal recollections, numerous interviews, and much of the available literature on the subject, ends with a two-hundred-page section dedicated to answering thirty-five sensitive questions about the war. Critical readers may disagree with some of Aḥmad's conclusions—an exhausting series of speculative calculations ends up confirming the

[33] Ṣalāḥ al-Dīn al-Ḥadīdī, *Shāhid ʿalā ḥarb al-Yaman* (Cairo: Maktabat Madbūlī, 1984).

[34] Aḥmad Ḥamrūsh, *Qiṣṣat thawrat 23 yūliyū*, vol. 3, *ʿAbd al-Nāṣir wa-l-ʿarab* (Beirut: Al-Mu'assasah al-ʿArabiyyah li-l-Dirāsāt wa al-Nashr, 1974–), 227–69.

[35] Binder, "Gamal ʿAbd al-Nasser," 55.

official body count—but he deserves credit for grappling with such matters in earnest.[36]

Those with the greatest access to archival materials have proven the most disappointing in this regard. Sāmī Sharaf, Nasser's private secretary, waited three-and-a-half decades before reflecting on his time in office in *Years and Days with Gamal Abdel Nasser*, published in Cairo in 2005. Although Sharaf did offer a series of revealing insights into the origins of the intervention, his description of the war was a stale and apologetic compendium of other sources. As the closest official to Nasser for almost fifteen years, Sharaf missed a valuable opportunity to come to terms with the intervention and its place in Egyptian history.[37] But it was Muḥammad Ḥasanayn Haykal, celebrated Nasser confidant and former editor of *al-Ahrām*, who squandered the biggest opportunity to come to terms with the legacy of the intervention. By virtue of his proximity to the seat of power, and his prolific writing on the subject, Haykal has become the doyen of Nasser interpreters. But in his massive three-volume study of Egyptian foreign policy, completed in 1990, Haykal gave the Yemen war short shrift, playing down the significance of the intervention and treating it in the apologetic vein characteristic of his work. Since he could not ignore it entirely, Haykal tried to stitch the war into a broad historical canvas depicting an international conspiracy against the Egyptian revolution culminating in the "trap" of June 1967. Given his unparalleled access to state archives, Haykal's failure to grapple with the problem of Yemen was a major lost opportunity for a serious historical reckoning.[38]

The fall of Mubarak may well affect Egyptian attitudes toward the war in Yemen—as it may toward other failures of the Nasser regime. The pent-up frustrations released onto the streets of Cairo in January 2011 had built up steadily over the preceding half-century as a consequence of pathologies spawned during the Nasser years. Although it is still difficult for many Egyptians—and for many in the Arab world and in the West as well—to avoid a deep sense of nostalgia for the charisma of Nasser and the grandeur of his era, the historian cannot ignore Nasser's responsibility for the problems he bequeathed to his successors.

[36] Maḥmūd ʻĀdil Aḥmad, *Dhikrayāt ḥarb al-Yaman, 1962–1967* (Cairo: Maṭbaʻat al-Ukhuwwah, 1992).

[37] Sharaf, *Sanawāt wa-ayyām maʻa Gamāl ʻAbd al-Nāṣir*.

[38] Muḥammad Haykal, *Sanawāt al-Ghalayān (Cairo: Al-Ahrām, 1988); idem, 1967: Al-Infijār* (Cairo: Al-Ahrām, 1990).

Structure of the Book

Chapter one traces the course of events from Syria's decision to secede from the United Arab Republic in September 1961 to Egypt's decision to intervene in the incipient civil war in Yemen exactly one year later. Sparked by humiliation at the Syrian secession, the intervention was the culmination of a decade of support for revolutionary movements on the Arabian Peninsula ultimately aimed at toppling the Saudi monarchy. The hastily made decision to send military forces to Ṣan'ā' was taken under the cloud of a power struggle within the Nasser regime, which carried serious consequences for military preparedness in June 1967.

Chapter two draws on declassified sources in Russian and Arabic to tell the extraordinary tale of clandestine Soviet support for the dispatch of Egyptian forces to Yemen at the height of the Cuban missile crisis. The Egyptian intervention was made possible by logistical support from the Soviet government, which viewed the civil war in Yemen as an opportunity to advance the cause of revolution in a region critical for Western security. The joint intervention in Yemen turns out to have been the high-water mark of the Soviet-Egyptian revolutionary endeavor in the Middle East.

Chapter three analyzes the breakdown of Egypt's crucial relationship with the United States as a result of the intervention in Yemen. Contrary to conventional wisdom, which posits a later break in US-Egyptian relations over Lyndon Johnson's pro-Israel policy, this chapter highlights the primacy of the US-Saudi alliance and the early emergence of Yemen as the central bone of contention in the final year of the Kennedy administration. The resultant suspension of American aid placed Egypt and the United States on a collision course that led to the Six-Day War.

Chapter four investigates Egypt's growing dependence on the Soviet Union as a result of the war in Yemen. It explores the tensions that developed between the two countries after Khrushchev's ouster as the Soviet government began to exploit Egypt's difficulties in order to obtain basing rights that would even the playing field against the US Sixth Fleet in the Mediterranean. The uneasy dependency on Moscow, in conjunction with the rupture in relations with Washington, shattered the edifice of Egyptian neutrality, which stood at the foundation of Nasser's international clout in the 1950s, and set the stage for the crisis that produced the Six-Day War.

Chapter five explores the interplay between the battlefield in Yemen and the domestic front in Egypt. The chapter begins with a revisionist account of the Egyptian counterinsurgency campaign, based on Egyptian memoirs and captured documents, and then proceeds to discuss three Egyptian taboos—casualties, cost, and corruption—demonstrating that the pursuit of revolutionary politics abroad contributed significantly to the enfeeblement of the revolution at home. Although the direct cost of the war in lives and treasure may not have been as great as some have argued, the indirect costs of the war proved catastrophic for Egypt.

Chapter six studies the vicissitudes of Saudi-Egyptian relations as the two countries attempted to negotiate a peaceful settlement in Yemen. Based primarily on US diplomatic cables and Egyptian memoirs, it demonstrates how negotiations between Nasser and Faysal faltered over mutual mistrust, exacerbated by the perennial spoiling effect of Yemeni politics. The chapter also shows how the Egyptians and the Saudis used the Arab summits, ostensibly convened to discuss the Palestine question, as a camouflage for the mediation of the conflict between them.

Chapter seven brings the story of the Egyptian intervention to a close. Covering the momentous year of 1967, it exposes the little appreciated link between inter-Arab tensions and the Arab-Israeli conflict and provides a revisionist interpretation of the Six-Day War as an unintended consequence of the Saudi-Egyptian struggle over Yemen. Egypt's defeat forced Nasser to confront the necessity of withdrawing his forces from the Arabian Peninsula and accepting Saudi financial aid. Both acts presaged a crucial shift in the regional balance of power in the late twentieth century as a result of the civil war in Yemen: the decline of Egypt and the rise of Saudi Arabia.

*

The book that follows is not a comprehensive history of the Egyptian intervention in Yemen. Still less is it a history of the Yemeni civil war. It is primarily an attempt to situate an important but largely forgotten episode within the framework of Nasser's foreign policy in the 1960s. Even so, it necessarily reflects the limitations imposed on any historian of the modern Arab world. Given the impoverished nature of the secondary literature on the subject, a great deal of the research has been based on primary sources. Abundant foreign archival material has proven invaluable in reassessing Egypt's foreign relations. It has not, however, been particularly helpful in penetrating the fog shrouding the inner workings of the regime. Nor has it succeeded in illuminating the battlefield. Memoirs, interviews, and press materials have been extremely useful in providing context and filling in blanks but often offer little more than flashes of light in the dark. The military aspects of the campaign in particular remain murky, making it difficult for the historian to place political decision making in its proper battlefield context, let alone produce an informed account of the war effort. This is not a position the historian of the twentieth century is accustomed to occupying. Future scholars who endeavor to construct a full narrative of the Egyptian intervention in Yemen will have to find a way to get at the material presumably locked away in the archives of the presidency and the Egyptian armed forces. Perhaps now, with the embers of Nasser's legacy still glowing amid the ashes of Mubarak's regime, it will become possible to unlock the secrets of the past and come to terms with one of the darker chapters in the history of a great nation.

✷ CHAPTER ONE ✷

The Road to War

I sent a company to Yemen and had to reinforce it with 70,000 soldiers.
—*Gamal Abdel Nasser, in conversation with the historian Aḥmad Ḥamrūsh, 1967*

BEFORE DAWN ON SEPTEMBER 28, 1961, units of the Syrian military seized control of Damascus and put an end to the grand experiment in pan-Arab unity launched with Egypt more than three years before. Egypt's most famous journalist, Muḥammad Haykal, called Syria's unilateral secession from the United Arab Republic (UAR)—the infamous *infiṣāl*—"the greatest blow to the Arab revolutionary movement" since 1952.[1] In fact, the blow landed squarely in Egypt.

Nasser's star had been on the ascendant ever since 1955. With the formation of the United Arab Republic in February 1958, his influence in the Arab world attained its climax. To the crown of anti-imperialism he had won at Suez, the Egyptian president, in Damascus, added the mantle of Arab unity. And he did it without shedding a drop of blood. In the wake of his great victory in Syria, Nasser's inchoate call for unity seemed irresistible to many ordinary Arabs. Gripped by the quasi-messianic fervor that engulfed Nasser everywhere he traveled in the Arab world, they seemed ready to follow "Gamāl" wherever he might lead. Their leaders, however, had other ideas.

The union was an improbable one from the outset. Separated by sea and enemy territory, Egypt and Syria were widely disparate in terms of elite structure, ethnic makeup, economic foundations, and political culture. Egyptian policies compounded the structural weaknesses of the union. If the enormous disparities between the two states militated in favor of considerable autonomy, the Egyptians proved incapable of restraining the centralizing reflex of their regime. The appearance of a voluntary union between two equal entities masked a considerably less

[1] Haykal, *Sanawāt al-ghalayān*, 554, quoted in Podeh, *Decline*, 149.

appealing reality. Cast as an act of involuntary surrender to the will of the Arab masses, the wildly popular unity agreement concealed Egypt's stubborn insistence on preserving Cairo's seniority in the new partnership from the very beginning. Over time, the illusion of an independent Syrian voice in the joint conduct of affairs gave way to the reality of Egyptian control—in political, economic, and military affairs. And along with Egyptian rule came the less pleasant trappings of the Nasserist system of governance: cronyism, strong-armed security tactics, and an incipient trend toward radical nationalization.[2]

To the Syrians these deficiencies would only become apparent with time, producing alienation among the elite and eventually precipitating the military coup that ended the union. But the surrounding governments immediately appreciated the negative significance of the UAR. Notwithstanding the popularity of the union among ordinary Arabs everywhere, to Arab statesmen, the incorporation of Syria into Egypt represented a dangerous extension of Egyptian power into the Levant. The merger of these two ancient entities signaled Nasser's apparent intention to follow in the footsteps of Saladin and Muhammad Ali.[3] That geopolitical constants trumped ideological principle in this instance is demonstrated by Iraq's consistent opposition to the union both before and after the revolution of July 1958. In fact, when revolutionaries toppled the Hashemite monarchy in Baghdad in July, the new regime soon turned out to be just as hostile to Egypt as the old regime had ever been. Nevertheless, the momentum acquired by the nationalist juggernaut in Damascus posed a special threat to the Arab royal families. For the monarchs in Amman, Riyadh, and Baghdad in particular—already reeling from the shock waves of revolution emanating from Cairo for the better part of a decade—the UAR was a step too far.

Although King Sa'ūd bin 'Abd al-'Azīz, ruler of the oil kingdom of Saudi Arabia, was less outspoken than his counterparts in Jordan and Iraq, he had no less profound misgivings about the expansion of Nasser's power and was more in a position to orchestrate his demise. Whether or not the king had actually bankrolled an assassination attempt on Nasser in early 1958 or had merely funded attempts to subvert the union from its inception, it was the Saudis who emerged at the

[2] Podeh, *Decline*, 2–4, 21–24, 50–57, 64–66, 110–15, 179–90, and passim; Jankowski, *Nasser's Egypt*, 161–64, 172–73; Kerr, *Arab Cold War*, 11–16, 23–25.

[3] Elie Podeh, "'Suez in Reverse': The Arab Response to the Iraqi Bid for Kuwait, 1961–63," *Diplomacy and Statecraft* 14, no. 1 (2003): 104–5.

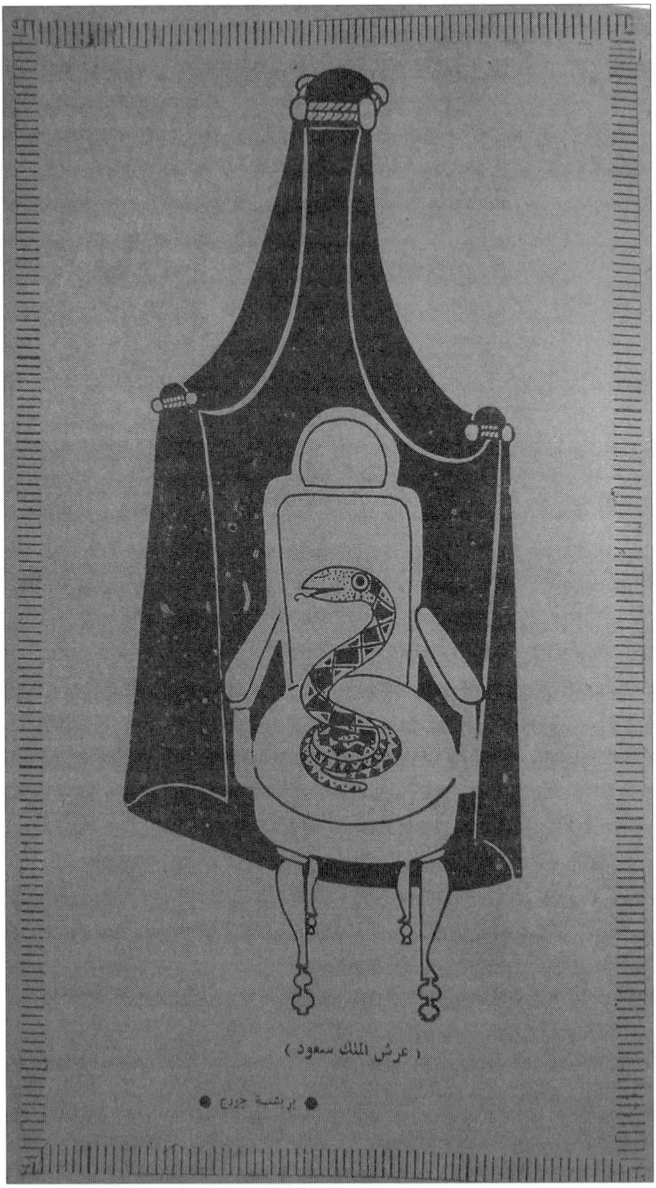

Figure 1.1 The throne of King Sa‘ūd as portrayed in the Egyptian newspaper *Rūz al-Yūsuf*, February 12, 1962. Drawing by George Barīsha.

forefront of the conservative forces opposing Egypt's aggrandizement.[4] Following the exposure of these bungled conspiracies in 1958, it became increasingly difficult for the Saudi leadership to evade Nasser's ire. Although a truce took root between Egypt, Jordan, and Saudi Arabia from 1959 to 1961, it was the tenuous product of fear and a common interest in opposing Iraqi expansionism. It did not survive the *infiṣāl*.[5]

Nasser apparently took the Syrian slap quite personally, and it was this blow to the president's prestige—and by extension, to Egypt's as a whole—that explains the bitterness of his reaction.[6] Reversing the long-standing policy of solidarity with other Arab regimes summed up in the slogan "unity of rank" (*waḥdat al-ṣaff*), he announced a new slogan: "unity of purpose" (*waḥdat al-hadaf*).[7] The purpose Nasser had in mind was revolution, and it was one aimed directly at the so-called reactionaries in Amman, Riyadh, and Ṣan'ā' as much as at rival revolutionaries in Damascus and Baghdad. Revolution, in other words, was henceforth to be a precondition for unity—where "revolution" designated rule by military officers with a pro-Egyptian orientation, while "unity" meant not so much territorial union as political solidarity under Egyptian leadership. Nasser's new posture posed a basic challenge to the very legitimacy of the postwar system of Arab states. "It was," in the words of Avraham Sela, "tantamount to a declaration of indiscriminate war against his Arab rivals, 'reactionaries' and 'revolutionaries' alike." The new policy "heralded the collapse of the Westphalian order struck by the foundation of the Arab League in 1945, whose most important principle was the commitment of its constituent members to respect

[4] Iraq's 'Abd al-Karīm Qāsim was Nasser's most powerful nationalist opponent. Kerr, *Arab Cold War*, 16–18; Haykal, *Sanawāt al-ghalayān*, 299–305, 542–50; Jankowski, *Nasser's Egypt*, 139; Sadat, *In Search of Identity*, 151, 157; Nadav Safran, *Saudi Arabia: The Ceaseless Quest for Security* (Cambridge, MA: Belknap Press of Harvard University Press, 1985), 85–87; Alexei Vassiliev, *The History of Saudi Arabia* (London: Saqi, 1998), 353–54; Hermann Eilts, "Saudi Arabia's Foreign Policy," in Brown, *Diplomacy in the Middle East*, 226–27.

[5] Kerr, *Arab Cold War*, 19–20, 26–27; Laura James, *Nasser at War: Arab Images of the Enemy* (Basingstoke, UK: Palgrave Macmillan, 2006), 52–53; Ḥadīdī, *Shāhid 'alā ḥarb al-Yaman*, 29; Podeh, "Suez in Reverse," 106–8 and passim.

[6] Kirk Beattie, *Egypt during the Nasser Years: Ideology, Politics, and Civil Society* (Boulder, CO: Westview Press, 1994), 158.

[7] Nasser speech, February 22, 1962, in United Arab Republic (hereafter UAR), *Majmū'at khuṭab wa-taṣrīḥāt wa-bayānāt al-ra'īs Gamāl 'Abd al-Nāṣir* (Cairo: Maṣlaḥat al-Isti'lāmāt, 196?), 4:8–9; Kerr, *Arab Cold War*, 25, 29; Avraham Sela, "'Abd al-Nasser's Regional Politics: A Reassessment," in Podeh and Winckler, eds., *Rethinking Nasserism*, 188; Vered, *Revolution and War in Yemen* (Hebrew) (Tel Aviv: 'Am 'Oved, 1967), 165–66.

each other's sovereignty." To the ruling elite in much of the Arab world, Nasser's aggressive posture posed a challenge of near-Napoleonic proportions.[8]

Nasser reacted to the dissolution of the UAR with resolve to export Egypt's revolution to his Arab rivals and determination to deepen the revolution in Egypt itself. In the immediate aftermath of the *infiṣāl*, the Egyptian leadership rededicated itself to shoring up the revolution at home. Further nationalizations, expropriations, and arrests of "reactionaries" followed within weeks. Within months the government dissolved the quasi-parliamentary National Union, soon to be replaced by the more regimented Arab Socialist Union (ASU). Then in May 1962 a new "national charter" (*al-mīthāq al-waṭanī*) was promulgated, which expounded the new socialist principles of Egypt's domestic revolution. But all this was carried out to the drumbeat of a defiant pledge to continue shouldering Egypt's revolutionary responsibilities abroad. Not unlike Stalin's "socialism in one country," Nasser's turn to radical socialism underlined the dual status of Egypt under the Free Officers: a pragmatic nation-state on the one hand, it was an interventionist revolutionary vanguard on the other. And if the rhetoric was anything by which to judge, it was only a matter of time before Egypt's domestic preoccupations came to an end.[9]

For exactly one year, Nasser smoldered as his enemies rejoiced at Egypt's misfortune. Of the major Arab states, only Algeria was on good terms with Egypt in the summer of 1962; Iraq, Jordan, Tunisia, Morocco, Syria, and Saudi Arabia were all arrayed against Nasser. For the self-proclaimed leader of the Arab world, the unprecedented regional isolation that followed the secession must have been intolerable.[10] The humiliating peak of Egypt's solitude came in August 1962, when the Egyptian delegation walked out of an Arab League summit in Lebanon, which had turned into a verbal lynching of the organization's putative

[8] Sela, "Nasser's Regional Politics," 189, 190; Jankowski, *Nasser's Egypt*, 177–78; Dawisha, *Egypt*, 35–36.

[9] Luwīs ʿAwaḍ, *Aqniʿat al-nāṣiriyyah al-sabʿah: Munāqashat Tawfīq al-Ḥakīm w a-Muḥammad Ḥasanayn Haykal* (Beirut: Dār al-Qaḍāyā, [1975?]), 155–56; Joel Gordon, *Nasser: Hero of the Arab Nation* (Oxford: Oneworld, 2006), 69–77; Robert Stephens, *Nasser: A Political Biography* (London: Allen Lane, 1971), 344–49; Kerr, *Arab Cold War*, 26, 30–31; Beattie, *Egypt*, 158–59, 162–66; Podeh, *Decline*, 192; Dawisha, *Egypt*, 146; Research Memo, Department of State, RNA-8, October 30, 1961, "The Outlook for Nasser," pp. 3–6, RG 59, CDF 1960–63, Box 2072, 786b.00/11-261, NARA; Haykal, "Marḥalat al-ṣarāḥah wa-l-wuḍūḥ," *al-Ahrām*, December 29, 1961.

[10] Adeed Dawisha, "Intervention in the Yemen: An Analysis of Egyptian Perceptions and Policies," *Middle East Journal* 29, no. 1 (1975): 47; Stephens, *Nasser*, 378.

Figure 1.2 As the propaganda battle heated up, the Egyptian media mercilessly ridiculed the Saudi leadership. Here King Sa'ūd collapses after reading about the Yemeni revolution in the paper. The doctor to Sa'ūd: "You must stay calm. What will you do when the revolution happens in Saudi Arabia?" *Akhbār al-Yawm*, October 6, 1962. Cartoon by Alexander Ṣārūkhān.

leader.[11] The loss of control over the Arab League, Cairo's principal instrument for the imposition of Egyptian-led solidarity, attested to the depth of Nasser's predicament. One month later, on the eve of the anniversary of the *infiṣāl*, events in Yemen provided a timely opportunity to strike back at Egypt's rivals, capture the moral high ground, and regain the initiative in the Arab Cold War.

The Coup in Yemen

On September 19, 1962, Imam Aḥmad bin Yaḥyā, iron-handed ruler of Yemen since 1948, passed away. His son, thirty-six-year-old Muḥammad

[11] Kerr, *Arab Cold War*, 39; Telegram, Badeau (Cairo) to Sec. State, no. 361, August 30, 1962, RG 59, CDF 1960–63, Box 2072, 786b.00/8-3062, NARA.

al-Badr, succeeded him. One week later, on September 26, 1962, a group of Yemeni army officers assaulted the Royal Palace in Ṣan'ā' and at the conclusion of a night-long bombardment declared the establishment of a republic. The rebels believed they had killed the young Imam; in fact, he had managed to escape. As the revolutionaries struggled to consolidate their hold on power in the major towns in the center and south of the country, many of the Zaydī tribes of the rural north of Yemen, upon which the Imamate had based its power for centuries, rallied around the deposed Ḥamīd al-Dīn royal family. Some of the republic's opponents were attracted by the cause of restoration; others were repelled by the personages, ideology, and behavior of the Republican government. All were subsequently lumped together under the banner Royalists, a misleading if indispensable shorthand designation for the various tribal forces opposed to the republic and the Egyptian presence in Yemen at any given moment. The Royalists stood in contradistinction to the so-called Republicans—likewise a motley crew of army officers, merchants, southern Shāfi'īs, and disaffected Zaydīs.[12] Yemen's difficult topography and deep social cleavages, along tribal, sectarian, and class lines, heightened the chances of indecision in the struggle for power, thereby raising the specter of civil war. The fact that this local contest took place in a regional context of great tension made armed conflict all the more likely.

Egyptian military aid followed so fast upon the coup that many foreign observers suspected, not unreasonably, that the "revolution" was an Egyptian concoction.[13] Indeed, the incredible speed of the Egyptian

[12] The terms *malakī* (royalist) and *jumhūrī* (republican) became common usage among Yemenis in late 1962. Aḥmad Aḥmad Faraj, *Rijāl fī khanādiq al-difā' 'an al-thawrah* (Ṣan'ā', 1995), 178.

[13] A similar point is made by Peter Mansfield, *Nasser* (London: Methuen, 1969), 130. For variants of the charge, see Dana Adams Schmidt, *Yemen: The Unknown War* (New York: Holt, Rinehart and Winston, 1968), 22–23; Edgar O'Ballance, *War in the Yemen* (Hamden: Archon, 1971), 84; Robin Bidwell, *The Two Yemens* (Boulder, CO: Westview Press, 1983), 169–96. By contrast, the director of Egyptian military intelligence at the time denies any Egyptian role in the coup, a version more or less accepted by then US ambassador to Egypt, John Badeau. Ḥadīdī, *Shāhid 'alā ḥarb al-Yaman*, 20, 25–26; Badeau, *The Middle East Remembered* (Washington, DC: Middle East Institute, 1983), 199; idem, *The American Approach to the Arab World* (New York: The Council on Foreign Relations, 1968), 127. But French intelligence concluded on the basis of intercepts that Egyptian intelligence stood behind the attempted assassination of the Imam in July 1962 and that Cairo had orchestrated the coup and its aftermath in a series of directives between September 20 and 28. Airgram, Paris to Department of State, no. A-361, "French Analysis of Nasser's attempts at subversion in other Arab states," August 14, 1962, p. 1, RG 59, CDF 1960–63, Box 2074, 786b.11, NARA; Cable, Paris to Secretary of State, no. 1792, October 13, 1962, RG 59, CDF

response, the suspicious coincidence of the coup with the anniversary of the *infiṣāl*, and the conscious emulation of Egypt by the self-styled Yemeni Free Officers all seemed to point in one direction: the revolution was a conspiracy hatched in Cairo. To what extent an Egyptian hand had guided the Yemeni revolutionaries is a question that may never be resolved. Oddly enough, both the Egyptian and Yemeni narratives of the revolution share an interest in portraying the coup d'état as a Yemeni affair—with the Egyptians emphasizing that they were merely responding to Yemeni pleas for protection from Saudi Arabia.[14] The truth probably lies somewhere between the two extremes: the Egyptians had known about preparations for the coup and prepared to aid it in advance, but they did not take an active role in the coup itself.[15] In any event, there was something more to the intervention than the seizure of an opportunity crafted by Yemeni agency.

The view of the intervention as Egypt's response to the *infiṣāl*, though it contains important elements of truth, fails to account for the considerable record of Egyptian subversion in Yemen well before the Syrian secession. According to an alternate interpretation, presented most compellingly by Sāmī Sharaf, Nasser's private secretary at the time, the explanation for Egypt's reaction to the events of September 1962 ought not to be sought in the tumultuous period that immediately preceded the revolution; rather, it is to be found in a decade of Egyptian support for national liberation movements in the Arab world in general and in Yemen in particular. Ever since the early 1950s, the Free Officers had volunteered their capital as a hub for the funding, training, and arming

1960–63, Box 2080, 786h.00/10-1362, NARA; Cable, Vered (Paris) to Head of Research, Middle East, October 25, 1962, HZ 3449/27, Israel State Archives (hereafter ISA), Jerusalem, Israel. See also James, *Nasser at War*, 56–60.

[14] See, e.g., Haykal, *Sanawāt al-ghalayān*, 621–22; ʻAbd Allāh Juzaylān, *Muqaddimāt thawrat al-Yaman* (Beirut: Manshūrāt al-ʻAṣr al-Ḥadīth, 1995), 28–32 and passim. Juzaylān sees locals (not least himself) as the prime movers of a revolution hijacked by exiles and their patrons in Cairo. For a Taʻizz-centered account that highlights Egyptian attempts to coordinate between the various conspirators, see ʻAbd al-Ghanī Muṭahhar, *Yawm wallada al-Yaman majdah: Dhikrayāt ʻan thawrat sibtimbir sanat 1962* (Cairo: Dār al-Bāz, 1984).

[15] This is the view held by the Soviet Foreign Ministry, and it is shared by the Egyptian general and historian Maḥmūd Aḥmad, by Nasser's secretary, Sāmī Sharaf, and by Egypt's head of foreign intelligence, Ṣalāḥ Naṣr. Memo, V. Kornev, "Polozhenie v Iemenskoi Arabskoi Respublike i Iemeno-OARovskie otnoshenia (spravka)," March 13 1964, f. 5, op. 30, d. 451, pp. 39–40, RGANI; Aḥmad, *Dhikrayāt ḥarb al-Yaman*, 264; Sharaf, *Sanawāt*, 2:622; Ṣalāḥ Naṣr, *Mudhakkirāt Ṣalāḥ Naṣr* (Cairo: Dār al-Khayyāl, 1999), 2:331–32.

of myriad Arab and African revolutionaries. Against this background of energetic activism, Egyptian policy toward the revolutionary movement in Yemen stands out as especially proactive. Yemen lay at the heart of plans formulated in 1953 by Egyptian intelligence to spread revolution throughout the Arab world. Soon after seizing power in Egypt, Nasser was already convinced that the collapse of the Imamate would do much to further the cause of revolution throughout the Arab world, and he was therefore determined to promote those who were capable of opposing it. It is in this context that we should consider the extensive record of Egyptian intelligence contacts with opposition elements in Yemen and in Cairo throughout the 1950s, a bungled coup d'état in 1955, and the dispatch of Egyptian military and police training missions to Yemen in 1954 and 1957.[16]

In other words, the overthrow of the Imamate, though primarily a Yemeni achievement, was also the culmination of nearly ten years of joint Egyptian-Yemeni efforts. The Egyptian government did not control the events of 1962. But its agents were in contact with all the main protagonists, most of whom had studied in Egyptian military institutions and operated under assurances of Egyptian support. Accordingly, when the Egyptian government received a call for help from a clique of Yemeni officers acting in evident emulation of Egyptian role models, there was no question of ignoring the appeal; the decision to support them had already been made.[17] Egypt responded, in other words, not on impulse, but by reflex, conditioned by nearly a decade of consistent policy.

This unapologetic depiction of the campaign as the natural product of Egypt's revolutionary foreign policy steers the debate about the origins of the intervention away from both the scholarly trope of post-*infiṣāl* trauma on the one hand and the Egyptian apologia of unanticipated reaction to Saudi meddling on the other.[18] Nevertheless, there is

[16] Sharaf, *Sanawāt*, 2:593–621; Maḥrizī, *al-Ṣamt al-ḥā'ir*, 8–105; ʿAbd al-Raḥmān al-Bayḍānī, *Miṣr wa thawrat al-Yaman* (Cairo: Dār al-Maʿārif, 1993), 47–48, 65–66; idem, *Azmat al-ummah al-ʿarabiyyah wa-thawrat al-Yaman* (Cairo: al-Maktab al-Miṣrī al-Ḥadīth, 1984), 260–66 and passim; Juzaylān, *Muqaddimāt*, 34–40 and passim; Aḥmad, *Dhikrayāt*, 256–64.

[17] Sharaf, *Sanawāt*, 2:617, 620; Vered, *Revolution*, 48–49. For a similar view, see Badeau, *Middle East*, 205–7. See also Naṣr, *Mudhakkirāt*, 2:334.

[18] For the former, see, e.g., Mansfield, *Nasser*, 128–31; Kerr, *Arab Cold War*, 40–41; and to a lesser extent Stephens, *Nasser*, 380, 385. For the latter, see Haykal, *Sanawāt al-ghalayān*, 619–22, 625–28; Anthony Nutting, *Nasser* (London: Constable, 1972), 320–22; and James,

no escaping the fact that the Syrian secession marked a turning point in Egyptian-Yemeni relations and in Egyptian attitudes toward the use of force.

Up until 1961, Egypt concealed its revolutionary intentions toward the Imamate beneath a veneer of friendly relations. The Egyptian military and police missions went to Yemen ostensibly to train the Yemeni armed forces to fight the British, not their sovereign. Moreover, Nasser's friendly relations with Aḥmad's chosen successor, Crown Prince Muḥammad al-Badr, seemed to indicate that differences between the two states arose out of specific policies, not a fundamental contradiction between two systems of government. This conclusion seemed all the more justified when, in March 1958, the Imam elected to join the UAR as a junior partner in what became known as the United Arab States, or UAS, thereby associating his ancient kingdom with the grandest pan-Arab experiment of the century.[19] But the chimera of two revolutionary republics joined to a deeply conservative kingdom had a complex psychological makeup. The Imam acceded to the UAR not out of a desire for self-immolation. Quite to the contrary, Aḥmad's primary goal was to move out of Cairo's line of fire by tethering himself to Egypt's revolutionary bandwagon.[20] Nor did Nasser's acceptance of the Imam reflect a genuine sprit of compromise. The need to generate momentum behind an expanding pan-Arab entity must have barely outweighed the embarrassment caused by introducing such a reactionary partner to the union.

Thus Yemen became one of Egypt's most obvious targets for retribution in the aftermath of Syria's secession—along with Syria itself. Relations between Egypt and Yemen came under strain even before the *infiṣāl* on account of the Imam's tacit support for Iraqi leader 'Abd al-Karīm Qāsim's annexationist ambitions in Kuwait in the summer of

Nasser at War, 56. Ḥadīdī's account combines elements of both strands. Ḥadīdī, *Shāhid 'alā ḥarb al-Yaman*, 9–31.

[19] Ḥamrūsh, *Qiṣṣat thawrat 23 yūliyū*, 3:201.

[20] Vered, *Revolution*, 14–15; Jankowski, *Nasser's Egypt*, 140; Aḥmad Ḥusayn Sharaf al-Dīn, *al-Yaman 'abra al-tārīkh: Dirāsah jughrāfiyyah tārīkhiyyah siyāsiyyah shāmilah* (Cairo: Maṭba'at al-Sunnah al-Muḥammadiyyah, 1964), 346; Naṣr, *Mudhakkirāt*, 2:330–31. He may also have wished to gain leverage over Yemen's peninsular opponents, Great Britain and Saudi Arabia. Podeh, *Decline*, 57–58; Clive Jones, *Britain and the Yemen Civil War, 1962–1965: Ministers, Mercenaries and Mandarins: Foreign Policy and the Limits of Covert Action* (Brighton and Portland: Sussex Academic Press, 2004), 33; Stanko Guldescu, "Yemen: The War and the Haradh Conference," *Review of Politics* 28, no. 3 (1966): 321.

1961.[21] After Syria seceded from the union, Yemen remained formally federated with Egypt. Within several weeks, however, the Imam, seeing that the tide had shifted against Cairo, summoned the courage to join in the monarchs' schadenfreude at Nasser's predicament. Aḥmad did so not by dissolving the union as Syria had done—secession would have posed too direct a challenge to his nemesis in Cairo—but rather, true to Arabian tradition, by expounding his position in verse.

In a sixty-four-line poem addressed "To the Arabs" in mid-December, the Imam attacked the noisy propaganda and socialist heresies of an unnamed regime, contrasting them sharply with the principles of Islam.[22] Nasser responded immediately. In his Victory Day speech at Port Sa'īd on December 23, the Egyptian president defended Egypt's socialist turn as inherent in the Islamic conception of justice and ridiculed the perversion of social justice Imam Aḥmad and King Sa'ūd practiced.[23] Three days later the Egyptian government announced its decision to terminate the association with the Imamate, politely citing the failure of the two governments to agree on social policy.[24] The dismissal, however civil, could not disguise Nasser's deep displeasure.

The dissolution of the UAS signaled open season on the Imamate in the Egyptian press, which began to host attacks on the Imam by prominent Yemeni exiles ensconced in Cairo. The Egyptian government's chosen instrument for this purpose was one of the most controversial figures associated with the revolution, Dr. 'Abd al-Raḥmān al-Bayḍānī. The educated son of a Yemeni émigré, Bayḍānī had insinuated his way into the corridors of power in Cairo in the early 1960s. Bayḍānī lacked the spiritual credentials or popularity of some of the better-known Free Yemenis resident in Cairo at the time, such as Aḥmad Muḥammad Nu'mān, a prominent Shāfi'ī notable and future prime minister, and Muḥammad al-Zubayrī, an influential Zaydī. But his close ties with Sadat made up for his lack of a political base in Yemen and won him a greater share in Egypt's revolutionary activities. In the period immediately preceding the revolution, Bayḍānī enjoyed varying degrees of co-

[21] Nutting, *Nasser*, 320.

[22] Sharaf al-Dīn, *al-Yaman*, 347–49; Aḥmad, *al-Dawr*, 76; Vered, *Revolution*, 18; Schmidt, *The Unknown War*, 45; Paul Dresch, *A History of Modern Yemen* (Cambridge: Cambridge University Press, 2000), 86. For the complete text, see Sharaf al-Dīn, *al-Yaman*, 349–52.

[23] UAR, *Majmū'at khuṭab*, 3:252–53.

[24] Sharaf al-Dīn, *al-Yaman*, 346, 352–53; Vered, *Revolution*, 19; Aḥmad, *al-Dawr*, 76.

operation with senior members of the regime, including Sadat, Nasser and ʿĀmir, Director of Military Intelligence Ṣalāḥ al-Dīn al-Ḥadīdī, and, to a lesser extent, Chief of General Intelligence Ṣalāḥ Naṣr.[25] First in the pages of *Rūz al-Yūsuf*, then over the airwaves of *Ṣawt al-ʿArab*, Bayḍānī led the crescendo of battle cries against the Imam from January to September 1962.[26]

Both the explanation of the intervention as a reaction to Syria's secession and the view that sees it as the logical issue of long-standing policy converge on the conclusion that Egyptian support for the revolution was inevitable. From here it is but a small leap to the conclusion that the intervention itself—and by extension, the war as a whole—was unavoidable once the conspirators struck in Ṣanʿāʾ. However, there is nothing in the nature of Egyptian preparations to suggest that support for the revolutionaries would take the form of direct intervention by the Egyptian military. It may be true that in parallel to the propaganda campaign of 1962, Egyptian intelligence agencies stepped up their efforts to collect information about Yemen and enhance military and financial cooperation with Yemeni opposition groups.[27] Nor is there any reason to dispute reports that by the end of August the Egyptian air force had a DC-3, loaded with arms and ammunition, on standby at Aswan airport ready to fly Bayḍānī and other exiled Yemeni leaders with a quantity of arms to Taʿizz (the anticipated locus of the revolution) at a moment's notice.[28] We can even accept that when revolutionary representatives from Yemen appeared in Cairo days before the revolution in order to ascertain the degree of Egyptian support, Nasser authorized his intelligence chief to tell the Yemenis that they could

[25] Bayḍānī, *Miṣr wa thawrat al-Yaman*, 79–81, 109–11; Ḥadīdī, *Shāhid ʿalā ḥarb al-Yaman*, 18–19. Bayḍānī's account points to a possible division within the Egyptian intelligence community concerning Yemen policy. As he tells it, military intelligence supported the northern revolutionaries enthusiastically, while the heads of the civilian agency undermined the republican cause, both before and after the intervention, by focusing on fomenting revolution in the British-controlled south of the country. This thesis gains some support from the disparaging portrayal of Bayḍānī and skeptical account of the intervention provided by Amīn Huwaydī, deputy chief of Egyptian general intelligence at the time. *Khamsūn ʿāman min al-ʿawāṣif: Mā raʾaytuhu qultuh* (Cairo: Markaz al-Ahrām li-l-Tarjamah wa-l-Nashr, 2002), 280–81.

[26] Ḥamrūsh, *Qiṣṣat thawrat 23 yūliyū*, 3:206–7; Vered, *Revolution*, 20. Bayḍānī authored a series of articles attacking the Imamate under the header "Secrets of Yemen." For the first, see *Rūz al-Yūsuf*, no. 1751, January 1, 1962.

[27] Ḥadīdī, *Shāhid ʿalā ḥarb al-Yaman*, 20; Ḥamrūsh, *Qiṣṣat thawrat 23 yūliyū*, 3:207–9.

[28] Bayḍānī, *Miṣr wa thawrat al-Yaman*, 81.

count on any quantity of arms and ammunition necessary for the success of the revolution.[29] But none of this pointed to war.

Far from indicating a plan for intervention, Egyptian preparations suggest intent to *avoid* direct intervention by adhering strictly to a course of indirect involvement. Thus while we may accept that the decision to support the anticipated revolution with money, weaponry, and political cover had fallen by the summer of 1962 (and possibly earlier), there is no evidence to suggest that serious thought had been given to the deployment of troops prior to the coup. Indeed, the record of piecemeal escalation and the utter lack of preparedness among Egyptian forces in the early months of the intervention cannot be explained as the products of incompetence alone: a near-complete absence of preparation is evident.[30] In other words, that Egypt would furnish military and financial aid to a successful revolutionary endeavor was almost a foregone conclusion by the summer of 1962, but the manner and extent of support was entirely unexpected—to Egypt's leaders as much as anyone else.[31]

Egypt's external conflict with most of the Arab regimes was the most obvious and indispensible ingredient in Nasser's decision to intervene in the civil war on behalf of the republic. Not surprisingly, it forms the backbone of familiar narratives of the war's origins. However, the regional context, which does establish the near certainty of Egyptian aid to a potential revolution in Yemen in 1962, is not sufficient to explain why Egyptian support took the form of direct intervention and how a five-year counterinsurgency resulted. That outcome was in fact far from inevitable; it was the result of decisions the Egyptian leadership made consciously, if hastily, in late September and early October 1962.

The view of the intervention as an inevitable counterstrike in the aftermath of the *infiṣāl* elides the historical policy choices open to the Egyptian leadership in response to the revolution in Yemen. The teleological chronicle of a disaster foretold conceals the fact that direct military intervention was only one of several policy alternatives available at the time, including indirect provision of aid. Indeed, given the near total unpreparedness of the Egyptian armed forces for war, direct inter-

[29] Naṣr, *Mudhakkirāt*, 2:332. Naṣr recalls discouraging hopes for the deployment of Egyptian troops.

[30] See chapter five.

[31] My conclusion accords with Aḥmad, *al-Dawr*, 111. See also Ali Abdel Rahman Rahmy, *The Egyptian Policy in the Arab World: Intervention in Yemen, 1962–1967: Case Study* (Washington, DC: University Press of America, 1983), 96, 98, 109.

vention appears on the face of it to have been the *least* likely response to the coup d'état in Ṣan'ā'. Thus the fact that an intervention occurred at all is a mystery demanding explanation. To begin to understand how, nevertheless, the war came about, it is necessary to examine a factor that has received far less scholarly attention than Egypt's external difficulties: the competition for political power *within* Nasser's regime.[32]

The Struggle for Power in Egypt

The complex relationship between Nasser and his deputy, 'Abd al-Ḥakīm 'Āmir, has been the subject of considerable speculation. In particular, the murky circumstances surrounding 'Āmir's death in September 1967, an apparent suicide under house arrest, have fueled rumors about an alleged plot against Nasser and have given rise to a considerable body of literature dedicated to tracing the origins of the rift.[33] The critical historian, however, cannot fail to take note of the fact that there is virtually nothing in the foreign diplomatic records of the time to suggest tensions between Nasser and 'Āmir prior to 1967. Nor can one ignore the record of extraordinary friendship between the two men up until 1967. These facts make the retrospective claims of a long-simmering rivalry baffling, to say the least, and raise the suspicion that the story of 'Āmir's treachery was invented in the aftermath of the 1967 war in order to clear Nasser of responsibility for the defeat. Indeed, in the absence of hard evidence one is tempted to conclude that Nasser's supporters manufactured the rift after the fact in order to cover up a conspiracy to sacrifice 'Āmir as a scapegoat. But since the framing—and possible murder—of the second most powerful man in Egypt could hardly have occurred without Nasser's blessing, the questions surrounding the relationship receive no easy answer under either scenario. Unfortunately, the layers of rumor that have accreted with time have only served to obscure the issue, to the point where it is now virtually impossible to tell fact from fantasy.

Although it would appear foolhardy to attempt a rational analysis of this anthology of gossip, there is no avoiding the issue entirely, given

[32] A notable exception is Laura James, *Nasser at War*, 49–52, 71–72. James senses the significance of the internal struggle for power but avoids grappling with its policy implications. Nasser's biographer, Robert Stephens, likewise appreciates the tensions within the regime but fails to explain their bearing on the decision for war (*Nasser*, 385).

[33] Typical of this genre is 'Abd Allāh Imām, *Nāṣir wa-'Āmir* (Cairo: Rūz al-Yūsuf, 1985).

the interconnectedness of the intervention in Yemen with deep structural tensions within the Egyptian regime. The best place to start is the memoir of Egyptian Vice President 'Abd al-Laṭīf al-Baghdādī, who recorded many of the events in this period in a diary replete with tidbits on the tortured relationship between the two men.[34] Baghdādī provides too much vivid detail for the rift to be purely an invention motivated by his obvious rivalry with 'Āmir, while his subsequent break with the president, also chronicled in these reminiscences, clears him of the suspicion that he might be serving up Nasserist apologetics. Moreover, the broad contours of Baghdādī's account have been substantiated recently by close Nasser aide Sāmī Sharaf and by the former chief of general intelligence, Ṣalāḥ Naṣr.[35] Taken together, these sources establish beyond reasonable doubt that a rift did develop between the president and his commander in chief after 1956, and that it carried profound implications for the behavior of the regime both at home and abroad throughout the decade leading up to 1967.[36]

A majority of the Free Officers were army buddies from the same 1938 cohort at the military academy in Cairo, while most of the others overlapped with them at the academy or at Staff College in the '40s.[37] The conspiracy that brought them to power was essentially an old boys' network of close personal friends, of whom Nasser and 'Āmir were the closest. But while trust and camaraderie were essential qualities for the successful launch of a conspiracy, they were insufficient for ruling a country of 30 million people. It was only natural that relations cemented among junior officers in the barracks would come under strain when burdened with the responsibilities of government. The process by which the Bolshevik brotherhood of co-conspirators degenerated into one-man dictatorship under Stalin offers a parallel to the corrosive effect of

[34] 'Abd al-Laṭīf al-Baghdādī, *Mudhakkirāt 'Abd al-Laṭīf al-Baghdādī*, 2 vols. (Cairo: al-Maktab al-Ḥadīth, 1977).

[35] Sharaf, *Sanawāt*, 1:407–37; Naṣr, *Mudhakkirāt*, 3:21–46. Echoes of the dispute can be found scattered throughout the memoirs of many of the leading figures of this period.

[36] See also Stephens, *Nasser*, 358–59.

[37] Igor Beliaiev and Evgenii Primakov, *Egipet: Vremia presidenta Nasera* (Moscow: Mysl, 1974), 35–37; Vatikiotis, *Nasser and His Generation*, 49; idem, *The Egyptian Army in Politics: Pattern for New Nations?* (Bloomington: Indiana University Press, 1961), 45–49; Sharaf, *Sanawāt*, 1:409; Eliezer Be'eri, *Army Officers in Arab Politics and Society* (New York: Praeger, 1970), 77, 79, 85, 122, 126–27; Imām, *Nāṣir wa-'Āmir*, 6.

power on the bonds among the Free Officers.[38] As in the Soviet Union, the process in Egypt was gradual, necessitating more than a decade to complete the arc from exuberant revolutionary egalitarianism to terror, exclusion, and submission.

In the long run, the brew of friendship and power proved costly to both men and to the regime they ran jointly for fifteen years. On a purely personal level, Nasser's Byzantine maneuvers to get his friend to resign without bringing down the regime can only be explained as the paralyzing product of love and fear.[39] But the story of a friendship gone sour overshadows a much more important *institutional* struggle for power within the Egyptian regime. The underlying structural factors made the conflict between the two leaders intractable.

The original decision-making body of the Free Officers, after they seized power in 1952, was the Revolutionary Command Council (RCC). Perhaps modeled on the Ottoman Committee of Union and Progress, its membership combined an egalitarian inclination toward collective rule with a conspiratorial preference for behind-the-scenes governance. Nasser apparently acquired the status of *primus inter pares* well before the revolution, but his emergence from the shadows as the public face of the conspiracy was nevertheless slow. His assumption of the premiership in 1954, and then the presidency in 1956, did not substantially alter the adumbral status of his colleagues. On the contrary, his rise shunted them further away from the limelight.[40] The so-called *Majmū'ah*, or ruling group, retained its consultative function but shed its decision-making capacity over time. Although Nasser increasingly relied on RCC members to fill key positions in the cabinet and bureaucracy, these shifted in and out of office without a permanent hold on executive power or any meaningful role in statecraft. Other than Nasser himself, this rule had one exception, forever resented and never accepted: 'Abd al-Ḥakīm 'Āmir.

Nasser selected 'Āmir early on for the all-important task of controlling the armed forces and securing their fidelity. 'Āmir's low rank was an obstacle easily swept aside. To pave the way for 'Āmir's appointment as commander in chief, Nasser engineering his promotion from

[38] Simon Sebag Montefiore, *Stalin: The Court of the Red Tsar* (New York: Vintage Books, 2005).

[39] Cf. Imām, *Ḥusayn al-Shāfi'ī*, 123.

[40] Tharwat 'Ukāshah, *Mudhakkirātī fī al-siyāsah wa-l-thaqāfah* (Cairo: Dār al-Hilāl, 1990), 1:13; and 2:129–30.

major to major general in a single go in the summer of 1953.[41] Not since Enver Pasha's promotion from lieutenant colonel to minister of war forty years before had the Middle East witnessed such a meteoric rise through the ranks. The result for Egypt was nearly as disastrous as it had been for the Ottoman Empire. ʻĀmir, who succeeded remarkably at pleasing the generals, turned out to be incompetent as their superior.[42] Sensitive, charming, and careless, he was a politically minded socialite not cut out for high military command. The former Soviet military attaché in Cairo, Sergei Khrakhmalov, records his first impression of the Egyptian general: "[His] views . . . struck me as exceedingly primitive. It seemed that in front of me [stood] not the supreme commander of a state's armed forces, but rather an infantry battalion commander of mediocre capacities."[43]

ʻĀmir's shortcomings became abundantly evident in the Suez War, a political victory that barely succeeded in concealing the scope of military disaster.[44] The inescapable conclusion from the events of October–November 1956 was that Egypt possessed neither an effective army nor commanders capable of reforming it. From the perspective of the national interest, there was no question: much of the high command, including the commander in chief, simply had to go in order to pave the way for major reform.[45] But the national interest was not the deciding factor in 1956. When, in the aftermath of Suez, Nasser confronted ʻĀmir with the imperative of change, ʻĀmir tied his own destiny to the fate of his senior commanders and threatened to resign. The president backed

[41] Baghdādī, *Mudhakkirāt*, 1:77; Imām, *Nāṣir wa-ʻĀmir*, 6–8; Be'eri, *Army Officers*, 322. A number of ʻĀmir's colleagues on the RCC, including Baghdādī, opposed his promotion. Sharaf, *Sanawāt*, 1:415.

[42] Nasser admitted this in conversation with Miles Copeland. R. M. Tesh (Cairo) to H. B. Walker (NEAD), November 14, 1967, FCO 39/235, PRO. See also ʻAwaḍ, *Aqniʻat al-nāṣiriyyah*, 164–66; ʻAbd Allāh Imām, *al-Iftirā' ʻalā thawrat yūliyū: Hazīmat yūniyū, mu'āmarat al-mushīr ʻĀmir wa- intiḥāruh, al-ṣulḥ maʻa Isrā'īl* (Cairo: Dār al-Khayyāl, 2003), 14; idem, *Nāṣir wa-ʻĀmir*, 13; Anwar al-Sādāt, *al-Baḥth ʻan al-dhāt: Qiṣṣat ḥayātī* (Cairo: al-Maktab al-Miṣrī al-Ḥadīth, 1978), 207.

[43] Sergei Krakhmalov, *Zapiski voennogo attaché: Iran-Egipet-Iran-Afganistan* (Moscow: Russkaia Razvedka, 2000), 93. See also ʻAbd Allāh Imām, ed., *al-Farīq Muḥammad Fawzī: Al-Naksah, al-istinzāf, al-sijn* (Dār al-Khayyāl, 2001), 19, 44–45, 56.

[44] Baghdādī, *Mudhakkirāt*, 1:337, 339, 344, 359; Krakhmalov, *Zapiski*, 94; Imām, *Nāṣir wa-ʻĀmir*, 10, 18, 20.

[45] Sharaf, *Sanawāt*, 1:421–24; Ṣalāḥ al-Imām, *Ḥusayn al-Shāfiʻī wa-asrār thawrat yūliyū wa-ḥukm al-Sādāt* (Cairo: Maktab Ūzīrīs li-l-Kutub wa-l-Majallāt, 1993), 120; Imām, *Muḥammad Fawzī*, 27–29.

down.[46] In part, he must have done so because the dismissal of his commander in chief would have exposed the reality of military failure lurking beneath the ballyhooed "victory" of Suez. But there was more to it than that.

Some of the most powerful men in Egypt favored 'Āmir's ouster: his comrades on the RCC. It was only natural for many of the original band of conspirators to regard 'Āmir's meteoric rise with envy.[47] While Nasser's ascent was both natural and beneficial, 'Āmir's must have seemed increasingly unjustified as the 1950s wore on, particularly to those who aspired to replace him and perhaps succeed Nasser himself one day. Men like 'Abd al-Laṭīf al-Baghdādī and Kamāl al-Dīn Ḥusayn, both competent military commanders relegated to the sidelines of Nasser's sham civilian government, chafed at 'Āmir's groundless persistence in power. In light of this opposition, the fact that Nasser decided to retain 'Āmir in the aftermath of the Suez debacle is all the more surprising.

A good part of the explanation has to do with the evolving balance of power within the regime. By 1956, 'Āmir's efforts to coup-proof the armed forces had produced networks of loyalty and patronage, which revolved around him and an expanding circle of acolytes.[48] 'Āmir's power grew in direct relation to the number of officers who owed their position to him. Conversely, the influence of this growing band of supporters, led by his calculating *chef de cabinet*, Shams al-Dīn Badrān, depended entirely on 'Āmir's continuation in office. As a result, the question of 'Āmir's future ceased to be a purely professional matter for decision by the political echelon and became tightly bound up in the cliquish politics of the military.

It is not quite clear who controlled whom in 'Āmir's fiefdom—the so-called power center (*markaz quwwah*) that grew up around him in the armed forces.[49] Over time the commander's opinions naturally came to reflect those of his constituency. The interests of 'Āmir's subordinates tended to reinforce his own proud resolve not to step down. The notion that 'Āmir ever seriously intended to mount a coup and seize power is probably unfounded. It was not that he ever seriously considered

[46] Baghdādī, *Mudhakkirāt*, 1:360–66; Imām, *Nāṣir wa-'Āmir*, 43–45, 47–49; Sharaf, *Sanawāt*, 1:426–28; Fawzī, *Ḥarb al-thalāth sanawāt*, 34.

[47] See, e.g., Nasser's comments in Haykal, *al-Infijār*, 847.

[48] Vatikiotis, *Nasser and His Generation*, 160; Baghdādī, *Mudhakkirāt*, 2:168; Nutting, *Nasser*, 309; Saïd Aburish, *Nasser: The Last Arab* (London: Duckworth, 2004), 190.

[49] For discussion, see Hannah Zubaydah, "The 'Power Centers' and the 'Intelligence State' [Hebrew]," in Shamir, *Decline of Nasserism*, 187–200.

replacing Nasser—although he may have certainly contemplated succeeding him—but that he was determined to hold on to his privileged position as number two.[50] And since Nasser could not be sure of the reaction of ʻĀmir's supporters, his loyalty mattered little as long as key elements in the military were prepared to revolt should their patron's powers be curtailed.[51]

Whether or not Nasser actually sought the removal of his trusted friend from the helm of the army at this stage is unclear; ʻĀmir's value as security watchdog may have outweighed his worthlessness as a commander in chief. But fear was certainly one ingredient of Nasser's decision to leave the military command structure intact in the aftermath of Suez. Even if the threat of a coup was overblown, there was still the real concern about the political costs of a fallout between the two icons of the revolution at a sensitive juncture in Egyptian history.[52]

Such weighty concerns would have been sufficient to override any objections from the RCC. At the same time the ease with which Nasser swept aside the national interest in 1956 suggests that additional factors played a role. Nasser's sympathizers like to portray him as the victim of his own security establishment, powerless to stop the chaos of competing interests pulsating within his dictatorship. A less charitable view holds that Nasser, far from helpless victim, served as Machiavellian puppet master of the regime's senior personalities. An inveterate gossiper and consummate intriguer, his favorite technique was to stir up conflict and then withdraw into a position of aloof neutrality. Appearing sympathetic to each of the feuding personalities and their fiefdoms, he would in fact manipulate their antagonisms from behind the scenes in order to perpetuate his own hold on power.[53] In other words, Nasser's apparent inability to resolve the power struggles within his regime may have masked a far more sinister truth: the instigation of a continu-

[50] Sharaf, *Sanawāt*, 1:536–38. See also Baker, *Egypt's Uncertain Revolution*, 52–53.

[51] For the contention that the problem lay with ʻĀmir's followers, not with ʻĀmir, see Imām, *Nāṣir wa-ʻĀmir*, 11, 22; idem, *Muḥammad Fawzī*, 22. For Nasser's fears, see Baghdādī, *Mudhakkirāt*, 2:171; Murād Ghālib, *Maʻa ʻAbd al-Nāṣir wa-l-Sādāt: Sanawāt al-intiṣār wa-ayyām al-miḥan: Mudhakkirāt Murād Ghālib* (Cairo: Markaz al-Ahrām li-l-Tarjamah wa-l-Nashr, 2001), 98–99.

[52] Sharaf, *Sanawāt*, 1:426–28. See also Gordon, *Nasser*, 124.

[53] Such is the interpretation given by Nasser's intelligence chief, Ṣalāḥ Naṣr. Naṣr, *Mudhakkirāt*, 3:38. For Nasser's belated mea culpa for letting the fiefdoms (*iqṭāʻiyyāt*) run wild in his kingdom, see ʻUkāshah, *Mudhakkirātī*, 2:390–91. See also Baker, *Egypt's Uncertain Revolution*, 55, 74.

ous competition for power constituted the essence of his conception of government.

Puppet master or not, there *was* something weak about letting all these competing ambitions play themselves out, often to the detriment of the national interest, and especially when it came to the armed forces.[54] Saïd Aburish may be on to something when he writes: "Nasser became a reluctant dictator overseeing a clutch of also-rans who lived in his shadow. His dictatorial ways didn't consist of eliminating old comrades, but of refusing to control them and having them accept their personal relationship with him as a way of retaining their freedom."[55]

Seen in this light, Nasser's " 'Āmir problem" may well have been the bloated by-product of his own attempts to play subordinates off against each other. In dealing with the revolutionary elite, the ever-present threat from 'Āmir and the military served as an argument for solidarity and an excuse for increasing presidential control, and when confronting the military, the dependable opposition from senior politicians such as 'Abd al-Laṭīf al-Baghdādī and 'Alī Ṣabrī constituted a civilian counterbalance to military might and a warning not to transgress the boundary separating fiefdom from fifth column.[56]

In any event, Nasser's reluctance to settle the issue in 1956 had far-reaching implications. Since no one paid a price for the rank incompetence the war revealed, the army remained complacent in its ineptitude. Incredibly, there was hardly any turnover in the Egyptian senior command in the entire decade leading up to the debacle of 1967.[57] Effecting change only became more difficult with time. After Suez, Nasser's feeble attempts to reform the military ran up against 'Āmir's burgeoning power base. As 'Āmir consolidated his position over the course of the 1950s, he became both the indispensible guarantor of the regime's security and a potential threat to its stability. Nasser's decision not to challenge 'Āmir throughout the period 1956–62 betrayed his priorities in this regard; stability came first, national security a distant second. The president's fear that what he had done to King Farouk would be done to him trumped his desire to create an efficient fighting machine. The consequence of this scale of priorities was grave: after 1956, the

[54] 'Ukāshah, *Mudhakkirātī*, 2:395.

[55] Aburish, *Nasser*, 190. Although one could quibble with the word *reluctant*, and several of those tossed off the revolutionary bandwagon at various stages of the journey might well dispute the benign characterization of Nasser's treatment of erstwhile comrades.

[56] See, e.g., Beattie, *Egypt*, 162.

[57] 'Abd Allāh Imām, *'Alī Ṣabrī yatadhakkar* (Cairo: Dār al-Waḥdah, 1988), 98.

Figure 1.3 Nasser and ʿĀmir in Yemen, April 1964. *Al-Quwwāt al-Musallaḥah*, May 1, 1964.

Egyptian military, for all intents and purposes, ceased to be a viable tool of state.[58] Without change at the top, there could be no reform; without reform, there must be no war. Although ostensibly the most power-

[58] ʿAwaḍ, *Aqniʿat al-nāṣiriyyah*, 127, 166–67; Sharaf, *Sanawāt*, 1:319, 536–37; Vatikiotis, *Nasser and His Generation*, 160. Cf. Dawisha, who takes Nasser's public expressions at face value and concludes that Nasser's overconfidence in the might of his armed forces led him into foreign adventures. Dawisha, "Perceptions, Decisions, and Consequences in Foreign Policy: The Egyptian Intervention in Yemen," *Political Studies*. 25, no. 2 (1977): 214; and Muḥammad Fawzī, who explores the military's bias toward internal security, but concludes it was still primarily oriented toward fighting. In fact, the preservation of an illusion of fighting capacity, as the army degenerated, may have been worse than a conscious slide toward impotence. Fawzī, *Ḥarb al-thalāth sanawāt*, 56–60; Imām, *Muḥammad Fawzī*, 29–31, 43–45, 53, 86, 93–94, 125.

ful Arab army in the Middle East, the Egyptian military, pride of the Free Officers' revolution, was thus effectively written off by its commander in chief, left to degenerate into a vestigial appendage of the state—important, like the Saudi military, for reasons of symbolism and internal security, but never seriously intended for use on the field of battle.

And yet, as we know, Nasser *did* commit the Egyptian military to large-scale action, not once but twice in the course of the 1960s. Explaining this paradox is one of the primary challenges facing any historian of the two wars of 1962 and 1967. The short answer is that both entailed massive miscalculation.

'Āmir continued to amass both military and political power in the late 1950s. In 1958, he received the new rank of field marshal (*mushīr*). After the establishment of the UAR, he became one of four vice presidents of the republic. In 1959, Nasser appointed 'Āmir as his personal emissary in Damascus, granting him wide powers in the administration of northern affairs and essentially making him governor of Syria. 'Āmir's record of intermittent rule in Syria between 1959 and 1961 is mixed, but his humiliating surrender to the secessionists in Damascus assured that he would bear a large share of responsibility for the disaster of the *infiṣāl*.[59] It was thus inevitable that the question of his future as commander in chief should arise once again in late 1961. By this point a majority of the leading members of the original Revolution Command Council (RCC) sought to get rid of 'Āmir, and two in particular seem to have been vying to succeed him: 'Abd al-Laṭīf al-Baghdādī and Kamāl al-Dīn Ḥusayn.[60] It appears that Nasser manipulated these ambitions in an effort to ease 'Āmir out of his place at the helm of the armed forces

[59] Haykal, *Sanawāt al-ghalayān*, 564–68; Sharaf, *Sanawāt*, 1:429–30; Huwaydī, *Khamsūn 'āman*, 54–56; Podeh, *Decline*, 98–101, 146; Beattie, *Egypt*, 159; Jankowski, *Nasser's Egypt*, 168; Muḥammad Fawzī, quoted in Imām, *Muḥammad Fawzī*, 120–21.

[60] Baghdādī, *Mudhakkirāt*, 2:174–75; Kamāl al-Dīn Ḥusayn, quoted in *Rūz al-Yūsuf*, August 4, 1975, 97; Huwaydī, *Khamsūn 'āman*, 193; Sādāt, *al-Baḥth*, 206–7; Sharaf, *Sanawāt*, 1:430–31; Naṣr, *Mudhakkirāt*, 3:41–42; Stephens, *Nasser*, 359; Imām, *Muḥammad Fawzī*, 39. It seems likely that Baghdādī's reticence concerning the likely replacement for 'Āmir, as well as Ḥusayn's maneuvering between Nasser and 'Āmir, stems from this rivalry. For Baghdādī's apparent rise to the number two position in the regime, see Airgram, Badeau (Cairo) to Sec. State, no. A-368, April 17, 1962, "An Estimate of the Relative Positions of UAR Leaders," RG 59, CDF 1960–63, Box 2072, 786b.00/4-1762, NARA. For interpretations of Baghdādī's fall that place emphasis on the rivalry with 'Āmir, see Telegram, Brant (Cairo) to Higgins (FO), June 5, 1964, FO 371/178579, PRO; Nutting, *Nasser*, 302–3.

and shift him gracefully into a civilian post far from the military.[61] As he had done after Suez, 'Āmir thwarted these designs—and any plans to retire senior commanders in the military—by threatening to resign and withdrawing ominously from the public eye. Ostensibly the very action the president desired, 'Āmir's sulky retreat created a dangerous situation in which the dispute threatened to become public and prompt action by his supporters within the military.[62] Nasser balked once again.

Tensions rose and fell throughout 1962. Then in August Nasser pushed through the revolutionary leadership one of his periodic experiments in government reorganization.[63] This reform, breathtaking in its ambition, amounted to an elaborate restructuring of the executive branch, entailing the establishment of a new Presidential Council (*majlis al-ri'āsah*, or PC), which would serve on top of the cabinet (or Executive Council, as it was henceforth to be called) as the highest decision-making body in the state.[64] Reminiscent of the proposal to dissolve the RCC in 1954 and the appointment of vice presidents with areas of supervisory responsibility in the summer of 1961, the move involved a collective decision on the part of the Free Officers to step down from positions of direct executive responsibility.[65] The idea was to place *all* members of the ruling group on an equal footing in purely supervisory roles, while lesser figures took on ministerial responsibilities.[66] Nasser

[61] Egyptian Ambassador to the USSR Murād Ghālib suggests that this was the motivation for tasking 'Āmir with political duties in Syria the year before. Ghālib, *Mudhakkirāt*, 98. See also Imām, *Nāṣir wa-'Āmir*, 64.

[62] Baghdādī, *Mudhakkirāt*, 2:124–33, 142–46, 158, 171, 174–77; Sadat, *al-Baḥth*, 206–8.

[63] Naṣr, *Mudhakkirāt*, 3:26, 28–29; Baghdādī, *Mudhakkirāt*, 2:178; 'Ukāshah, *Mudhakkirātī*, 2:393. Robert Stephens and Muḥammad Fawzī are almost certainly mistaken in placing this reform in March 1962. Stephens, *Nasser*, 360; Fawzī, *Ḥarb al-thalāth sanawāt*, 32. Their error is duplicated in James, *Nasser at War*, 51. For more on the possible origins of this erratum, see below.

[64] The resemblance to the Soviet Politburo was not lost on some contemporaries. That this reform coincided with the birth of the Arab Socialist Union may indicate conscious emulation of the Soviet model. Despatch, Arthur (Cairo) to Lord Home, no. 56 Confidential, October 2, 1962, "Reorganisation of the Government of the United Arab Republic," 2–3, FO 371/165350, PRO.

[65] For the historical precedents, see Vatikiotis, *Nasser and His Generation*, 140–46; Baghdādī, *Mudhakkirāt*, 2:173–74.

[66] The text of the eventual decree made this distinction clear by assigning specific areas of responsibility to all members of the Executive Council, and none to any member of the Presidential Council. Despatch, Arthur (Cairo) to Lord Home, no. 56 Confidential, October 2, 1962, Annex B, FO 371/165350, PRO. Nevertheless, PC members later received general areas of supervisory responsibility in six subcommittees. Despatch, Hawley (Cairo) to Laurence, VG 1015/138, October 5, 1962, FO 371/165350, PRO.

himself, under this arrangement, was to surrender his powers to the PC. This exercise in reform, little understood at the time, had little to do with efficacy and everything to do with power. Couched in terms of an idealistic move to collective leadership and indirect rule by the elders of the revolution, the formation of the council was in fact a sophisticated scheme to enhance presidential power.[67] Nasser never had any intention of relinquishing his presidential powers or vesting the PC with real authority. Quite the opposite: his aim was to strip his colleagues of their executive authority while pretending to bestow upon them the power of the presidency. Beyond Nasser himself, the main winner from this arrangement was his henchman, ʻĀlī Ṣabrī, the prospective president of the Executive Council.[68] Although there were a number of losers in the new order, there was none bigger than ʻAbd al-Ḥakīm ʻĀmir. And it was his potential loss that guaranteed RCC support for the maneuver.

There can be little doubt that the reform's primary objective was to pry ʻĀmir away from the armed forces and reassert the president's control over the military.[69] A key understanding concerning the Presidential Council exposed Nasser's true intentions in this regard. In order to strengthen the principle of civilian government, Nasser proposed that the powers over the promotion, transfer, and retirement of officers above the rank of battalion commander—a legal prerogative of the president exercised de facto by ʻĀmir—should be vested in the Presidential Council.[70] In the circuitous manner typical of Egyptian elite politics in

[67] See, e.g., Naṣr, *Mudhakkirāt*, 3:40. The reform's significance was lost on the British chargé, Geoffrey Arthur, who argued that its primary purpose was to allow Nasser and his colleagues "to devote more of their time to the formation of the Arab Socialist Union." His boss, Ambassador Harold Beeley, correctly perceived that the reform entailed the stripping away of executive power from the vice presidents but wrongly identified its primary targets as Baghdādī and Muḥyī al-Dīn. "Reorganisation of the Government of the United Arab Republic," 3; Despatch, Beeley (Cairo) to FO, no. 4, January 24, 1963, pp. 10–11, FO 371/172857, PRO. Robert Stephens underestimates Nasser's cunning in this episode (*Nasser*, 360–61).

[68] Many of the former RCC members, including ʻĀmir, opposed this appointment. Nutting, *Nasser*, 308–9; ʻUkāshah, *Mudhakkirātī*, 2:145–46.

[69] ʻĀmir certainly viewed it that way, and Nasser acknowledged as much in discussing the 1961 reforms. Sharaf, *Sanawāt*, 1:430–31; Baghdādī, *Mudhakkirāt*, 2:173–74, 183. See also Imām, *Nāṣir wa-ʻĀmir*, 64–67; idem, *Muḥammad Fawzī*, 121–22; Ḥamrūsh, *Qiṣṣat thawrat 23 yūliyū*, 2:212; Beattie, *Egypt*, 160. Fawzī indicates that he himself was slated to replace ʻĀmir, which is plausible in light of the sequence of events following the Six-Day War (*Ḥarb al-thalāth sanawāt*, 33); Sadat, *Search*, 160.

[70] Naṣr, *Mudhakkirāt*, 3:26, 28; Baghdādī, *Mudhakkirāt*, 2:193; Sharaf, *Sanawāt*, 1:431; Ṭāriq Ḥabīb, *Milaffāt thawrat yūliyū: Shahādāt 122 min ṣunnāʻihā wa-muʻāṣirīhā* (Cairo:

this period, the reform's basic function was to circumvent the need for the president to fire 'Āmir by compelling him to yield to the principle of collective rule or step down. As a face-saving technique, this was perhaps ingenious, but to those in the know, the subterfuge was painfully transparent. As 'Āmir reportedly told Ṣalāḥ Naṣr, chief of general intelligence at the time:

> "The issue is clear ... the order [*tanẓīm*] that Gamāl is forming is nothing but a device for his attainment of supreme power after the dissolution of the Presidential Council and the transfer of its responsibilities to the President ... Has Gamāl forgotten the crisis of March 1954 and the demands of [then president] Muḥammad Nagīb for the powers to appoint the commanders of formations down to the level of battalion commanders, as well as [the power] to promote officers and transfer them and appoint military attachés? Has he forgotten [what] the position of the Revolutionary Council [was] concerning this [demand]?"[71]

Full implementation of the proposed reform would have spelled not only the end of 'Āmir's career as commander in chief but also the dissolution of his power base in the armed forces. Behind the slogans of "collective rule," in other words, loomed the specter of a massive purge. Not surprisingly, the formation of the Presidential Council precipitated a crisis of the utmost gravity. On September 20, 'Āmir, professing fatigue and lack of interest in a nonmilitary role in public affairs, submitted his resignation to Nasser and then disappeared without a trace.[72] In a radio address on September 24, the president went ahead and announced the heralded reorganization of government under the banner of collective leadership.[73] Two days later, Yemen was engulfed in revolution.

Markaz al-Ahrām li-l-Tarjamah wa-l-Nashr, 1997), 231–32; Imām, *Ḥusayn al-Shāfi'ī*, 120–21. Control over personnel changes in the armed forces had apparently been the subject of contention for some time. Baghdādī quotes Nasser (p. 171) as saying that he had agreed to delegate to 'Āmir the president's legal powers to make promotions to the rank of major general and above at some point in the past, presumably before the launch of the reforms. We may speculate that this temporary delegation of powers had become entrenched over time, with the result that when it came time to reclaim them, Nasser found it necessary to resort to the stratagem of transferring the powers to a neutral body. Perhaps this is why Sadat misattributes this entire affair to 1961. Sadat, *Search*, 160.

[71] Naṣr, *Mudhakkirāt*, 3:31.

[72] Baghdādī, *Mudhakkirāt*, 2:178; 'Ukāshah, *Mudhakkirātī*, 2:393–94.

[73] Telegram, Arthur (Cairo) to FO, no. 94 Saving, September 25, 1962, FO 371/165350, PRO; Baghdādī, *Mudhakkirāt*, 2:77–81. A constitutional decree to this effect was announced on September 27 or 28. Telegram, Arthur (Cairo) to FO, no. 97 Saving, September 27, 1962,

The threat of a debilitating public scandal, or worse, a military coup, hung over the Egyptian leadership in those critical days in late September when the newly baptized Presidential Council met to debate the response to the coup d'état in Ṣan'ā'.[74] A majority of the senior civilian leaders stood aligned with the president against the general commander of the armed forces, in turn supported by a powerful faction in the military. 'Āmir's resignation placed Nasser in a bind. Publicly committed to announce the new order of government within days, he could no longer retreat.[75] If, on the other hand, he chose to go forward with the announcement in the absence of an arrangement with 'Āmir, he could not be sure of the army's reaction. And yet the president could not negotiate with a gun pointed at his head. In the event, Nasser decided to proceed with the reforms, thereby throwing the political future of his country into deepest uncertainty just as news began to trickle in of dramatic developments in Yemen.

The Accidental Intervention?

When news of the successful coup d'état in Ṣan'ā' reached Cairo in the early hours of September 27, 1962, it fell upon an Egyptian leadership united mainly by its determination to restore Egypt's position in the Arab world. Although a vigorous response seemed probable, large-scale military intervention in Yemen was highly unlikely.[76] How, then, did it come about? It is impossible to provide a full answer to this question without access to the archives of the Egyptian presidency. Nevertheless, the broad contours of what transpired in Cairo in late September and early October 1962 can be gleaned from the testimonies of several participants.

The death of the Imam, however desirable from Egypt's perspective, nevertheless seems to have caused confusion in Cairo. Badr was considered to be more reform minded than his father. Moreover, he had

---

FO 371/165350, PRO; Aḥmad, *al-Dawr*, 98. For the text, see "Reorganisation of the Government of the United Arab Republic," Annex A.

[74] Telegram, Badeau (Cairo) to Sec. State, no. 672, October 23, 1962, RG 59, CDF 1960–63, Box 2072, 786b.00/10-2362, NARA; Baghdādī, *Mudhakkirāt*, 2:207–8.

[75] Baghdādī, *Mudhakkirāt*, 2:181–82.

[76] This crucial point is appreciated by Aḥmad, *al-Dawr*, 111. According to Amīn Huwaydī, Egyptian general intelligence considered Yemen a "bottomless pit," geographically and demographically, and therefore opposed direct intervention (*Khamsūn 'āman*, 280).

been closely associated with Nasser in the 1950s. Although *Ṣawt al-'Arab* had been blasting Yemeni airwaves with incendiary propaganda for several months, much of it had been directed at Imam Aḥmad personally. Egypt's broader antimonarchic campaign notwithstanding, the Imam's sudden death on September 19, followed by the succession of his pro-Egyptian son, must have given Nasser and his associates pause.[77] The Egyptian president, apparently exasperated by the repeated postponement of plans for a coup and convinced by Badr's supporters in Cairo to give the new Imam a chance, reportedly ordered a halt to all hostile propaganda directed at the Imamate on September 21. But the moment of hesitation was brief. On September 25, Nasser gave his approval for one last fateful transmission. The next evening, the revolutionaries struck.

The first officially recorded meeting of senior decision makers in Egypt in connection with the crisis in Yemen took place on the morning of September 29, when the new Presidential Council met for the very first time and decided to recognize the Yemen Arab Republic (YAR).[78] By this point, things still seem to have been going according to plan. According to the account of the chief of Egyptian military intelligence at the time, a handful of Yemeni exiles together with an Egyptian communications team and Brigadier General 'Alī 'Abd al-Khabīr departed that evening for Ṣan'ā' aboard their preassigned DC-3, loaded with gold, a small quantity of arms, and a radio transmitter.[79] Their mission, apparently restricted to the provision of technical advice and the formulation of an assessment of the regime's military needs, was to last several weeks, based on the optimistic assumption that the regime would swiftly stabilize without the need for external protection.[80] There is no

[77] Bayḍānī, *Azmat al-ummah*, 304–7; Ḥamrūsh, *Qiṣṣat thawrat 23 yūliyū*, 3:208–9; Aḥmad, *Dhikrayāt*, 258, 260; Vered, *Revolution*, 21–22.

[78] In fact this was the very first foreign policy decision the PC made. Despatch, Arthur (Cairo) to Lord Home, no. 56, October 2, 1962, "Reorganisation of the Government of the United Arab Republic," p. 2, FO 371/165350, PRO; *New York Times*, "Cairo Recognizes Regime in Yemen," September 30, 1962, 5.

[79] Ḥadīdī, *Shāhid 'alā ḥarb al-Yaman*, 21–22; Aḥmad, *Dhikrayāt*, 277, 484n; Juzaylān, *Tārīkh*, 139–40. But Bayḍānī, perhaps based on an erroneous misquote of Ḥadīdī, cites the date of departure as the twenty-eighth, while Aḥmad Ḥamrūsh has the plane arriving at dawn on the twenty-eighth, which would entail departure late at night on the twenty-seventh. Bayḍānī, *Miṣr wa-thawrat al-Yaman*, 85–87; idem, *Azmat al-ummah*, 322; Ḥamrūsh, *Qiṣṣat thawrat 23 yūliyū*, 3:216; Aḥmad, *al-Dawr*, 111. Both Egyptian and Yemeni chronicles of the war suffer from a propensity for chronological imprecision.

[80] Ḥadīdī, *Shāhid 'alā ḥarb al-Yaman*, 22.

indication in Ḥadīdī's account that anything beyond the provision of advice, diplomatic support, and material aid was under consideration at this point. Yet within several days, a company of one hundred Egyptian commandos arrived in Yemen, followed within weeks by thousands more.

The factors that determined the dynamic of rapid escalation once Egyptian forces had been sent are fairly clear: the unanticipated intensity of tribal resistance, coupled with the weakness of the new regime in Ṣan'ā', necessitated ever-greater reinforcements to extend Republican control to the periphery and prevent the capital from being overrun. But the timing, process, and rationale of the initial decision to dispatch troops are all rather mystifying. The dominant narrative belongs to journalist Muḥammad Haykal, who portrays the decision to intervene as a belated, thoroughly defensive response to Saudi meddling, adopted at Sadat's insistence and against his own judgment.[81] The many irregularities in this account invite considerable skepticism: Haykal obfuscates the date and specifics of the decision, makes an unsuccessful attempt to portray the revolution as a near-total surprise to Egypt, and engages in a transparent bid to shift the blame for what ensued from Nasser's shoulders to Sa'ūd's (and to a lesser extent, Sadat's). Unfortunately, he is the only witness to have described the decision in any detail.

As Haykal tells it, news of the revolution sparked a three-day debate inside the Egyptian leadership, with opinion divided over two main options.[82] The first group, headed by Sadat, called for direct intervention in support of the revolution. This point is authenticated by Sadat, whose account of his own role in the decision is surprisingly candid: "when the Presidential Council met in Cairo to support the Yemeni request for assistance, I was the first to support it. I convinced the Council of the necessity for supporting the Yemeni Revolution, and we did so."[83]

[81] Haykal, *Sanawāt al-ghalayān*, 618–28; Nutting, *Nasser*, 320–22. The defensive outlook of the official narrative colors Adeed Dawisha's analysis of the Egyptian response ("Intervention in the Yemen," 49–50). For further scrutiny of the Egyptian government's official position, see James, *Nasser*, 56–57, 64.

[82] Haykal, *Sanawāt al-ghalayān*, 626–27. For reasons that will become apparent in chapter two, Haykal postdates this debate, attributing it to early October. The US ambassador to Egypt at the time recalls hearing about "a good deal of debate within the Presidency as to whether and to what degree Egypt should get involved." He too assesses the time it took to reach a decision at three days. Badeau, *Middle East*, 199.

[83] Sadat, *Search*, 162. In the Arabic original, Sadat portrays himself as the preeminent enthusiast (*awwal al-mutaḥammisīn*) of direct intervention. *Al-Baḥth*, 211. See also Naṣr,

The argument for this course of action, according to Haykal, rested on evidence of Saudi interference and an optimistic appraisal of tribal attitudes toward the revolution. The problem with this explanation is that the Saudi decision to arm the Royalists on any meaningful scale almost certainly came *in response* to the Egyptian dispatch of troops, which preceded it.[84] Nasser aide Sāmī Sharaf offers the following tripartite rationale for direct intervention: first, the security and future of the Arab nationalist movement as a whole hung in the balance; second, the situation did not brook hesitation, since any delay would lead to the collapse of the republic; and third, a task force comprised of a small number of commandos and assault aircraft would suffice to secure the regime in Ṣan'ā'.[85] According to PC member Ḥasan Ibrāhīm, Nasser cited the fear of potential Saudi intervention as the primary justification for dispatching a token deterrent force, which would cause the Saudis to think twice before challenging the republic.[86]

A second group within the senior leadership apparently called for the provision of arms and ammunition only. Their case rested on the assumptions that any actual fighting by Egyptian forces would be con-

---

Mudhakkirāt, 2:332; Aḥmad, *Dhikrayāt*, 278; Maḥmūd Riyāḍ, *Mudhakkirāt Maḥmūd Riyāḍ, 1948–1978* (Cairo: Dār al-Mustaqbal al-'Arabī, 1986), 2:271. It is hard to imagine that Nasser would have allowed himself to be persuaded by any individual to launch combat operations, however limited, against his own judgment.

[84] The heads of Egypt's civilian and military intelligence agencies both admit as much. Naṣr, *Mudhakkirāt*, 2:333; Ḥadīdī, *Shāhid 'alā ḥarb al-Yaman*, 43. See also James, *Nasser at War*, 65.

[85] Sharaf, *Sanawāt*, 2:620. See also Vered, *Revolution*, 50; Nutting, *Nasser*, 350. According to Ḥasan Ibrāhīm, the decision was adopted unanimously (Ḥamrūsh, *Qiṣṣat thawrat 23 yūliyū*, 3:220).

[86] Quoted in Ḥamrūsh, *Qiṣṣat thawrat 23 yūliyū*, 3:220. That deterrent calculations governed the thinking of Egyptian decision makers in the early phases of the intervention is evident from the decision to publish reports of the departure of the first Egyptian ship bearing military aid for Yemen. The information was released only after the ship had safely docked at the Yemeni port of Ḥudaydah. Telegram, Arthur (Cairo) to FO, no. 722, October 5, 1962, FO 371/162945, PRO. But in the course of a conversation with US ambassador to Egypt John Badeau the very morning after the coup, Anwar Sadat seemed more concerned about possible Saudi pressure on the United States to support the Royalists than any independent effort by Saudi Arabia. Indeed, the way Sadat framed his concerns seemed to Badeau to indicate an Egyptian perception of Saudi vulnerability, and even an expectation that the revolutionary contagion would soon spread to Riyadh. Telegram, Badeau (Cairo) to Sec. State, no. 510, September 27, 1962, RG 59, CDF 1960–63, Box 2079, 786h.00/9-2762, NARA.

strued as foreign intervention, and that the Egyptian army was unprepared for guerilla warfare in an unknown country. Although this line of argument sounds a trifle too prescient, we cannot exclude the possibility that it was voiced at the time.[87] Nasser allegedly leaned toward the first group but was apparently swayed by Sadat's recommendation, based on a quick visit to Yemen, that they follow the British practice by deploying a squadron of aircraft to assault the tribes from the air.[88] However, the squadron required a company for its protection, the company a battalion, and the intervention soon took on a life of its own.

Other accounts cast doubt on the existence of a meaningful debate in the PC. Then Chief of General Intelligence Ṣalāḥ Naṣr alludes to several days of deliberations between Nasser, ʻĀmir, and Sadat. He too reports that Sadat played a key role in overturning the consensus against intervention, building on the unexpected news that the Imam had survived, which transformed Egyptian appraisals of the situation.[89] Another senior member of the Egyptian ruling group, Vice President Zakariyyā Muḥyī al-Dīn, claims that no free debate about armed intervention took place, although there was some discussion of precautionary measures to avoid getting embroiled in war.[90] Others go further, suggesting that the decision was made even before the PC convened. ʻAbd al-Raḥmān al-Bayḍānī, for one, insists that Nasser had already agreed to send one hundred men and several planes by the time Bayḍānī left for Yemen.[91] A still more startling counterpoint to Haykal's narrative is Yemeni leader ʻAbd Allāh Juzaylān's assertion that Nasser and Sadat approved his request for an entire brigade several days *before the coup*.[92] If, in fact, Nasser approved orders to send Egyptian military units of any size to Yemen within a day or two of the coup, there would have been little

[87] Haykal, *Sanawāt al-ghalayān*, 627.

[88] According to Muḥammad Fawzī, Sadat recommended sending a sizeable Egyptian task force (*Ḥarb al-thalāth sanawāt*, 22).

[89] Naṣr, *Mudhakkirāt*, 2:332–34. For reasons that will become apparent in chapter two, Naṣr, like Haykal, pushes the debate into October, thereby enabling him to portray the intervention as a belated response to a request from Sallāl.

[90] Quoted in Ḥamrūsh, *Qiṣṣat thawrat 23 yūliyū*, 3:220.

[91] Bayḍānī, *Azmat al-ummah*, 321–22; idem, *Miṣr wa-thawrat al-Yaman*, 84–85. This question will be taken up in chapter two.

[92] Juzaylān, *Tārīkh*, 89–90. Even this larger contingent, Juzaylān stresses, was primarily intended to serve a deterrent purpose. If he is correct, it is likely that Nasser accepted the request in principle but decided to cut down the size of the task force from one brigade to a single company.

room for debate when the PC convened on the morning of the twenty-ninth.[93]

Although Haykal's account is problematic, it succeeds in highlighting the alternatives open to the Egyptian leadership at the end of September 1962. The first was to make do with indirect aid. The Egyptian government could have elected to restrict its support to money, materiel, advice, training, and diplomatic backing. In fact, indirect support was the most likely alternative simply by virtue of being the existing plan. This course of action carried two strong advantages: it minimized the risk to Egypt posed by any direct involvement in hostilities, and it placed a damper on the potential for escalation. The disadvantage was equally plain: by shunning the deployment of Egyptian forces, this option elevated the danger to the republic's survival. Absent outside support, the new regime could crumble swiftly in the face of tribal resistance and Saudi intrigue.

The second path open to the Egyptian government in the aftermath of the coup in Ṣan'ā' was to furnish air support in addition to material aid, thereby strengthening the Republican defenses in the one critical combat function that local forces could not fulfill. Whether or not elements of the Egyptian Air Force would have been sufficient to save the republic in the fall of 1962 is uncertain, but it is an intriguing possibility to consider. Under such a scenario, any ground forces sent to protect or service the air force would be prohibited from engaging in offensive operations.

A third alternative was to supplement air support with a token contingent of ground troops, which would send a stronger signal of commitment to the new regime and might serve as a more effective deterrent to tribal resistance and foreign intervention. Given the weakness of the republic and the distinct possibility of tribal opposition, it made sense to send a message of Egyptian resolve and commitment to the republic in order to deter outside intervention and crush any attempt to restore the Imamate at the outset. For such a force to serve as anything more than a trip wire, however, it would have to be sizeable.

Thus the fourth and final option was to send Egyptian ground forces in such vast numbers that resistance to the republic would become unthinkable, and any military contest would be decided rapidly and decisively. This course of action presented enormous planning and logistical

[93] This is essentially the conclusion Aḥmad Yūsuf Aḥmad reached (*al-Dawr*, 111–13, 119–20). Cf. Aḥmad, *Dhikrayāt*, 278.

challenges, which, as we shall see in the next chapter, were probably insuperable at the time. Nevertheless, the option of initiating rapid escalation backed by massive force, seemingly a gamble of the greatest proportions, might well have been preferable to the pattern of piecemeal escalation that took place.

Like many statesmen faced with similar choices before and since, Nasser, in 1962, opted for the dangerous middle road. Unfortunately for Egypt, the decision to send a token deterrent force gravely underestimated the revolution's effect on Yemen's neighbors. Saudi Crown Prince Faysal put it crisply to Ambassador Adlai Stevenson on October 2: "Yemen [is] too important to let slide."[94] Even the Foreign Office—the least militant among the British foreign policy bureaucracies—rapidly reached the conclusion that "the consolidation of the republican regime in the Yemen would be a serious threat to our interests in Aden, and thus also in the Persian Gulf."[95] If Nasser had thought that a small armed presence on the peninsula would serve to deter Saudi and British meddling, he badly miscalculated. Far from deterring Yemen's neighbors, Egypt's military intervention reinforced the fears of Nasser's regional foes, drove them together, and cemented their determination to oppose him, thereby fueling the very escalation the show of force was meant to avert.[96] And since—unlike Egypt—Saudi Arabia and Great Britain could conduct their war entirely by proxy, there was little disincentive for doing so.

Moreover, the decision to send a single company reflected a serious underestimation of the threat hostile Zaydī tribes posed to the new regime. Given the scale of conflict that ensued, even a brigade might not have sufficed to nip the resistance in the bud. Such a small force was clearly insufficient for combat on any scale and could only have been intended as a deterrent trip wire, a protective force for Egyptian aircraft, or security detail for the revolutionary leadership in the capital.[97] The Egyptian historian Aḥmad Yūsuf Aḥmad makes the plausible suggestion

[94] Stevenson (New York) to Sec. State, no. 1044, October 3, 1962, RG 59, CDF 1960–63, Box 2079, 786h.00/9-2762, NARA.

[95] Memo, Walmsley to Private Secretary, "Talking Points on the Yemen for Cabinet Meeting on Tuesday, October 9," October 8, 1962, FO 371/162947, PRO.

[96] Aḥmad, *Dhikrayāt*, 486–87; Safran, *Saudi Arabia*, 94; F. Gregory Gause, *Saudi-Yemeni Relations: Domestic Structures and Foreign Influences* (New York: Columbia University Press, 1990), 59–62; Jones, *Britain and the Yemen Civil War*, 33–53.

[97] Ḥadīdī, *Shāhid 'alā ḥarb al-Yaman*, 38; Aḥmad, *Dhikrayāt*, 278, 487; Aḥmad, *al-Dawr*, 117. Cf. Muḥammad Fawzī, quoted in Imām, *Muḥammad Fawzī*, 33–34, 36–37.

that Nasser conceived of the war—perhaps on the basis of Egypt's own revolutionary experience—as a localized struggle for the capital city and other urban centers, thereby ignoring the historical predominance of the northern highlands in Yemeni politics and the Ottomans' bitter experience in Yemen.[98] In any event, the decision represented a bad compromise between abstaining from direct support and launching a massive intervention. The danger implicit in this compromise was accentuated by the inexplicable decision to place the company of commandos under the command of Yemenis, who had every incentive to embroil the Egyptians in hostilities. Once Egyptian troops were committed to battle and began to take casualties, it became extremely difficult to halt the spiral of escalation from Cairo. Within weeks the Egyptian leadership responded to the spread of hostilities with a decision to reinforce the lonely company in Yemen with a full infantry brigade.[99]

Several additional factors seem to have produced this unfortunate outcome. First, the bitter experience of Syria's unopposed secession from the UAR one year earlier was still fresh in Egyptian minds. The failure to quell the uprising in Syria and prevent the stabilization of the secessionist regime had stemmed not so much from a failure of will as from the lack of a long-distance capacity to project coercive power.[100] Egypt had dispatched a similarly token force of paratroopers aboard Egyptian transport aircraft on the evening of September 28, 1961, but they were arrested upon landing, and the entire operation was subsequently aborted. The small task force turned out to be too small and unprotected to counter the secessionists' fait accompli, the reversal of which would have required massive military intervention. Without adequate military transport aviation or long-range bombing capabilities, an invasion of Syria was unlikely on purely military grounds—let alone the political repercussions of such an act.[101] Judging by the pattern of hardware acquisition in the interim, the Egyptian leadership seems to

[98] Aḥmad, *al-Dawr*, 116.

[99] Ḥadīdī, *Shāhid 'alā ḥarb al-Yaman*, 40–43; Ḥamrūsh, *Qiṣṣat thawrat 23 yūliyū*, 3:228.

[100] Sela, "Nasser's Regional Politics," 189; Baghdādī, *Mudhakkirāt*, 2:112–19, 123–24. Cf. Podeh, *Decline*, 151, 157; Haykal, *Sanawāt al-ghalayān*, 571–72; Jankowski, *Nasser's Egypt*, 169–70; Krakhmalov, *Zapiski voennogo attaché*, 84–86.

[101] This was Khrushchev's opinion, and he did not hesitate to share it with the Egyptian ambassador. Memcon, Khruschev, and Amb. Ghālib, October 9, 1961, in Vitalii Naumkin et al., eds., *Blizhno-vostochnyĭ konflikt: Iz dokumentov Arkhiva Vneshnei Politiki Rossiiskoi Federatsii* (hereafter *BVK*) (Moscow: Mezhdunarodnyi fond "Demokratia," 2003), 2:366.

have resolved not to let distance get in the way of a rapid response in the future.[102]

The new resolve to employ force was strengthened by the failure of Egypt's persuasive power. Up until 1961, Egypt's influence in the Arab world had rested mainly on what is today termed *soft power*. Throughout the 1950s, the main threat to Nasser's rivals came not from Egyptian military capabilities but from the powerful pull of propaganda emanating from Cairo. Up until the *infiṣāl*, fighting words had been the weapon of choice in Egypt's struggle for leadership of the Arab world. They had been marvelously effective and would continue to be deployed freely throughout the 1960s. But the humiliation inflicted upon Egypt by the Syrian secessionists diminished Egypt's status and weakened the appeal of Nasser's call. The diminution of Egyptian soft power made coercion an attractive alternative. Thus when the anointed leader of the revolution, Colonel ʿAbd Allāh al-Sallāl, cabled Cairo with a request for urgent Egyptian military support in late September 1962, the experience of the past year raised the probability that his appeal would fall on receptive ears.[103]

The failure of the Egyptian intelligence community to paint an accurate picture of the battlefield exacerbated the miscalculations inherent in the decision to intervene and reinforced the inclination to let unfounded optimism win the day. The breathtaking shortcomings of Egypt's intelligence efforts in previous years—its commandos went off to Yemen equipped with maps that would have embarrassed a tourist—ensured that in the moment of crisis the Egyptian leadership did not have at its fingertips the necessary facts upon which to base a critical decision.[104]

The effects of the knowledge deficit were amplified by the failure to seek out contrarian wisdom from those who knew the country well. Aḥmad Abū Zayd, a former Egyptian intelligence liaison to the Yemeni revolutionaries, had served more than three years in Yemen under official cover as deputy commander of the Egyptian military

[102] See, in particular, Yael Vered's discussion of the decisions to purchase the Tu-16 long-range bomber, to expand the paratrooper and commando forces, and enhance Egypt's military transport aviation (*Revolution*, 165). See also Baghdādī, *Mudhakkirāt*, 2:118; and chapter two.

[103] Naṣr, *Mudhakkirāt*, 2:334.

[104] Aḥmad, *Dhikrayāt*, 482–85; Ḥadīdī, *Shāhid ʿalā ḥarb al-Yaman*, 19–20; Dawisha, "Intervention in the Yemen," 48–49, 61; idem, "Perceptions, Decisions, and Consequences," 215; James, *Nasser at War*, 66.

Figure 1.4 Egyptian propaganda harped on the contradictions between reactionary monarchs and their people. Here King Sa'ūd and Imam al-Badr march confidently "To Reaction," unaware that the Arab army behind them has taken the turn "To Freedom." Sa'ūd and al-Badr: "We are secure as long as the entire Arab army is behind us." *Akhbār al-Yawm*, November 10, 1962. Cartoon by Alexander Ṣārūkhān.

mission. He recalls being summoned to 'Āmir's office immediately after the revolution, whereupon the *mushīr* and his deputy, Shams Badrān, interrogated him about the advisability of sending Egyptian forces to Yemen.[105] Abū Zayd advised against direct intervention on the grounds that the Saudi-supported opposition would prove too formidable. As Abū Zayd tells it, 'Āmir and Badrān rejected his warning, which they attributed to "Yemen-fatigue."

An even more telling testimony is that of the former chief military instructor in Yemen, Ṣalāḥ al-Dīn al-Maḥrizī, who remains convinced that a straightforward presentation of Yemeni realities to the president would have averted the intervention. Maḥrizī recalls attending a meeting between the Egyptian chief of military intelligence, Major General Ṣalāḥ al-Dīn al-Ḥadīdī, and the commander of the Third Army Division, Major General 'Abd al-Mun'im Ḥusnī, shortly after the coup. Egypt's chief of military intelligence shocked Maḥrizī with his assessment that all the Yemeni government required was "a limited number of commando teams and paratroopers [armed with] megaphones, smoke-

[105] Aḥmad, *Dhikrayāt*, 256–59, 486. On Abū Zayd, see also Juzaylān, *Muqaddimāt*, 34–39.

generators and firecrackers, [in response to which] the tribes would immediately be seized with fear and halt their challenge." Maḥrizī launched into a lengthy riposte, beginning with a history lesson about the loss of four Ottoman divisions to guerilla warfare in the Yemeni highland, and ending with a dramatic appeal to leave the defense of Yemen to the Yemenis and make do with moral and material aid. These words of wisdom met a chilly response. One level-headed officer, the future commander of the Eastern Front in Yemen, Brigadier General ʻUthmān Naṣār, praised Maḥrizī for speaking up and urged him to get other members of the mission to counter the "crazy stream of thought" holding sway at the top. But when Maḥrizī asked his former superior in Yemen, Ḥasan Fikrī, whether his advice had been solicited, Fikrī responded bitterly that it had not.[106]

Maḥrizī then made the mistake of approaching his cousin, journalist Muṣṭafā Amīn, with a request to deliver his contrarian appraisal of the situation to the president. Maḥrizī stressed that the traditional balance of political and military power in Yemen tilted heavily toward the Zaydī tribes, who would resist the weak government in Ṣanʻā' and any foreign army sent to support it. He also reportedly emphasized the futility of using conventional force against the tribes, who could be expected to employ guerilla tactics from the security of mountain strongholds. This report made its way to ʻĀmir's desk, where it was treated as an act of insubordination for which Maḥrizī, one of the few field commanders with any experience of Yemen, was grounded in Egypt as the intervention unfolded.[107]

Strategic considerations also militated in favor of direct intervention. Ultimately, Egyptian interest in regime change in Yemen was derivative; there was nothing intrinsically valuable about Yemen itself. The Imamate was simply the weakest link in the chain of largely conservative hostility that surrounded Egypt in the aftermath of the *infiṣāl*. If it collapsed, other monarchies might be expected to follow. That southern Yemen hosted the last outpost of British imperialism in the Middle East was certainly a bonus. But the most important consideration, in Egyptian

[106] Maḥrizī, *al-Ṣamt al-ḥā'ir*, 109–11. Another senior veteran of the mission to Yemen, Governor Kamāl Abū al-Futūḥ, apparently offered his services, but was ignored. Ḥamrūsh, *Qiṣṣat thawrat 23 yūliyū*, 3:230.

[107] Bayḍānī reports obtaining a promise from Nasser in late September that Maḥrizī would be sent out to join him in Yemen along with the first company of Egyptian troops. Bayḍānī, *Azmat al-ummah*, 321, 323. On the relationship with Muṣṭafā Amīn, see Maḥrizī, interview with Aḥmad al-Muslimānī, "al-Ṭabʻah al-ūlā," Dream 2 TV, November 6, 2008.

minds, was undoubtedly the proximity of Saudi Arabia. As Sadat succinctly put it: "[The outbreak of civil war in Yemen] was a good opportunity to teach King Sa'ūd a lesson. He had financed the breakup of the union with Syria, and led the campaign against Egypt, while his country had common borders with Yemen."[108] But precisely what form was the "lesson" to have taken?

The chief of Egyptian military intelligence at the time, Ṣalāḥ al-Dīn al-Ḥadīdī, insinuates that the primary motive behind Operation 9000 (the code name given to the intervention) was to place Egyptian troops on the Saudi-Yemeni border so as to mount a credible military threat to the Saudi regime.[109] The claims of such a high-placed general cannot be dismissed lightly. Nevertheless, it is not clear to what such a presence would have amounted. The paltry forces sent in the first few months of the war were woefully insufficient to mount an invasion of a country as vast and desertic as Saudi Arabia. At best they might have been capable of launching a raid or seizing a sliver of territory across the border. Moreover, open war with the Saudis was out of the question, given US security guarantees to the kingdom and the strength of the US-Egyptian relationship at this time. Ḥadīdī points to the northern bias in the pattern of early Egyptian troop deployments as evidence for his claims. Yet much of the tribal resistance to the republic, including Badr's headquarters, *was* based in the north of the country, close to the Saudi border. To be sure, strengthening the potential domino effect of the Yemeni revolution on both Saudi Arabia and Aden must have been high up on the list of Egyptian strategic objectives. But the role military action by Egyptian forces could play in such a scenario was limited. Ultimately, the domino effect rested on Egypt's ability to establish a model republic on the Saudi frontier. In order to do this, the revolution had to be rendered irreversible, and its writ extended to the locus of tribal resistance.[110]

As we have seen, the decision to intervene was taken in an extraordinary political context. The coup d'état in Ṣan'ā' took place a mere six days after the commander in chief of the Egyptian armed forces resigned in protest at the president's attempt to erode his authority.

[108] Sadat, *Search*, 162. The proximity of oil may have fired the imagination of Egyptian war planners, but vast deserts separated Yemen from the petroleum of the Persian Gulf.

[109] Ḥadīdī, *Shāhid 'alā ḥarb al-Yaman*, 29–30, 44, 83–84.

[110] Egyptian Vice President 'Abd al-Laṭīf al-Baghdādī testified that the intervention did not bear an anti-Saudi character at the outset, but that it swiftly became so when the Saudis, feeling threatened, decided to oppose the Egyptian presence. Quoted in Ḥabīb, *Milaffāt*, 242.

In fact, the acute crisis that seized the senior levels of the Egyptian government in late September served to enhance the odds of direct intervention.

The Denouement of the Crisis in Cairo

The news from Yemen descended upon the paralyzed Egyptian leadership like a bombshell. One effect of the sudden emergency in national security was to drive the estranged parties together. Events in Yemen demanded an immediate response, and that response clearly had to have both political and military components. Thus the external crisis seems to have functioned as a catalyst for hurried reconciliation. On September 26 or 27, in an apparent effort to avert confrontation, Nasser proposed to appoint ʻĀmir deputy supreme commander of the armed forces (*nā'ib al-qā'id al-aʻlā li-l-quwwāt al-musallaḥah*) with broad military responsibilities and a prominent role in an envisioned National Defense Council.[111] Although this ostensible promotion barely succeeded in masking the implicit attempt to clip ʻĀmir's wings by granting him a title devoid of meaningful authority, it was apparently sufficient to woo him back.[112] Within a couple of days of the Yemeni coup, he agreed. There must have been additional components to the temporary arrangement hammered out between Nasser, ʻĀmir, and their respective camps in tense late-night sessions in the final days of September, but details are murky. In any event, the resulting compromise was tenuous. On the one hand, Nasser's desired reform of the executive branch had gone through and the new institutions were up and running. At the same time, he had not clarified the balance of power between the PC and the military. ʻĀmir was no longer general commander of the armed forces; he was now deputy supreme commander of the armed forces. But what

[111] Naṣr, *Mudhakkirāt*, 3:32; ʻUkāshah, *Mudhakkirātī*, 2:394; Imām, *al-Iftirā'*, 22; Airgram, Cairo to Dept. of State, no. A-275, October 2, 1962, "UAR's National Defense Council," RG 59, CDF 1960–63, Box 2072, 786h.5/10-262, NARA; "Reorganisation of the Government of the United Arab Republic," Annex B. According to Baghdādī, this was a temporary solution until the formation of a new legislature (the National Assembly) and the appointment of a minister of war, who would be responsible for the armed forces in the Executive Council. Nasser apparently tried to lock ʻĀmir into this course by publicizing the appointments in *al-Ahrām* on September 27. Baghdādī, *Mudhakkirāt*, 2:187–89, 193.

[112] Nasser contemplated a similar maneuver with ʻĀmir in June 1967. Haykal, *al-Infijār*, 884–85.

did this mean? Who in fact commanded the military? And what of the crucial authority to confirm promotions, transfers, and retirement of senior officers? These essential questions were left hanging.[113]

Not surprisingly, ʻĀmir and his dependents seized upon the opportunity presented by the Yemeni crisis with gusto.[114] This is not to suggest that senior officers in the military engineered the coup in order to give their leader a new lease on life, or even that ʻĀmir's support for direct military intervention stemmed from considerations of a purely personal nature. But one cannot ignore the fact that in the heady days of late September and early October 1962, when it looked like a handful of commandos could erase the stain of the *infiṣāl* in a matter of weeks, Yemen presented a golden opportunity for ʻĀmir and his followers to escape the ax.[115] By committing their government to a miniwar, which, presumably, they had every chance of winning, ʻĀmir and his circle could avert the looming confrontation with the president and secure their position at the pinnacle of the Egyptian power structure. The model of indirect aid to the FLN in Algeria would not do in this instance. For the army—and its commander—to receive credit for success in this revolutionary endeavor, direct intervention by Egyptian forces was imperative. It is not surprising that so little attention was paid to contrarian opinions within the military. The Egyptian high command refused to apply its institutional brakes on the government's rush to war in part because it had a vested interest in military action.

The decision to intervene set in motion a chain of events that made it virtually impossible for ʻĀmir to step down. As the task force grew, the theater of operations expanded, and a small-scale mission morphed into wide-scale war, the exigencies of daily operations practically guaranteed ʻĀmir's survival. The political and military logic of war in Nasser's Egypt militated strongly against an extraordinary act to replace the acting commander in chief in time of war.[116] A Lincoln, or a Hitler,

[113] ʻUkāshah, *Mudhakkirātī*, 2:394.

[114] Ḥadīdī, *Shāhid ʻalā ḥarb al-Yaman*, 37; Muḥammad Fawzī, quoted in Imām, *Muḥammad Fawzī*, 34. For a contrary view, see Aḥmad, *Dhikrayāt*, 560–62. Aḥmad emphasizes Sadat's culpability, insists that the dispute between Nasser and ʻĀmir did not extend to foreign policy, and exonerates ʻĀmir from the charge of warmongering. However, the fact ʻĀmir stood at the forefront of subsequent peace efforts does not prove his lack of enthusiasm at the war's outset.

[115] This point is appreciated by Aḥmad, *al-Dawr*, 120, 131.

[116] Kamāl al-Dīn Rifʻat, for instance, reportedly told Nasser in November 1962 that it would be unwise to curtail ʻĀmir's authority on account of the deleterious impact such a step would have on the morale of the armed forces. And Sāmī Sharaf lists a series of for-

would have certainly replaced ʻĀmir—but then they would have done so years before. Ever since 1956, Nasser had displayed consistent incapacity to confront his incompetent deputy. Only a calamity on the scale of the Six-Day War would change that—and even then the path chosen was characteristically torturous.

The coincidence of the coup in Yemen with the struggle for power in Egypt tethered ʻĀmir's political destiny to the fortunes of the budding military campaign. On a personal and institutional level, failure was not an option.[117] ʻĀmir, apparently determined not to leave things to chance, adopted the campaign as a pet project early on. Ḥadīdī recalls ʻĀmir paying uncharacteristic attention to operational details at the outset of the intervention, while Nasser and Bayḍānī report ʻĀmir asserting ownership over contacts with the Yemeni government—a political function that belonged to Sadat.[118] In other words, the sense of vulnerability with which the Egyptian high command went to war tended to perpetuate the campaign, once underway, and reinforced the government's inclination to pursue an uncompromising drive to victory.

The war opened up fresh opportunities for ʻĀmir's supporters to block plans to subordinate the military to civilian control. Several weeks into the campaign, ʻĀmir exploited the pressures of wartime decision-making to demand the presidential powers of appointment, promotion, transfer, and dismissal of officers above the battalion level for a period of six months—thereby challenging Nasser's dormant proposal that those powers be placed in the hands of the Presidential Council.[119] Nasser agreed, on condition that the powers in question be vested in the Permanent Committee of the National Defense Council for a period

---

eign and domestic crises and concerns, including Yemen, which made a showdown consistently undesirable. Sharaf, *Sanawāt*, 1:432, 536–37.

[117] Nasser hinted at this in a psychological analysis of his estranged friend in early December 1962. Baghdādī, *Mudhakkirāt*, 2:211–12. For a dismissal of this argument, see Aḥmad, *Dhikrayāt*, 560–62.

[118] Ḥadīdī, *Shāhid ʻalā ḥarb al-Yaman*, 37; Bayḍānī, *Miṣr wa-thawrat al-Yaman*, 92, 108; Baghdādī, *Mudhakkirāt*, 2:193. However, the Egyptian commander in Yemen at the time, Major General Anwar al-Qāḍī, implies that the domestic crisis in Egypt *distracted* ʻĀmir from close management of the campaign in its crucial early months ("Asrār yūniyū 67," *Ākhir Sāʻah*, June 6, 1988, 8–11, 61).

[119] In Nasser's report of the conversation, ʻĀmir used the operations in Yemen as a pretext (*ḥujjah*) for his demands. Nasser's contention that the matter had been settled in his September compromise with ʻĀmir is doubtful. A more likely explanation is that it had been set aside by tacit consent of both parties. Baghdādī, *Mudhakkirāt*, 2:193; Sharaf, *Sanawāt*, 1:431; Ḥabīb, *Milaffāt*, 232.

of three months. But as the weeks went by, ʻĀmir refrained from convening the committee, thereby effectively appropriating its powers.[120] This was an issue upon which the president was determined not to give in, and he accordingly resolved to bring the matter before the PC, where both principle and power tilted his way.[121]

Nasser also asked the PC to arbitrate the campaign's ballooning financial requirements. Baghdādī reports Nasser complaining in late November 1962 about what he considered to be ʻĀmir's excessive demands for extrabudgetary funds. ʻĀmir made matters worse by refusing to subject these requests to the National Defense Council for deliberation. At the outset of the intervention, the *mushīr* had allegedly specified a sum of approximately E£1.5 million ($3.75 million) to be set aside for operations in Yemen. Soon thereafter, however, he doubled his estimate, then he revised it up to E£5 million, and then again to E£15 million. By mid-November 1962, ʻĀmir was asking for E£21 million ($52.5 million): E£14 million to cover the costs of the campaign through February 1963 and an additional E£7 million if operations continued into the spring.[122] The spectacular growth of expenditure estimates over the course of little more than six weeks speaks volumes about the unintended—and uncontrolled—nature of the escalation that ensued from the decision to intervene.

While ʻĀmir's demands may have been perfectly reasonable from an operational perspective, the explosive context in which they were presented rendered a reasoned debate on the merits impossible. On November 21, 1962, Nasser used the PC to stage a debate between ʻĀmir and his colleagues on these issues, hoping to force him to concede to majority opinion.[123] On the matter of finances, Nasser proposed that the council approve a much smaller sum than ʻĀmir had requested—thereby implicitly signaling his disapproval of the campaign's expansion.[124] On the matter of promotions, Nasser resorted to a typical ruse,

[120] Its members were ʻĀmir himself, Baghdādī, Muḥyī al-Dīn, and Kamāl al-Dīn Ḥusayn. Airgram, Cairo to Dept. of State, no. A-275, October 2, 1962, RG 59, CDF 1960–63, Box 2072, 786b.5/10-262, NARA; Nutting, *Nasser*, 310.

[121] Ṣalāḥ Naṣr blames Nasser on this score (*Mudhakkirāt*, 3:33–34).

[122] In addition, he requested substantial sums to fund the completion of two new infantry divisions. Baghdādī, *Mudhakkirāt*, 2:191–92; Naṣr, *Mudhakkirāt*, 3:33.

[123] Baghdādī, *Mudhakkirāt*, 2:194–98, 210–11; ʻAbd al-Magīd Farīd, quoted in Ḥabīb, *Milaffāt*, 232; Muḥammad Fawzī, quoted in Ḥabīb, *Milaffāt*, 232. See also Munīr Ḥāfiẓ, "al-Tārīkh al-sirrī li-ḥukm Gamāl ʻAbd al-Nāṣir," *Rūz al-Yūsuf*, May 31, 1976; Imām, *Nāṣir wa-ʻĀmir*, 67–69; Imām, *Ḥusayn al-Shāfiʻī*, 121; Naṣr, *Mudhakkirāt*, 3:34.

[124] Baghdādī, *Mudhakkirāt*, 2:191–92.

obscuring the vital issue by framing it within the broader question of appointments in general—in the military, the police forces, and the foreign and civil services. Characteristically, the president stayed away from the cockfight he had arranged. In his absence, the council members were unable to reach a unanimous decision. Although a slim majority favored accepting a slightly modified version of the proposed law, both ʿĀmir and Kamāl al-Dīn Ḥusayn left the meeting in evident displeasure, and it was clear that a split vote would not suffice to decide such a momentous issue. After the meeting adjourned, Nasser revealed some of the larger implications of the debate in a debriefing session with several of his colleagues: "The issue is not [that of] postponing [the debate] or agreeing to the decision. Rather, the issue is that ... ʿĀmir is not convinced [of the need for] collective rule. He has placed a veil around the army. And I—is it logical that I should operate in a secret manner in order to obtain intelligence about the army? Are we to allow [ʿĀmir's secretary] ʿAlī Shafīq to command the army? This is the truth. Is it acceptable that [Lieutenant Colonel Galāl] al-Huraydī be appointed assistant military attaché in Washington after what happened with him in Syria during the *infiṣāl*?"[125]

The real issue was not the principle of collective leadership or even the authority to promote officers; it was ʿĀmir's continued command of the armed forces.[126] The next day, ʿĀmir grudgingly accepted the need to nominate a replacement. But he also canceled orders for the dispatch of a senior commander to Yemen and leaked the contents of the PC meeting to several officers.[127] Several days later he rescinded his offer to step down.[128] Over the next three weeks, intelligence surfaced concerning incipient organizational activities within the military in support of ʿĀmir's position, rumors circulated of resignations by top military officials, and there was even talk of an assassination plan.[129]

[125] Quoted in ibid., 198. See also Imām, *al-Iftirāʾ*, 100. Huraydī was commander of the paratrooper force charged with halting the Syrian secession in September 1961.

[126] See, for instance, Ḥabīb, *Milaffāt*, 231–32.

[127] Ibid., 200, 206. The officer in question, Brigadier General ʿUthmān Naṣār, though initially skeptical of the intervention, became commander of the eastern front in Yemen. Maḥrizī, *al-Ṣamt al-ḥāʾir*, 111, 126–28. It is not clear why Naṣār's remaining in Egypt was considered so ominous. Perhaps it signaled the possibility of a coup.

[128] He claimed it had not been seriously issued in the first place. Ḥabīb, *Milaffāt*, 202.

[129] Baghdādī, *Mudhakkirāt*, 2:207, 214; Imām, *Nāṣir wa-ʿĀmir*, 74–75, 79–80; Muḥammad Fawzī, quoted in idem, *Muḥammad Fawzī*, 38–39; Ḥamrūsh, *Qiṣṣat thawrat 23 yūliyū*, 2:213; Ḥabīb, *Milaffāt*, 232.

Nasser, taking a page from 'Āmir's playbook, began to speak of resigning as president in favor of a position in the ASU, possibly in the hope that his estranged friend might thereby be persuaded to follow suit.[130] Once again, he was outmaneuvered. On December 1, 1962, 'Āmir sent Nasser a personal letter of resignation containing a litany of grievances and accusations. A three-page indictment of the regime for having promised the people freedom only to have withheld it, 'Āmir's letter was a hypocritical but potentially explosive document clearly written for publication in the event it was accepted.[131] As such, it was a terrible threat. The danger was underscored by the submission of a second letter of resignation on December 4, this one from the chief of general intelligence, Ṣalāḥ Naṣr, 'Āmir's former *chef de cabinet*.[132] On December 6, Shams Badrān met with Nasser to demand a response to his boss's letter.[133] The next day, 'Āmir and Nasser met, but they found no way out of the impasse. Most of the rest of the council apparently favored postponing the confrontation and maintaining the status quo. This is in fact what occurred.[134]

On December 11, 1962, Nasser and 'Āmir met again in an emotional session that lasted nine hours.[135] Once again the president reportedly attempted to persuade 'Āmir that the question was one of principle, not personalities. The revolutionary leadership as a whole had taken a strategic decision to step down from positions of executive authority; this would be taken a step further by the next anniversary of the revolution in July 1963, and the armed forces would be no exception. 'Āmir protested but eventually conceded the point. The meeting ended with an

[130] Baghdādī, *Mudhakkirāt*, 200, 202–3, 205, 208, 211, 216. Leaks about Nasser's intention to resign as president baffled foreign diplomats in Cairo. See, for instance, the British ambassador's report of a conversation with Haykal. Beeley (Cairo) to Stevens (Foreign Office), July 26, 1963, VG 1015/21a, FO 371/172862, PRO.

[131] Nasser and his colleagues make much of the fact that 'Āmir made a typewritten copy (and several photographs) of the handwritten letter he sent to the president. 'Āmir protested that he had done so for the sake of posterity. But 'Āmir did publish this condemnation of Nasser's autocracy in the turbulent aftermath of June 1967. Baghdādī, *Mudhakkirāt*, 2:206, 210–11; Naṣr, *Mudhakkirāt*, 3:34–37; Sharaf, *Sanawāt*, 1:432; Ḥāfiẓ, "*al-Tārīkh al-sirrī*"; Fawzī, *Ḥarb al-thalāth sanawāt*, 34; Imām, *Nāṣir wa-'Āmir*, 71–74; 'Ukāshah, *Mudhakkirātī*, 2:394.

[132] Naṣr, *Mudhakkirāt*, 3:38–39.

[133] Baghdādī, *Mudhakkirāt*, 2:209.

[134] Ibid., 213; Muḥammad Fawzī stresses that Nasser was content with the compromise. Imām, *Muḥammad Fawzī*, 40–41.

[135] Baghdādī, *Mudhakkirāt*, 2:214–17; Imām, *al-Iftirā'*, 22–23.

agreement that 'Āmir would retain the new title of deputy supreme commander of the armed forces.[136] However, the two men agreed to appoint a new general commander (*qā'id 'āmm*) for the armed forces, who would report to 'Āmir, in March 1963, "*after the Yemen war ended* [emphasis added] and the debate over the subject in dispute had subsided, particularly among the army officers." Baghdādī explains that they thought the delay necessary because "the appointment of a new supreme commander under the [current] circumstances ... would affect 'Abd al-Ḥakīm's position."[137]

The war, however, did not end within three months; it was to last another five years. Thus yet another temporary arrangement became permanent with time. A seemingly innocuous constitutional amendment in 1964 confirmed de jure what had taken place de facto more than a year earlier: the powers of the general commander of the Egyptian armed forces—'Āmir's pre-1962 position—were transferred to the deputy supreme commander of the armed forces—his position in the post-1962 order.[138] This act formally undid the damage done to 'Āmir's authority by his "promotion" to deputy supreme commander at the outbreak of the war. 'Āmir, a master at Nasser's version of musical chairs, always managed to end up on the seat of the commander in chief.

The other agreement reached between Nasser and 'Āmir in the meeting of December 11 resolved the impasse over the promotion of officers with a face-saving compromise: beginning in July 1963, 'Āmir would be obligated to present to the Presidential Council appointments, promotions, transfers, and dismissals of officers above the brigade level

[136] Sharaf, *Sanawāt wa-ayyām ma'a Gamāl 'Abd al-Nāṣir*, 1:432; Baghdādī, *Mudhakkirāt*, 2:216–17. In Nasser's version of this incident, as reported by Tharwat 'Ukāshah, the agreed date was July 1963. 'Ukāshah, *Mudhakkirātī*, 2:394–95.

[137] Although the choice of a new commander would not be 'Āmir's, he was to make the announcement. Baghdādī, *Mudhakkirāt*, 2:217. In Ṣalāḥ Naṣr's telling, the meeting ended simply with the restoration of 'Āmir's authority (*Mudhakkirāt*, 3:38–39). Aḥmad Ḥamrūsh claims that the agreement centered on removing the commanders of the UAR's land, air, and sea branches from their posts. Another subject of dispute was reportedly the future of Major General Anwar al-Qāḍī, 'Āmir's right-hand man in Syria, who assumed command of the war in Yemen shortly before this crisis. Ḥamrūsh, *Qiṣṣat thawrat 23 yūliyū*, 2:213–14. For further consideration of the impact removal of 'Āmir would have had on the forces in Yemen, see Imām, *Nāṣir wa-'Āmir*, 70; idem, *al-Iftirā'*, 99–100.

[138] Fawzī, *Ḥarb al-thalāth sanawāt*, 36. Subsequent decrees in 1966 subordinated the minister of war to the deputy supreme commander and united the offices of the chief of staff and the deputy supreme commander of the Egyptian armed forces. Sharaf, *Sanawāt*, 1:434–35.

only.[139] The violation of executive authority involved in the concession was made worse by the fact that the agreement was never executed. Nasser's willingness to ride roughshod over the council decision he had pushed for less than one month earlier doomed the young institution to irrelevance within weeks of its establishment.[140] In any case, it had been little more than an empty vessel, created by Nasser, like so many other state institutions, ad hoc and with little enduring commitment.

The consequences of 'Āmir's victory were dire. Nasser's divide-and-rule tactics assured the failure of the PC at the outset, thereby shattering the illusion of collective leadership and generating demoralization and disillusionment among its members. Two of the most influential figures in the Egyptian leadership—Kamāl al-Dīn Ḥusayn and 'Abd al-Laṭīf al-Baghdādī—lost faith in Nasser's sincerity and began a long march toward eventual withdrawal from public life in 1964.[141] More importantly, 'Āmir's successful stand in the fall of 1962 left him in full control of the armed forces until the fateful summer of 1967.

In less personal terms, the intervention in Yemen postponed the showdown between 'Āmir's military fiefdom and the civilian establishment by five years. As 'Alī Ṣabrī, former Egyptian prime minister and head of the ASU, put it: "There is no doubt that the complete change, in light of the circumstances of the Yemen war ... put off the confrontation, which, in my opinion, was going to take place. Either the military establishment would relinquish the powers it inherited on the night of the 23rd of July [1952], or it would launch a coup."[142] As Ṣabrī explains, this need not have been an overt seizure of power by the military, but rather a silent, forceful assertion of the military's exclusive authority in all matters pertaining to the leadership of the armed forces.[143] In the event, the decision to postpone the nomination of a replacement for 'Āmir and the appropriation of authority over military promotions—both of which

[139] Baghdādī, *Mudhakkirāt*, 2:217–18.

[140] Ibid.; Ḥamrūsh, *Qiṣṣat thawrat 23 yūliyū*, 2:220–22, 232; Be'eri, *Army Officers*, 122–23. On the dwindling of the Presidential Council's influence over the course of 1963, see Baghdādī, *Mudhakkirāt*, 2:225–26, 232–33; Aḥmad, *al-Dawr*, 257–59. The Presidential Council, a supreme executive body, was abolished officially in February 1964 and was replaced, somewhat illogically, by the legislative National Assembly, chaired by Anwar Sadat. In time the National Assembly came to serve as Nasser's preferred rubberstamp for matters of vital national interest. Aḥmad, *al-Dawr*, 257–59, 264.

[141] Cf. Aḥmad, *al-Dawr*, 259.

[142] Imām, *'Alī Ṣabrī yatadhakkar*, 100.

[143] For examples of this jealous regard for the sanctity of military jurisdiction, see Huwaydī, *Khamsūn 'āman*, 195.

would have resulted in an immediate and massive purge of the senior command[144]—dragged on indecisively until June 1967. In a sense, the events of September–November 1962 served as a dress rehearsal for the similar crisis that gripped Egypt in the aftermath of the Six-Day War. Then the president had the *mushīr* and his entourage arrested to prevent 'Āmir's return to power on the army's bayonets and a public airing of differences on the eve of Nasser's capitulation to Faysal at Khartoum. Domestic critics of the intervention in Yemen have tended to focus on the diversion of scarce resources and attention from the Sinai front.[145] But the war's most pernicious effect may have been to perpetuate the calcified command of the Egyptian armed forces by a crucial half-decade.[146]

*

The decision to send Egyptian troops to Yemen in the fall of 1962 resulted from a host of factors, including the open wound of the *infiṣāl*, the principled commitment to the export of Egypt's revolution, the competition with Saudi Arabia, and the internal contest for power within the Egyptian regime. Faulty planning precluded the emergence of direct intervention as a viable policy option until the coup took place, by which point it was too late to make up for the lack of preparation; as a consequence, an ill-advised decision to commit token forces to battle was adopted in haste. That decision ignored the true balance of forces on the ground in Yemen and underestimated the Saudi response to an Egyptian armed presence on the peninsula. Large-scale intervention emerged inadvertently as a by-product of that initial decision, as reinforcements for a badly outnumbered force became necessary. By the time the Egyptians appreciated the depth of their strategic predicament—the weakness of the republic, the relative strength of the royalist cause, and Saudi determination to oppose the change in the status quo—their political and military commitment to the YAR was too great to make a reversal of policy affordable.[147] The war, in other words, may be attributed in the first place to a colossal failure of judgment on the part of the Egyptian leadership. As Nasser himself later admitted, "Yemen was a miscalculation. We never thought it would lead to what it did."[148]

144 Baghdādī, *Mudhakkirāt*, 2:213.

145 See, e.g., Muḥammad 'Abd al-Ghanī al-Gamasī, *Mudhakkirāt al-Gamasī: Ḥarb uktūbir 1973* (Paris: al-Manshūrāt al-Sharqiyyah, 1990), 62–63.

146 For a similar assessment, see Stephens, *Nasser*, 361.

147 Dawisha, "Intervention in the Yemen," 50.

148 "Nasser admits he was wrong," *The Times* (London), March 5, 1968, 9.

✷ CHAPTER TWO ✷

The Soviet-Egyptian Intervention in Yemen

IN OCTOBER 1962, at the very peak of the Cold War, as Soviet warships laden with nuclear missiles headed west for Cuba, a second drama was unfolding far away in the rugged boondocks of the eastern hemisphere. As if to underline that his boldness in the Caribbean was the rule, not an exception, Khrushchev had authorized the dispatch of Soviet planes and pilots to the Middle East to help Egypt project force onto the distant battlefield in Yemen, more than 2,000 kilometers away. As world attention remained riveted on Cuba, thousands of Egyptian soldiers poured into the Arabian Peninsula. Night after night the air bridge continued; huge Antonov-12 transport planes, painted with the red, white, and black of the Egyptian air force, but piloted by Soviet aircrews, rolled off the tarmac at Cairo's al-Māẓah airbase, laden with everything from MiGs and men to mail and mousetraps. After a brief pit stop at Aswan, the planes continued on their nocturnal journey, heading south over the Red Sea in darkness and radio silence. Turning inland just before daybreak north of the port city of al-Ḥudaydah, the aircraft descended at the crack of dawn onto a rough airstrip perched precariously on the mountainous outskirts of Ṣan'ā', 7,200 feet above sea level. Within weeks the Antonovs would be joined by Tupolev-16 long-range bombers manned by mixed Soviet-Egyptian crews that, out of their base in Cairo West, would fly bombing missions over Royalist targets in northern Yemen and on occasion across the border into Saudi territory.[1]

[1] Parts of this chapter appeared in the author's "Soviet Support for Egypt's Intervention in Yemen, 1962–63," *Journal of Cold War Studies* 10, no. 4 (2008): 5–36. The story of this little-known episode in Soviet-Egyptian military relations has been pieced together from the following sources: Memo, V. Kornev (Deputy Director, Near East Department, Soviet Ministry of Foreign Affairs), "Polozhenie v Iemenskoi Arabskoi Respublike i Iemeno-OARovskie otnoshenia (spravka)," March 13, 1964, f. 5, op. 30, d. 451, pp. 39–40, RGANI; Lev Bausin, *Spetsluzhby mira na Blizhnem Vostoke* (Moscow: Olma-Press, 2001), 128–30; A. Fursenko, ed., *Prezidium TSK KPSS 1954-1964: Chernovye protokol'nye zapisi zasedanii, stenogrammy, postanovlenia* (Moscow: ROSSPEN, 2004), 1:596; Nikita Khrushchev, *N. S. Khrushchev: Vospominania—vremia, liudi, vlast'* (Moscow: Moskovskie novosti, 1999), 3:446; Sergei Pavlenko, "*Bez grifa 'Sekretno': Spetszadanie za predelami rodiny*," *Krasnaia Zvezda*, November 19, 1994; Andrei Pochtarev, "*Pod chuzhym flagom*," *Krasnaia Zvezda*, August 16,

The extraordinary tale of Soviet-Egyptian cooperation at the outset of the campaign in Yemen is a little-known chapter in Cold War history. The pages that follow lay out the origins, characteristics, and motivations of Soviet assistance to Egypt, without which the intervention would not have been possible.

The Nature of Soviet Relations with Egypt and Yemen

On the face of it, the extent of Soviet participation seems baffling. After all, Yemen, from the Soviet perspective, was an inconsequential backwater. Its remote mountain villages hosted few Communists for the party ideologues to nurture; its ancient tribal system held little promise for mobilization on the basis of class solidarity; it had few resources of value to the Soviet Union. Above all, Yemen—unlike Cuba or Berlin—was unimportant to the chief Soviet adversary, the United States. Why, then, was it worth the risk? To begin to answer this question, we must examine the historical foundations of the triangular relationship between Egypt, the Soviet Union, and Yemen.

2003; Yevgeny Primakov, *Russia and the Arabs: Behind the Scenes in the Middle East from the Cold War to the Present* (New York: Basic Books, 2009), 95–96; I. Shishchenko, ed., *Smoliane-Internatsionalisty: Sbornik vospominanii voinov-internatsionalistov Smolenshchiny* (Smolensk: Smiadyn', 2000), 172; V. Zolotarev, ed., *Rossia (SSSR) v' local'nykh voinakh i voennykh konfliktakh vtoroi poloviny XX veka* (Moscow: Kuchkovo Pole, 2000), 180; Aḥmad, *Dhikrayāt*, 508–9; Abū Dhikrī, *al-Zuhūr*, 11, 26, 31–32; Fawzī, *Ḥarb al-thalāth sanawāt*, 23–24; Ḥadīdī, *Shāhid 'alā ḥarb al-Yaman*, 48–49, 55–56; Mohrez Mahmoud El-Hussini, *Soviet-Egyptian Relations, 1945–85* (New York: St. Martin's Press, 1987), 120–21; 'Abd al-Mun'im Khalīl, *Ḥurūb miṣr al-mu'āṣirah fī awrāq qā'id maydānī: 1939–45, 1948–49, 1956, 1962–67, 1967, 1968–70, 1973* (Cairo: Dār al-Mustaqbal al-'Arabī, 1990), 58–59; Naṣr, *Mudhakkirāt*, 2:373; Oleg Peresypkin, *al-Yaman wa-l-yamaniyyūn fī dhikrayāt diblūmāsī rūsī* (Beirut: Dār wa-Maktabat al-Hilāl, 2005), 173–75; *al-Quwwāt al-Musallaḥah*, no. 417, July 16, 1964, p. 9; Memo, M. S. Weir (Cairo) to P. H. Laurence, VG 1226/1, November 20, 1962, "Egyptian Air Force: Record of a Conversation with a Wing Commander of the Indian Air Force," FO 371/165401, PRO; Airgram, Cairo to Secretary of State, no. A-288, "Joint Weeka no. 40," October 9, 1962, p. 4, RG 59, CDF 1960–63, Box 2073, 786b.00/10-962, NARA; Tom Bower, *The Perfect English Spy: Sir Dick White and the Secret War, 1935–1990* (London: William Heinemann, 1995), 250; Muḥammad Haykal [Mohamed Heikal], *Sphinx and Commissar: The Rise and Fall of Soviet Influence in the Middle East* (New York: Harper and Row, 1978), 118; Schmidt, *Yemen*, 168–69; "The Aerial Actions in Yemen," in Top Secret, The United Arab Republic, Supreme Command of the Armed Forces, Division of Instruction, Branch of Educational Institutions, *The Operational Military Lessons from Yemen* (undated document captured in Sinai in June 1967, Hebrew trans.; hereafter *OMLY*), ShM ?/586.140, Intelligence and Terrorism Information Center, Gelilot, Israel.

Soviet policy toward Yemen must be seen in the context of a larger pattern of behavior in the Middle East in which relations with Egypt were central. Given its size, strategic value, and anti-imperialist bearing, as well as its influence in Africa, the Arab world, and the nonaligned movement, Egypt was the natural entry point for Soviet involvement; it quickly became the hub of Soviet interests in the region. The USSR's Arab policy in the mid-1950s revolved around Nasser, who facilitated the creation of Soviet spokes reaching out to emerging allies such as Syria or Yemen and demarcated—in accordance with his interests, not theirs—no-go zones around antagonists such as Jordan and Iraq. In the diplomatic correspondence of the Soviet foreign ministry of the 1950s, Nasser comes across as a consultant to the Soviets on Arab affairs, an instructor for the newly initiated in the labyrinth of Oriental politics. The reverse was also true; to most Arab leaders, Cairo, not Moscow, was the gateway to the USSR, and Nasser made appropriate introductions when it suited him. As Libyan leader Muammar Qaddafi later recalled in conversation with Mikhail Gorbachev: "during Nasser's time, we all left the development of Soviet-Arab relations to him.... Even after the victory of the Libyan Revolution [in 1969], we went to Nasser and through him—to Moscow."[2]

Although Soviet-Yemeni relations date back to 1928, when Yemen became the first Arab state to conclude a treaty with the USSR, they were largely devoid of content until Khrushchev reengaged the Arab world in the mid-1950s. With Yemen, as with other Soviet allies in the Arab world, Nasser led the way. Relations, as usual, revolved around the supply of weapons, showcasing Nasser in his newly empowered role as regional arms dealer whose reward was not money but influence. In Soviet eyes the main anticipated benefit associated with arming and befriending the Yemenis was their resistance to Britain's colony in Aden to the south. Egypt shared Soviet hostility toward the British and had championed efforts to evict British power from the Middle East well before the revolution. But a consideration of more recent provenance was rapidly coming to the fore: the gradual transformation of

[2] Karen N. Brutents, *Tridtsat' let na Staroi ploshchadi* (Moscow: Mezhdunarodnye Otnoshenia, 1996), 369. Cf. Ben Bella's alleged remark to Khrushchev in May 1964: "Your relations with Egypt and with Gamal Abdel Nasser are the measure [*mi'yār*] of your relations with the Arabs as a whole." Haykal, *Sanawāt al-ghalayān*, 753. See also Horst Mahr, *Die Rolle Ägyptens in der amerikanischen und sowjetischen Aussenpolitik: Von der Suez-Krise 1956 bis zum Sechs-Tage-Krieg 1967: Exkurs, Sadats Umkehrung der Allianzen 1974* (Baden-Baden: Nomos, 1993), 41–60, 67–72, 94–102.

Yemen's neighbor to the north, Saudi Arabia, from key ally in the Arab Cold War to principal regional antagonist. By arming the Yemenis, Nasser was meddling in the Saudis' backyard and purchasing influence over their historically troublesome neighbor.

On March 21, 1956, Soviet Ambassador Evgenii Kiselev consulted President Nasser on a recent Yemeni appeal for arms.[3] Nasser responded cautiously. Yemen, after all, was very unstable. There was also the danger that the British might seize on the arms deal as a pretext to conquer Yemen, thereby securing their position in Aden. Moreover, King Sa'ūd, within whose sphere of influence much of Yemen fell, had expressed discomfort with the idea. On the other hand, Nasser stressed, the decision was a Soviet one, and something in the way he said this gave his interlocutor the impression that the Yemeni request should not be turned down. In another conversation with the Soviet ambassador eight weeks later, Nasser confided that he was being pulled into a complex battle with Saudi Arabia, where King Sa'ūd, evidently fearing he might share the fate of King Farouk, regarded Egypt with suspicion. In a transparent bid to squash Soviet hopes for the establishment of diplomatic relations with Riyadh, Nasser reported that, alas, all his attempts to persuade Sa'ūd of the harmlessness of Soviet ties had been to no avail. In this context Nasser expressed his full support for the Soviet plan to sell arms to Imam Aḥmad of Yemen.[4] However odd this must have sounded to Soviet ears, given that Egypt had concluded a mutual defense pact with Yemen and Saudi Arabia scarcely three months earlier, Nasser was already scheming to undermine the Saudi monarchy, as he had been doing for over a year to Sa'ūd's erstwhile rivals in Jordan and Iraq. Again, there was nothing intrinsically valuable about Yemen; it was Yemen's neighbors that mattered.

With Nasser's blessing, the deal was concluded officially during Crown Prince Muḥammad al-Badr's visit to the Soviet Union in July 1956. The weaponry—including aging tanks, armored personnel carriers, airplanes, helicopters, light artillery, light arms, explosives, and ammunition—was festively paraded before cheering crowds at the port city of Ḥudaydah later that year. Although the deal boosted Badr's domestic status considerably, the arming of the Imamate, by strengthening its restless army, served to hasten its demise.[5] A Soviet military

[3] *BVK*, 1:396–97.

[4] Ibid., 416. See also Juzaylān, *Tārīkh*, 23.

[5] Juzaylān recalls plotting the revolution while unloading the first shipment of arms from a Soviet ship with fellow revolutionary Ḥammūd al-Jā'ifī (*Tārīkh*, 23–28, 30–38). See

mission followed close upon the heels of the arms shipment and set up shop in Ṣan'ā'.[6] An Egyptian mission arrived soon afterward.[7] The two delegations divided the work between them, with the Soviets responsible for weapons maintenance and training, and the Egyptians instructing on strategy and tactics at the new military college in Ṣan'ā'. The crisis in Soviet-Egyptian relations between 1958 and 1961 spurred the Egyptian commander to demand that the college be split in two, but the Yemenis apparently succeeded in convincing him that politics should not be allowed to intrude into the military affairs of a mutual ally.[8] While the Egyptians were forced to leave Yemen as a result of the rift between Nasser and the Imam in the fall of 1961, the Soviet mission remained until the revolution. As a result the Soviets had the only significant foreign military presence in the country during the early days of the civil war.

A second result of Badr's visit to Moscow was a decision to open diplomatic missions in Ta'izz and Moscow in the course of 1958.[9] It was typical of the Soviet modus operandi in the Third World, of the centrality of Cairo in its evolving web of relations in the Arab world, and of the KGB's surprising role in diplomacy, that the man charged with building Soviet-Yemeni relations from the mid-1950s onward was the deputy KGB resident in Cairo, Vadim Kirpichenko. There is a parallel between the part played by Kirpichenko in Yemen and that of fellow agent Aleksandr Alekseyev in Cuba. Kirpichenko's main achievement was the development of a close relationship with Crown Prince Muḥammad al-Badr; so close, in fact, that on one occasion in 1957, the prince report-

---

also Stephen Page, *The USSR and Arabia: The Development of Soviet Policies and Attitudes towards the Countries of the Arabian Peninsula, 1955–1970* (London: Central Asian Research Centre, 1971), 33, 37; UAR, "From the Operational Military Experiences in the Theatre of Battle in the Yemeni Arab Republic," 23–24, in *LMOY*. Khrushchev mistakenly places Prince Badr's visit in 1955 (*Vospominania*, 3:444).

[6] Peresypkin, *al-Yaman*, 161, 181–82. The KGB, too, maintained a presence in Ṣan'ā' around the time of the revolution. The residency, however, appears to have been located at the embassy in Ta'izz, at least from September 1965 onward, when it was headed by Aleksandr Zaitsev, formally first secretary at the embassy. Bausin, *Spetsluzhby mira*, 134; Vladimir Sakharov and Umberto Tosi, *High Treason* (New York: G. P. Putnam's Sons, 1980), 166–68; Embassy of the USSR to Ministry of Foreign Affairs of the YAR, no. 306, December 23, 1966, f. 88, op. 18, pap. 11, d. 3, pp. 203–5, AVPRF.

[7] See chapter one. A small Egyptian military mission existed in Yemen since 1954, although its activities were circumscribed by the suspicions of the Imam. Ḥamrūsh, *Qiṣṣat thawrat 23 yūliyū*, 3:200.

[8] Juzaylān, *Ta'rīkh*, 37–38.

[9] The Soviets also stationed a trade representative and several doctors at Ḥudaydah and Ṣan'ā'.

edly refused to travel to London to meet the queen without the Soviet spy at his side.[10] As Kirpichenko's role indicates, Egypt's centrality in the USSR's Yemen policy was a physical reality as much as it was an abstract conception. When formal relations between the USSR and Yemen were established in 1958, it was Soviet ambassador to Egypt Kiselev who traveled to Yemen to be accredited by the Imam. Up until the eve of the revolution, the USSR's Yemen policy continued to be managed out of Cairo, while the Soviet legation in Ta'izz was entrusted to a chargé d'affaires.[11] By telling contrast, the US State Department managed relations with Yemen for the most part out of Jiddah.[12]

A third result of Badr's trip to Moscow in the summer of 1956 was an interest-free loan of 13.5 million rubles. The bulk of this credit was expended on the construction of a modern port at al-Ḥudaydah, which was completed in April 1961.[13] Built primarily for commercial purposes, the port—symbol of Soviet-Yemeni cooperation in the prerevolutionary years—would serve as the primary point of disembarkation for Egyptian men and materiel during the civil war. It was linked to the Yemeni interior by the first paved road between Ṣan'ā' and al-Ḥudaydah, a rival project executed by the Chinese and inaugurated in January 1962. Here, as elsewhere in the Third World at this time, growing competition with China was a significant factor in the making of Soviet policy—and in the calculations of local leaders.

The Egyptian Appeal and the Soviet Response

The military coup that ousted Badr on September 26, 1962, apparently caught the handful of Soviet policy makers attuned to that part of the

[10] Vadim A. Kirpichenko, *Iz arkhiva razvedchika* (Moscow: Mezhdunarodnye Otnoshenia, 1993), 30–31, 45–54. Kirpichenko seems to slip easily between work as official translator for visiting Arab dignitaries and liaising with their intelligence chiefs. Ibid., 60. On Alekseyev, see Aleksandr Fursenko and Timothy Naftali, *One Hell of a Gamble: Khrushchev, Castro, and Kennedy, 1958–1964* (New York: Norton, 1997), 25–33.

[11] V. Kornev, "Otnoshenia mezhdu SSSR i Iemenom (spravka)," sent March 13, 1964, f. 5, op. 30, d. 452, p. 31, RGANI. For an amusing account of Kiselev's reception by the Imam, see Kirpichenko, *Iz arkhiva razvedchika*, 50–53.

[12] The years 1958–60, during which relations were run out of Cairo, formed the exception in the postwar, prerevolutionary period.

[13] M. Suslov, Dep. Chairman of the Government Committee for Foreign Economic Relations of the Ministerial Council of the USSR, to N. A. Muhietdinov, CPSU Central Committee, no. 2-34/3106, June 3, 1961 [material on Soviet aid to underdeveloped countries], f. 5, op. 30, d. 371, pp. 130–32, RGANI.

world unawares.[14] As we have seen, the Egyptians were somewhat less surprised. Egypt's intercession on behalf of the fledgling republic came too rapidly to be merely a reaction to the unexpected, or to lightning Saudi intervention, as Nasser later alleged.[15] Soviet actions were similarly precipitate. Nikolai Sulitskii, Soviet ambassador to Yemen, was away on vacation when the coup took place. Several days later, Valentin Kamenskii, the chargé d'affaires, and Oleg Peresypkin, an attaché, flew from Ta'izz to Ṣan'ā' to meet the members of the new leadership. On the basis of these meetings, they then had to make a recommendation to their government: to recognize or not to recognize? In a revealing passage from his memoirs, Peresypkin recalls agonizing with Kamenskii over the content of their cable to Moscow:

> We had good relations with the Yemeni Kingdom. And even Khrushchev had expressed sorrow at the attempted assassination of Imam Aḥmad in al-Ḥudaydah on March 26, 1961 and his death on March [*sic*] 19, 1962, yet several indications showed that Moscow had reacted favorably to the change of the royalist regime and its replacement with a republic.... This was reflected in the arrival of the military aircraft that we saw at al-Raḥbah [airport], the information of the Soviet military experts concerning communications with the Egyptians in Ṣan'ā', the trusting request for aid by Sallāl [*vide infra*], and even the fact of the assault by Soviet-made T-34 tanks on Dār al-Bashā'ir.... After a short deliberation, Kamenskii wrote: "Taking into account the nature of the political changes, the Embassy is of the opinion that it would be best to recognize the republican regime in Yemen and extend it moral-political and other forms of aid and support it requires."[16]

[14] Khrushchev, *Vospmoninania*, 3:446; Peresypkin, *al-Yaman*, 166–67.

[15] See, for instance, Nasser's speech at Port Sa'īd on December 23, 1962, in UAR, *Majmū'at khuṭab*, 5:261–63. The only way for Nasser to make his usual justification of a purely reactive policy in this case was to push the date of Saudi intervention on behalf of the Royalists back to September 27, the very morning after the revolution. That said, it is plausible that the subsequent decision to broaden the scale of intervention in the first days of October was taken with Saudi actions foremost in mind. For opposing views, see Haykal, *Sanawāt al-ghalayān*, 626–27; Robin Bidwell, *The Two Yemens* (Boulder, CO: Westview Press, 1983), 198–99.

[16] Peresypkin, *al-Yaman*, 176. Cf. the tug of war between the British minister to Yemen, who came to favor recognition, his colleagues in Aden, who opposed it from the beginning, and his superiors in London, who eventually decided against it. Christopher Gandy, "A Mission to Yemen: August 1962–January 1963," *British Journal of Middle Eastern Studies* 25, no. 2 (1998): 247–74.

Peresypkin subsequently heard that this cable made it to Khrushchev's desk on the night of September 30. After reading the document with care, the Soviet leader allegedly pronounced: "Monarchy is by nature a reactionary regime. They have toppled it, and established a republican regime, which is naturally more progressive. Therefore, we should support the republicans and offer them aid."[17] As Peresypkin tells it, the diplomats, seeing where the wind was blowing based on the evidence of incipient military cooperation, opted for recognition, thereby anticipating Khrushchev's response yet somehow shaping it at the same time. In any event the Soviet Union officially recognized the Yemen Arab Republic on October 1. It was the first non-Arab state to do so.[18]

That the air bridge formed the central theme of Soviet-Egyptian cooperation in the early days of the intervention is not surprising. Long-range transport aircraft were crucial for rapid dispatch of men and materiel to the battlefield at a time when the republic existed in name only and the tribal forces amassing to crush it held a potentially fatal advantage. The two most pressing needs were Special Forces to defend

[17] Peresypkin, *al-Yaman,* 176. There are two problems with this account. First, if the cable was sent from Ta'izz on October 1, as Peresypkin contends, there is no way it could have reached Khrushchev on September 30. Second, the US and British representatives in Yemen place the first visit of the foreign diplomatic corps to Ṣan'ā' on October 2 and 3, respectively. The origins of *this* discrepancy are unclear, but given Gandy's communication difficulties in the aftermath of the coup, the American version seems more reliable. Cable, Gandy (Ta'izz) to Foreign Office, October 2, 1962, BM 1015/54, FO 371/162945, PRO; Cable, Stookey (Aden) to Secretary of State, no. 40, October 3, 1962, RG 59, Box 2080, 786h.00/10-362, NARA. See also Gandy, "A Mission to Yemen," 260.

[18] According to some sources, the USSR was in fact the very *first* state to recognize the Yemen Arab Republic (YAR) on September 28—the day before Egypt recognized the new republic. According to others, Soviet recognition came either simultaneously with Egyptian recognition on the twenty-ninth or immediately thereafter. O'Ballance, *War in the Yemen,* 73; Sulṭān Nājī, *al-Tārīkh al-'askarī li-l-Yaman 1839–1967* (Beirut: Dār al-'Awdah, 1988), 220 (which draws on O'Ballance); Richard E. Bissell, "Soviet Use of Proxies in the Third World: The Case of Yemen," *Soviet Studies* 30, no. 1 (1978): 91; Bruce Porter, *The USSR in Third World Conflicts: Soviet Arms and Diplomacy in Local Wars, 1945–1980* (Cambridge: Cambridge University Press, 1984), 74. However, Khrushchev's telegram of recognition, as quoted in *Pravda* of October 2, 1962, bears the date October 1. The source of the discrepancy is a transmission by Ṣan'ā' radio on September 29, which anticipated the essentials of Khrushchev's telegram. "Regime Reports Support," *New York Times,* September 30, 1962, 5; *al-Ahrām,* September 30, 1962, 1. Assuming the Yemeni broadcasts had some basis in fact, it is possible that the telegram of recognition was postdated in the Soviet press or that the Soviet government extended recognition in some unofficial manner on September 28 or 29. This is the sense one gets from *al-Ahrām,* October 2, 1962, 1.

the capital, and attack aircraft to strike at inaccessible tribal outposts.[19] In theory these could have been shipped by sea. In fact, this is how most subsequent supplies were transported; the Egyptian merchant marine, though stretched, was pressed into service on October 1. Over the course of the first year of operations, eighteen ships were to make a total of 122 trips (an average of 2.34 ships per week) between the ports of Adabiyyah in Egypt and Ḥudaydah in Yemen, ferrying upward of half a million metric tons of supplies to the front.[20] Had it been merely a question of tonnage, transport by sea would have been not only sufficient but also vastly superior to transport by air. For one, the largest Egyptian commercial vessels carried 8,000 tons, outperforming the biggest transport aircraft of the age by a factor of roughly 400. Moreover, Yemen's Soviet-built port, though designed for commerce, not war, could, with difficulty, handle three medium-sized ships or four small-sized ships simultaneously. By contrast, Yemen's airports at the time of the revolution were hardly worthy of the name; consisting of dirt strips 800 to 1,200 meters in length, they were suitable for nothing larger than a lightly loaded DC-3.[21]

In the event, speed was the crucial consideration. The trip by sea took an average of four days, followed by a dangerous 220-kilometer drive along the winding road connecting Ḥudaydah with the capital, Ṣan'ā'. Egypt's prospective point man in Yemen, 'Abd al-Raḥmān al-Bayḍānī, recalls telling Nasser, before boarding an Egyptian DC-3 bound for Ṣan'ā' on September 28, that if reinforcements took more than four days to arrive by sea, the president might as well order them to return to port as soon as he heard "that our heads had been strung up on the trees of Yemen and were being torn to bits by birds of prey."[22] Clearly, an airlift was necessary. But the twin-engine Il-14s (equivalent to US DC-3s) in possession of the Egyptian air force had a small cargo bay and could not make it to Yemen without multiple refueling stops.[23] Given Sudan's refusal to provide staging facilities,[24] transport by Il-14

[19] Fawzī, *Ḥarbal-thalāth sanawāt*, 23–24.

[20] UAR, "Logistical Matters in the Theatre of Operations in Yemen," 8–9, in *OMLY*.

[21] Ibid., 9; "The Aerial Operations in Yemen," 4; Parker Hart, *Saudi Arabia and the United States: Birth of a Security Partnership* (Bloomington: Indiana University Press, 1998), 140.

[22] Bayḍānī, *Miṣr wa-thawrat al-Yaman*, 85. Cf. idem, *Azmat al-ummah*, 322.

[23] See, for example, Kirpichenko's multileg trip to Yemen in January 1958. Kirpichenko, *Iz arkhiva razvedchika*, 47. See also Bayḍānī, *Azmat al-ummah*, 287.

[24] Cable, Arthur (Cairo) to Foreign Office, no. 721, October 5, 1962, FO 371/162945, PRO; Memcon, Dept. of State, "Mr. Talbot's Private Meeting with Crown Prince Faysal," October 4, 1962, RG 59, CDF 611.86b, M1855, roll 114, NARA.

was not a realistic option. The four-engine An-12 (equivalent to the American C-130), by contrast, was ideal. With a range of 3,400 kilometers with a 10-ton payload, it could almost make the round-trip flight from Egypt to Yemen without refueling.[25] Moreover, the An-12's lift capacity of 20 tons enabled it to carry up to ninety troops, several vehicles, or even a number of disassembled fighter aircraft, while its reversible-thrust engines enabled landing on rough airstrips only 500 meters long. But the Egyptians had none of these state-of-the-art flying trucks, nor did they have pilots trained to fly them. This was the context for the Egyptian appeal to the Soviet Union in the immediate aftermath of the coup in Ṣan'ā'.

Details of the deliberations in Cairo and in Moscow in late September and early October remain murky. Khrushchev provides merely the general contours of what happened: "Nasser wished to transport several military units from the UAR to Yemen, but he did not have airplanes. We sold the UAR several Antonov military transports.... However, Egypt did not have suitable pilots either. Nasser appealed to us with a request to provide this help as well. We responded to his appeal and urgently outfitted planes with our crews. Now Egypt was capable of supporting Yemen."[26] Egyptian chief of military intelligence at the time, Major General (subsequently Lieutenant General) Ṣalāḥ al-Dīn al-Ḥadīdī, elaborates:

> [The Egyptian authorities] scheduled an urgent meeting between Marshal ['Abd al-Ḥakīm] 'Āmir, the First Vice President of the President of the Republic, and the Deputy Supreme Commander of the Armed Forces, and the senior Soviet military advisers in Cairo, [headed by Lieutenant] General [Aleksandr] Pozharskii. Marshal 'Āmir began the meeting with an explanation of the circumstances endured by the Yemeni people under the regime of the Imams, and Egypt's obligation toward this fraternal people, which was given the opportunity to rid itself of the reactionary regime, from which it had suffered greatly. Then Marshal 'Āmir continued his speech, disclosing the difficulties the Egyptian forces were facing in their fighting with the tribes,

[25] Initially, the Antonovs were refueled in an awkward procedure on the ground using scarce barrels of fuel. Eventually, spare fuel tanks were installed, which enabled the planes to make the round trip from Aswan without refueling. "The Aerial Actions in Yemen," 7; John W. R. Taylor, ed., *Jane's All the World's Aircraft* (New York: McGraw-Hill, 1964–65), 314; idem, *Jane's All the World's Aircraft* (New York: McGraw-Hill, 1965–66) 322; Nikolai Iakubovich, "*An-12: Sorok let v stroiu,*" *Kryl'ia Rodiny*, no. 3 (1997): 5.

[26] Khrushchev, *Vospominania*, 3:446.

and the supplies flowing in to these tribes over the Saudi border, [and] explaining that at the top of the problems vexing the Egyptian command was the long distance separating Cairo from Ṣan‘ā’, and the pressing need for long-range, heavy-cargo military transport aircraft. Then Marshal ‘Āmir entered directly into the matter when he said that he had heard of the Russian-made.... Antonov planes, which he thought would serve the purpose [*tafī bi-l-gharaḍ*], and that Egypt would greatly appreciate the attitude of the Soviet Union, [if she] helped in easing the mission of the Egyptian forces by supplying her with a number of these planes at the earliest possible opportunity. Before the end of the visit, the senior adviser, who recorded ‘Āmir's speech in writing, promised to convey to the Soviet government the import [*faḥwā*] of what had transpired in the meeting, and added that he expected an answer in the immediate future.

A second meeting did in fact place between the two [men] *before forty-eight hours had elapsed* [*qabla murūr thāmānī wa-arba‘īn sā‘ah*], based on a request by the Soviet general, who opened it by saying—he was reading from a memo prepared in advance—that the Soviet government supported the policy Egypt was pursuing in Yemen, and agreed with the step that she had taken there, as well as with her desire to aid the Yemeni people, and had decided to grant [*ihdā’*] a quantity of food supplies sufficient for 5000 men for a period of one month, as well as military uniforms for the same number, in addition to a quantity of rifles and suitable ammunition. Then the advisers [*sic*] requested that Egypt undertake to send these supplies from her own storehouses in Soviet stead [*niyābatan ‘anhā*], until the Soviet Union could compensate her, in view of [Soviet] interest in their speedy delivery [on the one hand], and so as to simplify the transport operation on the other hand. General Pozharskii continued, saying, or rather reading: ‘As for the Antonov planes, which it is desired that the Soviet Union supply to Egypt, my government has asked me to inform you that it agrees to this request in principle, along with certain provisos necessary in the interest of all parties.

First: It is essential to begin by holding a training course on flying and maintaining this type of aircraft, [which would be] attended by a number of Egyptian pilots—on the condition that this course be held in Egypt. The Soviet Union is prepared to send the training team within one week so as to save time. After the end of the course, ten Antonov planes will arrive in Egypt as a first installment, after which the requisite number will be determined in a final manner.

> Second: If the Egyptian government sees the need to begin the flights of these planes to Yemen before the end of the pilots' training period, then *the government of the Soviet Union is prepared to send the crews required for operation and maintenance of ten Antonov planes, which would operate, temporarily, under Egyptian command, on the line Cairo-Ṣan'ā'*. In the event of your agreement on this, *the Soviet government asks that its pilots be supplied with personal identification establishing that they are civilians working in the service of the Egyptian government in aerial transportation operations, i.e. far from combat military actions* [*ba'īdah 'an al-a'māl al-'askariyyah al-qitāliyyah*].
>
> In the event, an agreement was struck on the principles proposed, and an agreement was reached on the details concerning the financial [fn. in original: "naturally: that they be at Egypt's expense"] and administrative sides, including the determination of the times of the planes' arrival, and the beginning of the training course, and other subjects warranted by the course of events.[27] (Emphases added)

Pozharskii, so we are told by this source, consulted with his superiors in Moscow and responded favorably to 'Āmir's appeal less than forty-eight hours after it was made. In addition to the grant of war materiel, the senior military adviser was authorized to launch a crash training program for Egyptian pilots on the Antonov 12. In the meantime, Soviet crews, disguised as civilians, would fly these top-secret missions on a task force of ten planes under Egyptian command and at Egypt's expense.[28]

Although Ḥadīdī does not date these meetings or the launch of the air bridge, the context of 'Āmir's plea places it *after* the initial influx of forces, at a time when Egyptian forces were already engaged in fighting on the ground in Yemen, that is, sometime in early or mid-October. The omission of a date in this instance may reflect no more than carelessness,

[27] Ḥadīdī, *Shāhid 'alā ḥarb al-Yaman*, 54–56. On Pozharskii, commander of Soviet military personnel in Egypt, see also Krakhmalov, *Zapiski voennogo attaché*, 66.

[28] Egypt's chief of general intelligence at the time, Ṣalāḥ Naṣr, presents a more streamlined version that differs from Ḥadīdī's in several key respects. In Naṣr's recollection, it was President Nasser who made the appeal in a phone call to the Soviet ambassador; the Soviets responded with twenty-five Antonovs, and the main sticking point concerned Egypt's intentions in Yemen. Once assured Nasser did not intend to seek unity (as he had with Syria), Khrushchev acquiesced. Naṣr does, however, echo Ḥadīdī's emphasis on the speed of the Soviet response. So too does Muḥammad Haykal, who writes that the Antonovs started to arrive in Cairo only three days after the request was made. Naṣr, *Mudhakkirāt*, 2:373; Haykal, *Sphinx and Commissar*, 118.

yet it is odd that elsewhere Ḥadīdī is quite specific about the beginning of the intervention. It began, he writes in another passage of his memoirs, on the night of October 2, with the departure for Yemen of the Egyptian SS *Sudan*, carrying one hundred commandos (disguised as civilians), a quantity of light arms and ammunition, and a pair of Yak airplanes.[29] According to this version, the first Egyptian unit to land in Yemen was a seaborne company of commandos, which arrived at Ḥudaydah on October 5. However, there is reason to question the authenticity of the arguments Ḥadīdī attributes to ʻĀmir, and the precedence of naval forces over the airlift more generally.

The most important alternative account is in a pedagogical lecture on the aerial operations in Yemen preserved in a series of Egyptian military documents the Israelis captured in 1967. The document portrays the beginning of the intervention in the following terms: "Immediately with the declaration of the instigation of the revolution on September 26, 1962, the armed forces of the United Arab Republic stood ready to provide any aid within their means, in order to help this revolution when asked to do so.... On September 30, 1962, after the regime of the revolutionaries in Yemen had stabilized, evidence showed that several foreign countries were intervening in order to thwart this revolution. In accordance with the request of the people of the Yemeni revolution, our armed forces began to send several units to strengthen the Yemeni revolution and support it." A subsequent passage provides further details: "Those responsible in Egypt decided to send to Yemen several units with their full equipment in order to support the forces of the Yemeni revolution and aid them. *These forces, in addition to the force of aircraft necessary to support them, were transported speedily by air* [emphasis added]. The rest of the forces and aircraft were transported in rounds by sea and air."[30]

[29] Ḥadīdī, *Shāhid ʻalā ḥarb al-Yaman*, 38–39. A similar version is presented by ʻAbd al-Raḥmān al-Bayḍānī in *Miṣr wa-thawrat al-Yaman*, 82–87. Bayḍānī, who justly takes Haykal to task for fudging the issue (*Sanawāt*, 622–28), himself commits serious sins of omission in describing the events in question. After setting the stage, on September 28, for a four-day cliffhanger in Yemen spent waiting for reinforcements (see above), his narrative jumps to the arrival of the *Sudan* on October 5. See also Bayḍānī, *Azmat al-ummah*, 389.

[30] "The Aerial Actions in Yemen," in *OMLY*, 2, 5. The document is undated but makes clear that the air bridge was still underway at the time of composition. In the absence of the Arabic original, I rely on the Hebrew translation of the captured document, the accuracy of which is impossible to assess.

The document registers unambiguously that the urgent dispatch of commandos by air *preceded* the slower deployment of reinforcements by sea. Less certainly, it places the date of intervention on or shortly after September 30—but in any case prior to the arrival of the *Sudan*.[31] This sequence of events is confirmed by Israeli military intelligence, which registered the first flight of Egyptian "equipment and advisers" on October 2,[32] and by Soviet diplomat Oleg Peresypkin, who reports that the first Soviet-piloted aircraft bearing Egyptian troops landed at night on September 29.[33] If Peresypkin's date is correct, Egypt's request

[31] The arrival of the *Sudan* on or around October 5 is not in doubt. US chargé Robert Stookey reported on October 10 that "[The] UAR supported coup within [a] day or two with military planes and pilots[,] which [are being] used [to] reduce internal resistance.... [A s]mall UAR cargo vessel[, the] STAR OF SUDAN[,] arrived in Hodeida several days ago with army uniforms, "C" rations, [a] few Ramses cars, and [an] estimated 50 teachers and advisors on government organization and administration.... No UAR troops disembarked [at] Hodeida, and no UAR war ship [is] believed [to] have arrived."Cable, Stookey (Ta'izz) to Sec. State, no. 124, October 10, 1962, RG 59, CDF 1960–63, 786h.00/10-1062, NARA. But British diplomats estimated that a force of at least battalion and possibly brigade strength had departed aboard the *Sudan* and a second ship, the SS *Taludi*, on October 3. Telegrams, Arthur (Cairo) to FO, Nos. 721, 732, October 5 and 8, 1962, FO 371/162945, PRO. Thus it is possible that the first company of commandos discussed in the sources arrived by air around September 30, while the infantry battalion or brigade of reinforcements arrived by sea around October 5. Bayḍānī asserts that the *Sudan* arrived on October 5 (*Miṣr wa-thawrat al-Yaman*, 86). For perceptive discussions of this question and of the launch of the intervention in general, see James, *Nasser at War*, 56–60, 64–65; Aḥmad, *al-Dawr al-miṣrī*, 111–13.

[32] Aman, Special Intelligence Survey 36/62 (Hebrew), no. 137/586.130.1/0, October 22, 1962, "The Revolution in Yemen—An Interim Summary," p. 2, in HZ 3449/27, ISA.

[33] He refers to the "night" of the twenty-ninth, which may in fact depict the early hours of September 30. Peresypkin's own first sighting of a Soviet-piloted An-10 [*sic*] at Ṣan'ā' airport allegedly occurred on the morning of October 1, when he returned to Ta'izz along with the rest of the diplomatic corps after meeting with members of the new regime. However, as discussed above, the diplomats returned from their first trip to Ṣan'ā' on October 3, not October 1. Moreover, Christopher Gandy refers to a strikingly similar airport encounter on a subsequent visit to Ṣan'ā on October 8. That he would have neglected to report such an occurrence five days earlier is implausible. These discrepancies necessarily cast some doubt on Peresypkin's dating of the first flight. Peresypkin, *al-Yaman*, 174; Cable, Gandy to FO, no. 163, October 9, 1963, FO 371/162947; Cable, Bushell (Aden) to FO, no. 213, October 11, 1962, FO 371/162947. However, September 29 is also the date specified in Wagīh Abū Dhikrī's fictionalized account of the war. He refers to landing at dawn on the twenty-ninth, which would entail departure from Cairo around midnight on September 28 (*Al-Zuhūr*, 10–12). The journalist Edgar O'Ballance asserts that the first Egyptian contingents arrived in Yemen by air on September 28, followed the next day by

for the Antonovs must have taken place on September 28 at the latest; given that at least a day probably elapsed between the Egyptian request and the Soviet response, the twenty-seventh—the very day after the nocturnal coup—is more likely.[34] In any case, the exchange between Cairo and Moscow almost certainly took place in late September.

Why, then, might Ḥadīdī have postdated the initiation of the air bridge? Perhaps because to acknowledge otherwise would undermine the official Egyptian narrative of the war, which centers on the notion of a response to Yemeni appeal made *in reaction* to a tangible threat from Saudi Arabia. If transport by air in fact preceded shipment by sea, then the launch of the air bridge also dates the launch of the intervention as a whole, and the closer the date of the intervention gets to September 26 (the date of the coup d'état in Ṣan'ā'), the less tenable the Egyptian narrative becomes. An early date would not only expose the extent of Egypt's dependence on the Soviet Union in launching the intervention; it would lend credence to speculation that the intervention was premeditated, and that Egyptian actions preempted rather than reacted to Saudi interference. We may speculate that exposure of this guarded secret went too far for Egypt's former chief of military intelligence, whose account of the war is otherwise revelatory.[35] Notably, other Egyptian writers share this tendency to delay the date of Egypt's military intervention. For instance, Nasser's foremost apologist, Muḥammad Haykal, though deliberately vague on the matter, leaves the reader with a distinct (and false) impression that the decision to intervene fell three days *after* the notorious defection to Egypt of Saudi planes bearing arms for Yemen on October 2, 3, and 8.[36] Similarly, Vice President 'Abd al-Laṭīf

a ship carrying "troops, tanks, guns, vehicles and military stores." He is almost certainly incorrect on both counts (*War in the Yemen*, 84). His version is reproduced in Arabic by Nājī, *al-Tārīkh al-'askarī li-l-Yaman*, 221. For other accounts that place the launch of the air bridge within days of the coup, see Lon Nordeen and David Nicolle, *Phoenix over the Nile: A History of Egyptian Air Power, 1932–1994* (Washington, DC: Smithsonian Institution Press, 1996), 188; and Sharaf, *Sanawāt*, 2:620.

[34] This assumes that Egypt's request was not made *before* the revolution, and that there were no An-12s on the ground in Egypt at the time of the coup. The latter assumption, in particular, is questionable.

[35] Ḥadīdī is, for example, similarly reticent on the sensitive issue of Egyptian casualties (*Shāhid 'alā ḥarb al-Yaman*, 161).

[36] It is impossible to tell which of the three dates marks the beginning of the alleged three-day deliberation period. Ṣalāḥ Naṣr also posits a three-day debate, but asserts that "the first of the units began to ship out of Egypt on October 5, i.e. eight [*sic*] days after the

al-Baghdādī, though silent on the issue in his memoirs, refers elsewhere to a platoon sent by sea a full fifteen days after the coup.[37]

In any event, one characteristic of Soviet decision making stands out already: like Egypt's, it was remarkably fast. Official Soviet recognition came within ninety-six hours of the change in regime, while Soviet aircrews flew the first contingent of Egyptian commandos to Yemen within one week of the coup—and probably much sooner. The impulsive alacrity of the Soviet response was vintage Khrushchev; *on s'engage, et puis on voit*. In this sense, the Soviet decision to support Nasser in Yemen was the logical corollary to the aid extended to Castro in Cuba. The traditional, and not illogical, view that the Soviet leadership was so absorbed with Operation Anadyr that it did not get around to dealing with the events in Yemen until after the missile crisis was peacefully resolved is false. Far from "restrained" or "distracted" by the mounting crisis over Cuba, as conventional accounts[38] have it, Khrushchev's reaction to the revolution in Yemen was swift, vigorous, and complementary to his aggressive policy in the Caribbean.

In order to avoid exaggerating the gravity of the decision to accede to Egypt's request, it is important to recognize that the leadership in the Kremlin almost certainly miscalculated the scale and duration of the commitment they were undertaking in Yemen. Following Egyptian estimates, they presumed that the need for intervention would be short lived and the operation limited. As the former chief of Egyptian military intelligence emphasizes in his memoirs, initial expectations were that the new regime would swiftly stabilize without the need for outside military support.[39] When, nevertheless, a company of commandos was sent to Ṣan'ā' several days after the coup, the Egyptian ambassador, who came to greet them at the airport, reportedly told them that their mission would last no more than a few weeks.[40] Soviet airmen were being told similar things. One military translator assigned to the

revolution took place." In discussing the air bridge, he mentions September 26 as the origin of Egypt's need for transport aircraft, but not necessarily the date of Nasser's appeal. Haykal, *Sanawāt al-ghalayān*, 625–26; Naṣr, *Mudhakkirāt*, 2:332–33, 373.

[37] Quoted in Ḥabīb, *Milaffāt*, 240. See also Riyāḍ, *Mudhakkirāt*, 2:271.

[38] Page, *The USSR and Arabia*, 74–75; Haykal, *Sphinx and Commissar*, 118; Stephens, *Nasser*, 391; Bissell, "Soviet Use of Proxies," 92.

[39] Ḥadīdī, *Shāhid 'alā ḥarb al-Yaman*, 22.

[40] Abū Dhikrī, *al-Zuhūr*, 12. 'Āmir reportedly said much the same thing in private. Rahmy, *Egyptian Policy*, 195.

Figure 2.1 An Egyptian Antonov An-12. Photo courtesy of Günter Grondstein.

Cairo-Ṣan'ā' shuttle recalls flying out to Egypt in October 1962 for a mission of several days. He would remain for three years.[41]

The Soviet decision to provide transport aircraft and crews to fly them preceded the still bolder decision to enable Soviet pilots to participate in bombing missions over Yemen by several weeks. We know little about the background for this second Egyptian request. That it was made in the second week of October suggests that the immediate background was the fall of Ma'rib on October 8, and the consequent extension of the Egyptian war efforts eastward to the Khawlān and northward toward the Saudi border in an attempt to interdict the incipient flow of supplies from Saudi Arabia. This dramatic expansion in the target area of Egyptian operations, which had hitherto focused on the im-

[41] Personal interview, Vladimir Shubin, Moscow, November 3, 2005.

mediate vicinity of Ṣan'ā', gave rise to the need for air cover as far as 150 kilometers to the east of Ṣan'ā' and some 300 kilometers to the north. Theoretically, the twin-jet Il-28 bomber in service in the Egyptian air force could have fulfilled this new role out of one of the airbases in the vicinity of Ṣan'ā'. This solution was, in fact, attempted but proved ineffective for two reasons. For one, the thick stone structure of Yemeni walls and fortresses required heavier ordnance than a light bomber could carry. Second, and more importantly, the only suitable airfield in Yemen—the rough, 3-kilometer dirt airstrip at al-Rawḍah, some 15 kilometers north of Ṣan'ā' and more than 7,000 feet above sea level—proved dangerous for the Il-28s to negotiate. Accordingly, flights were curtailed or suspended outright until construction of a new military airport at Ḥudaydah could be completed in the second half of February 1963.[42] In the interim, a solution was needed that did not depend on Yemen's shaky aviation infrastructure.

The Tupolev Tu-16 twin-jet bomber was just being introduced into the Egyptian air force at the time. With a range of 4,800 kilometers when fully loaded, it could easily make the round-trip flight from Cairo to practically any point in Yemen without refueling.[43] But Egyptian pilots were still in training on the Tu-16 when the war broke out and so were unable to fly these missions on their own for quite some time.[44] We may accordingly surmise that the original Egyptian appeal sought permission to employ the Egyptian trainees and their Soviet instructors in combat missions as an extension of the training program. If so it was a highly irregular request, made all the more sensitive by the fact that it involved sending Soviet pilots to participate in deliberate acts of war that could not be concealed as "volunteer" work of a noncombat nature. Moreover, the sorties, for the most part, targeted supply convoys originating in Saudi Arabia or arms depots located on or beyond the Saudi-Yemeni border. By attacking Saudi territory, these missions risked invoking the US defense pledge to the oil kingdom, leading to a potential military clash between Soviet and American airmen. Clearly, this was not a decision to be taken lightly.

Not surprisingly, the Egyptian appeal was initially rejected. Notes from the Presidium meeting of October 11, 1962, record Khrushchev's

[42] "The Aerial Actions in Yemen," 5. Even the single-engine YAK trainers, which the Egyptians converted into light attack aircraft at the very beginning of the intervention, had a hard time with Ṣan'ā' 's shorter "paved" runways (Ḥadīdī, *Shāhid 'alā ḥarb al-Yaman*, 48).

[43] Taylor, *Jane's All the World's Aircraft* (1965–66), 335.

[44] Weir, "Egyptian Air Force."

one-word response to ‘Āmir’s request to use the Tu-16 in Yemen: “*nevozmozhno*” (impossible).[45] It is not clear what overturned this categorical “no” within a matter of weeks, but approval was granted soon thereafter. Code-named “*mubārak*,” after squadron commander (and subsequent president) Hosni Mubarak, flights began in late October or early November.[46] In his memoirs, Khrushchev glosses over the initial negative: “it turned out that Nasser did not have the military aviation necessary for operations against Royalist troops assembled in neighboring countries, where Arab princelings, fearing for their own well-being, sought to return the throne to the king of Yemen. We sold Nasser excellent Tu-16 bombers. He again did not have pilots, and he appealed to us once more with a request to dispatch our pilots. These were volunteers. Without announcing anything in the press, they travelled to Egypt, and from there were transferred to Yemen.”[47] We may speculate that at the Presidium meeting of October 11, a decision was made to send General Markov at the head of a military delegation to ascertain more precisely Egypt’s expanding military needs. Markov, who spent October 15–27 in Egypt, must have returned with a positive recommendation. If this hypothesis is correct, it is all the more remarkable that Khrushchev approved this risk-fraught escalation *after* the onset of the crisis in Cuba on October 22.

Explaining Soviet Behavior

To begin to understand Soviet motivations we must first acknowledge how extraordinary Egypt’s initial appeal really was. After all, requesting a new weapon was one thing; asking for foreign nationals to operate them in combat was another altogether. Why, then, did the USSR support Egypt’s military intervention on the Arabian Peninsula so readily?

[45] Fursenko, *Prezidium*, Protokol no. 58, 596.

[46] Khalīl, *Ḥurūb Miṣr*, 58; Ḥadīdī, *Shāhid ‘alā ḥarb al-Yaman*, 48; Shishchenko, *Smoliane-Internatsionalisty*, 172. The actual participation of Tu-16s in the fighting is recorded as early as November 8, 1962. Memo, J. P. Waterfield, “Russians in the Yemen,” November 8, 1962, FO 371/162955, PRO; Cable, Col. E. R. Paterson (Tel Aviv) to Lt. Col. H. G. Niven, MA/11/5/62, (Report of Briefing by Israeli Director of Intelligence, Brig. Gen. Meir Amit, November 9, 1962), November 13, 1962, FO 371/162959, PRO. See also Bower, *The Perfect English Spy*, 250; and “The Aerial Actions in Yemen,” 6, 14.

[47] Khrushchev, *Vospominania*, 3:446.

The answer to this question reflects the volatile mixture of revolutionary fervor and strategic calculation that made up Soviet foreign policy under Khrushchev.

One must begin with an appreciation of the framework of Soviet policy toward the Third World in general. It was Khrushchev who, from 1955 onward, led the revival of Soviet interest in the Third World. In many ways this was a return to the spirit of the Congress of the Peoples of the East, held at Baku in September 1920. Born of the frustration with the pace of the revolution in Europe in the early 1920s, interest in the revolutionary potential of colonized Asians and Africans subsided during the great struggle for Europe in the 1930s and 1940s. But as the conflict in Europe congealed to produce a hostile standoff across a divided continent, the Cold War struggle found outlets in other parts of the globe, particularly in Asia. Whereas under Stalin Soviet foreign policy was guided primarily by the ceaseless quest for security,[48] and hence tended to focus on regions bordering the Soviet Union, under Khrushchev ideologically motivated support for national liberation movements in the Third World became a priority.[49] And while Stalin too had been known to aid nonsocialist movements primarily because they were anti-British—Soviet aid to Turkey in the 1920s and to Israel in the late 1940s come to mind—Khrushchev turned it into an ideologically sanctioned obligation.

In a famous speech on January 6, 1961, Khrushchev argued that it was the *duty* of the socialist camp to aid peoples struggling for their freedom from colonial domination and newly independent nations, even if they were not yet socialist by any stretch of the imagination. Received in some circles as a declaration of war over the Third World, Khrushchev's speech made it clear that a struggle with new forms of imperial domination was underway in Asia, Africa, and Latin America, from which the Soviet Union could not remain aloof. If the Communists did not reach out to the colonized, the capitalists would succeed in driving a wedge between the socialist camp and the newly independent states

[48] Vojtech Mastny, *The Cold War and Soviet Insecurity: The Stalin Years* (New York: Oxford University Press, 1996).

[49] Aleksandr Fursenko and Timothy Naftali, *Khrushchev's Cold War: The Inside Story of an American Adversary* (New York: Norton, 2006), 57, 80–82, 292–95, and passim; Odd Arne Westad, *The Global Cold War: Third World Interventions and the Making of Our Times* (Cambridge: Cambridge University Press, 2005), 67–70, 158–67; William Taubman, *Khrushchev: The Man and His Era* (New York: W. W. Norton, 2003), 348, 354, 487.

and eventually add them to the capitalist camp.[50] These ideas found increasing support in a body of social science produced by a new generation of Soviet theorists who saw grounds for optimism concerning the prospects for the rapid development of socialism in the Third World once the shackles of foreign exploitation had been removed.[51] Following in Khrushchev's footsteps, these ideologues placed a seal of approval on a broad category of newly independent states, which followed the so-called noncapitalist road of development.[52]

Whether by coincidence or design, these ideas were increasingly in harmony with the way Soviet realists believed the Cold War with the United States ought to be waged. In the summer of 1961, the party leadership approved a plan drawn up by the KGB and designed to create "a situation in various areas of the world that would favor dispersion of attention and forces by the United States and their satellites, and would tie them down during the settlement of the question of a German peace treaty and West Berlin." A key component of the plan called "to activate by the means available to the KGB armed uprisings against pro-Western reactionary governments" in Latin America, Africa, and the Middle and Far East, and "to cause uncertainty in the government circles of the United States, England, Turkey, and Iran about the stability of their positions in the Middle and Near East."[53] It was not long before these notions found concrete expression in policy. Soviet military aid to Lumumba in Congo, Castro in Cuba, and Kong Le in Laos in the course of 1960–61 traces a pattern of support for beleaguered revolutionaries in the Third World. Defeat in the Congo, and near setbacks in Laos and Cuba, must have made Soviet policy makers determined to be more prompt and decisive with military aid in similar situations in the future.[54] Although the Soviet foreign ministry, Soviet military intelligence (the GRU), and the KGB all maintained contacts with Yemeni individu-

[50] N. S. Khrushchev, "Za novye pobedy mirovogo kommunisticheskogo dvizhenia," *Kommunist*, no. 1 (January 1961): 25–29.

[51] Westad, *Global Cold War*, 166–67. For a contemporary and pioneering study of the problem of colonialism on the Arabian Peninsula, see Evgenii Primakov, *Strany Aravii i kolonializm* (Moscow: Gosudarstvennoe Izdatel'stvo Politicheskoi Literatury, 1956).

[52] The Yemen Arab Republic was swiftly hailed as belonging to this category. See P. Demchenko, "Veter peremen nad Iemenom," *Pravda*, November 22, 1962, 7.

[53] Shelepin to Khrushchev, July 29, 1961, f. 4, op. 13, d. 81, p. 130, RGANI, quoted in Vladislav Zubok, "Spy vs. Spy: The KGB vs. the CIA, 1960–1962," CWIHP Bulletin no. 4 (1994): 28–29. See also Christopher Andrew and Vasilii Mitrokhin, *The Mitrokhin Archive II: The KGB and the World* (London: Allen Lane, 2005), 150.

[54] Fursenko and Naftali, *Khrushchev's Cold War*, 292–337.

als opposed to the Imam and the British presence in Aden,[55] the coup that toppled the Imamate in September 1962 had nothing to do with Soviet intrigue. It did, however, take place in a climate in which Soviet support for wars of liberation in the Third World, particularly in circumstances where Western interests might be undermined, was axiomatic.

The rapidity with which the leadership in the Kremlin dropped their progressive prince for a dubious republic proved just how malleable the new doctrine of Third World interventions could be. To be sure, even from a purely ideological perspective, the emergence of a praetorian republic could be justified as "objectively progressive," in Marxist terms, when compared to the medieval Imamate. Still, Khrushchev's apologia—according to which Badr, as Imam, disappointed the Soviets with his pursuit of the reactionary policies of his father—is ludicrous, considering that Badr managed to reign all of eight days after the death of his father before being overthrown by a junta scarcely more enlightened or humane.[56] Indeed, if hues of dogma colored Soviet perspectives on Yemen in 1962, they were to be found at that edge of the spectrum where ideology shades into *realpolitik*.[57]

There was, in fact, a compelling strategic rationale for seizing the opportunity the revolution in Yemen presented—although it was perhaps not as strong as in the Cuban scenario. The most important strategic interest at stake in Yemen was the seven-year-old relationship with Egypt. From the arms deal of 1955 to the giant dam at Aswan, Khrushchev's foreign policy was marked by a record of extraordinary commitment to Egypt. During his time at the helm, Egypt received nearly a quarter of the total amount of Soviet economic aid dispensed abroad.[58] This need not surprise us: what Castro was for Latin America, and Lumumba might have been for Africa, Nasser personified in the Middle East. For policy makers in Moscow, a muscular Egypt under Nasser's magnetic leadership provided the best guarantee imaginable that their

[55] Peresypkin, *al-Yaman*, 154, 162; Krakhmalov, *Zapiski voennovo attaché*, 92; Bausin, *Spetsluzhby mira*, 127; Memo, V. Kornev, "*Kharakteristika na ministra kommunikatsii Iemenskoi Arabskoi Respubliki polkovnika Abdallu Dobbi*," sent March 13, 1964, fond 5, op. 30, d. 452, p. 23, RGANI.

[56] Khrushchev, *Vospominania*, 3:445. In fact, the new Imam announced a number of progressive reforms in his first and only week in office.

[57] Cf. Khrushchev rethinking military aid to Somalia in 1963, taking into consideration the change of regime in Kenya, and the potential use of Soviet weapons against new African allies. Fursenko, *Prezidium*, Protokol no. 305, December 23, 1963, 802.

[58] Charles R. Dannehl, *Politics, Trade, and Development: Soviet Economic Aid to the Non-Communist Third World, 1955–89* (Aldershot: Dartmouth, 1995), 86.

American and British counterparts would continue to lose sleep over the Middle East. Although ties between the two countries had recently suffered from differences over Syria, Iraq, and Arab Communists (1958–61), their broad strategic underpinnings were bound to reassert themselves with the passage of time and cooling of tempers.[59] Indeed, given the context of Soviet policy toward the Third World in general and Egypt in particular, for the Soviet leadership of 1962 to have failed to support Egypt in a revolutionary endeavor *anywhere* seems in retrospect scarcely conceivable.

The fact that the endeavor in question took place in Yemen made Soviet support all the more likely. For one, Yemen, unlike Syria or Iraq, lay so far outside the Soviet defensive perimeter that potential differences over policy must have seemed unlikely. At the same time, the country's location imparted considerable strategic significance. Situated along the shores of the Red Sea—sandwiched between oil giant and US ally Saudi Arabia to the north and the British Empire's last outpost in the Middle East, Aden, to the south—Republican Yemen, supported by the full weight of Nasser's political commitment and Soviet military might, was a potential revolutionary dagger in the heart of the conservative Anglo-American order in the Middle East. In the row of tottering monarchies that made up that order, the Mutawakkilite Kingdom of Yemen was the weakest link. The spread of revolution from Yemen threatened to undermine the Anglo-American position in the Persian Gulf, and with it the steady supply of oil upon which the Western economies depended.

That more tangible military objectives drove Soviet decision making in this crisis is unlikely. The eviction of "imperialist" bases from the region—including the important British position at Aden—constituted a paramount Soviet objective in the Middle East and may well have influenced Soviet calculations at this stage. But it would be wrong to anticipate the transformation of Aden into one of the major Soviet naval bases in the Indian Ocean in the 1980s. To be sure, the long-anticipated threat of a surprise attack on the Soviet industrial heartland by US Polaris submarines patrolling in the Mediterranean was only months away from materializing in the fall of 1962, and Soviet defense planners, led by Admiral Sergei Gorshkov, may have already begun to for-

[59] On the turbulence in Soviet-Egyptian relations in the late 1950s, see Khrushchev, *Vospominania*, 3:400–403, 409–10; Haykal, *Sanawāt al-ghalayān*, 424–37; Oleg Smolansky, *The Soviet Union and the Arab East under Khrushchev* (Lewisburg, PA: Bucknell University Press, 1974), 125–56.

mulate a new strategy of forward deployment designed to track and destroy enemy submarines preemptively.[60] But the basing requirements for such a strategy in the early 1960s concentrated primarily on the eastern Mediterranean littoral, where Syria and Egypt constituted the only plausible candidates, for political as much as geographical reasons. Indeed, if Egypt's embroilment in Yemen did present Soviet strategists with the prospect of naval gains, the opportunity lay in Egypt, not on the Arabian Peninsula.[61] Yemen itself had poor natural harbors—with the notable exception of Aden, at that time still very much under British control. Could Soviet strategists have foreseen the eventual withdrawal of the British from the Peninsula as far back as 1962, and aspired to fill the void they would leave in their wake? This is possible, but unlikely. Soviet interest in south Yemeni affairs seems to have begun only in the aftermath of the British withdrawal from Aden in December 1967, while pressure for a military presence materialized much later.[62] It is certainly possible, even probable, that the prospect of naval facilities beckoned to Soviet defense planners. So too did potential access to air bases on Yemeni soil, which offered the beginnings of a solution to the problem of power projection into Africa. Such purely military considerations would certainly have carried weight in Leonid Brezhnev's Politburo; whether they won the day in Khrushchev's Presidium is doubtful. But their existence guaranteed that Khrushchev could expect little resistance from the Soviet military over active participation in the Egyptian intervention in Yemen.

In sum, Soviet support for the projection of Egyptian military power into Yemen was the result of an array of factors that could be loosely grouped under the heading "political-strategic" considerations. While military calculations were not insignificant and would become increasingly important with time, more mundane, vaguely ideological impulses at the pinnacle of the Soviet power structure seemed to generate initial participation in the revolutionary adventure in Yemen. Again, the word *ideological* is used advisedly; it is not that the decision to get involved

[60] However, Gorshkov's planning gained momentum only after Khrushchev left office. See, for instance, I. M. Kapitanets, *Bitva za Mirovoi okean v "kholodnoi" i budushchikh voinakh* (Moscow: Veche, 2002), 210–11; and Michael MccGwire, "Turning Points in Soviet Naval Policy," in *Soviet Naval Developments: Capability and Context*, ed. Michael McCGwire (New York: Praeger, 1973), 203.

[61] For further discussion of Soviet naval objectives in Egypt prior to 1967, see chapter four.

[62] For the beginnings of Soviet snooping in Aden, see Bausin, *Spetsluzhby mira*, 344–72.

stemmed from a Marxist analysis of the class structure of Yemeni tribes or a careful study of the potential for Communism in the Arabian Peninsula, but that it fit in with a broad worldview in which "revolution" was a step forward, to be encouraged and applauded. Soviet support for the intervention was born neither of doctrinaire ideological concerns nor of concrete strategic objectives; rather, it issued from the impulse to defend revolution where possible. If, arguably, this was the case when it came to the placement of nuclear missiles in Cuba, so, a fortiori, it was when the question arose of flying Egyptians to Yemen.[63] And if most of the risk could be born by a revolutionary proxy, so much the better.

Forms of Early Soviet Involvement

Although the Soviets' participation in the conflict seems extraordinary, it is important to bear in mind that they channeled the bulk of their aid through Cairo and at Egypt's behest.[64] For a brief window of time at the very beginning of the revolution, the Soviet advisers in Ṣan'ā' supported the Republican government without Egyptian mediation. Thereafter, the Soviets followed Nasser's lead. From Moscow's perspective, the struggle in Yemen was a classic war by proxy.[65]

Given the vast distance between Egypt and Yemen, the urgency of military aid, and the existence of an established Soviet military mission in Yemen at the time of the revolution, it was natural for the new regime to turn to the Soviet Union directly for support.[66] Soviet attaché Oleg Peresypkin recalls that Colonel 'Abd Allāh al-Sallāl appealed to him and his colleague for military aid within days of the revolution. Hand-

[63] Vladislav Zubok and Constantine Pleshakov, *Inside the Kremlin's Cold War: From Stalin to Khrushchev* (Cambridge, MA: Harvard University Press, 1996), 260. For versions of the Cuban missile crisis that place greater emphasis on the military-strategic rationale, see Taubman, *Khrushchev*, 535–37; Fursenko and Naftali, *Khrushchev's Cold War*, 431–44; Dmitri A. Volkogonov, *Autopsy for an Empire: The Seven Leaders Who Built the Soviet Regime* (New York: Free Press, 1998), 236–37.

[64] Strictly speaking, Soviet engagement in Yemen may be said to have transcended mere *involvement* to constitute *intervention*. The theoretical distinction is made by Efraim Karsh in *The Cautious Bear: Soviet Military Engagement in Middle East Wars in the post-1967 Era* (Boulder, CO: Westview Press, 1985), 6–11.

[65] See Bissell, "Soviet Use of Proxies," 87–106.

[66] The instigators of the coup were, in fact, for the most part students of the Soviet military advisers resident in Ṣan'ā' (Juzaylān, *Tārīkh*, 132).

ing the diplomats a blank piece of paper with his signature at the bottom, he allegedly asked them to compose a wish list for military aid in consort with the Soviet military specialists resident in Ṣan‘ā’. This they prudently refused to do.[67]

Nevertheless, there is little doubt that the Soviet advisers assumed an active though limited role in the conduct of combat support operations in the first few weeks of the war—until the Egyptian army, with Soviet support, was able to air- and sealift sufficient forces to carry out the defense of the major cities of Yemen on behalf of the Republican regime. Here again, Soviet involvement was most evident in the air. The regime's most glaring military deficiency was the absence of trained pilots, a legacy of the Imam's crippling policy of grounding the air force. One of the vital functions performed by Soviet airmen—presumably members of the Soviet advisory team already on the ground in Yemen—was the transport of supplies from the capital to outlying outposts. One Soviet-piloted Mi-4 helicopter, carrying two YAR officials and a shipment of money to the eastern town of Ma'rib on October 3, 1962, was captured upon landing. Narrowly escaping execution by hostile tribesmen, the three-man crew and translator were taken prisoner and subsequently transferred to the British at Aden. After traveling on to London and Moscow, they soon returned to active duty in Yemen.[68]

Although the new regime continued to seek direct military and other aid from Soviet officials in Yemen, the principal scene of decision making shifted quickly to Cairo—where it was to remain, under jealous Egyptian guard, until 1967. The chief axis of cooperation involved coordination of the air bridge. The Soviet point man on this, as on other operational matters, was apparently Pozharskii, who was based in Cairo. His counterpart in Yemen, chief military adviser Major General S. A. Kuzovatkin, played a subordinate role. At the very inception of the air bridge, Kuzovatkin and his advisers received short notice of the incoming Antonovs from Cairo and had only several hours to prepare a runway of suitable length. Employing Yemeni soldiers and schoolchildren, they managed to clear boulders off a flat field, which they proceeded to illuminate with the headlights of several dozen cars parked at intervals along the 3-kilometer strip. The Soviet diplomats posted in

[67] Peresypkin, *al-Yaman*, 171, 181.

[68] Ibid., 178–81; Ḥadīdī, *Shāhid 'alā ḥarb al-Yaman*, 54; Dana Adams Schmidt, *Yemen: The Unknown War* (New York: Holt, Rinehart and Winston, 1968), 65. Yemeni dependence on Soviet pilots continued for some time. See, for example, War Minister of the YAR to Soviet Embassy, May 19, 1963, f. 585, op. 6, pap. 5, d. 7, p. 104, AVPRF.

Yemen heard about the commencement of the air bridge only after the fact.[69]

About fifteen An-12 aircraft were apparently supplied to Egypt over the course of the first year of the war. By October 9, less than two weeks after the coup in Ṣan'ā', at least seven of these were already on the ground at al-Māẓah.[70] Ten days later the British military attaché reported the arrival of five additional An-12s, bringing the total to twelve.[71] In the first few months of the intervention, the crews—some or all of which originated in the Cherkasy military transport aviation regiment based at Krivoi Rog in the Ukraine[72]—maintained an intensive flight schedule of between five and seven sorties per day, reflecting the urgency of the initial influx of manpower. The semidaily, and sometimes daily, routine of long nocturnal flights (nearly eleven hours round-trip) proved taxing on the men and their machines. To avoid excessive strain, the crews rotated every few months, while the aircraft were flown back periodically for maintenance on Soviet soil. By early March 1963, at which point the Egyptian task force stabilized at around 30,000 men, the frequency of flights had declined to an average of two sorties every twenty-four hours.[73] This reflected the conversion of the air bridge into a routine supply line for forces already in the field. It did not, however, reflect any decline in urgency. For an army still dependent on home supplies of everything from bullets to vegetables, the Antonovs provided the only reliable means of transporting perishables to Yemen and evacuating the wounded to Egypt.[74]

[69] Peresypkin, *al-Yaman*, 173–75, 181; interview, Oleg Peresypkin, Moscow, November 11, 2005. To a certain extent, this may be attributed to the factor of distance. The Soviet military advisers in Ṣan'ā' led a separate existence from the Soviet diplomatic corps, headquartered like most of the other foreign legations in Ta'izz, 350 kilometers (a bumpy twenty-hour drive) to the south. Institutional factors were also undoubtedly at work.

[70] Airgram, Cairo to Department of State, no. A-288, "Joint Weeka no. 40," October 9, 1962, p. 4, RG 59, CDF 1960–63, Box 2073, UAR Internal Political, 1962–63, NARA.

[71] Beeley (Cairo) to FO, no. 775, October 20, 1962, FO 371/162950, PRO.

[72] Pavlenko, "Bez grifa 'Sekretno'." Cf. Iakubovich, "An-12," 4, which almost certainly relies on Pavlenko.

[73] Weir, "Egyptian Air Force"; Airgram, Ta'izz to Department of State, no. A-81, March 2, 1963, "Observations from Sanaa," p. 4, RG 59, Box 4147A, POL 26-27 Yemen, NARA. See also Pavlenko, "Bez grifa 'Sekretno'." The Indian Air Force was apparently the only other non-Soviet air force already operating the An-12 at this time. Iakubovich, "An-12," 3.

[74] Vegetables arrived daily by air from Egypt, until a decision was taken to import seeds and plant vegetable patches next to each unit. "Logistical Affairs in the Operational Theatre in Yemen," 7; Aḥmad, *Dhikrayāt*, 23–24.

The effort to prepare the Egyptian air force for taking over the flights turned out to be one of the more challenging aspects of the Soviet mission. To begin with, the heavy workload imposed by the ongoing operations in Yemen on both Soviet and Egyptian pilots left little time for training.[75] A more serious problem was that the An-12 was a notoriously difficult plane to fly. As a result, the first operational solo flight by an Egyptian took place more than a year after the revolution, on October 17, 1963. It ended in disaster.[76] Only in the course of 1965 did the Egyptian air force finally take over running the air link between Cairo and Ṣan'a'—such was the degree of Egyptian dependence on Soviet capabilities in this domain.[77]

Another area of close cooperation encompassed the top-secret Tu-16 bombing missions over Yemen and southern Saudi Arabia. As Egyptian pilots were still training on the Tu-16 when the intervention began, they probably continued their instruction with live ammunition over Yemen. By the beginning of 1963, two squadrons of Tu-16s were stationed at Cairo West airport.[78] A Soviet radio operator, Colonel E. A. Aslanov, recalls: "From October 1962 to April 1963 I was on a special mission in the United Arab Republic Egypt. I participated in acts of war providing international aid to the Yemeni Republic. The crews of the regiment, together with crews of the ARE [UAR], performed combat flights on Tu-16 aircraft.... I completed more than thirty sorties."[79] Since the Egyptian pilots had not yet flown solo on the Tu-16 in late November 1962, the story of mixed crews presumably masks a more substantial role of Soviet airmen in these first sorties.[80]

That initial transport missions were flown exclusively by Soviet airmen does not mean that they fell under Soviet military authority. Quite

[75] Weir, "Egyptian Air Force"; personal interview, Vladimir Shubin, November 3, 2005, Moscow; Pochtarev, "Pod chuzhym flagom."

[76] American Embassy (Cairo) to Department of State, Joint Weeka no. 43, November 20, 1963, RG 59, Box 4075, POL 2-1 UAR, NARA; *Akhbār al-Yawm*, July 10, 1965; personal interview, Vladimir Shubin, October 25, 2005, Moscow. Over the course of the war, four An-12s, two crews, and several dozen Egyptian soldiers were lost to accidents—all over Egyptian territory. For the most catastrophic, see Pavlenko, "Bez grifa 'Sekretno'."

[77] The last Soviet crew apparently returned to the USSR in January 1966. See the testimony of Major Boris Riabokon' in Pavlenko, "Bez grifa 'Sekretno'."

[78] Brig. Mossman (British Military Attaché, Cairo) to Amb. Beeley, "Annual Report on the Armed Forces of the United Arab Republic for the year 1962," January 29, 1963, FO 371/172937, PRO.

[79] Shishchenko, *Smoliane-Internatsionalisty*, 172.

[80] Weir, "Egyptian Air Force."

the contrary: Soviet aerial operations in Yemen were executed completely under Egyptian command.[81] This was not a fiction designed to mask Soviet involvement in the war (although secrecy *was* an important consideration), but rather an operational reality. The Antonovs, for instance, were incorporated into the Egyptian Air Force (EAF) as Squadron 14 of the 32nd Air Brigade, and apparently took orders from EAF Commander Ṣidqī Maḥmūd in person.[82] The subordination of Soviet servicemen to Egyptian command was indicative of the broader pattern of interaction between Soviets, Egyptians, and Yemenis throughout the civil war, in which Egyptians led the way, Soviets followed, and Yemeni leaders incessantly tried to circumvent the Egyptian gatekeeper to deal with the USSR directly. For the duration of the Egyptian presence in Yemen, the Soviet military and diplomatic establishments, far from manipulating a dependent client, carefully deferred to Egyptian primacy.[83]

To solidify the foundations of the air bridge at the Yemeni end, the Soviet government undertook to construct a military and civilian airport suitable for jet aircraft at al-Raḥbah, north of Ṣan'ā'. For this purpose a construction battalion of nearly five hundred Soviet servicemen and women set sail for Yemen in the spring of 1963. Working rapidly over the course of the summer, they completed the project in late September 1963. Even before the facilities at al-Raḥbah were complete, however, the Antonov transports were directed to a makeshift runway at nearby al-Rawḍah, even though this necessitated wetting and compressing the airstrip day and night in order to harden it sufficiently for use at dawn. Upon completion of what was to become al-Raḥbah International Airport, the Egyptian squadron of MiG-15s, which had hitherto operated out of the Egyptian-constructed airport at Ḥudaydah (completed in February 1963), moved to Ṣan'ā' and was henceforth able to provide air cover for most of the area of operations.[84]

[81] Pochtarev, "Pod chuzhym flagom"; Naṣr, *Mudhakkirāt*, 2:373; Ḥadīdī, *Shāhid 'alā ḥarb al-Yaman*, 56; personal interviews, Vladimir Shubin, October 25, 2005 and November 3, 2005, Moscow.

[82] Pochtarev, "Pod chuzhym flagom"; personal interview, Vladimir Shubin, November 3, 2005.

[83] See, for example, Ḥadīdī, *Shāhid 'alā ḥarb al-Yaman*, 57–58.

[84] Memo, V. Kornev, "Otnoshenia mezhdu SSSR i Iemenom (spravka)," sent March 13, 1964, fond 5, op. 30, d. 452, pp. 34–35, RGANI; Cable, Hart (Jiddah) to Sec. of State, no. 1086, June 16, 1963, RG 59, Box 4147B, POL 27 Yemen, NARA; Peresypkin, *al-Yaman*, 192–93; Schmidt, *Yemen*, 80, 167; O'Ballance, *War in the Yemen*, 108; Letter, Vice President Ḥasan al-'Amrī to the Embassy of the USSR in the YAR, October 9, 1963, f. 585, op. 6, pap. 5, d. 8, p. 100, AVPRF; "The Aerial Actions in Yemen," 6–8.

Soviet support for the Egyptian project in Yemen had one other crucial component. Soon after the war began, the two governments reached an agreement whereby the Soviet Union would replace equipment the Egyptian army used in Yemen. Pozharskii had initially promised to equip 5,000 men with a month's supply of foodstuffs, uniforms, small arms, and ammunition.[85] In a prelude to future agreements on financing the campaign, the Soviets asked that the Egyptians tap into their own supplies and anticipate replenishment from Soviet stockpiles later.[86] How this arrangement was modified with time is not known, although there is reason to believe it persisted in some form for several years.[87] In 1963, the British ambassador to the USSR, Humphrey Trevelyan, reported from his Egyptian colleague that Marshal ʿĀmir, in his visit to Moscow in June 1963, reached "an agreement regulating the supply of spare parts and replacements, etc. of Soviet military material already held by the U.A.R., and for repayments under existing arms agreements to be spread evenly over a number of years."[88] A Soviet report from early 1964 refers to the agreement in similarly ambiguous terms: "In providing military aid [to Yemen], the United Arab Republic enjoyed cooperation from the Soviet Union (air crews), and also used Soviet special equipment delivered to Yemen. Additionally, an agreement was reached between the UAR and the USSR that the Soviet Union would

[85] Ḥadīdī, *Shāhid ʿalā ḥarb al-Yaman*, 55–56. Whether or not the Antonovs were provided free of charge is unclear. But the Egyptians bore the cost of operations and training. Ibid., 56n. Subsequent agreements may have taken the form of an aid package to the YAR, in which Egyptian equipment used in Yemen was to be granted eventually to the Yemeni armed forces. See, for instance, P. H. Laurence, F. O. Minute, "Discussion with Mr. Elliott, Canada House," November 7, 1963, FO 371/172864, PRO.

[86] Egyptian Ambassador to the USSR Murād Ghālib reports that Khrushchev authorized a similar arrangement in response to Ben Bella's request for military aid to fight Morocco (*Mudhakkirāt*, 75).

[87] It is even possible that the arrangement persisted, in various mutations, throughout the war. See Memcon between Richard Parker and Patrick Seale, May 5, 1966, in Airgram, Cairo to Dept. of State, May 9, 1966, RG 59, Box 3028, POL 27 Yemen, NARA; Ford (Cairo) to External 415, May 6, 1964, RG25, Vol. 8885, File 20-UAR-1-3, Library and Archives Canada (hereafter LAC), Ottawa, Canada; Ḥamrūsh, *Qiṣṣat thawrat 23 yūliyū*, 3:268–69; Sharaf, *Sanawāt*, 2:651; Airgram, Cairo to Department of State, July 3, 1965, "The Economic Cost to the UARG of Its Involvement in the Yemen," in FO 371/179864, PRO; Airgram, Taʿizz (Cortada) to Secretary of State, "UAR Influence in the YAR," June 9, 1963, RG 59, Box 4148, POL UAR-YEMEN, NARA; Vered, *War and Revolution in Yemen*, 111.

[88] Trevelyan (Moscow) to Earl of Home, Despatch no. 80, 10342/20/6, June 20, 1963, FO 371/172868, PRO.

replace for the UAR that part of the special equipment supplied in an urgent fashion by the UAR to Yemen [*Sovetskii Soiuz vozmestit OAR chast' spetztekhniki, postavlennoi v srochnom poriadke iz OAR v Iemen*]."[89]

Sergei Krakhmalov, Soviet military attaché to the UAR (and GRU representative) from July 1958 to January 1963, handled Egyptian requests for material aid in the early months of the campaign. In his memoirs, Krakhmalov reports a constant stream of Egyptian requests for help with logistics: for construction of an airbase at al-Ḥudaydah, for warm clothing to conduct mountain warfare, for spare parts. In the initial phases of operations in Yemen, Krakhmalov and 'Āmir would meet often, at times twice daily.[90] The readiness to resupply the Egyptian army in Yemen carried important logistical and financial implications. Even in periods of relative calm, the nature of the theater of operations imposed quickened maintenance tempos and elevated replacement costs on the military. The usable lifespan of work clothes and boots, for example, went down to a third of the normal expected lifespan in the Yemeni highlands.[91] Similarly, the attrition rate for vehicles on Yemen's rough mountain tracks was extraordinarily high.[92] The increasing effectiveness of insurgent attacks on Egyptian convoys further increased the need for spare parts for armored and nonarmored vehicles.[93] The possibility of resupplying such items efficiently and freely reduced shortages and cut costs. By eliminating the replacement cost of equipment worn out or destroyed on the battlefield, the Soviet-Egyptian understanding transferred a substantial portion of the added financial burden

[89] Memo, V. Kornev, "Polozhenie v Iemenskoi Arabskoi Respublike i Iemeno-OARovskie otnoshenia (spravka)," sent March 13, 1964, fond 5, op. 30, d. 452, pp. 39–40, RGANI. See also idem, "Otnoshenia mezhdu SSSR i Iemenom (spravka)," 34.

[90] Krakhmalov, *Zapiski voennogo attaché*, 93. Krakhmalov was replaced by Ryzhkov in January 1963.

[91] "Logistical Affairs in the Operational Theatre in Yemen," 24; Khalīl, *Ḥurūb Miṣr*, 65.

[92] One report cites the life expectancy of a truck in Yemen as a mere 10,000 miles; of a jeep, 30,000 miles. "High Cost of Yemeni Operation to U.A.R.," *Financial Times*, July 8, 1963. If the needs of the Yemeni republican army are any guide, inner tubes and truck tarps were the items most in demand for Soviet vehicles. Letter, Ministry of Foreign Affairs of the YAR to the Embassy of the USSR, no. 30, February 17, 1966, f. 88, op. 18, pap. 11, d. 4, pp. 26–30, AVPRF.

[93] Johnny Cooper, with Anthony Kemp, *One of the Originals: The Story of a Founding Member of the SAS* (London: Pan Books, 1991), 174–75; Khalīl, *Ḥurūb Miṣr*, 60–61. The French experience in Algeria emphasizes the seriousness of maintenance problems for a mechanized army operating in a similarly rough environment. See Charles R. Shrader, *The First Helicopter War: Logistics and Mobility in Algeria, 1954–1962* (Westport, CT: Praeger, 1999), 53–100.

associated with maintaining the Egyptian army in the field (as opposed to keeping them in their barracks at home) to the Soviet Union. To what extent these early understandings were sustained over the course of the war is a question to which we shall return.

*

The military aid readily authorized by the Soviet government at the outset of the conflict in Yemen enabled the rapid projection of Egyptian force onto the Arabian Peninsula, thereby making it possible for policy makers in Cairo to launch and sustain a major expedition more than 2,000 kilometers away. The extent of Soviet involvement in the intervention is all the more remarkable given the coincidence of the outbreak of war on the Arabian Peninsula with the Cuban missile crisis. Contrary to traditional narratives of the war, the crisis in Cuba did not distract decision makers in the Kremlin from attending to the parallel crisis in the Middle East. Indeed, Krushchev responded to Egypt's extraordinary request for military aid in the fall of 1962 with boldness and alacrity. The Kremlin's audacious reaction to the revolution in Yemen provides a neat historical parallel to the more familiar narrative of Soviet actions in Cuba, and should be seen as part of a larger pattern of Soviet behavior in the Third World at that time.

The joint revolutionary project in Yemen marked the triumphant emergence of the Soviet-Egyptian relationship from the slump of 1958–61, during which bitter disagreements over Arab Communists, the Qāsim regime in Iraq, and Egypt's union with Syria cast a pall over the partnership inaugurated at Suez. The myth of Suez notwithstanding, the silent support provided to Egypt in late 1962 and early 1963 proved incomparably more substantial than the saber rattling of 1956. Accordingly, when Khrushchev chose to bestow the highest honorary title in the Soviet repertoire, Hero of the Soviet Union, upon President Nasser and Marshal 'Āmir at the Aswan Dam on May 14, 1964, he was celebrating the revolutionary tidal wave set off in the region by a partnership newly tested in battle.

But flirting with the Kremlin had its costs. First was Egypt's growing dependence on the Soviet Union, which would become apparent after Khrushchev's ouster in the fall of 1964. Second was the penalty for breaking the unwritten rules of nonalignment. By the time of Khrushchev's historic visit to Egypt, the new warmth between Cairo and Moscow paralleled a palpable chilling in relations with Washington.

✷ CHAPTER THREE ✷

Food for "Peace"

THE BREAKDOWN OF US-EGYPTIAN RELATIONS, 1962–65

> Our political attitude toward national liberation movements explains the return of the traditional American policy, which looks on economic aid as an instrument of pressure and imposing conditions.
> —*From a memorandum of the Egyptian Foreign Ministry, January 1965*

FOOD AID WAS THE TAPROOT of American-Egyptian relations in the early 1960s.[1] Egypt, the focal point of Kennedy's Middle East policy, depended on a steady supply of wheat and other food products from the United States under the terms of the Agricultural Trade Development and Assistance Act of 1954, also known as the "Food for Peace" program, and commonly referred to as Public Law 480 (hereafter PL 480). Although the program included grant provisions, its largest and most successful component was an arrangement for the sale of surplus food products by the US Department of Agriculture to developing countries. The terms included payment in local currency and a substantial rebate in the form of loans and grants. Heretofore dominated by complicated technical aid programs on a relatively small scale, the US aid program to Egypt took off in the late 1950s with PL 480.

Egyptian need for American agricultural products stemmed from the coincidence of three factors: a rapidly growing population, a limited amount of arable land, and dwindling foreign currency reserves. To be sure, there were alternatives to American supply. But the purchase of grain on the world market entailed higher prices and, more impor-

[1] The story of US-Egyptian relations and the aid question is recounted expertly by William Burns in *Economic Aid and American Policy toward Egypt, 1955–1981* (Albany: State University of New York Press, 1985).

tantly, payment in scarce foreign currency. Buying US grain for Egyptian pounds enabled the Egyptians to free up considerable resources needed to fund the ambitious development plans of the 1960s, which depended to a large extent on foreign capital and expertise. The significance of PL 480 to Egypt during the period in question was enormous. By 1962 Egypt was importing roughly 50 percent of its consumption of wheat, more than 2 million tons annually; practically all of it came from the United States.[2] The value of this arrangement to the Egyptian government may be appreciated from the fact that the alternative cost of purchasing this aid on the global market was approximately $180 million at a time when Egypt's foreign currency reserves were nearly exhausted, and total annual foreign currency earnings—largely made up of Suez Canal revenues, cotton exports, and tourism—were in the neighborhood of $500 million.[3] Had anyone suggested to Nasser in September 1962 that his support for the revolutionaries in Ṣan'ā' would end up endangering this lifeline, he might well have laughed. But this is in fact what occurred, with consequences that were anything but amusing, over the next half-decade.

A fundamental assumption underlying the provision of massive assistance to Egypt was that it would solidify the basis for a long-term relationship founded on mutual interests. In practice, just the opposite occurred: US aid fostered an unhealthy dependency, which rendered relations with Egypt susceptible to serious crisis in the event of disruption.[4] Another key expectation in Washington was that sustained aid would provide a modicum of leverage over Egyptian policy makers, enabling the United States "to moderate the behavior of the Egyptian government along lines which are at least not inimical to United States interests," as one USAID study put it.[5] That assumption too proved to be of extremely limited validity. Aid, and especially the process of negotiation for aid contracts, turned out to have some moderating influence

[2] "U.S. Assistance to the United Arab Republic," in M.P.V. Hannam (Cairo) to J. M. Edes (Foreign Office), March 23, 1962, no. 11211/62, FO 371/165357, PRO; Burns, *Economic Aid*, 126.

[3] The Free Officers inherited close to $1 billion in foreign currency from the monarchy at the time of the revolution. By December 1962, scarcely $16 million were left, excluding the untouchable gold reserves needed to back the Egyptian pound. Waterbury, *Egypt*, 95; Ikram, *Egypt*, 340; Bent Hansen and Karim Nashashibi, *Foreign Trade Regimes and Economic Development: Egypt* (New York: Columbia University Press, 1975), 17, 89.

[4] Badeau, *Middle East*, 241–43.

[5] Quoted in Burns, *Economic Aid*, 2. See also Badeau, *Middle East*, 204.

on Egyptian behavior as long as the linkage was not made explicit or pressed too far. Beyond a certain point, however, aid as a political weapon backfired.[6] Given the multiplicity of complicating factors outside the direct control of the executive branch in either country, and the proud and impulsive nature of Egypt's leaders, it was almost impossible to calibrate the pressure correctly. Spasmodic generosity was no way to restrain a determined revolutionary.

Anyone who has read the diplomatic correspondence between Cairo and Washington in the 1960s in conjunction with the reminiscences of several of its key participants can have little doubt that US-Egyptian relations foundered principally over the problem of Yemen.[7] Yet this conclusion is hardly appreciated in the historiography of the period.[8] To be sure, there were other important differences between the two countries during this time period. Some, such as Egyptian military support for Algeria against Morocco in 1963, or for the Stanleyville governments in the Congo in 1960 and 1964, flared up for a while and then died down; others, notably policy toward Israel and the Soviet Union, were more enduring, but fell into the category of issues upon which it was agreed to disagree and which were accordingly placed, for the time being, "in the icebox."[9] It was the seemingly unimportant question of Yemen, which, in a manner surprising and frustrating to both governments, persisted in undermining any attempt at keeping relations on an even keel.

It was therefore ironic—and of unintended consequence—that Egypt's intervention in the civil war in Yemen coincided with the conclusion

[6] Badeau, *American Approach*, 72–73.

[7] See, e.g., 'Abd Allāh Imām, *Ṣalāḥ Naṣr yatadhakkar: Al-Thawrah, al-mukhabbarāt, al-naksah* (Cairo: Dār al-Khayyāl, 1999), 191, 196. Haykal, *Sanawāt al-ghalayān*, 645–62; idem, *al-Infijār*, 110–18 and passim; Sharaf, *Sanawāt*, 2:623–27; Badeau, *Middle East*, 199–215, 240–41; Hart, *Saudi Arabia*, 161 and passim; Lyndon Johnson, *The Vantage Point: Perspectives of the Presidency, 1963–1969* (New York: Holt, Rinehart and Winston, 1971), 290.

[8] Notable exceptions include Warren Bass, *Support Any Friend: Kennedy's Middle East and the Making of the U.S.-Israel Alliance* (New York: Oxford University Press, 2003), 98–143; Burns, *Economic Aid*, 122, 134, 139; James, *Nasser at War*, 55; and Malcolm Kerr, "'Coming to Terms with Nasser': Attempts and Failures," *International Affairs* 43, no. 1 (1967): 78.

[9] The phrase, ubiquitous in the diplomatic correspondence of the period, apparently originated with the Egyptian ambassador to the United States, Muṣṭafā Kāmil. Badeau, *Middle East*, 179.

of an unprecedented "Food for Peace" deal with the United States. This massive aid package, signed on October 8, 1962, committed the US government to the sale of some $390 million worth of wheat and other foodstuffs over a three-year period ending in October 1965.[10] Optimistically based on the premise that a long-term aid commitment would foster Egypt's inward focus on domestic development, increase its stake in regional stability, and solidify the trend of increasingly friendly relations with the United States, it was the last gasp of an outdated policy. Skeptics, particularly in the United Kingdom and Saudi Arabia, observed that the long-term commitment deprived the administration of the leverage associated with the hitherto semiannual negotiating process.[11] They were proven correct much sooner than they could have imagined. As relations between the two countries deteriorated, American policy makers felt compelled to wield more damaging weapons in the hope of bringing Egyptian policy to heel—including the suspension of aid and the threat to avoid renewal of existing aid packages. These tools proved counterproductive.

In theory, the provision of economic aid to Egypt and military aid to Saudi Arabia provided the United States with leverage over both—a symmetry absent from Soviet policy. In practice, this advantage proved elusive. On the one hand, aid to the warring parties, as with the Arab-Israeli conflict, placed Washington at the center of negotiations over a settlement. On the other hand, it provided an illusion of influence that proved at best ineffective and at worst incendiary. In vain did hawkish statesmen in Saudi Arabia and Great Britain rail against the stupidity and futility of the American balancing act. For them, it was just so much shortsighted appeasement and wishful thinking; Nasser should be isolated, threatened with loss of aid, and perhaps eliminated. But the lofty vantage point of a great power is always clouded by considerations not evident to lesser powers. One of the unavoidable side effects of superpower obligations, the contradiction in US policy toward the conflict in

[10] Department of State to various embassies, Circular no. 624, October 8, 1962, RG 59, CDF 1960–63, 611.86b, M1855, Roll 115, NARA. The figure given is for calendar years 1962–65. The fiscal-year figure is even higher: $431.8 million. Burns, *Economic Aid*, 134.

[11] For the Johnson administration's return to a "short-tether" aid policy, see Kristin Ahlberg, "'Machiavelli with a Heart': The Johnson Administration's Food for Peace Program in India, 1965–1966," *Diplomatic History* 31, no. 4 (2007): 665–701. For the argument that a version of this policy should have been adopted earlier with Nasser, see Transcript, Lucius D. Battle, *Oral History Interview* no. 1, November 14, 1968, pp. 20–22, LBJL.

Yemen was never fully resolved by American statesmen. It was eventually decided for them by the Egyptians, who tired of the charade and ended it.

As the Egyptian intervention deepened, US policy makers found themselves in the unfortunate position of subsidizing a Soviet-armed liberation campaign.[12] Indeed, Washington soon found itself providing vital support to *each* of the principal antagonists in the war while simultaneously deploring the actions of both. And yet despite its myriad contradictions, American policy was not entirely devoid of logic or success. After all, an Egypt unrestrained by the rewards of US aid was capable of serious damage to American interests throughout the Middle East. And though this saga ends with the collapse of US-Egyptian relations in 1967, US policy makers in 1962 and 1963 did manage to ward off a potent threat to what was arguably the most vital US interest in the region: the integrity of Saudi Arabia.[13]

Recognition

The battle for recognition of the new government in Ṣan'ā' highlighted the centrality of Washington in the considerations of all the principal actors in the Yemeni drama over the coming years. It also showcased the limits of American influence and the hazards of exaggerated expectations. From the very beginning Nasser saw in Washington a lever with which to exert pressure on Riyadh. The Saudis applied the same formula in reverse.[14] The spectacle of two Arab leaders each beseeching American diplomats to restrain the other was a recurring one throughout the war. Disappointment in US efforts was inevitable and mutual, but carried different consequences for either side. The Saudis, having few options, remained frustrated but constant allies to the United States throughout the war—although they did diversify their portfolio of allies to include the British as a counterbalance to US pressure. The Egyptians, with Khrushchev staunchly at their side, drifted steadily eastward.

[12] Commander of the UNYOM, Major General Carl von Horn, put it in characteristically blunt terms: "The real position was that Nasser's intervention was being armed by Russia and financed (whether they liked it or not) by America." Carl von Horn, *Soldiering for Peace* (New York: David McKay, 1967), 314.

[13] Badeau, *American Approach*, 145; Robert Stookey, *America and the Arab States: An Uneasy Encounter* (New York: John Wiley, 1975), 187.

[14] Badeau, *American Approach*, 141.

There was a rough parallel in the initial reaction within the US and British foreign policy establishments to the appearance of an Egyptian army in Yemen. In both countries, representatives on the ground in Yemen, strengthened by influential officials within the foreign service, played down the threat posed by Egypt's intervention and, fearing the dangers of escalation, urged rapid recognition of the new regime.[15] At the same time, elements of the security establishment in both countries, and of the Colonial Office in the United Kingdom, argued the opposite case, citing the threat posed by Yemeni-Egyptian radicalism to peninsular stability.[16] Although this institutional equivocalness never disappeared completely from either regime, it fizzled out more rapidly in London, where the advocates of appeasement lost out to the proponents of confrontation because of the immediacy of the threat to Aden. For Washington, by contrast, Aden was an important but ultimately secondary consideration; the House of Saʿūd came first.

Although the threat to Saudi Arabia was no less potent than the threat to Aden, the Americans maintained a course of appeasement vis-à-vis Egypt much longer than the British did in large part because of the different nature of their responsibilities. Ever since the Second World War, the United States had been assuming more and more of the former British obligations in the region; nowhere was this more apparent than in Cairo, where Britain had lost both stake and influence in 1956, and where Washington was locked in fierce competition with Moscow. With important interests in both Cairo and Riyadh, the United States, unlike the United Kingdom, was not free to make a binary choice when its two allies came to blows in Yemen, nor was it truly capable of remaining aloof.[17] This also explains why the United States proved central to

[15] E.g., Stookey (Taʿizz) to SecState, no. 134, October 15, 1962, RG 59, CDF 1960–63, Box 2080, 786h, NARA; Gandy (Taʿizz) to Foreign Office, no. 160, October 8, 1962, FO 371/162948, PRO. See also Hart, *Saudi Arabia*, 119–23.

[16] See, e.g., Sir Johnston (Aden) to the Secretary of State for the Colonies, no. 1077, November 13, 1962, FO 371/162956, PRO; Hart, *Saudi Arabia*, 121, 137; Stookey, *America and the Arab States*, 182–83, 187. See also Schmidt, *Yemen*, 190–91; Tom Little, *South Arabia: Arena of Conflict* (London: Pall Mall, 1968), 94–96; Bidwell, *The Two Yemens*, 200; Bass, *Support Any Friend*, 108.

[17] For a succinct presentation of this dilemma, see Memo from Komer (NSC) to Talbot (State), October 12, 1962, in *FRUS*, 1961–63, vol. 18, doc. 79; Kerr, "Coming to Terms with Nasser," 78. The perspective on policy varied with the institution. In the US embassy in Cairo, for instance, preservation of US aid to Egypt sometimes seemed to be a goal in and of itself. In this view the principle obstacles to successful foreign policy in the region were oilmen and hostile congressmen.

mediation of Saudi-Egyptian differences, whereas the United Kingdom turned out to be peripheral. Bereft of influence in Cairo, and more concerned by the effect of Egyptian actions on Aden, the British, in league with their newfound friends, the Saudis, drifted toward a policy of open confrontation with Nasser.

Although the three-year aid package postponed the real crisis in US-Egyptian relations until 1965–66, cracks began to appear much sooner. In a memorandum dated October 5, 1962, influential National Security Council (NSC) staffer Robert Komer cautiously recommended that President Kennedy approve the agreement. At the same time he acknowledged its negative implications in the context of the delicate situation in Yemen and toyed with the idea of postponement.[18] With the benefit of hindsight, we may conclude that the decision to push through the multiyear aid agreement, under pressure from the State Department, was not only irrelevant but also dangerous, given the new reality taking shape in the Arabian Peninsula. With the conclusion of PL 480 negotiations in early October, the Kennedy administration entered the long struggle for an end to hostilities in Yemen shorn of an important political weapon. The first stage in this saga surrounded the question of US recognition of the new regime, with the Saudis and, to a lesser extent, the British pressing for nonrecognition, and the Egyptians, together with the Yemeni Republicans, pushing for rapid recognition. Although the threat of US recognition (for the Saudis) or nonrecognition (for the Egyptians) was considerable on its own, Kennedy's unsuccessful campaign for military disengagement might have packed more punch—with both parties—had a portion of the aid package still hung in the balance.

Throughout the early months of the conflict, US officials were mostly concerned about the danger of domestic instability posed to the Saudi and Jordanian regimes by their unpopular sponsorship of what the Americans considered to be hopeless attempts to turn back the revolutionary tide in Yemen. Although some authors have cited the threat of Egyptian expansionism on the oil-rich peninsula as a major strategic concern, in fact it was a comparatively insignificant consideration in Washington.[19] Initial diplomatic efforts were, accordingly, directed primarily at restraining Kings Hussein and Sa'ūd. They proved ineffective.

[18] Memorandum from Robert W. Komer of the National Security Council Staff to President Kennedy, Washington, October 5, 1962, *FRUS*, 1961–63, vol. 18, doc. 70. See also Bass, *Support Any Friend*, 105.

[19] Badeau, *American Approach*, 132–35.

Egypt's brazen launch of air and sea attacks on Saudi targets across the Yemeni border on November 2, 5, and 6 altered the situation fundamentally. This was not so much because of the damage done, but because the raids represented a test of US resolve to uphold its defense guarantee to Saudi Arabia. The attacks prompted the Saudis to sever diplomatic relations with Egypt and transformed the situation almost overnight: America's two main allies in the Middle East, the twin pillars of its Arab policy, were effectively at war with each other. Although the bombing of Saudi territory was designed ostensibly to end aid to the Royalists, its more important objective was to engage the kingdom's protectors in Washington. By demonstrating the likely alternative to Saudi restraint—open war between Egypt and Saudi Arabia, and a disastrous US-Egyptian clash on the peninsula—Nasser upped the ante and forced the Kennedy administration to the bargaining table.[20] As he would demonstrate repeatedly throughout the conflict, Nasser preferred to conduct negotiations with a cloud portending imminent military escalation hanging visibly overhead. By manufacturing a potent menace to US interests, Nasser skillfully transformed a bilateral dialogue over US recognition, in which the Americans held the only card, into a trilateral negotiation on disengagement, in which he could leverage US power against his adversaries in Yemen and link speedy recognition to Saudi restraint. At a minimum, Nasser must have calculated, the reminder of Egypt's nuisance value would hasten US recognition and stimulate American pressure on Riyadh and Amman; at best, Saudi and Jordanian intransigence would drive a wedge between the two Arab monarchies and their great power ally.[21]

In the short run, Nasser must be judged successful in this maneuver. US proposals, transmitted in a letter from Kennedy to the leaders of Jordan, Saudi Arabia, Egypt, and the Yemen Arab Republic, revolved around rapid recognition of the YAR—an entity wholly rejected by the Saudi and Jordanian monarchs—in exchange for conciliatory declarations of goodwill by the governments in Cairo and Ṣan'ā'.[22] Recognition

[20] See, for instance, Rusk to Cairo (and other embassies), no. 514, November 14, 1962, RG 59, CDF 1960–63, Box 7080, 786h, NARA; Hart, *Saudi Arabia*, 118, 145. That Nasser saw in the bargain over recognition part of a larger US-Egyptian understanding over Yemen policy is evident from Haykal, *Sanawāt al-ghalayān*, 646–50.

[21] Rusk to Cairo (and other embassies), no. 490, November 7, 1962, RG 59, CDF 1960–63, Box 7080, 786h, NARA; Badeau (Cairo) to SecState, no. 726, November 9, 1962, in ibid; Rusk to Cairo (and other embassies), no. 506, November 10, 1962, in ibid.

[22] For the text, see Rusk to Cairo (and other embassies), no. 525, November 16, 1962, CDF 1960–63, Box 7080, 786h, NARA.

was to be followed by a process of reciprocal disengagement. As the bitter responses of King Hussein and Crown Prince Faysal to Kennedy's proposals demonstrated, Nasser had won this round almost before it began.[23] That the United States was prepared to afford the revolutionary regime recognition without any tangible demonstration of Egypt's willingness to withdraw appalled the rulers of Jordan and Saudi Arabia. It also produced discomfort in London. The prolonged negotiations over the terms of US recognition, which ensued in late November and the first half of December, were largely irrelevant. What mattered was that the government of the United States had been forced to commit itself to the quest for a solution in Yemen; that it had done so in a manner that highlighted US dependence on Nasser's good will and good offices in Ṣan'ā'; and that the resultant process was sure to deepen the divergence of opinion between Washington on the one hand and London, Amman, and Riyadh on the other.[24]

For Egypt, the US recognition of the Yemen Arab Republic on December 19, 1962, entailed a substantial broadening of the moral foundations of the new regime, which rendered its subversion by the Saudis and their allies less acceptable and therefore more difficult. Although the public side of the US-Egyptian deal over recognition entailed conciliatory declarations by the governments of Egypt and Republican Yemen, which could be read as concessions to US pressure, it was the hidden dynamic of US efforts on behalf of Egyptian objectives in Riyadh, which constituted Nasser's second principal gain from the exercise.[25] Nasser

[23] Amman to SecState, no. 277, November 20, 1962, CDF 1960–63, Box 7080, 786h, NARA; Jiddah to SecState, no. 401, November 19, 1962, in ibid.; Hart, *Saudi Arabia*, 146–49; Bass, *Support Any Friend*, 108. Jordanian reactions made out of earshot of US officials were even more vitriolic. See, e.g., Amman to Foreign Office, nos. 1436, 1438, December 22, 1962, FO 371/1629625, PRO; Amman to Foreign Office, no. 1454, December 31, 1962, FO 371/168786, PRO; and also Gause, *Saudi-Yemeni Relations*, 60–62.

[24] For British reservations about US recognition in exchange for "mere words," see Macmillan to Kennedy, November 14, 1962, in Foreign Office to Washington, no. 8199, November 14, 1962, FO 371/162956, PRO; Macmillan to Kennedy, November 15, 1962, in Foreign Office to Washington, no. 8257, November 15, 1962, FO 371/162957, PRO; Kennedy to Macmillan, November 15, 1962, in Foreign Office to Washington, no. 8290, November 16, 1962, FO 371/162957, PRO. See also Schmidt, *Yemen*, 190. In the short run, to be sure, the Egyptian bombing campaign *postponed* US recognition of the YAR. Dept. of State to Jiddah, no. 225, November 17, 1962, in *FRUS*, 1961–63, vol. 18, doc. 91.

[25] The initial draft of the Egyptian statement submitted for US consideration was quite the opposite of conciliatory. It was a long-winded tribute to the heroic intervention of "Arab forces" in defense of the long-suffering Yemeni people, who had just freed themselves "from the shackles of under-development and reaction," only to be subjected to "border invasion" bent on "dragging [them] ... in spite of themselves back to the dark-

did not yet know that in order to secure Saudi commitment to disengagement, the US government would have to cut a separate deal with Crown Prince Faysal, who by this point had all but succeeded the ailing King Saud. This would involve the deployment of a squadron of the US air force on Saudi soil as a deterrent against further Egyptian attacks.[26] Nor did anyone foresee how difficult the process of disengagement would turn out to be. That Nasser, not Kennedy, sat in the driver's seat was underscored by the resumption of air raids on the Saudi border towns of Jīzān and Najrān a mere eleven days after the announcement of US recognition and the accompanying promises of goodwill from Cairo. Although Egypt's armed forces continued to take awful casualties on the battlefield, its statesmen had gained the upper hand, for the moment.

In the long run, however, the arm-bending exercises of November and December damaged Egypt's relations with the United States. True, recognition of the YAR forced Washington onto a path of confrontation with Riyadh; it was hardly possible for the United States to protect a safe haven for attacks on a government it recognized. But it led to an even deeper conflict with Egypt. From Cairo's perspective, this was largely the result of a misunderstanding. The special relationship between Washington and Riyadh obscured both behind-the-scenes pressures on the Saudi leadership to desist and the simple fact that US influence over Saudi behavior was limited. The Egyptian leadership, failing to recognize these facts, mistook invisibility for absence and incapacity for collusion.[27] The long delay in US recognition of the YAR, a consequence of deference to Saudi and British interests, provoked irritation

---

ness of pre-Islamic days and the despotic rule of the Middle Ages." The operative paragraph read: "If the government of the Arab Republic of Yemen should feel certain that outside aggression had ended, if Saudi Jordanian aggression coordinated with the Sherif of Beihan was halted, if other outside help extended to the mercenaries to foment trouble and menace the Yemeni people stopped, and if the foreign concentrations on the Yemeni borders were withdrawn, the United Arab Republic would express her readiness to withdraw her armed forces gradually from Yemen then or whenever the Government of the Arab Republic of Yemen should make such request." As US Secretary of State Dean Rusk commented, "[the] statement as drafted would be worse than no statement at all." The final draft was largely an American concoction. Cairo to SecState, no. 773, November 26, 1962, RG 59, CDF 1960–63, Box 7080, 786h, NARA; Rusk to Cairo, no. 556, November 26, 1962, in ibid; Badeau, *Middle East*, 209; Hart, *Saudi Arabia*, 152.

[26] The force of eight F-100Ds arrived in Saudi Arabia in June 1963 and remained until January 1964.

[27] See, for instance, comments made by Prime Minister 'Alī Ṣabrī to Ambassador Badeau in Cairo and by Marshall 'Āmir and Vice President Sadat to Policy Planning Council member William Polk in Ṣan'ā'. Cairo to SecState, no. 1034, January 19, 1963, RG

in Cairo and raised suspicions that the United States was siding with the Saudis and the British in a conspiracy to undermine the fledgling republic. These suspicions were reinforced by the US Navy's deterrent show of force in the Red Sea, by reports of US arms flown to the front aboard chartered airplanes piloted by Americans, and by the apparent inability of the US government to bring to a halt Saudi aid to the Royalists. In an extraordinary display of mistrust, Nasser wrote to 'Āmir in Yemen a mere two days before the announcement of US recognition: "I am now strongly convinced that we must attack Najrān and Jīzān and take our battle from defense to offense. In my opinion, the US mediation was of fraudulent intent, designed to dampen our enthusiasm and our spring to action, and to prevent us from carrying out any action against bases of concentration in Saudi Arabia."[28] The very next day, having become convinced that US recognition was indeed imminent, he reversed himself: "I believe that, after the US recognition, what was said in my response of yesterday has now become premature or in need of reappraisal. In my opinion, we need to try again diplomatically to reach a cessation of Saudi activity. If this is not achieved, the next step will be a warning to destroy the bases of aggression."[29] Nasser, though skeptical, was willing to give Kennedy a chance to exercise his influence in Riyadh.

The US-Saudi alliance was more durable than the bridge of illusions erected between Washington and Cairo in the early 1960s because it was grounded in shared interests. But differences in style also worked to Saudi advantage. Faysal's mantra worked like a charm on US diplomats: "I implore you to understand and appreciate my position. Get Nasir out of Yemen and our fears would cease, but don't pressure me, your constant friend, to sacrifice my honor, prestige and standing with my people for Nasir, who has all along acted contrary to US interests in this area."[30] As time progressed, the Americans became convinced that that their mediation effort was being undermined more by Egyptian noncompliance than by Saudi foot-dragging. The crucial factor in the

59, CDF 1960–63, Box 2081, 786h, NARA; Cairo to SecState, no. 1227, February 9, 1963, RG 59, CF, Box 4146, POL Yemen, NARA.

[28] Letter from Nasser to 'Āmir, December 17, 1962, in Haykal, *Sanawāt al-ghalayān*, doc. 42, 924–25, quoted on 651.

[29] Letter from Nasser to 'Āmir, December 18, 1962, in Haykal, *Sanawāt al-ghalayān*, doc. 43, 926–27, quoted on 651–52.

[30] Quoted in Hart (Jiddah) to SecState, no. 600, January 25, 1963, RG 59, CDF 1960–63, Box 2081, 786h, NARA.

decline of Nasser's stock in Washington was the failure of the disengagement agreement presidential envoy Ellsworth Bunker brokered in March and April of 1963.

Disengagement

In November 1962, in conjunction with the US proposal to recognize the YAR, President Kennedy set forth his proposed principles for an end to hostilities in a letter to the relevant heads of state: "1) phased but expeditious withdrawal of external forces from Yemen; 2) termination of external support to the Royalists; and 3) phased but expeditious withdrawal of forces introduced after the revolt in Yemen into the vicinity of the Saudi-Yemeni borders." Implementation, Kennedy envisaged, would entail "direct contact between the parties concerned, the good offices of a third party, or possibly observation or supervision of the disengagement process by the United Nations."[31] There was a great deal of wishful thinking in all of this.

Perhaps the biggest flaw in the US-Egyptian bargain over recognition was that it excluded the Saudis—not to mention the Ḥamīd al-Dīn royal family and its tribal backers, who were doing the actual fighting against Egyptian and Republican forces in Yemen. Prince Faysal, suspicious of the process that led to US recognition and resentful of the fact that the associated disengagement plan excluded the deposed Imam, assumed no commitment whatsoever to reduce Saudi support for the Yemeni Royalists. On the contrary, the international recognition accorded the YAR only doubled his resolve to fight Nasser tooth and nail on the peninsula.[32] Not surprisingly, what ensued was the opposite of disengagement.

The second fault in US diplomacy in late 1962 was the failure to launch an aggressive push for disengagement immediately following the recognition initiative. Whether or not either party could have been persuaded to disengage in late December is highly uncertain. However, in the absence of an agreement with the Saudis, time was of the essence. Yet for more than two months the administration shunned direct involvement in the negotiations, instead placing vain hopes in mediation

[31] Dept. of State to Amman, November 16, 1962, in *FRUS*, 1961–63, vol. 18, doc. 100.

[32] Hart (Jiddah) to SecState, no. 509, December 28, 1962, in *FRUS*, 1961–63, vol. 18, doc. 122; Hart, *Saudi Arabia*, 118, 149.

by a personal representative of UN Secretary General U Thant.[33] Most accounts fault the United Nations for its sluggish supervision of the agreement's implementation in April–July 1963.[34] But the earlier delay in negotiating the deal, for which the United States, as author of the disengagement plan, bore primary responsibility, was at least as fateful.

The three-month interval between US recognition in December and the launch of negotiations over disengagement the following March was a bloodbath. In late January 1963, tribal forces armed and funded by Saudi Arabia began to close in on Ṣan'ā' from multiple directions. By early February the capital was essentially under siege from the north, east, and south. Tribal leaders sympathetic to the Royalist cause began to speak of "crushing the head of the snake."[35] Frustrated with the lack of political progress—"we cannot wait another five months for disengagement," Nasser later complained to the US ambassador—the Egyptians responded with escalation.[36] In violation of their commitment to abstain from further attacks on Saudi territory, the Egyptians resumed deadly air raids on Jīzān, Najrān, Khamīs Mushayṭ, and Abhā[37] and conducted a sensational (if somewhat quixotic) air drop of weapons and ammunition, presumably intended for Saudi dissidents, on the coastal

[33] Nasser, for one, had reservations about letting the United Nations try where the United States had failed. When in early March he suddenly voiced preference for a UN representative, he was almost certainly trying to buy time for the unity talks with Syria and Iraq to come to fruition. Faysal probably felt the same way, although on one occasion he too voiced preference for a UN representative, since it would entail less pressure on him. In any case, the Kennedy administration clung to the notion of UN mediation far beyond the point of reason—indeed, well after Bunker's own mission was underway. Badeau (Cairo) to SecState, no. 1089, January 24, 1963, in *FRUS*, 1961–63, vol. 18, doc. 141; Hart (Jiddah) to SecState, no. 600, January 25, 1963, RG 59, CDF 1960–63, Box 2081, 786h, NARA; Hart, *Saudi Arabia*, 168–69, 174–77, 179, 188.

[34] See in particular Badeau, *American Approach*, 143–45. Badeau emphasizes that the fundamental US objective was not to liquidate the conflict but to contain it. But he acknowledged the failure of early US efforts to restrain the Saudis: "Having based containment [of the] Yemen conflict on [the] hope of reciprocal action, we now find ourselves out on [a] limb because we have been unable to secure SAG cooperation." Badeau (Cairo) to SecState, no. 1360, March 3, 1963, RG 59, CF, Box 4147b, POL 27 Yemen, NARA.

[35] Schmidt, *Yemen*, 161; O'Ballance, *War in the Yemen*, 97; Parkes (Amman) to FO, no. 168, February 8, 1963, FO 371/168790, PRO.

[36] Nasser to Badeau, in Badeau (Cairo) to SecState, no. 1379, March 5, 1963, RG 59, CF 1960–63, Box 4147b, POL 27 Yemen, NARA.

[37] See, e.g., Badeau (Cairo) to SecState, no. 959, January 9, 1963, in *FRUS*, 1961–63, vol. 18, doc. 131; Hart, *Saudi Arabia*, 154–56, 172–73.

road north of Jiddah.[38] Within Yemen itself, the Egyptian military embarked on a massive influx of men and materiel, which more than doubled the size of the expeditionary force and altered its pattern of deployment fundamentally. By the time disengagement talks got underway in March, there were 28,000 Egyptian troops in Yemen, up from between 10,000 to 15,000 at the time of US recognition.[39] Moreover, Egyptian forces, hitherto concentrated principally around Ṣan'ā', were now scattered across the northern mountains and eastern desert in an effort to interdict supplies flowing into the insurgents from Saudi Arabia. This dispersion complicated any withdrawal plan immensely. With the war raging at its most ferocious intensity yet, the prospects for peace seemed dim.

There were, however, two factors that made successful disengagement in March more likely than before. The first, somewhat paradoxically, was the situation on the battlefield. The Egyptians' offensive in late February and early March was probably their best effort of the entire war.[40] A concerted effort to end Royalist resistance by conquering all the major towns of Yemen and cutting off the supply routes from Saudi territory, the so-called Ramadan Offensive was a major, if temporary, success. The operation formed a natural counterpoint to the diplomatic process. Its basic political objective was to extend Republican dominion to the northeast of the country, thereby establishing a fait accompli of Republican control over most of the territory of Yemen. This, it was hoped, would bring the war to an end and establish a favorable platform for the launch of peace negotiations.[41] The capture of Ma'rib

[38] Hart, *Saudi Arabia*, 157–60; Haykal, *Sanawāt al-ghalayān*, 662; Rahmy, *Egyptian Policy*, 148; Memo, Komer (NSC) to President Kennedy, February 21, 1963, in *FRUS*, 1961–63, vol. 18, doc. 160; Ẓahrān to SecState, no. 240, March 3, 1963, RG 59, CF, Box 4147b, POL 27 Yemen, NARA; Memcon, Donald Bergus and Gen. Ṣalāḥ Ayyūb, November 14, 1966, "UAR Airdrop into Saudi Arabia: Footnote for Future Historians," RG 59, CF, 1964–66, Box 3029, NARA.

[39] Jerusalem to Washington (and other embassies), kh.o.z.m. 66, January 9, 1963, HZ 3449/28, Teman inyanei pnim, Part II (10/62–12/63), ISA; Ḥadīdī, *Shāhid 'alā ḥarb al-Yaman*, 81; Aḥmad, *Dhikrayāt*, 290; Vered, *Revolution*, 111, 113; Stookey (Ta'izz) to SecState, no. 325, February 12, 1963, RG 59, CF, Box 4147b, POL 27 Yemen, NARA; Badeau (Cairo) to SecState, no. 1314, February 25, 1963, in ibid.; Badeau (Cairo) to SecState, no. 1379, March 5, 1963, in ibid.

[40] See chapter five.

[41] Cairo to Foreign Office, no. 181, March 11, 1963, FO 371/168793, PRO; J.C.W. Bushell (POMEC) to A. R. Walmsley, BM 1015/134, February 25, 1963, FO 371/168792, PRO; Aḥmad, *al-Dawr*, 210, 212–13; Haykal, *Sanawāt al-ghalayān*, 654–55.

in the east coincided almost exactly with the visit of UN envoy Ralph Bunche, who was whisked off to see the ancient city by Egyptian military escort.[42] In fact, it was the Egyptian sense of triumph (however ephemeral) in the beginning of March, which, more than any other factor, made the moment an auspicious one for negotiations. Victory alone—or at least the illusion thereof—permitted Egypt's leadership to entertain the thought of withdrawal with honor.[43] As Nasser wrote to ʻĀmir in Yemen on March 7: "The important thing now is how we acquit ourselves politically in the conflict [*kayfa nukhalliṣu anfusana siyāsiyyan fī al-maʻrakah*] so that we can leave a small force in Yemen while the rest of the force returns home as soon as possible."[44] By the time ʻĀmir and Sadat returned home on March 10 after forty days in Yemen, the headlines had been screaming "victory!" for over a week.[45] From Cairo's perspective, the time was ripe for peace—on Egyptian terms.

If military success strengthened Nasser's hand, so too did political developments in the region. On February 8, a coup d'état in Baghdad toppled the hated regime of ʻAbd al-Karīm Qāsim (known derogatively in Nasserist parlance as "Qāsim al-ʻIrāq," Divider of Iraq). Exactly one month later, the secessionist regime in Damascus fell to a similar coup.

[42] Schmidt, *Yemen*, 192–93; Manfred Wenner, *The Yemen Arab Republic: Development and Change in an Ancient Land* (Boulder, CO: Westview Press, 1991), 206–7.

[43] My view accords with that of Aḥmad, *al-Dawr*, 212–13, 246–47, and Gause, *Saudi-Yemeni Relations*, 63. For evidence that the senior Egyptian commanders felt the same way, see Aḥmad, *Dhikrayāt*, 526; Ḥadīdī, *Shāhid ʻalā ḥarb al-Yaman*, 91. For the opposite argument, see Safran, *Saudi Arabia*, 99; Stephens, *Nasser*, 399; and Badeau, *American Approach*, 143. There is an apparent contradiction between Badeau's assertion that both Saudis and Egyptians seemed ready to throw in the towel in March 1963 and his contention that their agreement to embark on the path of disengagement resulted purely from "American pressure," and "did not represent a change of heart in either party." Badeau seems to be arguing that US policy makers overestimated the war weariness of the parties, and therefore seized the moment to thrust disengagement upon them, when in fact Nasser and Faysal were determined to pursue the war regardless of any agreement, to which they committed only grudgingly. However, US pressure notwithstanding, it is likely that both parties saw the offer of US mediation as a low-risk opportunity to end the conflict on advantageous terms.

[44] Nasser (Cairo) to ʻĀmir (Yemen), March 7, 1963, in Haykal, *Sanawāt al-ghalayān*, doc. 48, 939.

[45] E.g., *al-Gumhūriyyah*, March 3, 6, 7, 1963; *al-Akhbār*, March 1, 3, 5, 1963. Most of the battlefield gains of the Ramadan Offensive were reversed over the course of April and May. Vered, *Revolution*, 114–15; Schmidt, *Yemen*, 169–70; Aḥmad, *al-Dawr*, 268.

Change was in the air.[46] In Cairo, the erasure of the stain of the *infiṣāl* was like a dream come true. The news from Syria captured the headlines and dominated them for a month. The coup in Damascus and subsequent tripartite unity talks among Egypt, Syria, and Iraq completely overshadowed the news from Yemen, underscoring once again that the war was one move in a match of greater political stakes. With revolutionary (read: pro-Egyptian) forces back in the saddle in Ṣan'ā', Baghdad, and Damascus, and negotiations for the resurrection and expansion of the UAR in full swing, Egypt in the spring of 1963 appeared to have broken out of the deep isolation of the previous year. The favorable military situation the Ramadan Offensive produced, in conjunction with the regional atmosphere fostered by regime change in Damascus and Baghdad, created near-ideal circumstances for an honorable Egyptian withdrawal from Yemen.[47] It is probably no coincidence that the triumphant declaration of tripartite unity among Egypt, Syria, and Iraq on April 17 formed the backdrop for the conclusion of the Bunker Agreement.

Although negotiations over disengagement began with mediation by UN envoy Ralph Bunche, and implementation revolved around supervision by a UN mission of observers, the seen and unseen hands of American power guided the process throughout. After Bunche toured Republican Yemen with an Egyptian escort but shunned Royalist representatives, the Saudis refused to receive him, thereby nullifying his mission. Ever mindful of the realities of power, the Saudis understood that the guarantees they wanted could only come from the Americans; they therefore sought to engage them more directly in the process. Ostensibly in support of Bunche, but effectively in his stead, Kennedy dispatched seasoned diplomat Ellsworth Bunker to the region in early March.[48] As all subsequent diplomatic processes between Egypt and Saudi Arabia over the course of 1962–67 revolved around the commonsense ideas ironed out by Bunker in the spring of 1963, it is worthwhile going into them in some detail.

[46] As Nasser wrote to 'Āmir in Yemen: "The situation in the Arab world has changed in a decisive manner after the Iraqi revolution. Nevertheless, I continue to worry." Quoted in Haykal, *Sanawāt al-ghalayān*, 680.

[47] Stephens, *Nasser*, 399–400.

[48] For the circumstances surrounding the birth of Bunker's mission, see Department of State to London, no. 4902, March 16(?), 1963, RG 59, CF, Box 4147b, NARA; Badeau, *Middle East*, 210–11; Hart, *Saudi Arabia*, 152–54, 166–69.

Bunker's mission began on March 6 in the town of al-Damām on the shores of the Persian Gulf, where he met a skeptical Prince Faysal to try and gain Saudi agreement to a cessation of aid to the Royalists.[49] Two days earlier, Ambassador Badeau had supplied the necessary prerequisite for the talks, clinching Nasser's agreement to suspend cross-border raids as long as negotiations were underway.[50] Unbeknownst to Nasser, Bunker brought two additional incentives with him to Saudi Arabia; one, a pledge to put US influence to work in Cairo toward the end of a speedy withdrawal of Egyptian forces, the other, an offer to deploy a US Air Force unit on Saudi territory so as to deter further Egyptian attacks on Saudi Arabia and begin to develop an indigenous deterrent capability.[51] Although Faysal raised several objections, Bunker concluded there was sufficient basis to move forward.

After a two-week delay due to Egyptian preoccupation with the unity talks, Bunker proceeded to Cairo. Nasser did not reject Bunker's proposals outright. But he raised three critical concerns that would continue to dog diplomats on all sides of the issue in the years to come. First, and most seriously, Nasser worried that the Saudis would continue to fund the insurgency regardless of any commitment to the contrary. Since Faysal's fears revolved around similar concerns over Egyptian withdrawal,[52] it became clear that success of the disengagement plan hinged on the establishment of an independent mechanism of verification. The second obstacle, common to mediations of this sort, was the chicken-and-egg problem: who, Nasser wanted to know, would take the first step? The answer Bunker gave was "both." Third, Nasser demanded the removal of the Ḥamīd al-Dīn family from Yemen. Since the Royalist cause, to which Saudi Arabia was publicly committed, centered on the legitimacy of the Imam and his family, this was a matter of principle, which went far beyond the technicalities of arranging a cease-

[49] Horner (Ẓahrān) to Department of State, March 7, 1963, *FRUS*, 1961–63, vol. 18, doc. 180; Hart, *Saudi Arabia*, 169–72.

[50] Badeau (Cairo) to SecState, no. 1379, March 5, 1963, RG 59, CF, Box 4147b, POL 27 Yemen, NARA; Hart, *Saudi Arabia*, 172–73.

[51] Bunker returned from consultations in the middle of March bearing authorization to make these commitments (Hart, *Saudi Arabia*, 174–78); "Terms of Reference: Presidential Emissary to Prince Faysal," in Memo, Brubeck to Bundy, February 28, 1963, in *FRUS*, 1961–63, vol. 18, doc. 170; Bunker's account of his March 17 meeting with Faysal in Meyer (Beirut) to SecState, no. 847, March 19, 1963, RG 59, CF, Box 4147b, NARA.

[52] Horner (from Bunker, Ẓahrān) to Department of State, March 8, 1963, *FRUS*, 1961–63, vol. 18, doc. 181.

fire. For the moment, however, the question was buried under a clause calling for the suspension of Royalist activity from Saudi territory.[53]

With Nasser's comments and proposed amendments in hand, Bunker flew back to Saudi Arabia for talks with Faysal at Jiddah. The most important issue debated in the sessions of April 5 and 6 was the question of a timetable for the withdrawal of Egyptian forces from Yemen. For the Saudis, a schedule was essential; to the Egyptians, it was unthinkable. This would surely have resulted in deadlock had not Faysal accepted US pledges to hold Nasser to an "expeditious" withdrawal. Although the crown prince raised several further objections, he proved unexpectedly malleable, perhaps because he desired to transfer the onus for anticipated failure onto Nasser.[54]

In a first indication that Nasser's attempt to embroil the United States of America in his private war with the House of Sa'ūd might backfire, Bunker cabled to Washington: "Faysal has placed all his faith in us re this exercise and there is no question [the] USG must use [the] full force [of] its influence and suasion [to] get Nasser [to] carry out in good faith and expeditiously his part of [the] bargain once [a] final agreement [has been] achieved. Otherwise, we will have suffered serious loss of confidence, honor, prestige and good will in this country."[55] All Faysal had done was to make an easily reversible commitment to halt transborder

[53] Telegrams from Badeau (Cairo) to SecState, Nos. 1632, 1645, 1655, April 1–3, 1963, RG 59, CF, Box 4147b, NARA; Badeau to Department of State, April 3, 1963, "Memorandum of conversation between ... Nasser ... Bunker, and ... Badeau [in Cairo on April 1]," in ibid; Badeau to Department of State, April 3, 1963, "Memorandum of conversation between ... Nasser ... Bunker, and ... Badeau, with ... Ali Sabri attending [in Cairo on April 2]," RG 59, CF, Box 4147a, NARA; Badeau to Department of State, April 6, 1963, "Memorandum of conversation between ... Nasser ... Bunker, and ... Badeau, with ... Ali Sabri attending [in Cairo on April 3]," RG 59, CF, Box 4147b, NARA; Badeau to Department of State, April 10, 1963, "Memorandum of Conversation on Negotiation of Resolution of Yemeni Conflict [in Jiddah on April 6, 1963]," in ibid; Badeau to Department of State, April 20, 1963, "Memorandum of conversation between ... Nasser ... Bunker, and ... Badeau, with ... Ali Sabri attending [in Cairo on April 9]," in ibid. See also Gause, *Saudi-Yemeni Relations*, 62; Hart, *Saudi Arabia*, 224.

[54] For a detailed account of these talks, see Badeau (Cairo) to Department of State, April 10, 1963, "Memorandum of Conversation on Negotiation of Resolution of Yemen Conflict [in Jiddah on April 5, 1963]" and "Memorandum of Conversation on Negotiation of Resolution of Yemeni Conflict [in Jiddah on April 6, 1963]," RG 59, CF, Box 4147b, NARA; Hart, *Saudi Arabia*, 185–89.

[55] Hart (from Bunker, Jiddah) to Secretary of State, no. 819, April 7, 1963, RG 59, CF, Box 4147b, NARA.

smuggling. Yet he had succeeding in convincing Kennedy's top deal maker that US requests taxed his limits. This was a testament to Faysal's skill as a negotiator. But the prince's achievement owed more to the centrality of Saudi Arabia in US calculations. The Saudi-American relationship, grounded as it was in the bedrock of common interests, would weather the strains imposed upon it by the Egyptian involvement in Yemen; Egypt's ambivalent relations with the United States, henceforth held hostage to the vicissitudes of guerilla warfare, would bear the brunt of the storm.

Bunker returned to Cairo on April 9 to find Nasser equally amenable to rapid conclusion of the negotiations. After a skillful presentation of Faysal's concessions to date, Bunker managed to secure Nasser's agreement to all but one of the amendments worked out at Jiddah.[56] With that, his mission came to an end. The so-called Bunker Agreement consisted of the following principal points:[57]

1. Termination of Saudi support for the Royalists, and prohibition of the use of Saudi territory for carrying on the struggle in Yemen
2. Phased withdrawal of Egyptian forces from field activities to their bases pending departure from Yemen; withdrawal [from Yemen] to begin simultaneously with the Saudi cessation of aid, and to be executed as soon as possible
3. Cessation of Egyptian attacks on Saudi territory
4. Establishment of a 40-kilometer-wide demilitarized zone on the Saudi-Yemeni border
5. Stationing of impartial observers in the DMZ, one of whose responsibilities would be to travel outside the DMZ to verify Saudi and Egyptian adherence
6. Cooperation of the Saudi and Egyptian governments with a UN or other mediator on the process and verification of disengagement
7. Agreement by the Egyptian government to use its good offices with the government of the YAR to get it to desist from inflammatory speeches and reaffirm its commitment to peace

[56] Badeau (Cairo) to SecState, no. 1707, April 9, 1963, RG 59, CF, Box 4147b, POL 27 Yemen, NARA.

[57] For the precise text, see United Nations Security Council, *Official Records*, 1963, Supplement no. 1, doc. S/5298; Badeau (Cairo) to SecState, Nos. 1706, 1707, April 9, 1963, RG 59, CF, Box 4147b, POL 27 Yemen, NARA; Airgram, Cairo to Dept. of State, "Memorandum of conversation between … Nasser … Bunker, and … Badeau, with … Ali Sabri attending [in Cairo on April 9, 1963]," in ibid.

This agreement, even if executed fully, stopped well short of providing a comprehensive formula for peace. Most obviously, the deal did not stipulate a timetable for the withdrawal of UAR forces, omitted provisions for a full cease-fire, neglected the porous eastern borders of the YAR, and all but ignored the Yemeni side to the dispute.[58] Nevertheless, it was a big step in the right direction.

Much now depended on swift action by the United Nations. Unfortunately, the United Nations, as Ambassador Badeau put it, "moved as slowly as cold molasses."[59] It took several weeks to obtain UN agreement to sponsor the disengagement process, and a further two months to deploy and equip the requisite team of observers, thereby delaying implementation by a fateful three months. By the time the first major contingent of the United Nations Yemen Observation Mission (UNYOM) appeared in Yemen in July, patience was wearing thin on all sides, much blood had been spilled, and confidence in the United Nation's ability to intervene effectively had already been undermined.[60]

Contrary to expectations in Washington and Cairo, the fruitless quest for disengagement in Yemen continued to dominate US-Egyptian relations throughout 1963—invariably topping the agenda in letters exchanged between Presidents Nasser and Kennedy, in conversations between US ambassador to the UAR John Badeau and various Egyptian officials, and in the parallel talks of UAR ambassador to the United States Muṣṭafā Kāmil with US officials. Implementation proved a greater obstacle than anyone (in Washington, at least) had imagined for a number of reasons. At the most basic level, neither Nasser nor Faysal were quite ready to throw in the towel.[61] But even if one assumes the sincerity of both leaders, the flaws inherent in the agreement, aggravated by the fecklessness of execution, were more than sufficient to undermine it.

[58] Aḥmad, *al-Dawr*, 241.

[59] Badeau, *Middle East*, 212.

[60] For a firsthand account of UNYOM's misadventures in Yemen, see Von Horn, *Soldiering for Peace*, 308–93. For discussion and relevant documentation, see Rosalyn Higgins, *United Nations Peacekeeping, 1946–1967: Documents and Commentary* (London: Oxford University Press, 1969), 605–68. See also Michael Bishku, "The Kennedy Administration, the U.N. and the Yemen Civil War," *Middle East Policy* 1, no. 4 (1992): 122–28; Schmidt, *Yemen*, 194–99; Vered, *Revolution*, 126–31; Badeau, *American Approach*, 143–44; O'Ballance, *War in the Yemen*, 100–105, Bidwell, *The Two Yemens*, 204–5; Wenner, *Yemen Arab Republic*, 207–10; Aḥmad, *al-Dawr*, 219–40, 242–44; Hart, *Saudi Arabia*, 202–34.

[61] Safran, *Saudi Arabia*, 99.

At a deeper level, the failure of plans for reciprocal disengagement was grounded in the nature of the conflict itself. Although mutual accusations of bad faith abounded, the suspicions that underlay them were of greater significance.[62] These, in turn, were bred by a fundamental asymmetry in the structure of the conflict: the enormous distance between Egypt and the battlefield contrasted sharply with Saudi proximity to northern Yemen. This meant that "disengagement" was much less easily reversible for the Egyptians (for whom it entailed costly withdrawal) than it was for the Saudis (for whom it entailed a mere suspension of aid).[63] As early as February 1963, Policy Planning Council member William Polk predicted that mutual disengagement was doomed to failure because Nasser and Faysal both knew that if successful it would lead to the collapse of the republic.[64] This observation lay at the root of the conflict's intractability.[65]

The negative implications of this geostrategic asymmetry for Egypt were exacerbated by two factors. The first was the nature of the battlefield.[66] The diffuse, episodic nature of counterinsurgency—with its strong resemblance to police work—does not lend itself to rapid or decisive outcomes, as many a conventional army has learned (and in some cases has had to relearn) in recent decades. If the success of the Ramadan Offensive had misled some into thinking victory was around the corner, the gradual resurgence of Royalist activity over the course of April–June 1963 must have disabused any but the dullest observer of the notion of a swift or total victory.[67] Commander of the Egyptian forces in Yemen, Lieutenant General Anwar al-Qāḍī, recalls (somewhat conveniently) pressing Nasser in May 1963 to declare victory and pull the troops out of Yemen as soon as possible. Otherwise, he feared the gradual expansion of operations into the Jawf, where tribal affinities with Saudi Arabia presaged a protracted war that could not end well

[62] Egypt's public campaign to distort the contents of the agreement and paint it as the result of Saudi capitulation did not help. Hart, *Saudi Arabia*, 190–91.

[63] Aḥmad, *al-Dawr*, 246; Hart, *Saudi Arabia*, 178.

[64] Horner (Ẓahrān) to SecState, no. 215, February 13, 1963, RG 59, CF, Box 4147a, NARA. For Nasser's appreciation of this fact, see "Asrār yūniyū 67," *Ākhir Sāʿah*, June 6, 1988, 9. For a similar acknowledgment by the Egyptian prime minister, see Ḥamrūsh, *Qiṣṣat thawrat 23 yūliyū*, 3:242.

[65] A similar conclusion was reached by the commander of the UN observers at the end of 1963. Hart (Jiddah) to Department of State, "Final Talk with General Gyani, Retiring UNYOM Chief [on November 7, 1963]," November 14, 1963, RG 59, CF, Box 4147a, NARA.

[66] See chapter five.

[67] Aḥmad, *al-Dawr*, 268; Maḥrizī, *al-Ṣamt al-ḥāʾir*, 143–44.

for Egypt. Nasser allegedly refused to consider this, saying withdrawal would lead to the revolution's collapse.[68]

To the difficulties of antiguerilla warfare was added a second, closely related problem: the complexity and autonomy of local politics. The initial obstacle in Yemen had appeared essentially military in nature; if Saudi aid were halted and the tribes subdued, the insurgency would dry up, fighting would cease, and the Egyptians could go home. But as time wore on, the problems facing the Egyptian expeditionary force in the YAR took on an increasingly political coloring.[69] In part this merely reflected a belated realization of the obstacle faced by all of Yemen's would-be occupiers: ingrained hostility to centralized power, particularly when exercised by foreigners. Even though the Saudi-Egyptian row continued to provide the strategic impetus for intervention, Egypt's deferred appreciation of local agency, which, for the most part, lay beyond the control of meddling neighbors or foreign occupiers, begot the incipient realization that local instability threatened to undermine any agreement reached in Cairo or Riyadh. Even if Saudi aid to the tribes were to cease entirely, it was no longer evident by the summer of 1963 that the state would survive without heavy military, political, administrative, and economic involvement on Egypt's part. Given the fractious nature of Yemeni society, the Egyptian venture carried a high risk of failure on purely political grounds. The biggest challenge, in other words, was nonmilitary. The question was no longer the relatively straightforward one of bombing dissident tribes and smugglers into submission, but rather that of resolving the age-old conflict between central authority and tribal autonomy in Yemen. As such, it was not resolvable merely by the application of military force.[70]

The situation on the ground was especially conducive to skepticism. As the illusion of Republican unity disintegrated over the course of the summer of 1963,[71] the Egyptian military expedition, which originated as

[68] "Asrār yūniyū 67," *Ākhir Sā'ah*, June 6, 1988, 9. Qāḍī refers to the first contingent of soldiers withdrawn under the terms of the Bunker Agreement in May 1963 as "token forces."

[69] Cf. Badeau, *Middle East*, 213. For more on the political dimension of the problem, see chapter five.

[70] Boswell (Cairo) to SecState, no. 605, September 12, 1963, RG 59 CF, Box 4075, NARA; Hart, *Saudi Arabia*, 220, 222. Nasser admitted as much on at least two occasions. Badeau (Cairo) to SecState, no. 779, October 6, 1963, Box 4147a, NARA; "Asrār yūniyū 67," *Ākhir Sā'ah*, June 6, 1988, 9.

[71] For the disintegration of the republican camp and the birth of the "Third Force," see, e.g., Aḥmad, *al-Dawr*, 285–301, 361–63; Vered, *Revolution*, 137–38, 151–58.

a small-scale mission in support of a friendly government, morphed into a full-fledged occupation regime. With Egyptians holding key positions in every ministry and throughout the bureaucracy, and the YAR's economy increasingly tied to Egypt's, the military task force became an external prop for what was essentially an Egyptian-sponsored experiment in republican politics.[72] As indigenous support for the regime evaporated, the Egyptians faced an acute dilemma between broadening its political base and losing control.[73] The fragility of this arrangement immeasurably magnified the challenges Saudi involvement posed. In other words, wishful thinking did not translate into a successful exit strategy in the summer of 1963 primarily because the shakiness of the political situation in Yemen provided fertile ground for the growth of suspicions in Egyptian minds that withdrawal would lead to ignominious collapse of the republic in Ṣan'ā' at the hands of tribes rearmed through Saudi perfidy.

A final factor that served to undermine the Bunker agreement was the very fact of US mediation. The failure of disengagement demonstrated what seems obvious in retrospect: that US mediation, while perhaps a desirable component of any Saudi-Egyptian arrangement, was no substitute for direct Saudi-Egyptian negotiations. These, in turn, were useless without a political deal between the Yemenis themselves. Absent these components, the interposition of the United States as broker, although it staved off open war, actually delayed resolution of the conflict by enabling each of the parties to evade responsibility by complaining to the Americans about the other's infractions. As Ambassador Badeau noted at the time, the agreement encouraged the Egyptians "to temporize and to use tactics of high school debate and clumsy efforts to deceive."[74] To what extent all three parties realized the pointlessness of further US mediation is unclear, but the Bunker experience was not repeated. From this point onward, the antagonists would pursue peace either directly or by means of an Arab mediator.

Given the almost certainly disastrous consequences of withdrawal, it is not surprising that Nasser, however sincere his original intentions, did not carry out the agreement.[75] The hero's welcome that awaited

[72] Wenner, *Yemen Arab Republic*, 140–41, 144, and passim; Vered, *Revolution*, 138–42.

[73] Itamar Rabinovich, "The Embroilment" (Hebrew), in Shamir, *Decline of Nasserism*, 220, 222.

[74] Badeau to SecState, no. 1303, December 10, 1963, CF, Box 4147a, NARA.

[75] In early 1963, a leader of the Saudi-backed mercenaries in Yemen summarized the situation thus: "If the Egyptians do withdraw ... then the Royalists could have Sana in a week. But if they don't withdraw and the Saudis still suspend supplies, I don't think the

troops returning from Yemen could not hide the underlying reality of troop rotations masquerading as withdrawal.[76] In April, at the height of the US mediation effort, there had been approximately 30,000 Egyptian troops in Yemen; by the beginning of October that figure remained essentially unchanged.[77] With frustration mounting both in the White House and on Capitol Hill, Kennedy confessed to Nasser in mid-October:

> In the spirit of frank exchange[,] which I believe we have both come to value, I must tell you of my own personal concern over the UAR's failure to date to carry out its part of the Yemen disengagement agreement. I think it fair to say that the Saudis are carrying out their end of the bargain.... We are confident that the UKG and the SAG are honoring their assurances to us that they are not aiding the Royalists. I therefore have no leverage with Faysal when, having carried out his side of the bargain, he continues to see Egyptian troops in Yemen and hear expressions of UARG hostility from Cairo.[78]

Emphasizing the difficult position in which he found himself, as effective underwriter of the disengagement plan Kennedy demanded concrete steps to demonstrate Egypt's continued commitment to a peaceful resolution. "The alternative—a breakdown of disengagement, withdrawal of UNYOM, and probable renewal of direct Saudi-UAR confrontation—could not but lead to a situation in which the US and UAR, instead of moving closer together, would drift further apart. If we should let Yemen affect our larger interests in this manner, we would have lost our ability to shape events and have permitted events to dominate us."[79]

Royalists can hold out for more than a month. If, as seems most likely, the Egyptians stay and the Saudis resume supplies, we're in for a long war." David Smiley, *Arabian Assignment* (London: Leo Cooper, 1975), 151.

[76] See, e.g., *al-Ahrām*, August 12 and October 23, 1963; Maḥrizī, *al-Ṣamt al-ḥā'ir*, 137–40.

[77] Badeau (Cairo) to Department of State, "Memorandum of conversation between ... Nasser ... Bunker, and ... Badeau [in Cairo on April 1, 1963]," RG 59, CF Box 4147b, NARA; Cairo to SecState, no. 779, October 6, 1963, RG 59, CF, Box 4147a, NARA. The precise figure cited by US intelligence estimates for the latter date is 32,000.

[78] Oral message from Kennedy to Nasser in Rusk to Cairo, no. 1618, October 19, 1963, RG 59, CF, Box 4148, NARA. For Kennedy's growing frustration with Nasser in the weeks prior to his death, see Hart, *Saudi Arabia*, 228. *Pace* Kennedy, it is virtually certain that the Saudis had resumed clandestine support for the Royalists in the fall of 1963 and had violated the agreement on at least one prior occasion. See, for instance, Smiley, *Arabian Assignment*, 156; Hart, *Saudi Arabia*, 209–10, 217–18.

[79] Oral message from Kennedy to Nasser, October 19, 1963.

The Bunker Agreement and the UNYOM commission purchased a year of time in which the repeated extension of UNYOM's two-month commissions had the merit of keeping the Saudis and Egyptians from each other's throats. But as 1963 drew to a close the pace of action picked up again on the battlefield, and the ritual of renewal appeared increasingly futile. By December the Bunker Agreement was clearly dead, and US officials in Cairo were urging it pronounced so.[80] The disengagement process had stalled, and the White House was inclined to place most of the blame on Egypt. Meanwhile, Egypt's failure to withdraw from Yemen began to look like part of a pattern when, in mid-October 1963, Nasser, with Soviet encouragement, ordered Egyptian military units to Algeria in support of Algeria's border dispute with another Arab monarchy and US ally, Morocco.[81] There was little doubt that the continued pursuit of such policies would sooner or later be reflected in US aid.

In internal US documents it was acknowledged early on that Egypt's continued presence in Yemen would result in some reduction of aid, if only due to domestic political reasons. As one US diplomat in Cairo put it: "[The t]hreat to withhold US aid to [the] UAR has not had [the] effect of increasing [the] rate of withdrawal [of] UAR troops from Yemen. At [the] same time we recognize that, given [the] unsatisfactory UAR performance in Yemen as well as [the] atmosphere in congressional and other circles in [the] US, future US assistance to [the] UAR cannot but be affected by [the] Yemen situation."[82] Although the potential link between US aid and Egyptian foreign policy was rarely made explicit in conversations with Egyptian officials, threats of a looming crisis in US-Egyptian relations unless Egypt acted could mean little else.[83] The hints were clearly taken. In the course of a portentous conversation with Ambassador Badeau on October 27, 1963, Nasser—raising a theme that would be repeated with ever-growing frustration over the next three

[80] Boswell (Cairo) to Secretary of State, no. 1267, December 5, 1963, RG 59, Box 4147a, NARA; Badeau (Cairo) to Secretary of State, no. 1303, December 10, 1963, in ibid. Nevertheless, the disengagement agreement remained in force until the end of August 1964, when Faysal demonstratively refused to renew UNYOM's commission on the eve of his talks with Nasser at Alexandria.

[81] Ghālib, *Mudhakkirāt*, 75.

[82] Boswell (Cairo) to SecState, no. 1267, December 5, 1963, RG 59, CF, Box 4147a, NARA.

[83] See, for instance, Badeau's strong representations to 'Alī Ṣabrī in Cairo (Badeau) to Secretary of State, no. 966, October 26, 1963, RG 59, CF, Box 4076, NARA. The Egyptians were aware of the implicit linkage from the early 1960s. Burns, *Economic Aid*, 127; Badeau, *Middle East*, 195.

and a half years—vowed not to surrender to pressure. Disingenuously, he disavowed any particular interest in US assistance, which, he alleged, was sought by underlings operating without presidential encouragement. While grateful for American aid and appreciative of its utility, he claimed to be constantly searching for alternatives should it diminish or cease. Waving the red flag of Suez, he made a veiled allusion to Soviet potential in this regard. A meaningful reduction in aid would certainly cause "friction" between Egypt and the United States and temporarily affect Egyptian development plans, Nasser concluded, but if these were unavoidable, so be it. And yet, having lodged his protest, Nasser immediately proceeded to negotiate with Badeau over further Egyptian troop withdrawals, thereby implicitly accepting the linkage.[84]

In Congress, where the federal purse strings resided, pressure to penalize Nasser mounted. On November 7, the Senate passed the Gruening Amendment, which prohibited aid to a country the president deemed to be engaging in or preparing for aggression against the United States or any recipient of US aid. News of the amendment, clearly directed at Egypt, was received with fury in Cairo.[85] Against this ominous backdrop, Ambassador Badeau warned his Egyptian interlocutors of "most serious effects" for US-Egypt relations unless some dramatic action was taken to demonstrate progress in Yemen.[86]

The Suspension of US Aid

In Egyptian historiography, much of the blame for the growing crisis in US-Egyptian relations from the mid-1960s onward is placed on Lyndon Johnson's accidental assumption of the presidency.[87] Johnson, it is

[84] Badeau (Cairo) to Secretary of State, no. 969, October 27, 1963, RG 59, Box 4147a, NARA.

[85] Burns, *Economic Aid*, 145–46; Memorandum from the President's Special Assistant for National Security Affairs (Bundy) to Senator J. William Fulbright, November 11, 1963, in *FRUS*, 1961–63, vol. 18, doc. 357.

[86] See, for instance, Badeau's conversation with Sāmī Sharaf on December 9, 1963, in Badeau (Cairo) to Secstate, no. 1318, December 11, 1963, CF, Box 4147a, NARA. Sāmī Sharaf and ʻAlī Ṣabrī were two Nasser confidants to whom Badeau could convey a blunt message for the president without embarrassing him in person. Badeau, *Middle East*, 227–30.

[87] See, for instance, the memoirs of the former Egyptian foreign minister, Maḥmūd Riyāḍ, *Mudhakkirāt Maḥmūd Riyāḍ, 1948–1978* (Cairo: Dār al-Mustaqbal al-ʻArabī, 1986),

sometimes argued, reversed the friendly policy of his predecessor out of gratuitous animosity for Nasser, excessive sympathy for Israel, preoccupation with Vietnam, or the prioritization of oil interests. This interpretation has been adopted, in a more qualified manner, by most American students of the subject as well.[88] But such explanations ignore the historical record of US-Egyptian relations under the Kennedy administration. To be sure, President Johnson was more inclined than his predecessor had been to take his Egyptian counterpart to task for actions and rhetoric subversive of US interests in the region. He was also less patient with aid.[89] But his problem with Nasser was an inherited one.[90]

As this analysis has revealed, the roots of the later tensions between the United States and the UAR were planted squarely in the favorable soil of the Kennedy presidency.[91] In practice, economic assistance other than PL 480 came to a halt even before the end of the Kennedy administration over Egypt's failure to disengage in Yemen.[92] It was precisely the clash between mutual, misplaced expectations and the bitter reality of Egyptian-American discord over Yemen that made the eventual awakening so rude. From the American perspective, Egyptian behavior in Yemen was the root of the problem, not any imagined animosity in Washington. From Cairo's perspective, it was US determination to pick a fight over Yemen—a matter of immense national prestige—by tugging ever harder on the aid strings—a matter of national survival—that made a serious crisis seem increasingly unavoidable.[93]

2:272; Haykal, *Sanawāt al-ghalayān*, 772–76; Sharaf, *Sanawāt wa-ayyām ma'a Gamāl 'Abd al-Nāṣir*, 1:288; and Mohamed Auda, "Nasser: The Revolution Continues," *Arab Papers*, no. 8 (London: Arab Research Centre, 1981), 29–30. The perception was common among Egyptian contemporaries as well. Maitland (Cairo) to Scrivener (Foreign Office), VG 103145/2, February 20, 1964, FO 371/178591, PRO.

[88] See, e.g., William Quandt, "America and the Middle East: A Fifty-Year Overview," in *Diplomacy in the Middle East*, ed. Brown, 65; Gordon, *Nasser*, 89.

[89] Burns, *Economic Aid*, 149.

[90] See, for instance, Robert W. Komer, *Oral History Interview* no. 1, January 30, 1970, 55, LBJL.

[91] Ambassador Hart writes that President Kennedy was in the midst of stiffening Washington's posture toward Nasser at the time of his assassination. *Saudi Arabia*, 228.

[92] US Ambassador to the UAR, Lucius Battle, wrote toward the end of 1964 that "economic assistance other than technical assistance or PL-480 ... has now been in suspense (*primarily over Yemen*) [emphasis added] for more than one year." Battle (Cairo) to Sec. of State, no. 2016, December 9, 1964, RG 59, CF, Box 2768, NARA.

[93] Cf. Haykal's explanation, according to which a "shadow government" in Washington, in league with Arab reactionaries, oil moguls, and arms dealers, set out to destroy the

Several factors contributed to the further deterioration of US-Egyptian relations under Johnson. One was the growing domestic opposition to the provision of aid to Egypt, which tied the president's hands; another was the administration's increasing preoccupation with Vietnam.[94] Above all, a series of unfortunate events took place in the course of 1964, which diminished Johnson's inclination to indulge Nasser. We cannot here analyze in depth the entire sequence of events from the Arab Summit of January 1964 to the burning of the American embassy's library in Cairo in November of that year. Most of these developments share a common theme: each injected a new element of discord into an already tense relationship. Whether it was Nasser's call for the eviction of foreign bases from Libya in February,[95] Khrushchev's ostentatious visit to Egypt in May, conflicting policies toward the Congolese civil war in November, or the continued prosecution of Egyptian missile development program, Cairo and Washington drew increasingly apart as the year progressed.[96]

Yemen, on the other hand, was placed on the back burner for much of 1964. Although UAR forces did not depart, the fighting died down, and Nasser was busy for much of the year reaching out to his Saudi counterparts at the Arab summits and elsewhere in an apparently sincere effort to calm regional tensions and find a way out of Yemen.[97] Reporting to President Johnson at the end of January that the US deterrent air force contingent had been removed from Saudi soil, NSC official Bob Komer added optimistically: "our best guess is that the Yemen flap is about over ... and a UAR/Saudi reconciliation in the cards. I may be wrong but I think we can keep this messy little problem off your list of trouble spots."[98] On March 3, 1964, the UAR and Saudi Arabia announced the resumption of diplomatic relations. A new era seemed at hand.

Egyptian regime by employing a vast army of mercenaries to liquidate Nasser's army in Yemen while cutting aid to starve his people at home (*al-Infijār*, 110–19). This conspiracy theory has been echoed most recently by Sāmī Sharaf, *Sanawāt*, 623–24. For a rejection of the "army of mercenaries" thesis, see Aḥmad, *Dhikrayāt*, 117, 311.

[94] Badeau, *Middle East*, 242.

[95] UAR, *Majmū'at khuṭab*, 4:517–18.

[96] Kerr, "Coming to Terms with Nasser," 79. Cf. Haykal, *al-Infijār*, 178.

[97] See chapter six.

[98] Memo, Komer (NSC) to President Johnson, January 31, 1964, *FRUS*, 1964–68, vol. 21, doc. 321.

Figure 3.1 The trump card. [British PM] Macmillan: "How can I lose when I have all these cards left (Faysal, al-Badr, Hussein, and Sa'ūd)?" Abdel Nasser: "Because I have the winning card (the Arab people)." *Akhbār al-Yawm*, December 22, 1962.

It was not to be. For just as Nasser appeared on the verge of a deal with one major US ally in the region, he struck out at another. In the course of his sole trip to Yemen in April 1964, Nasser essentially declared war on the Federation of South Arabia and the British position at Aden.[99] The federation, an amalgamation of British-protected sheikdoms in southern Yemen, was scheduled to enter the British Commonwealth in 1968 as an independent state. Aden, host to the second-busiest port in the world and the headquarters of the United Kingdom's Middle East Command, constituted the last foothold of the British Empire in the Middle East and the linchpin of Anglo-American defense arrangements east of the Suez Canal.

Aden had been on the hit list of Cairo Radio since the late 1950s. After 1962 Sallāl and his fellow revolutionaries provided inspiration for their

[99] For the most relevant passages of Nasser's speeches in Yemen, see UAR, *Majmū'at khuṭab*, 4:551–52, 555, 562–63. For a US perspective on the visit, see Cortada (Ta'izz) to SecState, no. 602, April 28, 1964, RG 59, CF, Box 3024, POL 15 Yemen, NARA. See also chapter six.

Figure 3.2 Sallāl, Nasser, and 'Āmir during the Egyptian president's only visit to Yemen, April 1964. *Al-Quwwāt al-Musallaḥah,* May 1, 1964.

southern compatriots, who were sitting on a powder keg of migrant labor, tribal rivalries, and anti-British sentiment.[100] The Egyptians did not hide their sympathies with the revolutionary movement in the federation, nor did they discourage the Republicans from asserting Yemeni claims to the "Occupied South." Soon after the intervention, the deputy director of Egyptian general intelligence, 'Izzat Sulaymān, began to work with exiled activist Qaḥṭān al-Sha'bī to arm the more extreme of the Adeni nationalists and organize them into what became the National Front for the Liberation of South Yemen (NLF, sometimes referred

[100] For a superb discussion of the evolution of the revolutionary movement in the south and its relation to its northern counterpart, see Dresch, *A History of Modern Yemen*, 58–64, 71–77, 85–88, 96–114, and passim. See also Vitalii Naumkin, *Red Wolves of Yemen: The Struggle for Independence* (London: Oleander, 2004), 76–93; idem, *Natsional'nyi Front v bor'be za nezavisimost' Iuzhnogo Iemena i natsional'nuiu demokratiiu, 1963–1969* (Moscow: Nauka, 1980), 72–98; Aḥmad 'Aṭiyyah Miṣrī, *Tajribat al-Yaman al-dīmuqrāṭiyyah, 1950–1972* (Cairo, 1974), 253, 282; Joseph Kostiner, *The Struggle for South Yemen* (New York: St. Martin's Press, 1984); Bidwell, *The Two Yemens*, 130–94; Little, *South Arabia*, 100–137; and Gause, *Saudi-Yemeni Relations*, 38–43.

to simply as the National Front, or NF), the most influential political and military opposition group in the south.[101]

The British, for their part, embarked early on a covert campaign to destabilize the republic and make life difficult for the Egyptians—primarily by means of a clandestine organization of mercenaries sent into Yemen to train and advise Royalist forces. The mercenaries, led by veterans of the British Special Forces, never numbered more than forty. Because of the sensitivity of their mission, they received no support from the British government and depended entirely on Saudi funding. Nevertheless, they succeeded in lending a degree of coordination, determination, and imaginative leadership to an otherwise feckless resistance. Perhaps their most impressive achievement was to bring together two of the strangest bedfellows the Egyptian intervention in Yemen produced: the government of Israel and the Ḥamīd al-Dīn family. Just three weeks before Nasser's visit to Yemen, the mercenaries pulled off the first in a series of top-secret airdrops of supplies into the Yemeni highland executed by the Israeli air force. Had the origin of these missions leaked out, they would have compromised the Royalist cause and the Saudis' ability to support it.[102]

Ever since late 1962, tensions between the republic and the neighboring sheikhdoms had erupted into armed clashes among Egypt, Great Britain, and their local allies across the YAR's permeable eastern and southern frontiers. Since aid to the Royalists increasingly by-passed the UN-patrolled buffer zone in the north, entering Yemen instead from federation territory in the east (particularly Bayḥān), interdiction of this supply route necessitated confronting the British directly.[103] In a sense, therefore, there was nothing new about the Egyptian campaign. It was Nasser's high-profile commitment to unseat the British in April 1964 that signaled a qualitative shift in the nature of the confrontation.

[101] Bayḍānī, *Azmat al-ummah*, 471; Aḥmad, *Dhikrayāt*, 430–31; Ḥamrūsh, *Qiṣṣat thawrat 23 yūliyū*, 3:245; Dresch, *History*, 91; Little, *South Arabia*, 103, 137; Peresypkin, *al-Yaman*, 193; Naumkin, *Red Wolves*, 87; idem, *Natsional'nyi Front*, 78–81. Apparently, Sulaymān had begun to plan a terrorist campaign in Aden even before the revolution in Yemen (Bayḍānī, *Miṣr wa-thawrat al-Yaman*, 109–10).

[102] For details, see Clive Jones, *Britain and the Yemen Civil War, 1962–1965: Ministers, Mercenaries, and Mandarins: Foreign Policy and the Limits of Covert Action* (Brighton: Sussex Academic Press, 2004); Duff Hart-Davis, *The War That Never Was: The True Story of the Men Who Fought Britain's Most Secret Battle* (London: Century, 2011).

[103] Chapdelaine (Cairo) to External, no. 291, May 9, 1964, RG 25, Vol. 8885, 20-UAR-1-3, Vol. 2, LAC; Aḥmad, *Dhikrayāt*, 461, 652–53.

Although Nasser was jumping on the bandwagon of a revolution already underway in the federation since the outbreak of violence in Radfān in October 1963, the public launch of an overt anti-British crusade—under the code name Saladin—reflected his growing frustrations in Yemen. With the Saudis displaying increasing fortitude under US protection and the steadier hand of Prince Faysal, the spread of revolution northward must have seemed an increasingly remote prospect. Even withdrawal with honor was impossible as long as the Saudis refused to play ball. In this context the British to the south represented a convenient scapegoat for Egypt's failure to stabilize the republic in the north.[104] By throwing his weight behind the insurgency in the south, Nasser was effectively hedging his bets on the peninsula: instead of investing all in a doomed effort at counterinsurgency, he would diversify his peninsular portfolio with a stake in the neighboring insurgency. What better way to increase the chances of success and reduce the risks than by giving the British a taste of their own medicine?[105]

Although Nasser's campaign took aim at the emerging Anglo-Saudi axis, the opening of an old-new revolutionary front on the southern tip of the Arabian Peninsula also carried grave implications for relations with the United States. Nasser's trip to Yemen was arguably the single most important link in the chain of events leading to the suspension of US aid to Egypt. By declaring repeatedly and publicly that Egypt would act in consort with the Yemenis to evict the British from Aden, Nasser transformed what had been a clandestine policy of retaliatory subversion into open war against a major US ally. With time, success in the federation whet Egyptian appetites for further mischief in the vulnerable belt of emirates and sheikhdoms that extended east from Aden into the oil-rich territories adjoining the Persian Gulf. This was a dangerous game indeed.

Whether or not Nasser intended it, much of the initial ire in Washington was directed at the British. The United Kingdom's aggressive posture toward Nasser in Yemen did not find favor in the NSC or in the State Department, where British retaliatory policy—like Israel's—was viewed primarily through the lens of US-Arab relations.[106] Many US

[104] Battle (Cairo) to SecState, no. 2585, May 3, 1964, RG 59, CF, Box 2767, POL 1 UAR UK, NARA.

[105] See also chapter six.

[106] See, e.g., Memo, Bundy and Komer (NSC) to President Johnson, April 29, 1964, *FRUS*, 1964–68, vol. 21, doc. 334.

officials doubted the wisdom of the conservative government's belligerent policy toward Egypt and feared being dragged deeper into confrontation with Nasser for the sake of their Atlantic commitments.[107] When on March 28, 1964, British warplanes attacked a fort near the border town of Ḥarīb in retaliation for cross-border aggression by YAR forces, the US ambassador to the United Nations, Adlai Stevenson, was forced into an uncomfortable stance of isolated solidarity with his British allies under attack at the United Nations.[108] Stevenson's bosses, however, did not share his discomfort. As President Johnson told Dean Rusk in a telephone conversation on April 9: "He [Nasser] has not performed in Yemen, he is undermining us in the Wheelus [Air Force] Base [in Libya] and he's pitching this arms race into the Near East.... I think it's important for Nasser to know that ... he just mustn't take us for granted on these things ... an abstention on this is something of a warning to Nasser that we're ... coming close to the end of the trail on this business."[109]

In retrospect, the focus of many in Washington on restraining the British seems misplaced. Not only did they underestimate British obligations toward the rulers of the federation—regardless of who was in power in London—they failed to understand the extent to which Nasser's new campaign in the south represented a new strategic venture, not merely a temporary reactive measure. By April 1964 the train of all-out British-Egyptian confrontation on the peninsula had already left the station. From this point onward, the eviction of the British from Aden in particular and the Arabian Peninsula in general became an Egyptian obsession. Initially born of the search for a scapegoat for failure in the north, with time the eviction of the British from the peninsula became a paramount strategic goal in its own right. As his chief of intelligence testifies, Nasser came to see the liberation of South Arabia as essential to sustaining the momentum of the Arab revolutionary move-

[107] See, e.g., Memos from Komer (NSC) to Bundy, March 30, and April 28, 1964, *FRUS*, 1964–68, vol. 21, docs. 324, 333. It was ironic that officials in Washington and London each anticipated the others' policy toward Nasser to shift in their favor after the general elections of November and October, respectively. Nasser too held high hopes for British policy after a Labour victory. Memo, Komer (NSC) to President Johnson, April 29, 1964, *FRUS*, 1964–68, vol. 21, doc. 334; Greenhill (Washington) to Harrison (Foreign Office), VG 1022/28, August 27, 1964, FO 371/178582, PRO.

[108] For Rusk's position, see Memo, Bundy (NSC) to President Johnson, April 9, 1964, *FRUS*, 1964–68, vol. 21, doc. 326.

[109] Telephone conversation, Johnson and Rusk, April 9, 1964, 12:06 PM, Tape no. WH6404.05, Citation no. 2941, LBJ.

ment as a whole, to which the legitimacy of Egyptian leadership was inextricably bound.[110] As the rebellion picked up steam in the south with the help of Egyptian arms, training, and finance, the confrontational approach gained support in London. The new Labour government that assumed power in October tried to backpedal, but the persistent reality of terrorism in Aden soon eroded the will to appease.

If Nasser's aim in April 1964 had been to repeat the dynamic of late 1962, in which Egyptian escalation against a US ally generated American pressure to restrain that ally, he once again miscalculated the long-term effects of upping the ante. The British had been harping on Kennedy's pro-Nasser policy ever since the outbreak of the revolution in Yemen, but their protests acquired urgency when a major Western position came under direct threat. With Aden under siege, the British factor began to exercise an increasingly adverse effect on US policy. Since the existing Anglo-American defense system for the Persian Gulf depended largely on the British position at Aden, and Nasser's campaign against Western bases targeted the Anglo-American position in Libya as well, US policy makers, in the long run, could not fail to be concerned. Although there was still a core of die-hard Nasser fans in Foggy Bottom, they faced steadily growing opposition, not only from the White House, but from Capitol Hill as well.[111] Nasser's turn against Aden provoked a powerful voice to join the unlikely chorus of Saudis, Israelis, and oilmen already calling for a halt to US aid to Egypt. By doubling his bets in Yemen, Nasser lengthened his odds in Washington.[112]

Eager to avoid a repetition of the major disaster that followed the last time a US administration decided to withhold aid from Egypt, American policy makers looked warily on any scale back of aid to Nasser. But domestic pressures, and presidential ire, proved harder to ignore with the passage of time. In November 1964, the United States withdrew an offer for a $20 million commodity loan, in part because the UAR was not reducing its commitment in Yemen.[113] This marked the termination

[110] Imām, *Ṣalāḥ Naṣr yatadhakkar*, 196–98. See also Nasser's remarks to King Hassan of Morocco in September 1965, in Haykal, *al-Infijār*, 222.

[111] Ormsby-Gore (Washington) to Foreign Office, no. 3213, September 19, 1964, FO 371/178584, PRO.

[112] The danger inherent in this dynamic was appreciated early on by senior administration officials. See Memo, Komer (NSC) to Bundy, April 28, 1964, *FRUS*, 1964–68, vol. 21, doc. 333.

[113] Airgram, Cairo to Department of State, "Commodity Loan Conditions," September 25, 1964, RG 59, CF, Box 589, NARA; Talbott (State) to Battle (Cairo), no. 2794, November 14, 1964, in ibid; Battle (Cairo) to Talbott (State), no. 1696, November 16, 1964, in ibid.

of US economic aid to Egypt other than food, and it angered Nasser considerably. Still, as the end of 1964 approached there was no hint that PL 480, the cornerstone of the US-Egyptian relationship, would be discontinued. With negotiations over a new wheat deal soon to begin, one might have expected Nasser to try and appease the Americans. Instead, he chose to provoke them. In December, "a series of little horrors,"[114] some born of misunderstanding but all involving gross miscalculation in Cairo, swiftly dissipated the patience of the old-new US administration that came to power after the November elections, bringing about the surprising suspension of US food aid.

By 1964 Yemen had become the central battlefield of a war being waged on multiple fronts, in each of which the projection of Egyptian military power threatened US interests. One, as we have seen, was in Algeria. Another was in Aden. But the deathblow to US-Egyptian relations, when it came, arrived from Congo, where the two governments had been tacitly supporting opposite sides in a vicious civil war.[115] Here too Nasser had begun to flex his long-distance military muscle, flying armaments to the rebel government via Sudan. The peak came in November, when US planes carried Belgian troops to Stanleyville to help free hundreds of Western hostages held by the Simba rebels, as Egyptian planes ferried Soviet weapons to their captors. On Thanksgiving Day, 1964, in apparent retaliation for US involvement, a mob of African students in Cairo ransacked and burned the library of the US embassy, while Egyptian security forces stood idly by. Ambassador Lucius Battle, outraged by the apparent complicity of the regime in the attack, was even more incensed by the callous attitude evidenced by senior Egyptian officials in its wake. The incident could not have come at a worse time, just weeks before a scheduled White House review of aid policy toward Egypt.[116] As if this were not bad enough, on December 19, Egyptian air defense shot down a private plane belonging to US businessman John Mecom, killing all aboard. The alleged accident was treated with similar callousness by Egyptian officials. It was this inopportune moment that the deputy minister of supply, Ramzī Istīnū,

[114] Battle, *Oral History*, 13.

[115] Stephens, *Nasser*, 417–18; Mahr, *Die Rolle Ägyptens*, 237–38; Aḥmad, *al-Dawr*, 316.

[116] McGeorge Bundy, National Security Action Memorandum 319, "US Aid to the UAR," November 20, 1964, at http://www.lbjlib.utexas.edu/johnson/archives.hom/nsams/nsam319.asp; Battle (Cairo) to SecState, no. 1945, December 3, 1964, RG 59, CF 64–66, Box 2765, NARA.

chose to summon Ambassador Battle for a discussion of Egypt's supply problems.[117] Battle's angry rebuff was apparently distorted in Istīnū's report of the conversation to Prime Minister 'Alī Ṣabrī, who portrayed it to Nasser as a threat to cut off US aid.[118]

Perhaps sensing that the boat of US-Egyptian relations had already tipped too far,[119] or alternatively believing he could still right it with the threat of capsize,[120] Nasser jumped overboard. In a vitriolic speech at Port Sa'īd on December 23, 1964, with Alexander Shelepin at his side,[121] the president asserted the independence of Egyptian policy. He flaunted Egyptian supplies of weapons to liberation movements—including the Congolese opponents of Prime Minister Moise Tshombe, a "killer" and "imperialist stooge" working for American and Belgian interests—and contrasted Egyptian independence with the slavish subservience of Iran, an "American and Zionist colony." In what the CIA termed "Nasir's bitterest attack on the U.S. since 1956,"[122] the president let loose with vitriol usually reserved for the British:

> Our policy is an independent one; we say that we deal with the world powers on the basis that no one intervenes in our affairs. But if the

[117] Battle (Cairo) to SecState, no. 2162, December 22, 1964, RG 59, CF 64–66, Box 2767, POL 31-1 UAR-US, NARA; Battle, *Oral History Interview*, 15–17.

[118] Such, at least, was the exculpatory explanation given by Haykal to the US ambassador. Battle (Cairo) to SecState, no. 2452, January 15, 1965, RG 59, Box 590, NARA.

[119] Ibid.

[120] Burns, *Economic Aid*, 160. A research paper written in the Egyptian Foreign Ministry after the speech highlights Egyptian confidence that the United States had too much to lose by halting aid to Egypt. Ministry of Foreign Affairs, General Research Administration, "The Future of Our Relations with the United States Following President Jamal Abd al-Nasser's Speech on Victory Day," January 2, 1965, in "Weekly Review of General Information," trans. in CIA, Intelligence Information Cable, April 9, 1965, "UAR Foreign Ministry Study on the Future of UAR Relations with the United States," p. 6, in NSF, Country File, United Arab Republic, Box 159/1, Folder: United Arab Republic, Vol. 3, Memos [1 of 2], 11/64–6/65, LBJL.

[121] As Ambassador Battle notes, Nasser may have chosen to stage an anti-American show in part for the benefit of his guest, at a time when it was still not certain that the boat of *Soviet*-Egyptian relations could be righted after Khrushchev's ouster. But the Egyptians also clearly considered the threat to substitute Soviet for US aid a potent deterrent. Battle, *Oral History Interview*, 16; "UAR Foreign Ministry Study," 6. See also Kerr, "Coming to Terms with Nasser," 78–79.

[122] Memcon, "U.S.-U.A.R. Relations," December 23, 1964, *FRUS*, 1964–68, vol. 18, doc. 115n.

> Americans understood that they would give us aid so that they could come and dominate us and dominate our policy, I tell them, [we are] sorry! We are prepared to forego a little tea ... [and to] reduce our consumption of certain products to preserve our independence.... I tell [US Ambassador Battle] here: He who does not like our behavior can drink from the sea, and if the water of the Mediterranean is not enough for him, we offer him the Red [Sea] as well!... We are not prepared to accept [that kind of] talk from anyone. Anyone who [so much as] says a word to us, we shall cut off his tongue.... We have honor ... and we are not prepared to sell that honor for a billion pounds.

This affront had an immediate and drastic effect on US aid policy. Johnson, who was in any case opposed to the sort of long-term aid commitments his predecessor advocated, had had it. "Food for Peace" was delivering nothing of the kind. The Saudi argument, that the United States was in effect subsidizing Nasser's militant interventionism in Yemen, Congo, and Algeria, was beginning to make sense. With not even gratitude to show for all the costly aid showered upon Egypt at a time of depleted wheat surpluses in the United States, and the threat of real famine in India, there seemed little point in continuing the charade. Secretary of State Dean Rusk recalls: "We didn't expect Nasser to bow, scrape, lick our boots, and say, 'Thank you, Uncle Sam,' but we did expect him at least to moderate his virulent criticism of the United States. Instead, he got up before those big crowds in Cairo and shouted such things as 'Throw your aid into the Red Sea!' Nasser's fiery speeches persuaded Congress to move to do exactly that."[123] On January 5, President Johnson exercised his prerogative to postpone indefinitely sales of wheat to the UAR under the existing multiyear agreement. Negotiations for a new PL 480 aid package ground to a halt.[124]

Nasser apparently realized he had gone too far, for he sent peace feelers through Kāmil in Washington and Battle in Cairo. He also moved to cut Prime Minister 'Alī Ṣabrī out of the loop, taking personal charge of

[123] Dean Rusk, with Richard Rusk and Daniel S. Papp, *As I Saw It* (New York: W. W. Norton, 1990), 380.

[124] Burns, *Economic Aid*, 150, 160; Memcon between Dean Rusk, Phillips Talbot, and Rodger Davies, Washington, December 31, 1964, *FRUS*, 1964–68, vol. 18, doc. 117; Johnson, *The Vantage Point*, 224–25, 290. Cf. Haykal, *al-Infijār*, 178–79. A similar attitude characterized Johnson's India policy, except that the famine of 1965–66 made the sort of pressure applied to Egypt all but unthinkable; it also made India more desperate than Egypt to strike a deal. Nevertheless, the course of relations with both countries in these years is remarkably similar. Ahlberg, "Machiavelli with a Heart," 665–701.

Egypt's relations with the United States and directing that all telegrams from Ambassador Kāmil in Washington be sent directly to the presidency. But the damage was done.[125] From the beginning of 1965 onward, US aid to Egypt—and with it, relations between the two countries—hung by a thread. Although a full cutoff was still two suspenseful years in the future, the economic and political effects of the squeeze were already palpable.[126]

The Balance of Payments Crisis

The conflict brewing with the United States in late 1964 could not have come at a worse time for Egypt's economy. The internal manifestations and political repercussions of the supply crisis of 1964–65 will be discussed later.[127] But the crisis had an important external symptom of no lesser consequence: a critical shortage of foreign exchange. The combination of soaring trade deficits, rising defense expenditures, and converging debt payments made for a bleak picture in any case.[128] The rising costs of bribes in silver to the tribes in Yemen and other war-related expenses exacerbated the chronic shortage of hard currency.[129] But the halt to US food aid at the beginning of 1965 made a bad situation potentially disastrous.

[125] Memcon between Kāmil and Rusk in Department of State to Cairo, no. 4008, January 12, 1965, *FRUS*, 1964–68, vol. 18, doc. 120; Ḥasan Ṣabrī al-Khūlī to Embassy Officer in Boswell (Cairo) to SecState, no. 2514, January 21, 1965, RG 59, CF 64–66, POL 1 UAR-US, NARA; Amb. Kāmil to Davies in Department of State to Cairo, no. 4477, January 31, 1965, in ibid.; Battle (Cairo) to SecState, no. 2671, February 1, 1965, in ibid.

[126] Recalls David Nes, US chargé d'affaires in Cairo during the Six-Day War: "it was very obvious when I got there in June of 1965 that the relationship was not good and was deteriorating." Transcript, David G. Nes, *Oral History Interview* no. 2, March 25, 1983, by Ted Gittinger, p. 3, LBJL. For a good overview of the fluctuations in US-Egyptian relations during this period, see Burns, *Economic Aid*, 163–73.

[127] See chapter five.

[128] Egypt's trade deficit reached a record E£175 million ($403 million, or almost 9 percent of GNP *excluding* arms imports) in 1964. IMF, *Balance of Payments Yearbook*, 1962–66. According to the best available estimates, defense expenditures grew from 7.1 percent of GNP in 1961–62 to 12.2 percent of GNP in 1964–65. Nadav Safran, *From War to War: The Arab-Israeli Confrontation, 1948–1967* (New York: Pegasus, 1969), 148. See chapter four.

[129] Sādāt, *al-Baḥth*, 212; Ḥadīdī, *Shāhid 'alā ḥarb al-Yaman*, 71–72; Naṣr, *Mudhakkirāt*, 3:199; Vered, *Revolution*, 168; Moshe Efrat, "The Ten-Year Program and Its Results" (Hebrew), in Shamir, *Decline of Nasserism*, 66–67. See also chapter five.

Since Egyptian trade agreements with Soviet bloc countries usually featured a structured surplus representing debt repayment,[130] the overall deficit was almost exclusively with the West. Nearly half of the perennial deficit was covered by revenues from the Suez Canal.[131] Much of the rest of the deficit represented PL 480 food purchases from the United States, hitherto paid for largely in Egyptian currency. The cutoff of aid meant not only that this food would have to be purchased elsewhere at market prices, but also that it would entail foreign currency expenditure on a massive scale.[132] To make matters worse, the crisis hit the economy just as the second Five Year Plan, upon which the regime's prestige-laden development goals were staked, was set to begin. With the old regime's $1 billion treasure chest of sterling long since exhausted, all that money had to come from abroad.[133]

Over the course of 1965–66, Egyptian officials scoured the globe in a frantic bid to obtain moratoria from government creditors and short-term loans to feed the government's hunger for hard currency.[134] They achieved mixed results. One of the main problems was that the suspension of US aid eroded global confidence in Egypt's creditworthiness. As a result the Egyptians were forced to accept short-term European bank credits "at interest rates that even the Khedive Ismail would have found immodest."[135] Even so, the government fell into arrears on a number of its debt accounts. The effect of this desperate maneuvering was to defer the ultimate reckoning by a couple of years and amplify its magnitude considerably.[136]

The severity of the situation from late 1964 onward thrust upon Nasser and his colleagues the unsustainable nature of their policies. To stave

[130] Robert Mabro, "Egypt's Economic Relations with the Socialist Countries," *World Development* 3, no. 5 (1975): 316. See also chapter four.

[131] Hansen and Nashashibi, *Foreign Trade*, 116.

[132] The two theoretical alternatives were to purchase food from alternate Western sources for cash or to negotiate barter agreements with Communist countries. But barter entailed diversion of Egyptian exports from the free market and therefore represented an opportunity cost in foreign currency of equal magnitude.

[133] Waterbury, *Egypt*, 95; Haykal, *al-Infijār*, 181. Nasser blamed the United States explicitly for Egypt's economic troubles in a particularly bitter speech on February 22, 1967.

[134] See, for instance, Airgram, Cairo to Dep. of State, no. A-500, December 11, 1965, "U.A.R. Faces Drastic Foreign Exchange Situation," in NSF, Files of Robert W. Komer, Box 52, File UAR (Economic) December 1963–March 1966, Part 3, LBJL.

[135] Hansen and Nashashibi, *Foreign Trade*, 108–9; Egyptian intelligence chief Ṣalāḥ Naṣr cites a figure of 12 percent in his *Mudhakkirāt*, 3:199.

[136] Hansen and Nashashibi, *Foreign Trade*, 120; Ikram, *Egypt*, 344; Waterbury, *Egypt*, 95.

off the looming threat of default, they desperately needed to restructure the external debt. To fund imports, they needed to raise money. And to diminish the drain of foreign currency, they had to reduce the defense burden. All of these endeavors would be aided greatly by the reduction of Egyptian commitments in Yemen. They would also be served by the resumption of US aid. Ultimately, none of this could be achieved without an accommodation with Faysal. In the meantime, it was time to press Egypt's Eastern allies for a dramatic increase in aid.[137]

[137] Michael N. Barnett, *Confronting the Costs of War: Military Power, State, and Society in Egypt and Israel* (Princeton, NJ: Princeton University Press, 1992), 99. In April 1965, it was announced that the planned duration of the Five Year Plan would be extended to seven years due to adverse economic circumstances (Waterbury, *Egypt*, 96).

✷ CHAPTER FOUR ✷

Guns for Cotton

THE UNRAVELING OF SOVIET-EGYPTIAN RELATIONS, 1964–66

THE DEPENDABLE IF CAPRICIOUS NATURE of Khrushchev's generosity must have eased the troubled minds of Egypt's leaders in the months leading up to October 1964. But then, in a flash, he was gone. With some justification, Haykal writes that "in few countries can the news of the Russian leader's fall have been received with greater shock than in Egypt."[1] A US intelligence source records the Egyptian president's panicked reaction to the news: Khrushchev's ouster, exclaimed Nasser, "is a catastrophe for us." Indeed, "[it] is worse than Suez." The Soviet leader had recently promised more arms and aid, but now "all is gone."[2]

Within weeks, Marshal ʻĀmir was on a plane for Moscow, ostensibly to attend the festivities surrounding the anniversary of the revolution but in reality to try and secure continuity of the Soviet commitment to Egypt. ʻĀmir, according to another US intelligence source, carried with him a brief, handwritten by Nasser, that contained instructions on how to reestablish the strategic basis of Soviet-Egyptian relations with the new leadership.[3] The first section outlined the common strategic goals of the two countries. Topping the list was the destruction of Anglo-American influence in the region, followed closely by the destruction of Israel (head of the "imperialist spear"), the destruction of foreign monopolies, support for newly liberated African and nonaligned countries

Parts of this chapter appeared in the author's "Guns for Cotton? Aid, Trade, and the Soviet Quest for Base Rights in Egypt, 1964–1966," *Journal of Cold War Studies* 13, no. 2 (2011): 4–38.

[1] Haykal, *Sphinx and Commissar*, 138; idem, *al-Infijār*, 70–78. For a Soviet perspective, see Brutents, *Tridtsat' let*, 277–78.

[2] CIA Intelligence Information Cable, "Nasser's Reaction to Khrushchev's Ouster," October 26, 1964, in NSF, Country File, United Arab Republic, Box 159/1, Folder: United Arab Republic, vol. 2, Cables [2 of 2], 6/64–12/64, LBJL.

[3] CIA Intelligence Information Cable, "Nasir's Brief for Amir for His Trip to Moscow," [date excised], in NSF, Country File, United Arab Republic, Box 159/1, Folder: United Arab Republic, vol. 2, Cables [2 of 2], 6/64–12/64, LBJL.

in escaping from under the thumb of imperialism, and the gradual conversion of the Arab regimes to socialism. In the second section, Nasser listed the conditions necessary to reach those goals. First, "the UAR must have an army equipped with strong weapons." Second, "the UAR must have help to create industries and to raise its standard of living ... [to serve as] a model socialist regime." Third, "the UAR must have economic help to remove its hard currency crisis ... [which was the] result of US-UK and other Western pressure on the UAR because of the latter's political standing in Africa and Asia; *because the UAR army in the Yemen[,] 'as agreed on'[,] is the only way to destroy US-UK influence in the Arab Peninsula* [emphasis added]; because the UAR sent troops to Algeria to back Ben Bella's socialist regime against imperialist tools; and because it sent troops to Iraq to save the Arif government from falling into the hands of the 'old regime.'"[4] The centrality of the Yemen campaign in Nasser's rationale for Soviet aid is a subject to which we shall have occasion to return.[5] Suffice it to say that Egyptian instincts concerning the likely effect of Khrushchev's removal on bilateral relations were not entirely misplaced. Although the geostrategic logic of the alliance seemed virtually immune to personality changes at the top, the inevitable nuances of emphasis and interpretation under any successor posed a credible threat to the continuation of Khrushchev's blank check policy.

One of the best Russian students of Soviet involvement in the Middle East concluded simply that after Khrushchev, "cooperation with Egypt remained the cornerstone of Soviet Middle Eastern policy."[6] Indeed, there is little evidence of a deliberate reformulation of Soviet policy toward the Middle East until the 1967 war forced Khrushchev's successors to rethink fundamentals.[7] But that is not to say that there was no change in Soviet policy between October 1964 and June 1967. Inertia carried Khrushchev's policies a certain distance forward. But absent Khrushchev's predilection for Arab affairs, Soviet policy toward the

[4] The cable itself notes the ambiguity of the phrase "as agreed on." It is unclear whether the agreement referred to is between the UAR and the YAR, or between the UAR and the USSR. But the context strongly suggests the latter.

[5] See also the comments of Egyptian ambassador to the Soviet Union on this subject (Ghālib, *Mudhakkirāt*, 114–15).

[6] Alexei Vassiliev, *Russian Policy in the Middle East: From Messianism to Pragmatism* (Reading: Ithaca, 1993), 63.

[7] Vassiliev goes further: "I am convinced that during the whole history of the Soviet state no general conception of Soviet policy in the Middle East ... has ever been formulated" (ibid., 223).

Middle East became increasingly responsive to institutional pressures from outside the Presidium, especially the military.[8]

Guns for Cotton

Although the tensions between Cairo and Washington made the vulnerability of US aid more obvious, the supply line from Moscow was in fact no less tenuous. The Egyptian army's dependence on arms supplies from the Soviet Union paralleled the economy's dependence on food supplies from the United States. Given the incompatibility of Egyptian and Western interests at this time, there simply were no real alternatives to Soviet weapons. And since the security of the regime hinged on the robustness—and quiescence—of the armed forces, the acquisition of arms became the main benefit associated with the Soviet relationship. Soviet aid, though generously disbursed under lenient terms, was not free. And herein lay the precariousness of Nasser's Cold War balancing act on the Soviet side. Like other aid recipients, Egypt eventually had to fund its purchases out of a scarce pool of exports, of which cotton was the single biggest item.[9] Yet the growth of cash-earning exports was vital to funding the import-substituting industrialization drive of the 1960s.[10] Had efforts to expand exports throughout this period succeeded, the mortgaging of a share of Egyptian exports to pay for the steady acquisition of weapons and other equipment might not have become a serious problem. In the event, exports stagnated while arms purchases spiked—in large measure due to the intervention in Yemen. Egyptian planners were thus forced to allocate a growing proportion of stagnating exports to the repayment of mounting debt to the Soviet bloc.

The deleterious dynamic at work in Soviet-Egyptian economic relations in the 1960s stemmed principally from the schedule of service on

[8] On the listlessness of Brezhnev's statecraft, see Georgi Arbatov, *The System: An Insider's Life in Soviet Politics* (New York: Times Books, 1992), 125–27; Odd Arne Westad, *The Global Cold War: Third World Interventions and the Making of Our Times* (Cambridge: Cambridge University Press, 2005), 169; Arkady Shevchenko, *Breaking with Moscow* (New York: Alfred A. Knopf, 1985), 130.

[9] Yaacov Ro'i and David Ronel, "The Soviet Economic Presence in Egypt and Its Political Implications," Soviet and East European Research Centre, Hebrew University of Jerusalem, Research Paper no. 9 (September 1974), 21–22.

[10] Waterbury, *Egypt*, 84, 90.

Egyptian debt. By the mid-1960s, many of the sizeable obligations incurred in the late 1950s were beginning to fall due. Due dates for old debt coincided unhappily with a spike in military debt payments after 1964 due to the escalating war effort in Yemen. The huge arms deal of June 1963 alone was valued at over $200 million. In the three years leading up to 1967, Egyptian debt to the USSR captured center stage in relations between the two countries, introducing new tensions into a relationship hitherto dominated by common interests and the illusion of stringless aid.[11]

The convergence of economic and military debt repayment schedules in the mid-1960s produced a crushing burden on Egypt's economy precisely at a time when US aid was grinding to a halt, pulling the carpet out from under the development plan, the supply of food to the populace, and the economy as a whole. The added burden of the war in Yemen accelerated Egypt's advance toward a day of reckoning, which was probably inevitable in any case.[12] By 1965 Egypt's annual payments to the USSR for both economic and military debt amounted to about $80 million, representing approximately 12 percent of Egypt's total annual foreign currency earnings at the time. This figure accounts for about 35 percent of Egypt's annual foreign debt service, which consumed almost a third of the country's hard currency earnings and was estimated in 1965 at $230–255 million—roughly 5 percent of GDP.[13] Not surprisingly, by the end of 1964, Egypt was falling significantly behind schedule in repayments to the USSR. In December 1964, Deputy Prime Minister for Economic Affairs Dr. ʿAbd al-Munʿim al-Qaysūnī traveled to Moscow to request deferment on some $47 million in debt service overdue to the Soviet Union. He was refused.[14]

[11] For a more complete discussion of Egypt's debt repayment schedule, see Ferris, "Guns for Cotton," 9–16.

[12] See chapter five.

[13] CIA, NIE no. 26.1-65, "Problems and Prospects for the United Arab Republic," March 31, 1965, 7, in NSF, National Intelligence Estimates, Box 6, File 36.1 UAR, LBJL. Total foreign debt by this point topped $2.5 billion, more than half of Egypt's GDP. CIA, NIE no. 26.1-65, "Deficit Financing of Economic Progress in Egypt," 38, 40, in NSF, National Intelligence Estimates, Box 6, File 36.1 UAR, LBJL.

[14] Tadeush Theodorovitch (Economist, Soviet Aid Mission, Cairo) to M.P.V. Hannam on January 5, 1965, in M.P.V. Hannam (Cairo) to R. T. Higgins, January 6, 1965, FO 371/183926, PRO. Ustinov mentioned a sum of 39 million rubles in his November 7 talks with ʿĀmir (Haykal, *al-Infijār*, 80).

The rising pressure of debt service to the USSR and other creditors in 1964–65, on top of Egypt's widening rift with the West, made the possibility of economic meltdown a frightening reality. Under these circumstances Egyptian dependency on Soviet aid rose dramatically. But Egypt's predicament posed a number of dilemmas for the Kremlin. The first concerned Soviet attitudes toward the crisis in US-Egyptian relations. The competition for influence with the United States should have led Soviet leaders to desire a diminution, or even a cessation, of American aid. However, economic considerations militated against this approach. For it was well understood that US assistance, being fungible like all foreign aid, made it possible for Nasser's regime to stay afloat and meet its repayment obligations to the USSR. In the absence of US aid, it was unlikely that the Soviets would be prepared to uphold Egypt's faltering economy on their own. Nor were they in a position to make up more than a fraction of the deficit in grain.[15] This is why, for all the public hostility toward the US presence in Egypt, Soviet policy makers privately wished to avoid a complete rupture between Nasser and the Americans.[16] Eventually, they faced a choice between easing Egypt's debt burden and risking default or, worse, the collapse of Nasser's regime.[17] A second dilemma Egypt's difficulties posed was whether or not to exploit them for Soviet advantage. In fact, Egypt's increasing economic difficulties opened up a rare opportunity for the Kremlin to advance a strategic agenda of growing urgency. However, that agenda was so sensitive that its very mention in Egypt's moment of weakness carried the risk of tearing apart the Soviet-Egyptian relationship.

The Soviet Quest for Base Rights in Egypt

At the same time as the Egyptian campaign in Yemen was heating up in the spring of 1963, a new threat to Soviet security materialized in the Mediterranean. In April the submarine-launched Polaris nuclear missile made its Middle Eastern debut on board the USS *Sam Houston*. With a range of 2,700 kilometers, Polaris (A-2 version) presented the industrial heartland of the Soviet Union with the unprecedented threat of

[15] Haykal, *al-Infijār*, 80; H.F.T. Smith, "Soviet Policy toward the U.A.R.," January 14, 1965, VG 103138/2, FO 371/183896, PRO.

[16] See, for instance, Kohler (Moscow) to SecState no. 3529, May 18, 1966, RG 59, Box 589, NARA.

[17] B. G. Cartledge (Moscow) to P. H. Laurence, March 5, 1965, FO 371/183896, PRO.

surprise attack from a mobile underwater platform. Whereas inbound hostile aircraft could be interdicted, incoming missiles were unstoppable once airborne. The threat was foreseeable by the late 1950s; by the early '60s, it was a reality.

By 1964, countering the threat of a first strike by Polaris submarines lurking in the Mediterranean had become a major obsession for Soviet defense planners. Given the difficulties of detection, let alone of preemption, from afar, the only hope of success was to deploy sea and air assets in forward positions, so as to track and destroy enemy submarines before they could launch.[18] As one former Soviet admiral explained, the conceptual solution entailed "the deployment of units of battle-ready naval forces in remote regions of the oceans and seas well in advance in order to employ them immediately with the onset of acts of war."[19] But the time-consuming limitations placed on naval transit through the Turkish Straits by the Montreux convention,[20] coupled with the limited range of land-based submarine-hunting aircraft, meant that any sustained Soviet deployment in the Mediterranean required air and sea bases in the eastern Mediterranean basin. Onshore facilities were necessary in order to service the crews, repair the ships, and provide air cover. Of the likely host countries, Turkey, Lebanon, Israel, and Libya were all out of the question on account of their political orientation. Of the two remaining littoral states, Syria and Egypt, the latter was preferable by virtue of its relative political stability and superior geographical position, straddling the Mediterranean and Red Seas. The sheer logic of the strategic proposition was undeniable. The only obstacle was political.

There are several indications that Egypt's attractiveness in theory was also translated into the praxis of Soviet diplomacy. One such indication is the extraordinary attention lavished on Egypt by the commander in chief of the Soviet navy prior to the Six-Day War. As one student of the subject has remarked: "In retrospect, [Admiral Sergei] Gorshkov's series of four visits to Egypt (1961, 1965, 1966, 1967) was

[18] I. M. Kapitanets, *Na sluzhbe okeanskomy flotu 1946–1992: Zapiski komanduiushchevo dvumia flotami* (Moscow: Andrevskii Flag, 2000), 12–13, 23, 111, 165–71, and passim.

[19] I. M. Kapitanets, *Bitva za Mirovoi okean v "kholodnoi" i budushchikh voinakh* (Moscow: Veche, 2002), 210–11. See also Michael McCGwire, "Turning Points in Soviet Naval Policy," in *Soviet Naval Developments: Capability and Context*, ed. Michael McCGwire (New York: Praeger, 1973), 203.

[20] Ferenc Vâli, *The Turkish Straits and NATO* (Stanford, CA: Hoover Institution Press, 1972), 116.

unparalleled. He had made one only one previous visit outside of the Soviet bloc, to Indonesia in October 1961. And, except for his visit to Ethiopia in January 1967, Egypt is the only foreign country which he is known to have visited from October 1961 until his April 1967 visit to Yugoslavia."[21] It is unlikely that Admiral Gorshkov, mastermind of the Soviet fleet's transformation into a blue-water navy, traveled to Egypt to see the pyramids four times in little more than five years.[22]

But there is also some evidence of a harder nature. The most forceful exponent of the thesis that Soviet naval interests drove Soviet-Egyptian relations is a former Egyptian naval officer, Commodore Mohrez Mahmoud El Hussini. According to El Hussini, the central theme of Soviet diplomacy in Egypt throughout the 1960s was the attempt to secure basing rights through a combination of military and financial incentives, political pressure, and efforts to foster a state of military dependency. What the Soviets strove to obtain was essentially what they got in the aftermath of the Six-Day War: permanent storage facilities for fuel and spare parts in Alexandria and Port Sa'īd; permission for regular access to Egyptian harbors with twenty-four-hour advance notice and no diplomatic approval procedure; constant availability of repair facilities for maintenance and refitting of Soviet vessels; permanent deployment of auxiliary ships to Alexandria for logistical support; and establishment of early warning systems, including aircraft, on Egyptian soil under Soviet command. Contrary to conventional wisdom, El Hussini argues that the need for basing rights was not the sudden and unexpected product of Arab-Israeli hostilities. Rather, it was a long-standing Soviet ambition, achieved incrementally between 1962 and 1967 by Soviet negotiators who exploited Egypt's growing dependence stemming from the war in Yemen, the looming economic crisis, and deteriorating relations with the West.[23]

[21] George S. Dragnich, *The Soviet Union's Quest for Access to Naval Facilities in Egypt Prior to the June War of 1967* (Arlington, VA: Center for Naval Analysis, 1974), 50; Mahr, *Die Rolle Ägyptens*, 274, 287.

[22] Adam Ulam, *Expansion and Coexistence: The History of Soviet Foreign Policy, 1917–1967* (New York: Praeger, 1968), 745. See also Alvin Z. Rubinstein, "The Middle East in Russia's Strategic Prism," in *Diplomacy in the Middle East*, ed. Brown, 84.

[23] Mohrez Mahmoud El Hussini, *Soviet-Egyptian Relations, 1945–85* (New York: St. Martin's Press, 1987), 120, 177–78, and passim. A similar assessment of Soviet requirements in the 1960s is made by Michael MccGwire, "The Structure of the Soviet Navy," in *Soviet Naval Developments*, ed. MccGwire, 165–70. For an insider's account of the Soviet quest for basing rights in the aftermath of the defeat, see Huwaydī, *Khamsūn 'āman*, 229–30.

Although the Soviet campaign for base rights emerged as a central theme in relations in the post-Khrushchev era, it apparently originated much earlier. El Hussini relates how, in 1957, Soviet negotiators exploited discussions concerning Egypt's naval wish list to push through a proposal to build versatile repair yards at Alexandria harbor. In the course of 1958–59, they reportedly made two appeals for access to sea and air facilities, both of which Nasser rejected.[24] Two years later, in December 1961, Admiral Gorshkov made his first two-week visit to Egypt. The trip almost certainly originated with the Soviet-Albanian rift and the resultant loss of the Soviet navy's only base in the Mediterranean at Valona (Vlorë).[25] It was also undoubtedly related to the Soviet decision of 1961 to move to a strategy of forward naval deployment.[26] Although implementation of that strategy would not become feasible until the mid-1960s, the search for forward bases was already underway.

For Egypt the Soviet objective was a nonstarter on purely political grounds. After all, Nasser had solidified his position with an agreement to end the British occupation of the Suez Canal Zone; he had led the battle against Western military pacts in the 1950s and continued to argue vociferously and uncompromisingly for the closure of foreign bases throughout the Middle East and Africa—in places such as Cyprus, Aden, Libya, and Saudi Arabia. For him to countenance a permanent Soviet military presence in Egypt would be to accept the Saudi accusation that he was no more than a Communist stooge. By replacing one foreign military occupation with another, he would be pulling the rug out from under the anti-imperialist crusade that underlay Egypt's popularity throughout the developing world. Egypt's claims to nonalignment would disappear overnight, and with them the prospects of aid

[24] El Hussini, *Soviet-Egyptian Relations*, 75–76, 87, 93–94. These dates coincide with the landmark Soviet decision to interrupt the twenty-year postwar shipbuilding program and build a submarine fleet. Given the long lead times involved in developing and deploying naval platforms on the one hand (typically a decade from concept to production in the case of Soviet submarines) and the diplomatic difficulties associated with obtaining basing rights on the other, a foreign policy perfectly harmonized with a state's strategic objectives would set about obtaining them several years in advance of the planned date of use. See Franklyn Griffiths, "Forward Deployment and Foreign Policy," in *Soviet Naval Developments*, ed. MccGwire, 10.

[25] Dragnich, *Quest*, 17–20; Cairo (Chancery) to NEA Dept. 1031/61, January 1, 1962, "Visit of C. in C. of Soviet Fleet to the U.A.R.: Possible Soviet use of U.A.R. submarine facilities," FO 371/165356, PRO.

[26] Michael MccGwire, "Current Soviet Warship Construction," in *Soviet Naval Developments*, ed. MccGwire, 136.

from the United States. The delicate balance between East and West, upon which Egyptian foreign policy had stood since Nasser came to power, would collapse.

The naval question came to the fore almost immediately following Khrushchev's ouster, and continued to dominate the back rooms of Soviet-Egyptian relations for the better part of a decade thereafter. We can speculate that Khrushchev's personal investment in Egypt made significant political pressure from the Kremlin on the base issue inconceivable as long as he was in power. There is also the fact that the Polaris threat only became serious in the mid- to late 1960s. In any event, Soviet ambitions in this regard surfaced in the winter of 1964. A new, or at least newly overt, link emerged between Soviet aid and Egyptian defense needs in the post-Khrushchev era, exposing the hitherto absent linkage between foreign aid and political influence, so often touted by Soviets and Arabs alike as the principal advantage of Soviet over American aid.

Since trade negotiators were compartmentalized from military questions in the Soviet trade system, linkage between economic aid and security issues could only be made at the highest levels of government. However, lower-level military officials could conceivably pursue linkages between issues lying within the military sphere. This is how the story of overt Soviet pressure on the base question—a rare instance of documented linkage in the history of Soviet foreign policy—began.[27] When Marshal 'Āmir traveled to Moscow in November 1964 to attend the anniversary of the Bolshevik Revolution and sniff out the new leadership, he brought with him a long list of naval desiderata, geared to defending Egypt against the US Sixth Fleet. Negotiations continued in greater depth between Egyptian Admiral 'Izzat and Soviet Admiral Gromov in Alexandria in December, where, for the first time, the Soviets conditioned further aid on Soviet-Egyptian strategic cooperation. El Hussini translates from the meeting minutes of December 2, 1964: "In the event of the continuation of good relations between the two countries, full cooperation between the Egyptian C-in-C and the Soviet C-in-C, and a mutual understanding on the subject of full cooperation between the two navies in event of crisis, Egypt could rely on the USSR in building up a strong and efficient navy." Gromov then went on

[27] Cf. Randall Stone, *Satellites and Commissars: Strategy and Conflict in the Politics of Soviet-Bloc Trade* (Princeton, NJ: Princeton University Press, 1996), 63, 72–73, 90–91.

to list specific requests pertaining to the upgrade of facilities at Alexandria, the creation of new units and training of new cadres, the desirability of an Egyptian naval call on the port of Odessa, and the need for further negotiations between Admirals 'Izzat and Gorshkov in the USSR. Apparently, Marshal 'Āmir shot down these proposals, with the result that Egypt's naval requests remained unfulfilled for several months.[28]

However, the issue was of such importance to the Soviet military that Admiral Gorshkov got involved personally, making his second ten-day visit to Egypt in mid-March 1965. Although Gorshkov offered Egypt a generous package of new weaponry in exchange for accepting the Soviet conditions, his visit ended without a breakthrough.[29] Perhaps hinting at Nasser's steadfastness in an article the following month, *al-Ahrām* editor Muḥammad Haykal wrote: "The man [Politburo member Alexander Shelepin] and his great country are shrewder and smarter than [to engage in] maneuvers of imposing conditions, and clearly understand that Cairo's acceptance of any political conditions means—in truth and fact—Cairo's [unilateral] disarmament. *He who disarms vis-à-vis one party disarms vis-à-vis all parties, relinquishing all sources of his strength.*"[30] Egypt's rhetorical resolve, however, was beginning to crumble under the weight of economic reality.

From Jiddah to Moscow

In the summer of 1965, at that pivotal moment in US-Egyptian relations, and in Egypt's policy toward the Arabian Peninsula, debt service on Soviet aid had reached a critical point. The future of his army in Yemen was certainly on Nasser's mind as he proceeded to Moscow on August 27, 1965, just three days after the conclusion of the Jiddah summit with King Faysal; debt relief was most certainly another. Nasser must have realized he could no longer expect to get something for nothing.

[28] El Hussini, *Soviet-Egyptian Relations*, 143–45.

[29] Ibid., 148.

[30] "Shīlībīn wa-Burqībah," *al-Ahrām*, April 23, 1965. The quote refers specifically to rumors that Shelepin had pressured Nasser into inviting Walter Ulbricht to Egypt during his visit of December 1964, but was probably a camouflaged signal to the Soviets to back off on the naval issue as well.

Egypt's deepening economic problems and diminishing pool of foreign donors meant that concessions were necessary. The fitting and immediate prelude to his visit was the dramatized diversion of 100,000 tons of Odessa-bound Australian wheat to Alexandria on June 25, 1965[31]—and the far less publicized visit of a Soviet cruiser, two submarines, and a tanker to the distant Egyptian port of Sallūm on the Libyan border one week later.[32] Although Nasser devised the Soviet rescue act as a signal to the Americans that he had other options—the contemporaneous US decision to release some 400,000 tons of wheat suspended since the beginning of the year met with a "stony silence" in Cairo[33]—it was clear to all concerned that in the long run there was no Soviet substitute for US wheat. The Soviets, to be sure, were only too happy to jump into the fray and score points against the United States, but they stressed that this was a one-off deal and a last resort; the Soviet Union itself, after all, had become a net importer of grain in recent years.[34] Moreover, even for staging this small charade, they apparently claimed their price. Official protestations to the contrary notwithstanding, Egypt's leaders were beginning to lose their freedom of action in the international arena as a result of their country's political and economic woes. As Egypt drifted further into isolation and crisis, the stringlessness of foreign aid was fast being unmasked as a fiction in both its Western and Eastern guises, with consequences that would prove anything but pleasant.

At the time, little emerged from behind the closed doors of the Kremlin. More than a decade later, Sadat revealed something about the context surrounding Nasser's mysterious trip and its surprising results:

> In 1965 the domestic situation of the country reached a deplorable stage (*marḥalah yurthā lahā*) ... In the same year Johnson cut off Ameri-

[31] *Al-Ahrām*, June 26, 1965, 1. This was a first installment of 300,000 tons of wheat Kosygin promised to Nasser in June as a stopgap solution for the shortage produced by the American suspension of aid. Apparently, the Egyptians were to pay for the wheat in cotton and rice over two years. CIA, Intelligence Brief, "Soviet Wheat for the UAR," July 1965, in NSF, Files of Robert W. Komer, Box 52, File UAR (Economic) December 1963–March 1966, Part 3, LBJL; Airgram, Cairo to Dep. of State, no. A-439, November 25, 1965, "Discussion of UAR's Current Economic Situation," p. 4, in ibid.; Cairo to SecState no. 422, August 7, 1965, RG 59, Box 2762, NARA; Battle (Cairo) to SecState no. 4521, June 24, 1965, RG 59, Box 589, NARA; Haykal, *al-Infijār*, 181–82; Ghālib, *Mudhakkirāt*, 118.

[32] El Hussini, *Soviet-Egyptian Relations*, 149–50.

[33] Burns, *Economic Aid*, 165.

[34] Haykal, *al-Infijār*, 182.

> can aid to Egypt, and placed us in a critical position. Our plans were thereby jeopardized as we were reliant on America for the wheat we used to import from her in Egyptian pounds, which spared us about £80 million, which we used for our projects. Faced with the cutoff of American aid we found no option but to resort to the Soviet Union, and so we went to Moscow in September 1965.... *Our goal in visiting Moscow was to persuade the Soviets to postpone the installments we owed [on our debt] to enable us with the available funds to compensate for the cutoff of American aid to us* and also to complete our ambitious plans. In fact, the Soviets responded to our requests in a manner we had not anticipated. *Our debt amounted to £400 million—and they decided to forgive half of it*, so that what remained was a debt of only £200 million. As a result, the installments naturally fell.[35] (Emphases added)

Besides shedding light on the particular circumstances surrounding Nasser's trip to Moscow, Sadat's account reveals that in the summer of 1965 the Soviet leadership forgave one-half of Egypt's $1 billion debt to the USSR. To understand the magnitude of this gesture, consider that $1 billion in twelve-year debt translates into an average of more than $80 million (excluding interest) in annual installments—equal to about 10 percent of Egypt's total annual foreign currency earnings at the time. As a result of the cancelation, installments (again, excluding interest) fell to around $40 million annually. This sum was still far from insignificant but represented a return to the acceptable levels of the early 1960s. On the face of it, this impressive show of generosity appears to trash the theory of an October 1964 watershed neatly dividing Khrushchevian largesse from Brezhnevite parsimony.[36] And yet Brezhnev *was* no Khrushchev. To believe that the new hard-bargaining leadership in the

[35] Sādāt, *al-Baḥth*, 213–14. Nasser alluded cryptically to this agreement in a public speech almost three months later: "I say, without need to go into details, that our talks resulted ... in an understanding that saves the Egyptian people no less that two hundred million pounds (*tafāhum yuwaffiru 'alā al-sha'b al-miṣrī mā lā yaqillu 'an mi'atay miliyūn junayh*." Nasser speech, November 25, 1965, in UAR, *Majmū'at khuṭab*, vol. 5, 466. Further clues came in an article by Haykal in *al-Ahrām*, December 31, 1965. The *New York Times* reported a consensus among Western observers in Cairo that the Egyptians had indeed obtained a sizable reduction in their military debt. "Soviets Said to Ease Cairo's Arms Debt," *New York Times*, Decemer 30, 1965, 5.

[36] See, e.g., Elizabeth Valkenier, *The Soviet Union and the Third World: An Economic Bind* (New York: Praeger, 1983), 11–15; Carol Saivetz and Sylvia Woodby, *Soviet-Third World Relations* (Boulder, CO: Westview Press, 1985), 45–46; Dannehl, *Soviet Economic Aid*, 35. See also Anderson, *Public Politics*, 147–65.

Kremlin cut Egyptian debt in half without obtaining anything in return stretches credibility. Sadat's account is incomplete.

The second link in the chain of evidence exposing what transpired in Moscow is provided by Muḥammad Haykal. Like Sadat, Haykal says nothing about Egyptian concessions, but he does shed some light on the roots of Soviet beneficence. According to Haykal, the debt forgiven in Moscow was military, and much of it resulted from the continued fighting in Yemen.[37] While this is no doubt true, his explanation, according to which this extraordinary act of Soviet munificence was due solely to Nasser's ability to convince his interlocutors that the war in Yemen should be seen as an anti-imperialist campaign on behalf of a national liberation movement, seems, on the face of it, ludicrous. The war, as we know, was perceived as such in Moscow from the very beginning, which is why the Soviets had supported the Egyptian intervention so eagerly in the first place.

Still, Haykal's account contains a kernel of truth. For one, the leadership in the Kremlin had changed. While attributions of Khrushchev's ouster to his largesse abroad are certainly overblown, there was considerable criticism of the excesses of his foreign aid program, with both Cuba and Egypt cited as salient examples by his critics.[38] More generally, by 1965 the initial wave of Soviet enthusiasm for involvement in Third World revolutions had died down, under the cumulative impact of a row of spectacular failures beginning with China and ending in Congo.[39] In the Far East, the confrontation with the United States over Vietnam highlighted the dangers of excessive involvement, while in the Near East, the ouster of Ahmed Ben Bella in Algeria demonstrated the unpredictability of Soviet allies in the Third World. Within months, the fall of Kwame Nkrumah in Ghana and Sukarno in Indonesia would reinforce Soviet wariness of radical nationalists. In light of this, it is not implausible that Leonid Brezhnev and Aleksei Kosygin needed some convincing of the wisdom of continued support for a Vietnam-like situation that threatened to spiral out of control with little tangible benefit. More

[37] Haykal, *Sphinx and Commissar*, 146–47. A later version of the same episode refers merely to Soviet recognition of the burden Egypt shouldered in support of "the national liberation movement." This version also lists the amount of debt forgiven as 500 million *rubles*, which is almost certainly an error arising from confusion about the exchange rate of the ruble in 1965. Haykal, *al-Infijār*, 94.

[38] See, e.g., Ghālib, *Mudhakkirāt*, 82.

[39] Westad, *Global Cold War*, 167–69.

prosaically, it is likely that Khrushchev's successors had at best a dim awareness of events on the Arabian Peninsula and required some education on the matter if they were to continue shouldering the burden.

As we have seen, Yemen featured prominently in 'Āmir's efforts to justify continued aid to Egypt in his talks with the new leadership in the immediate aftermath of Khrushchev's ouster. Indeed, the military campaign had served as his chief justification for requesting debt deferral. At the time, Dimitri Ustinov had reportedly promised 'Āmir that he and his colleagues were "studying postponing the dates of settlement, based on your request, on account of the burden of Yemen," while Kosygin had voiced his appreciation for Egyptian national liberation movements, saying: "we know what you are doing in Yemen and Aden and Cyprus and Africa."[40] Yet when Minister Qaysūnī visited Moscow in December 1964 to follow up on 'Āmir's talks from the previous month, nothing had come of it. Nine months later, it must have been anything but evident to Egyptian policy makers that Soviet support would continue undiminished.

A hint as to which way the wind was blowing in Moscow was provided a week after the summit in a rare article on Yemen in the Soviet weekly journal of international affairs, *Novoe Vremia*.[41] In it the author traced the history of the civil war and the factors leading to the recent conclusion of the Jiddah Agreement. He argued that the United States and the United Kingdom were colluding "to get the U.A.R. bogged down in a lengthy conflict over the Yemen and thus prevent it from tackling its socio-economic problems." Indeed, they were eager to foment all-out war between Egypt and Saudi Arabia. Accordingly, it behooved those opposing the imperialists to frustrate their designs and root for peace in alignment with the interests of the "broad masses" of Yemen. A further indication that Soviet policy on Yemen had shifted in 1965 is betrayed by Nasser's tight summer schedule. The timing of his visit to Moscow, sandwiched between the Saudi-Egyptian summit days earlier and the pan-Arab summit in Morocco two weeks later, suggests not only that Nasser desperately wanted to reach the Arab summit with an agreement on Yemen in the bag, but that he was eager to demonstrate reduced commitments in Moscow as well. Why would Nasser be in

[40] Haykal, *al-Infijār*, 80, 82.

[41] F. Seiful-Mulyukov, "Yemen: Between War and Peace," *New Times*, no. 36, September 8, 1965, 10–12.

such a rush to ink a peace deal on Yemen if Brezhnev and Kosygin were as enthusiastic about the war as Khrushchev had once been?[42]

Moreover, as must have been clear to both sides, the initial Soviet commitment to support the intervention had been overtaken by events on the battlefield. Given that the original agreement between the two governments concerning the costs of intervention in Yemen pertained only to the initial influx of forces, it is quite possible that the subsequent costs of expanding the campaign in 1963, 1964, and 1965 were borne (in the form of debt) by the Egyptians. It should be recalled that a campaign of three brigades in November 1962 had morphed into a four-*division* affair by the summer of 1965.[43] It is doubtful whether the cost of equipment used over two and a half years in Yemen would have amounted to $500 million, but a substantial fraction of that figure is plausible.[44] This was no small sum in either Soviet or Egyptian terms. A key item on the agenda must have been the status of this debt and limitations on the accumulation of future debt. In this context, even though the assignation of "Yemen debt" to that particular half of Egypt's total military debt forgiven by the USSR in September 1965 may have been arbitrary, it was a significant statement of policy. The Soviet leadership, by appearing to buy Nasser's argument about the justness and utility of

[42] Aḥmad, *al-Dawr*, 330, 391; Ḥamrūsh, *Qiṣṣat thawrat 23 yūliyū*, 3:250–51. Faysal adviser Rashād Fir'awn recalled that Nasser's urgent appeal to Faysal to hold a summit in August mentioned specifically his desire to reach an agreement before his trip to Moscow. But he concluded conspiratorially that the talks in Jiddah had been a successful ruse on Nasser's part, which had enabled him to confront the bellicose Soviets with imminent withdrawal unless they bankrolled Egypt's continued occupation of Yemen. Memcon, Fir'awn, Dinsmore, and Seelye, Riyadh, January 7, 1966, p. 4, in Airgram, Jiddah to State, no. A-209, January 10, 1966, 3–6, RG 59, CF, 1964–66, Box 3028, POL 27 YEMEN, NARA. For the Soviet ambassador to Yemen's expression of support for the peace process, see Airgram, Ta'izz to State, no. A-120, October 16, 1965, p. 1, RG 59, CF, 1964–66, Box 3027, POL 27 YEMEN, NARA.

[43] IDF General Staff, Intelligence Division,"Special Intelligence Survey 39/62: Assessment of the Financial Burden Imposed on Egypt as a Result of Its Military Intervention in Yemen" (Hebrew), SD 586.150.1/M (?), November 20, 1962, HZ 3449/28, Part 2, ISA; Aḥmad, *Dhikrayāt*, 288.

[44] For discussion of the cost of the war, see chapter six. The Egyptian historian Maḥmūd Aḥmad cites a Soviet "discount" of more than E£250 million ($575 million) on the price of arms and equipment used in Yemen, but does not mention where and when the concession was granted (*Dhikrayāt*, 509). Elsewhere, he cites a precise figure of E£254 million (approx. $585 million) in forgiven Soviet debt, which was "sufficient" to cover the expense of arms, equipment, and ammunition consumed or destroyed in the war (*Dhikrayāt*, 609, 649). See also Safran, *Saudi Arabia*, 120.

the war in Yemen, was in fact endorsing, however reluctantly, the continued prosecution of the war effort. They undoubtedly understood this and probably prevailed upon Nasser to cut his expenditure in Yemen henceforth.

One perhaps unintended consequence of Soviet generosity was to undermine the economic rationale for ending the war within weeks of the landmark accord with King Faysal.[45] Although the Jiddah Agreement ultimately foundered, as we shall see, on its own ambiguity, on continuing distrust between Nasser and Faysal, and on the autonomy of local leaders in Yemen, the lifeline thrown to Nasser in Moscow cannot have strengthened his determination to end the campaign, regardless of the consequences. Coming as it did on the heels of Soviet promises of 300,000 tons of emergency wheat supplies in June, the belated US agreement to release a similar amount of wheat under the 1962 agreement and the success of Egyptian officials in obtaining a further 400,000 tons of wheat from Mexico on tolerable terms—all of which granted the Egyptian bread industry almost a year-long lease on life[46]—the debt relief renewed Nasser's freedom of action considerably. Still the question remains: were Brezhnev and Kosygin responding merely to Nasser's sweet talk?[47]

Nasser went to Moscow determined to maximize Soviet economic and military aid to Egypt without compromising Egyptian sovereignty. What was said publicly about the summit yields no insights. As the joint communiqué issued at the end of the visit indicates, one important concession extracted by the hosts, at little cost to their guests, was an Egyptian declaration of support for Soviet participation at the postponed Afro-Asian Conference in Algeria.[48] This was no doubt part of the price Nasser had to pay for Soviet forgiveness. But still heavier issues

[45] See chapter six.

[46] Zayn al-Dīn Shukrī, "Taḥqīq kāmil ʿan raghīf al-ʿīsh . . . wa-maʿrakat al-qamḥ," *Akhbār al-Yawm*, July 3, 1965, 3; ʿAlī al-Maghribī, "ʿIndanā qamḥ wa-dhurrah yakfīnā 11 shahran," *Akhbār al-Yawm*, July 24, 1965, 9.

[47] Haykal quotes Maḥmūd Fawzi remarking on the plane ride home that the Soviets were entering a phase in which considerations of cost would influence policy to a much greater extent than they had under Khrushchev. The comment makes no sense in the context of selfless generosity Haykal describes (Haykal, *al-Infijār*, 95).

[48] "Joint Communiqué on the Talks between the Soviet Union and the United Arab Republic," in Harrison (Moscow) to Foreign Office, no. 45 Confidential, September 10, 1965, FO 371/183896, PRO; "Sovmestnoe Kommiunike . . ." *Pravda*, September 2, 1965, 1. It is plausible that Nasser had been flirting with the Chinese in order to build up leverage over the Soviets. See below.

were afoot. Once again, El Hussini provides the missing link. At the summit, he reports, hard bargaining took place, in the course of which Nasser rejected a generous Soviet offer to provide cruisers in exchange for semimonthly reconnaissance missions by Soviet aircraft based in Egypt. But while he stood firm on any overt infringement of Egyptian sovereignty, Nasser did apparently compromise on the naval issue, in a way that enabled the Soviets to tighten their naval relationship with Egypt without the Egyptians giving ground on the question of regular access to facilities. It is very likely that Nasser agreed in Moscow to permit three naval visits per year to the lesser ports of Sallūm and Sa'īd. As a result, Soviet naval contingents called without publicity at Port Sallūm for the second time that year in September 1965, and at Port Sa'īd in November of that year.[49] Although the Soviets could not have been thrilled with this result (and were as a consequence less than forthcoming on Egyptian arms requests), the arrangement nevertheless constituted the first real breakthrough in their dealings with the stubborn Egyptians. The institutionalization of naval visits to Egyptian ports must have been a crucial factor both in the Soviets' agreement to waive half of Egypt's debt and in their decision to fulfill some of 'Āmir's arms requests from the previous November.[50]

The circle of linkage was now complete. Khrushchev's enthusiastic, no-strings-attached endorsement had enabled the Egyptian campaign in Yemen in the first place. However, the subsequent expansion of the campaign tethered Egypt militarily to the USSR and severed the aid bond with the United States. Three years later, with Egypt's economy in disarray and its sources of foreign aid dwindling by the day, the war became the source of leverage for a new Soviet government desperate for strategic gains. Although Nasser's concessions constituted the beginning of a slippery slope to loss of sovereignty, the gravity of Egypt's position was not yet apparent. For the price paid in Moscow was still

[49] El Hussini, *Soviet-Egyptian Relations*, 160–61. Former Egyptian minister of war, Shams Badrān, later referred to the Soviet demand for aerial headquarters in Alexandria, to which he submitted during his visit to Moscow in May 1967, as an "old demand." Shams Badrān, "U'linu mas'ūliyyatī al-kāmilah 'ammā yusammā . . . bi-l-ta'dhīb!," *al-Ḥawādith*, September 2, 1977.

[50] $100 million was the amount Nasser cited in his report to the Arab leaders at Casablanca several weeks later. But it is doubtful the Soviets agreed to fulfill 'Āmir's lengthy ("heavy" was the term Ustinov used) wishlist. Riyāḍ, *Mudhakkirāt*, 2:308; Haykal, *al-Infijār*, 80–81, 94.

miniscule in comparison with the magnitude of the benefit, and Cairo still seemed very much in control of the relationship.

Egypt's deepening economic crisis—and narrowing diplomatic options—called for resourceful leadership. Nasser proved equal to the challenge. In fact, his apparent triumph in Moscow was merely the crowning act in a series of dazzling displays of Cold War virtuosity performed over the spring of 1965.

In the Cracks of Cold War Geology

The Sino-Soviet rift was the first of several Cold War fault lines the Egyptians exploited in 1965. Throughout the year-long buildup to the Afro-Asian Conference, originally scheduled to be held in Algiers in March 1965, the Egyptians had refused to lend their weight to the Soviet position in the global tug of war then raging between the Soviet and Chinese foreign policy establishments over the question of Soviet participation.[51] Nasser's masterful exploitation of the Sino-Soviet split in 1964–65 came to an end, as we have seen, in Moscow—but not before he succeeded in prying an unprecedented loan of $80 million from the usually tightfisted Chinese, along with promises of desperately needed wheat and corn.[52]

The second Cold War deposit the Egyptians mined in 1965 lay in divided Germany. Sprinting to the head of the pack of "canny nonaligned leaders" who exploited the keen competition between Bonn and Berlin for foreign recognition in order to obtain material benefit, Nasser struck a body blow at the sacred cow of West German diplomacy, the Hallstein Doctrine.[53] Named after Walter Hallstein, the doctrine held that West Germany would not maintain diplomatic relations with any state that recognized East Germany. Up to that point West Germany had successfully outbid its rival for influence in the Arab world. Encouraged by the

[51] Haykal points to Egypt's principled support for the Chinese position as a major source of Soviet irritation. However, in his account of the summit in Moscow, he neglects to mention Nasser's capitulation on this point. Haykal, *Sphinx and Commissar*, 143–47, 150–51.

[52] Goldman, *Soviet Foreign Aid*, 79; Waterbury, *Egypt*, 97; Karen Dawisha, *Soviet Foreign Policy towards Egypt* (London and Basingstoke: Macmillan, 1979), 35.

[53] William Glenn Gray, *Germany's Cold War: The Global Campaign to Isolate East Germany, 1949–1969* (Chapel Hill: University of North Carolina Press, 2003), 4, 171–82.

United States, West Germany had showered aid upon Egypt in the late 1950s and early '60s—in amounts that poor East Germany could hardly hope to match. Paradoxically, both the threat of sanctions from Bonn and the need to keep the East German option open as a source of leverage over the West prevented Nasser from considering recognition of the German Democratic Republic (GDR) until 1965.[54] But disclosures about a West German tank deal with Israel, coming as they did at a time of conflict with the United States and economic crisis at home, created a unique opportunity to milk the German issue for all it was worth.[55]

On January 24, 1965, Egyptian newspapers announced that the Egyptian government had issued a formal invitation to first secretary of the Communist Party of the GDR, Walter Ulbricht, to visit Egypt the following month. In the circumstances of the time, this was a diplomatic earthquake, with consequences extending far beyond Cairo.[56] Ulbricht arrived on February 24 and was received with great fanfare. As a reward for this spectacle—and the promise to open consulates in East Berlin—Nasser squeezed more than $100 million in government and commercial credits from the GDR at a time when a slowing West German economy was tying the hands of aid officials in Bonn.[57] By handing the GDR its "greatest foreign policy victory since 1949"[58]—and for West Germany, its greatest defeat—Nasser struck a diplomatic coup of the first order. Not only did he expose, in brazen fashion, the hollowness of the Hallstein Doctrine, he also succeeded in forcing the West German government to capitulate ignominiously and cancel its arms deal with Israel while rallying most of the Arab states around Egypt's leadership on the most politically correct issue of all.[59] Finally, when the West Germans retaliated by establishing diplomatic relations with Israel in May, Nasser gave them a dose of their own medicine, persuading ten Arab states to sever relations with Bonn. It was a fine performance indeed.

[54] Gray, *Germany's Cold War*, 92–93, 129, 166–67.

[55] George Lavy, *Germany and Israel: Moral Debt and National Interest* (London: Frank Cass, 1996), 99–100. Note Nasser's claim to the West German ambassador, Georg Federer, in response to the threat of a cutoff of German aid: "We did not get aid from you or anyone else. You participated in industrial projects and we paid most of it at six percent interest. That is not aid!" For a different perspective on this episode, see Haykal, *al-Infijār*, 137–45.

[56] Rainer A. Blasius, "'Völkerfreundschaft' am Nil: Ägypten und die DDR im Februar 1965," *Vierteljahrshefte für Zeitgeschichte* 46, no. 4 (1998), 747–805.

[57] Ibid., 756; Goldman, *Soviet Foreign Aid*, 79; Gray, *Germany's Cold War*, 179–80.

[58] Gray, *Germany's Cold War*, 175.

[59] Riyāḍ, *Mudhakkirāt*, 2:298.

Thus as he reflected on the last six months of feverish diplomacy on his way home from Moscow, Nasser had reason to be content. He had successfully staved off economic disaster through a series of shrewd maneuvers that brought Egypt desperately needed aid and reduced its burden of debt. If the limited resumption of US wheat sales announced in July could be turned into a revivification of the PL 480 program, there was hope yet for avoiding Egypt's day of reckoning. Within weeks Nasser would exploit yet another of the fault lines of Cold War geopolitics, seizing the opportunity offered by Gaullist France to divide and conquer. In October 1965, letting Suez bygones be bygones, Marshall 'Āmir flew to Paris with an olive branch in hand. He returned with a package amounting to $50 million worth of development credits and wheat supplies.[60]

But there was hardly room for complacency. Debt to the USSR comprised only one piece, albeit a significant one, of a much larger picture of Egyptian obligations in which impatient Western creditors, both banks and governments, figured prominently. And if the Americans should decide to terminate their aid program, continued foreign financing on the scale needed to purchase wheat elsewhere was doubtful. In the event, the breakthroughs of the summer of 1965 provided but a temporary respite for Egypt. Within months the crisis would reach the boiling point once again.

There was only so far a developing country could get by exploiting the lesser fractures of the Cold War. Many of Nasser's antics actually reduced his range of maneuver on the global scene. The severance of relations with West Germany cut off an important source of aid, which the East Germans could not, in the long run, replace. Nor must Nasser's perfidy have sat well with the Chinese, who, in any case, stood on the verge of civil war and sharply reduced commitments abroad. Similarly, the break in relations with the United Kingdom in December—ostensibly over the unilateral declaration of independence by Ian Smith's government in Rhodesia, but in all likelihood intended, like the break with West Germany, as an indirect warning to the United States—deprived Egypt of any vestiges of goodwill by one of its most formidable adversaries in the region. Above all, the persistent inability to repair relations with the United States made disaster all but inevitable. Nasser's performance in 1965 was like a final burst of fireworks before the onset of a long night. With each flourish, Nasser gained short-term mileage at

[60] Haykal, *al-Infijār*, 292–99.

home, in the region, and in the nonaligned movement, but isolated himself still further on the broader international scene. And it was in that broader sphere that the keys to Egypt's financial security lay.

The Final Unraveling

The beginning of 1966 brought mixed news to Cairo. In January, American and Egyptian negotiators concluded a modest $55 million PL 480 food deal that postponed the possibility of famine in Egypt—and the explosion of US-Egyptian relations—by another six months. In February, the British government declared its intent to withdraw its forces from Aden by 1968, thereby handing Egyptian propagandists their greatest victory since the fall of Qāsim. But there were troubles on the horizon. The Jiddah understandings with King Faysal were being increasingly undermined by arguments about implementation and by the squabbles among the warring factions in Yemen.[61] Faysal's visits to Iran in December and Jordan in January, his calls for an "Islamic Conference," which sounded like a substitute for pan-Arabism under Egyptian leadership, and his conclusion of massive arms deals with the United States and the United Kingdom at the beginning of the year extinguished the faith rekindled at Jiddah. Nkrumah's ouster in February, and that of Sukarno the following month, removed two of Nasser's remaining allies in the nonaligned movement and sent a warning to Cairo. Finally, the installation of a new and radical regime in Syria in February brought a new element of unpredictability into the regional equation. From Nasser's vantage point, above all these hazardous developments hung the specter of CIA conspiracy and the uncertainty of US aid.[62] With Egypt's balance of payments situation worse than ever, an air of dangerous unpredictability set in.

This atmosphere of dramatic tension set the stage for Kosygin's first official trip outside the Communist bloc, to Cairo in May. The high-profile visit, from May 10 to 18, constituted the main event of 1966 in Soviet-Egyptian relations, and it set the tone for many subsequent developments in the region. Like many of the key events in Soviet-Egyptian relations from this period, here too a tight blanket of secrecy has prevented the leakage of anything but fragmentary information on what

[61] See chapter six.

[62] Battle (Cairo) to SecState, no. 1895, October 11, 1966, RG 59, CF, Box 589, NARA.

transpired between Kosygin and Nasser.[63] Haykal lists three unsurprising issues raised by the Egyptian president in the course of the summit: first, Nasser made a request for more arms; second, he sought postponement of Egyptian debt payments; and third, he asked for wheat—an issue of great concern, coming as it did on the eve of the American decision to withhold further aid from Egypt and the near exhaustion of Egyptian reserves.[64] The conventional interpretation, largely based on Haykal's original narrative of the summit, has it that Nasser got nothing out of Kosygin.[65] The truth is more complicated. Here again, there can be little doubt that the base issue formed a central part of the discussions. For Kosygin did not come alone. Besides Foreign Minister Gromyko, Minister of Power and Electrification Pyotr Neporozhny, and Chairman of the State Committee for Foreign Economic Relations Sergei Skachkov, the delegation included one other high-profile individual who stood out in this cast of political leaders: Admiral Gorshkov, commander in chief of the Soviet navy.[66]

The context of Gorshkov's third visit to Egypt was once again telling. In December 1965, Grechko, then commander in chief of the Warsaw Pact and deputy minister of defense, had traveled to Egypt at the head of a huge military delegation that included Admiral Nikolai Sergeiev, chief of staff of the Soviet navy. According to the rumor mill, Grechko, whose grand tour of Egypt included suspicious requests to visit Marsā Maṭrūḥ (the Greco-Roman Paraetonium), a port on the Mediterranean west of Alexandria, and Ra's Banās, a peninsula on the southern coast of the Red Sea featuring an ancient harbor (the Ptolemaic Berenice) and an adjacent air base, proposed a large package of economic aid in exchange for the construction of bases for wartime use by the Soviet military.[67] In February 1966, Admiral Sulaymān 'Izzat traveled to the USSR, probably to follow up on Grechko's visit in December. His trip ended with an agreement on three annual Soviet naval visits to Egypt, limited in scope,

[63] The official communiqué is useless. *Pravda*, May 19, 1966.

[64] Haykal, *Sphinx and Commissar*, 163–65.

[65] Waterbury, *Egypt*, 97.

[66] Mahr, *Die Rolle Ägyptens*, 275.

[67] Military Attache (Moscow) to TT CFHQ-DGI M39 DE OT (Ottawa), April 1, 1966, RG25, vol. 8885, File 20-UAR-1-3, LAC. An article along similar lines had been published in the *Jewish Observer and Middle East Review*, March 11, 1966. The British Ministry of Defence, which was usually skeptical of such rumors, took it seriously. Hugh Niven (Ministry of Defence) to R. Higgens (Foreign Office), DI 4(A)/EG 254(b), March 17, 1966, FO 371/190230, PRO.

duration, and location (Ports Sallūm and Sa'īd only) and strictly contingent upon prior approval. In return, the Egyptians obtained advanced R-class submarines. While the regularization of visits was a step forward, the deal fell far short of Soviet defense requirements; the facilities at Alexandria were still off limits, there were too many controls and limitations on the visits to make them operationally valuable, and no progress had been made on the crucial issue of air reconnaissance over the Mediterranean. It was in this context that Gorshkov accompanied Kosygin to Cairo in May.[68] The Soviet premier set the stage for these secret talks in his public address to the National Assembly on May 17, which stressed the threat to regional security presented by the unopposed presence of "warships belonging to powers situated far away from the shores of the [Mediterranean] ocean."[69]

One analyst has speculated that Gorshkov's mission was to get Nasser to agree to regular naval visits without the need to obtain prior authorization.[70] In fact, he was after much more. Ṣalāḥ Naṣr, chief of Egyptian intelligence at the time, recalls: "Moscow had asked [Cairo] in the spring of that year [1966] to grant some facilities [*ba'ḍ al-tashīlāt*] to the Soviet fleet at Port Sa'īd, giving her right of refuge [*ḥaqq al-lujū'*] and re-supply with petrol and water, and had also asked for cooperation in the field of long-range aerial reconnaissance, [meaning] that Egypt was to give the Soviets [access to] an airport along with its requisite facilities, provided that the Soviets would provide the planes, equipment, and pilots for this operation, in exchange for giving Egypt a picture of the results of the aerial reconnaissance."[71] A meeting between Gorshkov and commander of the Egyptian air force, Ṣidqī Maḥmūd, took place to discuss this, but 'Āmir rejected these demands in consultation with Nasser.

Naṣr, like Haykal, omits any mention of Egyptian concessions at the summit. Although both Haykal and Nasser subsequently denied that Egypt was prepared to allow "Russian bases" on its territory,[72] El Hus-

[68] El Hussini, *Soviet-Egyptian Relations*, 164–65.

[69] *Al-Ahrām*, May 18, 1966. Kosygin linked this threat to the formation of the Islamic Pact, on which more below.

[70] Dragnich, *Quest*, 31–33.

[71] Naṣr, *Mudhakkirāt*, 3:181.

[72] Battle (Cairo) to SecState no. 2971, May 16, 1966, RG 59, Box 2768, NARA; Battle (Cairo) to SecState no. 148, July 9, 1966, RG 59, Box 2768, NARA. Haykal later reiterated this denial in print, but then immediately proceeded to highlight Egypt's rejection of alleged US pressure to allow the Sixth Fleet to visit Egyptian ports. This article may well

sini is almost certainly correct in his estimation that the Egyptian president offered Kosygin to include Alexandria in the list of permissible ports. He may also have increased the number of permissible visits from three to six per year.[73] In return for Nasser's concessions, the Soviet government not only approved the Egyptian request for wheat,[74] it also made the dramatic gesture of postponing *all* Egyptian military debt installments due in 1967–70—a total of R154.4 million (about $171.5 million)—by four years.[75]

Egypt's ambassador in Moscow, Murād Ghālib, interprets the Soviet decision as a response to Nasser's convincing presentation of the campaigns in north and south Yemen as part of one anti-imperialist liberation struggle. Ambassador Ghālib's interpretation echoes Haykal's similar characterization of Soviet debt forgiveness in 1965.[76] It must have been a flattering notion, perhaps purposefully conceived as such, but it does not ring true. As we have noted before, it is certainly likely that Brezhnev, Kosygin, and others entered the Kremlin with less enthusiasm than their predecessor for an increasingly expensive and patently unwinnable campaign in the Arabian Peninsula, and that Nasser's persuasiveness played an important role in educating them. But by 1966, surely, the learning period was over.[77]

---

have been intended to deflect Soviet pressure while posing behind a facade of anti-Americanism. "*Risālah ilayhi fī Wāshinṭun,*" *al-Ahrām*, June 24, 1966.

[73] El Hussini, *Soviet-Egyptian Relations*, 166.

[74] Naṣr, *Mudhakkirāt*, 2:373. Naṣr mistakenly dates Kosygin's visit to March 1965. It is therefore possible that he is referring to earlier shipments of Soviet wheat in the summer of 1965; Ambassador Murād Ghālib (Moscow) to Secretary to the President for Information Sāmī Sharaf (Cairo), June 3, 1966, in Haykal, *al-Infijār*, 947.

[75] Kosygin to Nasser, May 31, 1966 [Russian original first page and Arabic translation of complete text], in Haykal, *al-Infijār*, 940–42. The Soviet proposal was in fact less charitable than it appeared. Kosygin's offer contained a qualification concerning the structure of Soviet-Egyptian trade that placed a significant damper on the expected benefits to Egypt from the proposed postponement of debt. Rather than eliminating the structured trade surplus by reducing planned Egyptian exports to the Soviet Union—which would have enabled the Egyptian to free up goods for sale on the global market in exchange for desperately needed hard currency—the Soviets opted for the less generous of the two paths to eliminating the trade deficit. Egyptian exports would continue to be directed at the Soviet economy in amounts designated in the multiyear trade agreement of 1965, while Soviet exports to Egypt would increase. See Ferris, "Guns for Cotton," 30–31.

[76] So much so that one wonders whether Haykal, writing more than a decade after the fact, may have been confusing the two events. Ghālib (Moscow) to Secretary to the President for Information Sāmī Sharaf (Cairo), June 3, 1966, in Haykal, *al-Infijār*, 946.

[77] My view accords with that of Aḥmad, *al-Dawr*, 426.

And yet Ghālib's interpretation, like Haykal's, cannot simply be dismissed. Two fundamental aspects of the situation in the Arabian Peninsula had changed since Nasser's last encounter with the Soviet leadership almost a year before. The first, having to do with the internal political situation of the YAR, was wholly negative. The disintegration of the all-Yemeni peace conference at Ḥaraḍ in December, as reported in the pages of *Pravda* by a young correspondent named Evgenii Primakov,[78] symbolized the irredeemably fractious nature of Yemeni politics and the hopelessness of Egypt's quest for stability. Egypt continued to maintain a sizable task force far from home, which imposed a "heavy burden on the Egyptian treasury and diverts large funds which could otherwise be used for development plans."[79] Moreover, the heavy-handedness of the Egyptian occupation, reminiscent of the twilight of Egyptian rule in Syria in 1961, looked increasingly like part of the problem rather than the indispensable key to its resolution.[80] Egypt's patent failure to stabilize the revolutionary regime in Yemen could not fail to dampen the enthusiasm of some in the Kremlin for the Egyptian project. Given this change in the fundamentals of the situation in Yemen, it is not implausible that the Soviet leadership sought assurances from Nasser on his capacity to deliver.

The second development in Yemen was positive for Egypt and the Soviet Union alike. Whereas Nasser's costly campaign in the north—the fabled Operation 9000—had failed to bring down the Saudi regime and held out little hope for stabilizing the Yemen Arab Republic, his campaign of terrorism and subversion in the south—code-named Saladin—had just scored a major victory. On February 22, 1966, the British government released a new defense white paper, which declared its intent

[78] Primakov was sworn to secrecy at the time, and his report appeared six weeks after the collapse of the conference. "Iemen: Problemy i nadezhdy," *Pravda*, February 2, 1966, 5.

[79] P. Demchenko, "Arab Differentiation," *New Times*, no. 34, 24 Aug. 1966, p. 6. See also Aḥmad, *al-Dawr*, 426–27.

[80] Doubts in Soviet circles about Egypt's management of the campaign in Yemen surfaced early on. For a KGB perspective, see Bausin, *Spetsluzhby mira*, 123. For the Foreign Ministry, see Kornev, "Polozhenie v Iemenskoi Arabskoi Respublike i Iemeno-OARovskie otnoshenia (spravka)," sent March 13, 1964, f. 5, op. 30, d. 451, p. 40, RGANI; for an expression of concern by the Soviet Ambassador in Cairo over the effects of the campaign on the Egyptian economy, see Battle (Cairo) to SecState, no. 4521, June 24, 1965, RG 59, Box 589, NARA. Journalistic expressions of disappointment in the republic can be found in *Pravda*, February 2, 1966; and *Novoe Vremia*, May 12, 1967—both of which are cited in Walter Laqueur, *The Struggle for the Middle East: The Soviet Union in the Mediterranean, 1958–1968* (New York: Macmillan, 1969), 106.

to evacuate Aden by 1968 at the latest. Although the British withdrawal from South Arabia was part of a broader process of realigning Great Britain's global responsibilities with tightening economic constraints, it was difficult to argue that the campaign of subversion and terrorism waged primarily by the NLF with Egyptian arms, training, and money was not the primary cause of a looming defeat for Great Britain.[81] The Soviets were in all likelihood not directly involved in Operation Saladin at this point, but they certainly stood to benefit from its success; the eviction of the most important US ally from its strategic base east of Suez would undermine the imperialist position throughout the oil-production belt surrounding the Persian Gulf.[82]

This mix of good and bad news from Yemen—probable failure in the north and incipient success in the south—may have led the Soviet leadership to the logical conclusion that the more successful of the two efforts ought to be reinforced. The Egyptians already appeared to be acting in this direction, having reduced their footprint throughout much of northern Yemen in a unilateral fashion in the early months of 1966 while declaring their intent to remain in the country until the last British soldier left Aden—as long as five years, if necessary.[83] But Egypt's primary adversary in this affair remained Saudi Arabia. The British retreat from Aden might conceivably serve as a fig leaf for an honorable withdrawal of Egyptian forces from Yemen, but not if the republic collapsed as a result. We can speculate that Kosygin suggested to Nasser in Cairo that he withdraw the bulk of his force from Yemen but maintain his small advisory team running Operation Saladin from Ta'izz, thereby effecting a major savings, cutting his losses in a losing battle in the north, and reinforcing the common Soviet-Egyptian efforts in the south.[84] But Nasser, as Ghālib's report emphasizes, argued for the inseparability

[81] Senior British officials were aware of the possible effects of such a decision upon Nasser in the crucial months following the Jiddah summit. However, a host of considerations overruled this concern. Defence and Oversea Policy Committee, OPD 66 (16), January 19, 1966, "South Arabia," CAB 148/27, PRO.

[82] Vladimir Sakharov, who served as Soviet Consul in Ḥudaydah in the summer of 1967, recounts that the KGB took over the training and financing of the peninsular liberation movements from Egyptian intelligence prior to the withdrawal of Egyptian forces from Yemen (Vladimir Sakharov and Umberto Tosi, *High Treason* [New York: G. P. Putnam's Sons, 1980], 166–68).

[83] See chapter six.

[84] Haykal hinted at this scenario in conversation with Patrick Seale in March. W.H.G. Fletcher (Cairo) to M. Weir (Foreign Office), BM 1015/59, March 28, 1966, FO 371/185447, PRO.

of the two fronts in the battle against reaction (Saudi Arabia) and imperialism (Great Britain). This presentation, we are led to believe, convinced Kosygin. In his speech before the National Assembly on May 17, the visiting premier declared that "the Soviet Union upholds the attitude of the UAR in the question of Yemen and welcomes the efforts of the leaders of your government in the search for a path leading to the settlement of the situation in Yemen [that will] ensure its independent and democratic development." The Cairo press seized on the statement as a straightforward affirmation of Soviet support for Egypt's Yemen policy and by implication, an endorsement of Nasser's tough talk on Saudi Arabia in the speech that immediately preceded Kosygin's.[85]

In fact, Kosygin's statement was a subtle endorsement of the peace process, which exposed a *divergence* of opinion between Cairo and Moscow on how to deal with Saudi Arabia. A new clash with the United States over Yemen at a time when confrontation was already in full swing in Vietnam must have been the last thing the Soviets wanted at this point. The war in Yemen, and its Saudi component in particular, continued to be more important to perceived Egyptian national interest than it ever had been in the Soviet perspective, where the question of air and sea facilities in the Mediterranean held pride of place as a matter of vital national security. But a cautious statement of support for Egypt's position in Yemen was a small price to pay for progress on the base issue.[86] Thus the Soviet-Egyptian debate in Cairo over the future of the Egyptian expedition in Yemen took place in the context of, and to a certain degree as a foil for, the more significant debate between Nasser and Kosygin over the reduction of Egyptian debt to the USSR and the pursuance of Soviet strategic interests in Egypt. If Kosygin appeared to have given in to Nasser's eloquent defense of the Yemen campaign, he did so to mask a truth less convenient for both parties.[87]

[85] Amembassy Cairo to Department of State, June 3, 1966, "Soviet Premier Kosygin Visits UAR President Nasser," RG 59, Box 2769, NARA; *al-Ahrām*, May 18, 1966; Aḥmad, *al-Dawr*, 430. Soviet officials seem to have been at pains to correct this dangerous misinterpretation in conversations with Western diplomats. Battle (Cairo) to SecState, June 10, 1966, "Soviet Attitudes toward the UAR," RG 59, Box 2769, NARA.

[86] In the same speech Kosygin called attention to the dangers posed by foreign navies cruising the Mediterranean. "Soviet Premier Kosygin Visits UAR President Nasser," p. 2, RG 59, Box 2769, NARA.

[87] Whether or not the question of Aden as a potential naval base entered Soviet calculations at this stage is impossible to say. The threat from US submarines bearing Trident missiles in the Indian Ocean was still some years away, whereas Polaris was a present danger.

The day after Kosygin and Gorshkov left Cairo, Soviet Deputy Foreign Minister Vasilii Kuznetsov directed Soviet Ambassador Dmitrii Pozhidaev to meet ʻĀmir and request a naval visit to Alexandria or Port Saʻīd in July. This was an effort to follow up on the conversations only just concluded in Cairo, and a move that Nasser and ʻĀmir must have anticipated. Pozhidaev duly met ʻĀmir on May 23, 1966, and presented the request. ʻĀmir's response was calculated: on the one hand, he professed to welcome the prospect of such a visit; on the other, he refused to commit to a date. In a sign of things to come, ʻĀmir then played the US card, revealing casually that the Americans too had been pestering the Egyptians for just such a visit. So far, the Egyptians had rebuffed American advances and might even be able to do so again, using arms deliveries to Israel as a pretext; in any case they would have to see to it that visits by the two navies did not coincide. The threat implicit in ʻĀmir's friendly confidences was to empty the evolving Soviet-Egyptian naval relationship of its content by equalizing the rights of the Soviet fleet with that of its principal rival in the region, the US Sixth Fleet.[88]

ʻĀmir's response to Pozhidaev contained the kernel of a new Egyptian policy of "Open Ports," implemented in the fall of 1966. The new strategy sought to deflect pressure from the Kremlin by yielding to the text of Soviet demands while subverting their spirit. It also attempted to mask the reality of having bowed to Soviet pressure by appearing not to have yielded on the fundamental question of national sovereignty. The idea was to allow further Soviet naval visits to Egypt's ports but drown them in a barrage of similar visits by rival navies. Another way to dilute the damage done by acquiescence to Soviet demands was to insist on reciprocity. Before the Soviets were permitted to conduct their first official visit to an Egyptian port, an Egyptian naval contingent paid an official visit to Sebastopol in the Black Sea on June 27. Thus when Vice Admiral Grigorii Chernobai led a five-ship contingent triumphantly into Alexandria harbor on August 6, 1966, this major achievement for Soviet diplomacy could be construed as no more than natural reciprocation for the Egyptian visit in June. The effect of the visit was diluted still further by the arrival, in quick succession, of naval units from Turkey (August 16), France (August 25), and the United States (September 2).[89]

[88] Pozhidaev (Cairo) to Ministry of Foreign Affairs, May 23, 1966, in *BVK*, 2:504–5.

[89] El Hussini, *Soviet-Egyptian Relations*, 166, 168. My view of the Egyptian visit to Sebastopol as a face-saving gesture accords with that of Dragnich, *Quest*, 33.

Given their recent display of generosity, the Soviet government must have been less than amused by these antics. Nor could the Egyptians have been happy with this new state of affairs; the days of deft manipulation of superpower rivalry were clearly over. It was in this atmosphere of "extreme tepidity"—in Ṣalāḥ Naṣr's understated description[90]—that 'Āmir led a high-profile delegation to Moscow on November 22, 1966. At the time, little information leaked out of sessions held in Moscow. Western diplomats speculated that 'Āmir had asked for wheat and arms and expressed wonder at 'Āmir's four meetings with Kosygin.[91] Ṣalāḥ Naṣr's recently published memoirs shed light on what transpired behind the scenes in Moscow.[92]

According to Naṣr, he and 'Āmir flew to Moscow, accompanied by Minister of Planning Labīb Shuqayr, Minister of War Shams Badrān, Commander of the Navy Sulaymān 'Izzat, Commander of the Air Force Ṣidqī Maḥmūd, and several other military commanders. They had two primary goals: first, to prod the Soviets into rapid delivery of arms; and second, to request urgent supply of 400,000 tons of wheat to make up for the deficit the Americans left.[93] We need not get into details of the arms discussions, carried out with Acting Minister of Defense Andrei Grechko, although it is here that Naṣr's account is most suspiciously self-serving; the emphasis on urgent requests for air defense technology and advanced MiG fighters capable of facing the Israeli Mirage seems too laden with foresight to be an accurate representation of the proceedings, and the depiction of Soviet intransigence seems a little overwrought, as if to lay the groundwork for a conspiracy theory blaming the USSR for the "trap" laid for Egypt in May 1967. In any case, the Soviets reportedly agreed to fulfill contracts already completed in the first quarter of 1967[94] but refused new requests for advanced weaponry.

[90] Naṣr, *Mudhakkirāt*, 3:181. See also Imām, *Ṣalāḥ Naṣr yatadhakkar*, 202.

[91] BJP Fall (Moscow) to NEAD, December 1, 1966, FO 371/190195, PRO; Guthrie (Moscow) to SecState, no. 2442, December 1, 1966, RG 59, Box 2762, NARA; Cairo to SecState, no. 3144, December 3, 1966, in RG 59, Box 2762, NARA.

[92] Naṣr was tried in the aftermath of the Six-Day War for complicity in 'Āmir's alleged conspiracy against the regime and spent a considerable number of years in prison as a result. Whether or not there was a conspiracy, and whether or not Naṣr was complicit in it, his tendency is liable to be exculpatory—toward himself and toward 'Āmir—and accusatory toward Nasser. Accordingly, all references to 'Āmir's involvement (and his own) in events leading up to the war should be treated with caution.

[93] Naṣr, *Mudhakkirāt*, 3:182.

[94] The weapons did not in fact arrive until after the Six-Day War, a delay to which Naṣr ascribes ominous significance (ibid).

A request for advanced tanks for a new armored division was similarly turned down, and old tanks were offered instead.

Soviet foot dragging continued in the economic sphere. And it was here that Soviet-Egyptian talks took a most intriguing turn. It should be noted that with US aid now on hold for more than six months, and the USSR thus far unwilling to make up much of the shortfall, Egypt was scheduled to run out of grain at some point in January 1967. In other words, the discussions in Moscow took place under the specter of imminent famine. The Soviets (unnamed in Naṣr's account, but presumably including Kosygin) knew this very well. Nevertheless, they responded to the Egyptian request for wheat with an initial negative, claiming that it came too late for consideration, and that even Communist countries had asked for wheat and been refused. This turned out to be merely a bargaining position. In the negotiations that ensued, the linkage between Soviet aid and Soviet strategic interests reared its ugly head once more. Exploiting Egypt's dire shortage of wheat, the Soviets again raised the question of naval facilities and bases for aerial reconnaissance. Left with little choice, War Minister Shams Badrān finally gave in. Acting on instructions from 'Āmir (and, one assumes, on the basis of a prior agreement with Nasser in Cairo), he agreed to grant the Soviet navy access to onshore facilities. However, Badrān stood his ground on the question of land-based aerial reconnaissance until it could be discussed with Nasser in Cairo. As a consequence, the Soviets agreed to provide a fraction of the amount of wheat requested in the near future, with the rest to follow in short order.[95]

Ṣalāḥ Naṣr's depiction of the atmosphere at the summit is considerably bleak. Beginning with furious accusations of malicious intent in the near crash of the delegation's aircraft on approach to the airport at Leningrad,[96] and ending with outrage at Brezhnev's ill-advised comparison of the hardware-hungry Egyptians to children in a gun shop, the visit was laden with tension and mishaps. Naṣr and Ghālib barely managed to restrain 'Āmir on two occasions from responding to Soviet provocations, which could have easily blown up the summit.[97] Even if

[95] Ibid.; Imām, *Nāṣir wa-'Āmir*, 141. El Hussini claims that the Egyptians held firm on both accounts (*Soviet-Egyptian Relations*, 174).

[96] The depiction of control-tower "error" as a deliberate attempt to kill off the Egyptian high command is implausible, although 'Āmir's furious reaction to the near crash is believable (El Hussini, *Soviet-Egyptian Relations*, 184).

[97] Ibid., 183. Cf. Ghālib's calming effect on Nasser during the latter's first encounter with Khrushchev (Ghālib, *Mudhakkirāt*, 33–34).

we subtract from this dark picture to compensate for anti-Soviet bias on the part of the author, there is little reason to doubt that ʻĀmir considered the summit a failure and returned home to Cairo in a fury. The explicit linkage made between Soviet food aid and access to Egyptian air and sea facilities could not have failed to outrage Nasser as well, who was always quick to respond to any perceived infringement of Egyptian national sovereignty.

The outrage in Cairo explains why Soviet-Egyptian relations hit an impasse at the end of 1966, from which they were only able to emerge in the vastly altered landscape of the post-Six-Day-War era. As Soviet defense requirements clashed with Egypt's national interest for the first time in the history of Soviet-Egyptian relations, the continued pursuit of the Soviet strategic investment in Egypt came to be seen in Cairo as an open threat to Egypt's national sovereignty.[98] By 1966 pressure over the basing issue was casting a pall over Soviet-Egyptian relations in an ominous parallel to the breakdown of US-Egyptian relations over the war in Yemen. At the point of maximum pressure, when Egypt, in its moment of grave weakness, seems to have been on the verge of capitulation to Soviet demands, Nasser ended the game. ʻĀmir and Badrān may have promised something in Moscow, but Nasser almost certainly overruled them upon their return. Six weeks after Chernobai's historic visit to Alexandria, on September 20, 1966, Soviet warships paid a secret five-day visit to Port Sallūm. It was to be their last call on an Egyptian harbor prior to the Six-Day War.[99] Admiral Gorshkov, who visited Egypt for the fourth time in January 1967 to conclude a deal on access to naval facilities, was turned down. For the moment, at least, Soviet pressure had backfired.[100]

*

[98] This remained a sensitive issue even after the Six-Day War. See, e.g., Marshal Grechko's cautious probing in Memcon, Amīn Huwaydī and Marshal Grechko, Moscow, November 10, 1967, in Huwaydī, *Khamsūn ʻāman*, 464–65.

[99] There may have been one unannounced stop by two Soviet destroyers at Port Saʻīd on March 14, 1967. Amembassy Cairo to Department of State, Airgram A-798, March 23, 1967, RG 59, 1967–69, Box 2553, NARA.

[100] El Hussini's hypothesis, according to which the Soviets suspended their naval presence in Egypt as a means of pressuring Nasser, is implausible. There is no doubt that the Soviets' inflation of the threat posed by the Sixth Fleet to Egypt and Syria served the purpose of heightening Egyptian dependence on Soviet protection, but it is unreasonable that they should have forsaken their presence in the Mediterranean to prove the point (*Soviet-Egyptian Relations*, 174–75).

As 1966 drew to a close, Nasser's painstakingly constructed edifice of neutralism lay in shambles. When added to the existing crisis in US-Egyptian relations, the tensions with Moscow in late 1966 represented a fundamental break in Egypt's relations with *both* superpowers at one of the most critical points in its history. Nasser had entered Yemen in late 1962 with the economic and military needs of his regime guaranteed by bountiful, string-free aid from both superpowers eagerly competing for his favors. Now, largely as a result of Egypt's continued involvement in Yemen, he stood on the verge of losing aid from one and was busy staving off assaults on Egypt's sovereignty by the other. Meanwhile, his people were fast approaching starvation.

✷ CHAPTER FIVE ✷

On the Battlefield in Yemen—and in Egypt

> The war in Yemen did not bear the character of an invasion but was meant to help a sister-Arab country. The government of Yemen at the time of the revolution as well as the Arab forces that came to defend this revolution from reactionary-imperialist infiltration stood before a dysfunctional, backward society in which fantastic tales, division and dissent proliferated. For this reason the armed battles were carried out in tandem with ... an attempt to instill in the Yemeni an awareness of the backwardness and dysfunction in which he lives.
>
> —*From a training manual of the Egyptian armed forces, ca. 1964*

THE OUTBREAK OF THE WAR IN YEMEN coincided with a sharp turn to the left in Nasser's domestic policies. Fueled in part by fear of right-wing opposition from members of the old regime in the aftermath of the *infiṣāl*, the adoption of a specifically Arab brand of socialism, embodied in the National Charter of 1962, presaged a radicalization in the regime's social and economic policies in the mid-1960s. The intensification of socialist reform and the frenetic drive to implement the development plan contributed to an atmosphere of perpetual crisis reminiscent of the Soviet Union in the 1930s. Although censorship and intimidation crippled public discussion of any sensitive subject, some criticism filtered through the allegorical works of select Egyptian intellectuals. The author Yūsuf Idrīs, for example, satirized the totalitarian ambitions of the burgeoning, sloganeering bureaucracy in his play *The Striped Ones*.[1] Mass arrests and rumors of torture spread disillusionment, apathy, and fear—phenomena wittily portrayed by Naguib Mahfouz in the novels *Babble on the Nile*, *Miramar*, and *Karnak*.[2] The war, however, escaped even

[1] Yūsuf Idrīs, *Al-Mukhaṭṭaṭīn* (al-Fajjālah: Maktabat Miṣr, 1984). The title, a play on words, also means "The Planned Ones." Originally published in 1968, it was never produced because of a government ban.

[2] Nagīb Maḥfūẓ, *Thartharah fawqa al-Nīl* (usually translated as "Adrift on the Nile") (al-Fajjālah: Maktabat Miṣr, 1965); *Mīrāmār* (Cairo: Maktabat Miṣr, 1967); *al-Karnak* (Cairo:

the pen of the most daring critics. Since public debate on the intervention was impossible—criticism of the war was grounds for imprisonment—it is easy to miss the connections between these deepening domestic pathologies and the war effort.

The commitment to deepening the revolution at home was the domestic concomitant to active support for revolution abroad.[3] As Nasser's armies battled the foot soldiers of "reaction" in the hills of Yemen, his security services crushed the remnants of "feudalism" along the banks of the Nile in order to lay the foundations for an industrial, egalitarian society. This linkage was not purely theoretical: failure in Yemen boded ill for the revolutionary experiment in Egypt, while success promised legitimacy and stability. In practice, the prosecution of the war in Arabia diverted badly needed resources from the domestic economy. The mounting death toll raised questions about the regime's judgment. And widespread corruption sparked a wave of discontent, which broke out into the open in the years following 1967. The export of revolution abroad, in other words, came at the expense of the revolution at home.

This was a truth the regime was most eager to suppress. Consequently, the historian, like the diplomat before him, is condemned to navigate between rumor and propaganda. As one US official serving in Cairo wrote in 1965: "Because of restrictions on contacts and the lack of reliable indicators of public feelings, such as a free press, it is difficult if not impossible for either outsider or insider to know what is really going on here. Thus, we doubt if anyone really knows how the Egyptians really feel about the regime, or how well or badly it is doing economically."[4] A detailed portrait of Egyptian society under the impact of the war has yet to be written. The following pages highlight some of the military, social, and economic consequences of the intervention and set

Maktabat Miṣr, 1974), a novel set in 1965–67. Other examples in this vein are Tawfīq al-Ḥakīm's plays *Bank al-qalaq* (Bank of worry) (Cairo: Dār al-Ma'ārif, 1966) and *Kull shay' fī maḥallih* (Everything in its place), in *Five Egyptian-Arabic One Act Plays: A First Reader*, ed. Karl Prasse et al. (Copenhagen: Museum Tusculanum, 2000), 36–61, originally published in 1966.

[3] Leonard Binder argues that the essential unity of the regime's domestic and foreign policy reflected a desire to neutralize opposition and maximize support from the same two contending forces (Communism and Capitalism, broadly speaking) held to be at play both within the state and in the international arena (*In a Moment of Enthusiasm: Political Power and the Second Stratum in Egypt* [Chicago: University of Chicago Press, 1978], 380–81).

[4] Richard Parker (Cairo) to Dept. of State, Airgram A-351, October 27, 1965, "The UAR in 1965: Revolutionary Malaise," RG 59, CF, 1964–66, Box 2765, NARA.

the stage for the peace negotiations discussed in the next chapter. Four controversial aspects of the war stand out: counterinsurgency, casualties, cost, and corruption.

Counterinsurgency

Counterinsurgency is arguably the most frustrating form of warfare. The blurred lines between friend and foe, between mission and routine, between the political and the military, and between tactical victory and strategic defeat make the planning and execution of effective counterinsurgency operations exceedingly difficult. If there is one sentiment that seems to have predominated among the Egyptians in Yemen throughout the five-year conflict, it is exasperation—with their slippery enemy, with their fickle friends, and, not least, with their own incompetence. It was a devilish enterprise, this Arabian adventure, consisting of grueling chases after perfidious tribesmen along winding goat paths in the mountains; interminable hours spent in the stifling rear of sluggish, unprotected armored carriers waiting for an ambush at the next bend; and long cold nights standing guard atop barren hilltops expecting an ever-imminent onslaught from the dark. One may evaluate, and critique, the performance of the Egyptians in Yemen, but one should never lose sight of the depressing dearth of good options imposed on the military by the political decision to intervene.

There is a tendency in the literature to dismiss Egyptian performance in the war, attributing "failure" to the rigid application of conventional methods to an unconventional war.[5] This argument, born in part of polemical attempts by Egyptian officials to disassociate themselves from failure in Yemen or in the subsequent Sinai campaign, overlooks several important factors. First, it disregards the evolution of Egyptian tactics over the course of the war. Second, it dismisses the enormous scope of the Egyptian political project in Yemen, erected to compete with, and supersede, the popular Royalist cause. Third, it ignores the gradual decline, and eventual extinction, of the rival cause the Ḥamīd al-Dīn royal family championed. Finally, it turns a blind eye to the emergence of something approaching a coherent counterinsurgency strategy by the

[5] Kenneth Pollack, *Arabs at War: Military Effectiveness, 1948–1991* (Lincoln: University of Nebraska Press, 2002), 57; Fawzī, *Ḥarb al-thalāth sanawāt*, 24; Sādāt, *al-Baḥth*, 211. On Sadat's attempt to evade responsibility for Yemen, see Aḥmad, *Dhikrayāt*, 565–66.

Figure 5.1 An Egyptian commando and his Yemeni guide. Northern Yemen, 1962. *Al-Quwwāt al-Musallaḥah*. December 12, 1962. Photo by Muḥammad Rashwān.

end of the war. Although the Egyptian armed forces may not deserve high marks for their achievements in Yemen, to dismiss their performance as a failure is to miss the gentle learning curve they ascended between 1962 and 1967.[6]

The early months of the intervention were indeed a string of unmitigated disasters that did much to shape the perception of contemporaries and historians of the war as a whole. As one unit after another shipped off to rescue those who had gone before them, it became clear that the Egyptian leadership had, at best, seriously underestimated the resistance to be expected in Yemen and, at worst, committed a strategic blunder of grave proportions. Despite years of intrigue in Yemen, the

[6] For a discussion of Egyptian operations and tactics based on much of the available memoir material, see David Witty, "A Regular Army in Counterinsurgency Operations: Egypt in North Yemen, 1962–1967," *Journal of Military History* 65 (April 2001): 401–40. See also Pollack, *Arabs at War*, 47–57.

Figure 5.2 Cliff climbing. *Al-Quwwāt al-Musallaḥah*. February 1, 1964.

military commanders who rushed to support the long-anticipated revolution in the fall of 1962 arrived without passable maps of the country they had been sent to occupy, let alone a sophisticated understanding of the people they were to defend and fight.[7] That small-scale catastrophe ensued is not surprising. The more interesting question is how the Egyptians dug themselves out of the pit of late 1962 and early 1963 and went on to achieve a modicum of stability with a reduced troop level in 1966–67. Part of the explanation lies in the evolution of Egyptian doctrine.

The tactical disposition of Egyptian forces in the field was unenviable. The diffusion of forces in small garrisons across the desert or in the mountains, which was deemed necessary to interdict the flow of supplies from outside Yemen and to hold the enemy at a safe distance from Ṣan'ā', rendered Egyptian units ever vulnerable to surprise attack by superior numbers.[8] The principal military countermeasures were aggressive patrolling and preventive ambushes, neither of which was practiced sufficiently. Dispersion transformed the protection of lines of communication into the vital issue of the war. Since garrisons could not survive without supplies of food, fuel, spare parts, and when necessary, reinforcements, the battle for the routes leading out from Ṣan'ā' to the various fronts and to the vital supply port at Ḥudaydah became a central feature of the war. Mines and ambushes constituted the principal danger on the roads. To counter them, regular reconnaissance and control of the surrounding high ground were essential. The latter, in particular, required infantrymen in huge numbers, which goes a long way toward explaining the quadrupling of the expeditionary force between 1962 and 1965.[9] Even so, it was impossible to control hundreds of kilometers of mountainous terrain along the key axes at all times. On top of it all, the indigenous population throughout much of these areas was martial in its bearing, fickle in its allegiances, and fiercely independent in its attitude toward central authority of any kind. In such a situation, even the most imaginative tactics an enormous force executed were not likely to bring lasting peace. The ubiquity of incompetence—occasional flairs of brilliance notwithstanding—made a bad situation worse.

[7] The lack of accurate maps is a common theme in the memoirs of participants. See, e.g., Aḥmad, *Dhikrayāt*, 482.

[8] For a good firsthand account, see Maḥrizī, *al-Ṣamt al-ḥā'ir*, 121.

[9] Pollack, *Arabs at War*, 55; Hart-Davis, *The War That Never Was*, 91; Ḥadīdī, *Shāhid 'alā ḥarb al-Yaman*, 48; Abū Dhikrī, *al-Zuhūr*, 31; Aḥmad, *Dhikrayāt*, 289–90, 294, 583n. Aḥmad estimates the portion of troops commissioned with road security at 50–60 percent of the entire task force (*Dhikrayāt*, 594).

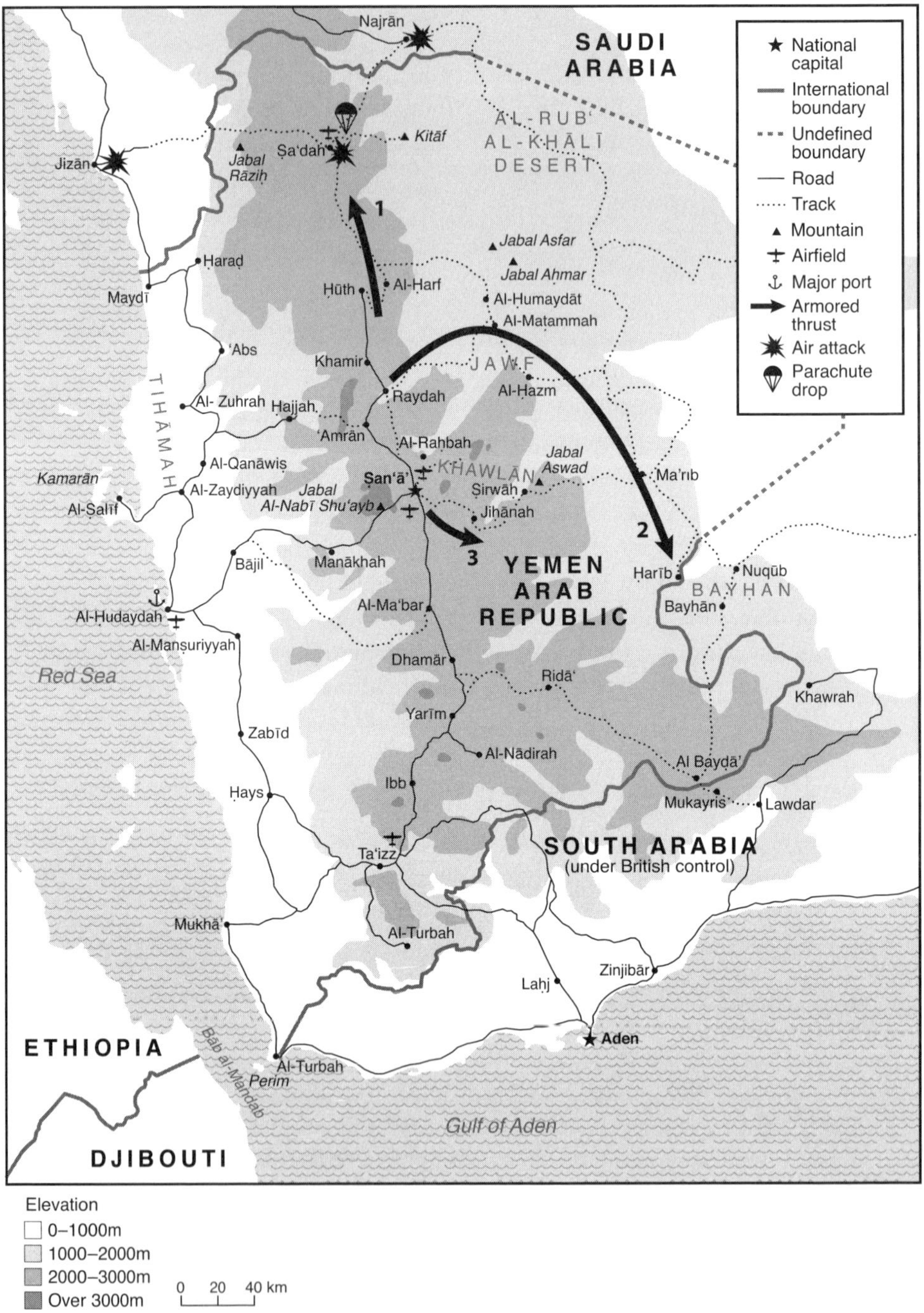

Figure 5.3 The Ramadan Offensive, January–February 1963.

The best conventional operation of the war was the Ramadan Offensive of January–February 1963. Over the course of three weeks, Marshal ʿĀmir oversaw a succession of armored thrusts out of Ṣanʿāʾ. The first struck north, opening up the road through Raydah and Khamir to the besieged town of Ṣaʿdah, unofficial capital of the Zaydī north. The second, spearheaded by an infantry battalion supported by artillery and tanks, swung northeast out of the Ṣaʿdah–Ṣanʿāʾ road deep into the Jawf desert, bypassing the blocked main road to Maʾrib in a major flanking movement executed under the protective screen of a diversionary effort along the road. At Ḥumaydāt, the force joined up with another heading down from Ṣaʿdah and proceeded to capture key junctions along the network of tracks that led from Najrān in Saudi Arabia into Yemeni territory before wheeling southward to seize the pivotal supply points of Maʾrib and Ḥarīb, near the border with the staunchly pro-Royalist Emirate of Bayḥān. A third force halted the westward advance of ʿAbd Allāh bin Ḥasan and Shaykh Nājī al-Ghādir toward Ṣanʿāʾ along the main road from Maʾrib via Ṣirwāḥ and Jiḥānah at Jabal Aswad. With Republican forces now ensconced in all the major towns of Yemen, the Royalist cause appeared to have suffered an irreversible setback.[10]

However, even this effective display of fire and maneuver could have no lasting effect if it were not followed by a concerted effort to win over the tribes. As long as the supply of money and arms from Saudi Arabia was guaranteed, it was a matter of months before the rebels could regroup and resume the insurgency by circumventing the new web of Egyptian positions along Yemen's long and porous frontiers. As the Ottomans' experience proved, absent a coherent strategy for integrating traditional tribal hierarchies into the modern mechanisms of state power—or granting them substantial autonomy—the gains achieved

[10] "The Mode of Operations in the Theatre and Explanation of Several of the Battles and Their Lessons," 43–47, *LMOY*; "The Airborne Divisions," 18–21, *LMOY*; "Logistical Affairs in the Theatre of Operations in Yemen," 16–17, *LMOY*; Cortada (Ta ʿizz) to Department of State, "Visit to Marib in Eastern Yemen [on Mar. 6, 1963]," March 16, 1963, RG 59, CF, Box 4146, POL 2 Yemen, NARA; Badeau (Cairo) to SecState, no. 1314, February 25, 1963, RG 59, CDF, Box 4147b, POL 27 Yemen, NARA; Badeau (Cairo) to SecState, no. 1360, March 3, 1963, RG 59, CDF, Box 4147b, POL 27 Yemen, NARA; Aḥmad, *al-Dawr*, 206–13; Rahmy, *Egyptian Policy*, 148–49; Maḥrizī, *al-Ṣamt al-ḥāʾir*, 121–25; Khalīl, *Ḥurūb Miṣr*, 62–63; Aḥmad, *Dhikrayāt*, 710; Schmidt, *Yemen*, 164–65; O'Ballance, *War in the Yemen*, 98, 108–9; Peter Somerville-Large, *Tribes and Tribulations: A Journey in Republican Yemen* (London: Robert Hale, 1967), 182–83; Smiley, *Arabian Assignment*, 115–16; Pollack, *Arabs at War*, 49–51; Witty, "Egypt in North Yemen," 414.

in any military offensive would inevitably erode with time. But nothing could have been further from the minds of Egyptian planners in the first year of the war.[11]

The full compass of the Egyptian political project in Yemen—from the drafting of a republican constitution to the construction, almost ex nihilo, of a modern bureaucracy—lies beyond the scope of this book. Suffice it to say that the megalomaniac dimensions of the Egyptian transformational project in Yemen complemented the mad rush toward socialism at home. The ambition to recreate Yemen as a modern republic in 1962 derived no doubt from an analysis of Egypt's failure to retain control of Syria the year before. But whatever the merits of a more thoroughly revolutionary approach to Syria, it was completely inapplicable to Yemen. Ultimately, the very notion of central government was irreconcilable with the independent traditions of tribal rule. This is why the enormous investment in building a modern republic from scratch in Ṣan'ā' from 1962 to 1966 seems to have done next to nothing to win over the rebellious Zaydī tribes of the north and northeast. On the contrary, it did much to deepen their resentment.

Arguably, even the most enlightened, abuse-free administration—of which Sallāl's regime was certainly not capable—would have done little to dent tribal resistance to the very fact of centralized rule, especially one foreigners supported so heavily.[12] It was only by abandoning the ideal of a modern, perfectly centralized republic, with its implied choice between adherence to revered traditions and conversion to alien practices, that the Egyptians were eventually capable of loosening their grip on the country.[13] To be sure, both the "Yemenization" of the conflict by building up the YAR security forces[14] and the development of the various organs of government were important. However, it was the grudging acceptance of tribal reality—not merely of the tribes as a factor demanding representation but as a permanent feature of the social landscape to which a considerable degree of autonomy must be ceded—that constituted the crucial psychological breakthrough that enabled

[11] For a study of the tribes of Yemen, see Paul Dresch, *Tribes, Government, and History in Yemen* (New York: Oxford University Press, 1989).

[12] Stookey, *Yemen*, 232–38.

[13] This conclusion is resisted by Ḥamrūsh, who faults Egyptian efforts at transforming Yemeni society for not being strenuous enough (*Qiṣṣat thawrat 23 yūliyū*, 3:265).

[14] For the official launch of Egyptian efforts to build an effective republican army in May 1963, see "The Yemeni Armed Forces," in *LMOY*, 26–27.

the handover of security responsibilities to the tribes themselves and a substantial reduction of Egyptian troops.[15]

The first obstacles to be overcome were the Egyptians' own ignorance, prejudice, and arrogance. A lessons-learned document from the operations in Yemen, composed by the military in 1964, is replete with assumptions and attitudes that betray the distorted ambitions of the Egyptian *mission civilisatrice* in Yemen. Although nonviolent engagement with the local population is listed as one of three most effective means for the conduct of operations,[16] many of the prescriptions for action reflect a blinkered view of the locals as inferior natives in need of conversion to the dogmas of revolutionary socialism. Yemenis were to be sent in large numbers to Cairo to observe the impact of socialism on society. Delegations were to be dispatched to Yemen to "fix the ways of thinking" of the people and win them over to the revolutionary cause. Radio broadcasts, newsletters, and pamphlets were to be deployed in the struggle to "instill consciousness" among the rebels and warn them of the consequences of resisting revolutionary principles.[17] Contact with the Egyptian soldier was to be encouraged so as to influence the local psyche and foster higher standards of health, cleanliness, and honorable conduct. Tribal conferences were to facilitate persuasion by loyal sheikhs. And so on.

On the face of it, the Egyptians in Yemen had more affinity with the local population than did the Americans in Vietnam, the Soviets in Afghanistan, or even the Ottomans in Yemen more than a century before.[18] Egyptians and Yemenis spoke a dialect of the same language, practiced the same religion, and shared many cultural attitudes. Nevertheless, at the outset, at least, the Egyptians in Yemen felt like complete aliens.[19] Most Egyptian field commanders knew little about the country or its population. When attacked by unidentified assailants indistinguishable

[15] This seems to have been a belated, partial, and almost accidental victory of common sense among the military commanders in Yemen over the centralizing instinct of Cairo. Nasser's baffling adherence to unpopular incompetents is discussed by Aḥmad, *Dhikrayāt*, 557, 576.

[16] The others being offensive forward deployment and efforts to split the enemy geographically so as to facilitate destruction of isolated pockets of resistance. "The Mode of Operations in the Theatre and Explanation of Several of the Battles and Their Lessons," *LMOY*, 29.

[17] Perhaps the soundest investment the Egyptians made in Yemen was to distribute as many as 100,000 transistor radios (Ḥadīdī, *Shāhid 'alā ḥarb al-Yaman*, 71n).

[18] Witty, "Egypt in North Yemen," 439.

[19] E.g., Ḥadīdī, *Shāhid 'alā ḥarb al-Yaman*, 19–20.

Figure 5.4 The cover of the Egyptian weekly *Ākhir Sā'ah*, on November 28, 1962: "We have won! And the Yemeni revolution has begun to turn toward internal building."

from the surrounding civilians, they reacted as foreign occupiers have always done: with indiscriminate punitive raids, in which the innocent and the sympathetic were inevitably mixed up with the perpetrators and their supporters.[20] The failure to discriminate between friend and foe was amplified by the Egyptian foot soldier's basic attitude toward

[20] Faraj, *Rijāl fī khanādiq*, 196.

locals, a mixture of fear and contempt.[21] The insurgents, by contrast, proved adept at turning Egyptian behavior to their advantage, driving a wedge between the foreign army and the undecided population. For these reasons the theoretical affinities between liberator and liberated, occupier and occupied mattered little in practice.

Initial attempts at tribal outreach by the high command were suffused with goodwill, plagued by wastefulness, and often undermined by punitive actions that exhausted the goodwill the provision of aid generated. The army's efforts to win over hearts and minds concentrated on the distribution of money and the provision of social and humanitarian services. One visitor recalls a regime-sponsored rally in the capital, at which the army distributed fistfuls of cash to an unruly crowd.[22] An Egyptian training manual explained: "At the beginning of the war it became clear that a great portion of the engineering capabilities should be dedicated to helping the inhabitants of the country, since this aid was the cornerstone of preserving the Yemeni revolution in tandem with military operations."[23] Engineering units dug dozens of wells in rural areas and outfitted them with pumps, built schools and hospitals, and distributed tractors. Medical teams offered free treatment, vaccinations, and instruction. Army clerics appeared in local mosques and religious clubs. And hundreds of Egyptian teachers arrived in Yemen to teach and restructure academic curricula.[24]

But still the insurgency raged on. The former Egyptian commander of military intelligence drops the blasphemous hint that senior Egyptian officers were so bewildered by what they faced in Yemen that they turned to the handbooks of British imperialism in search of guidance:

> It was clearly necessary to follow a different technique in order to win over the men of the tribes, [one] more alluring than digging water

[21] See, e.g., Somerville-Large, *Tribes and Tribulations*, 105; Aḥmad, *al-Dawr*, 140; Schmidt, *Yemen*, 87–88.

[22] Somerville-Large, *Tribes and Tribulations*, 111–13.

[23] "The Engineering Support for the Arab Forces in Yemen and the Lessons Learned," *LMOY*, 63.

[24] Ibid., 58, 68–69; "Logistical Affairs in the Theatre of Operations in Yemen," *LMOY*, 40; Ḥadīdī, *Shāhid ʿalā ḥarb al-Yaman*, 67; ʿAlī ʿAlī Sālim, "Dirāsah maydāniyyah ʿan al-awḍāʿ al-ṣiḥḥiyyah ʿinda qiyām al-thawrah al-yamaniyyah," in ʿAbd al-Munʿim Muḥammad ʿAlī, *Taṭawwur al-khadamāt al-ṣiḥḥiyyah bi-l-Yaman, 1962–1967* (Cairo, 1971), 102–18 and passim; Schmidt, *Yemen*, 208. For a survey of Egyptian civilian aid projects, see Aḥmad Fuʾād Abū al-ʿUyūn's "al-Risālah al-maʿūnah al-fanniyyah fī al-Yaman," in ʿAlī, *Taṭawwur al-khadamāt al-ṣiḥḥiyyah*, 20–52; Aḥmad, *Dhikrayāt*, 544–54.

> wells and treating the sick, yet there were no means of enticement other than gold. Indeed, we read a lot about the practices followed by Britain—in which Lawrence [of Arabia] succeeded to the greatest extent in winning over the tribes.... [We] were apparently affected by what we had read about Lawrence of Arabia, as he was called, and about the success he achieved about a half-century before in controlling the tribes and employing them in the service of the aims of the empire of that time, when [we] began to think about establishing an organization made up of several officers charged with actions related to the tribes, and with establishing relations of friendship and cooperation with their Sheikhs, their men and their youth, in order to acquire, thereby, better knowledge of their condition, their inclinations and the factors influencing their loyalty, in the hope that by this infiltration into their midst it would be possible to direct them towards that which would serve military goals and bring about a quick end of the war. This organization was the kernel of the Administration of Tribal Affairs, which later engaged in beneficial actions that led in many cases to the stabilization of affairs inside the loyal tribes.[25]

In late 1962 the Egyptians established an organ dedicated to handling relations with the tribes. As early as November 1962, special officers tasked with tribal affairs make their appearance on the battlefield, reflecting the attention the Egyptian military justly lavished on the tribal leadership from a relatively early stage.[26] By early 1963 the exchange of money—primarily silver coins in sachets termed "sacks of pebbles" (*akyās zalaṭ*)—had become central to these dealings.[27] According to one officer's account, at the first meeting with influential Sheikh Nājī al-Ghādir of the Khawlān, the latter received a "gift" of 5,000 silver riyals.[28] On subsequent occasions, he apparently received vastly greater sums in exchange for promises of future fealty.[29] Maḥmūd Aḥmad re-

[25] Ḥadīdī, *Shāhid 'alā ḥarb al-Yaman*, 70, 72.

[26] Faraj, *Rijāl fī khanādiq*, 159. The first director of the Office of Tribal Affairs in the headquarters in Ṣan'ā' was Brigadier General 'Abbās Fahmī (Bayḍānī, *Miṣr wa-thawrat al-Yaman*, 115–16).

[27] Aḥmad, *Dhikrayāt*, 577–78; Somerville-Large, *Tribes and Tribulations*, 184–85.

[28] Maḥrizī, *al-Ṣamt al-ḥā'ir*, 126–27. Similar encounters with tribal leaders were beginning to take place at the same time on other fronts. For the northeast, see, "The Airborne Divisions," *LMOY*, 21.

[29] As much as 250,000 riyals on one occasion, according to Abū Dhikrī, *al-Zuhūr*, 73–74. For other reports of negotiations with Ghādir, see Khalīl, *Ḥurūb Miṣr*, 63; Aḥmad, *Dhikrayāt*, 744–45.

Figure 5.5 Sheikh Nājī al-Ghādir meets with Major General ʿUthmān Naṣār in the Khawlān, early 1963. Photo from the collection of Ṣalāḥ al-Dīn al-Maḥrizī. Courtesy of Ahmed El-Mehrezy.

calls accompanying General al-Qāḍī to Ṣaʿdah in the summer of 1963, where the Egyptian commander gave two allied sheikhs 100 gold guineas each.[30]

The payment of generous subsidies to prominent sheikhs in order to purchase their loyalty signaled the launch of a new political practice concomitant to military operations against the tribes.[31] This policy constituted the second stage in the evolution of Egyptian thinking on counterinsurgency in a tribal setting. The Ottomans had pioneered these techniques, blending stern punishment with amnesty and selective largesse in an ultimately vain attempt to ride the tribal tiger nearly a cen-

[30] Equal to about E£600, or $1,400 in 1963 dollars (*Dhikrayāt*, 577–78). General Khalīl mentions diverting funds designated for the tribes to purchase food for his troops (*Ḥurūb Miṣr*, 65).

[31] Ḥamrūsh, *Qiṣṣat thawrat 23 yūliyū*, 3:230–31; Huwaydī, *Ḥurūb ʿAbd al-Nāṣir*, 131–32. ʿĀmir himself apparently drove the change in policy in response to the death of a squad of Egyptian commandos at the hands of perfidious tribesmen at the end of November 1962 (Bayḍānī, *Miṣr wa-thawrat al-Yaman*, 122).

tury before.[32] The Saudis and the British, Egypt's new neighbors in Yemen, also provided inspiration for Egyptian tactics.[33] Results of this policy were mixed, and the cost-benefit yield doubtful. On the one hand, money purchased temporary respites from attack and enabled a more efficient deployment of forces. On the other, pledges of allegiance to the republic rarely proved lasting, and enormous sums were expended in the process. Worse, in some cases money provided a perverse incentive to revolt, as wily sheikhs already on the payroll realized they could instigate their allies to rebel and then profit from further funds by promising to pacify them.[34] The fact that there were at least two sides to be played in this game—the Saudis and the Egyptians—made it all the more profitable. Nonetheless, the bribes did represent a coherent attempt to step outside the boundaries of conventional thought and deal with the source of resistance off the battlefield. More importantly, the meetings established a pattern of direct engagement between Egyptian military commanders and the traditional agents of authority in the country, which bypassed the weak government in Ṣan'ā'. These interactions eventually issued in a far more sophisticated approach to the tribes in the final eighteen months of the Egyptian presence.

In the summer of 1966, 'Āmir appointed Major General Ṭal'at Ḥasan 'Alī commander of Egyptian forces in Yemen. It was he who oversaw the withdrawal of Egyptian forces from the periphery to the urban centers of central Yemen—the so-called Long Breath Strategy discussed in the next chapter. The concentration of Egyptian forces was made possible by two changes in Egypt's approach to the war. First was an increasing reliance on air power to subdue the foci of resistance on the periphery. Anecdotal evidence from British sources points to an increase of over 300 percent in the number of bombing sorties against Royalist targets between September and October 1966. A number of these involved the use of poison gas. The most violent attack took place on January 5, 1967, when Egyptian planes targeted the Royalist headquarters at Kitāf, killing hundreds.[35]

[32] Caesar Farah, *The Sultan's Yemen: Nineteenth-Century Challenges to Ottoman Rule* (London: I. B. Tauris, 2002), 63–64, 83–84, 91, 96, 106–7, 175, 234, and passim.

[33] Aḥmad, *Dhikrayāt*, 325.

[34] Bayḍānī, *Miṣr wa-thawrat al-Yaman*, 125. Of a similar situation in Waziristan, Akbar Ahmed writes: "To create a problem, control it, and terminate it is an acknowledged and highly regarded yardstick of political skill." *Resistance and Control in Pakistan* (London: Routledge, 2004), 25.

[35] Hart-Davis, *The War That Never Was*, 283, 303, 320–21.

The stick of aerial bombardment was complemented by a carrot of tribal aid. This final stage in the evolution of Egyptian COIN involved a new pattern of relations with the Yemeni tribes centered upon a web of decentralized "political offices" (*makātib siyāsiyyah*) embedded in the tribal habitat. The Egyptians who manned these stations, usually one officer and two noncommissioned officers, belonged to a secret unit of the branch of tribal affairs. Typically, these were men of rural background who were closer in mindset to their Yemeni hosts. They immersed themselves completely in tribal society, sharing the tribesmen's food and learning their manners, adopting their dress and speaking their dialect. In addition to their intelligence mission, the political officers were charged with incremental dispensation of aid in return for specific services. No longer was aid lavishly showered upon a prominent sheikh, to do with it what he pleased; instead, money went to the installation of a water pump, the establishment of a medical clinic, or the construction of a school, in return for security responsibility over a swath of territory or a segment of road. If a given tribe failed to stand by a particular commitment, it was held directly accountable.[36]

If there was a way to win the war on the ground, surely this was one of its most promising components.[37] The establishment of a Special Forces outfit dedicated to the penetration of tribal society demonstrated considerable sophistication. So too did the decentralized model of tribal liaison offices and the careful—and accountable— dispensation of aid. To be sure, the strategic paralysis imposed by hostile neighbors conspiring with impunity across porous borders undercut the utility of these initiatives. So too did the unrestrained use of air power. More importantly, Nasser's dogged determination to prop up Sallāl's corrupt junta in Ṣan'ā' pegged Egyptian policy to an unpopular regime. This negative political context undermined the military's efforts to win over disaffected tribes. But the chronic deficiencies of judgment in Cairo need

[36] Aḥmad, *Dhikrayāt*, 318–19, 326, 531; Ḥamrūsh, *Qiṣṣat thawrat 23 yūliyū*, 3:253–35, 263; Ḥadīdī, *Shāhid 'alā ḥarb al-Yaman*, 72–73; Abū Dhikrī, *al-Zuhūr*, 72; O'Ballance, *War in the Yemen*, 180; Aḥmad, *al-Dawr*, 441–42; Maḥrizī, *al-Ṣamt al-ḥā'ir*, 172–73, 181; Nasser, Speech, May 2, 1967. This new strategy seems to have been accompanied by an intensification of efforts to extend medical treatment to outlying rural areas. Dr. Nasīm Ādam Khalīl, "al-Amrāḍ al-sā'idah fī al-Yaman," in 'Alī, *Taṭawwur al-khadamāt al-ṣiḥḥiyyah*, 294, 298–306. A useful comparison may be made between the Egyptian political offices in Yemen and the British/Pakistani "Political Agents" of Waziristan. See Ahmed, *Resistance and Control in Pakistan*, 36–39.

[37] See, e.g., David Galula, *Counterinsurgency Warfare: Theory and Practice* (New York: Praeger, 1964), 110–13, 116, and passim.

not obscure the increasing sophistication of thinking among at least some of Egypt's military planners in Ṣan'ā' toward the end of the war.

By the eve of the Six-Day War, Egypt was holding on to Yemen with around 40,000 troops, little more than half the number needed scarcely two years before. This achievement owed as much to the enemy's weakness as it did to Egyptian strength. Once concentrated, Egypt's conventional forces had little to fear from tribal resistance that continued to lack coordination, discipline, or persistence. Moreover, enthusiasm for the Ḥamīd al-Dīns among the tribes hostile to the republic had waned considerably by this point in the war. By the summer of 1966, the fate of the Royalist cause lay entirely in the hands of the Saudis who, for reasons that will be discussed in the next chapter, were decreasingly eager to help as time went by. Nevertheless, some credit is due to the more imaginative of Egypt's military commanders.

Casualties

Although official Egypt portrayed the war as an uninterrupted chain of battlefield successes, the truth could not be hidden for long. Ghastly funerals for headless corpses, whispered rumors of heavy losses, and foreign reportage of setbacks all contributed to the widening gap between official rhetoric and popular perception.[38] In an attempt to bridge it, Nasser made an effort to come clean in a heart-to-heart talk with the Egyptian people at Port Sa'īd on "Victory Day," December 23, 1962. Up to that point, there had been official silence on specifics concerning the expeditionary force—its size, the date of its dispatch, and especially the loss of human life. Stories of individual heroism motivated by passionate belief in the justice of the cause dominated news coverage of the war effort. Representative of this genre was the tale of one patriotic pilot who set out on his first combat sortie within half an hour of his arrival in Yemen and was depicted climbing coolly into the skies between two peaks manned by Royalist marksmen with Voice of the

[38] "Yemen: Ears, Noses, and Lips," *Time*, December 21, 1962, 28–29; Clark (Alexandria) to Dept. of State, Airgram no. A-122, January 29, 1963, "Local Opinion on U.A.R. Economic and Political Conditions and U.A.R. Involvement in Yemen," RG 59, CDF 1960–63, Box 2072, NARA; American Consulate (Port Sa'īd) to Dept. of State, Airgram A-53, November 6, 1962, "U.A.R. Casualties in Yemen," RG 59, CDF 1960–63, Box 2076, NARA; Somerville-Large, *Tribes and Tribulations*, 103; Abu Dhikrī, *al-Zuhūr*, 26–28 and passim; Aḥmad, *Dhikrayāt*, 115, 297, 588; Badeau, *Reminiscences*, 215.

Arabs blaring in the cockpit.[39] Thus when Nasser described the escalation of Egypt's intervention from an initial company of 100 men on October 5 to 2,000 eleven days later and revealed that a total of 136 men had died thus far in the war ("each one of their boots more noble than the crown of King Saud and King Hussein"), the Egyptian media presented these belated half-truths as startling revelations.[40]

Thirty-two-year-old Lieutenant Nabīl Bakr al-Waqqād, honored by the president as the war's first martyr, received a front-page piece and photo in the next day's *al-Akhbār*.[41] Waqqād, who died at some point in October in the eastern desert near Ma'rib, was first mentioned in the obituaries six weeks earlier.[42] Son of a retired supervisor in the Ministry of Education, he was representative of the few men whose death slipped past the censor and into public consciousness by way of the obituaries column. Both the list of wishers and addressees in such death notices usually indicated considerable social status; the death in combat of the peasants who made up the bulk of the Egyptian armed forces passed for the most part without mention.[43] Condolence messages printed in Egyptian dailies judiciously avoided any overt mention of the circumstances of death. Well-wishers (or their editors) rarely referred to the deceased by the traditional appellate for war dead, "*shahīd*" (martyr), instead opting for the neutral "*marḥūm*" (deceased);[44] nor did they specify the time, place, or manner of death. Usually the only clue to a dead man's connection with Yemen was the appendage of a rank to the name and the occasional use of phrases such as "*faqīd al-wājib wa-l-sharaf*" (casualty of duty and honor). Such was the case with Waqqād. It was only after the president transformed Waqqād, posthumously, into a na-

[39] Musa Ṣabrī, "*Sirr intiṣārinā fī al-Yaman*," *Akhbār al-Yawm*, December 22, 1962, 3.

[40] Nasser speech, December 23, 1962, in UAR, *Majmū'at khuṭab*, 4:263–64; "Asrār ḥarbinā fī al-Yaman," *al-Akhbār*, December 24, 1962. On the question of dating, see chapter two. The casualty figures are plausible but almost certainly low.

[41] December 24, 1962.

[42] See, for instance, *al-Akhbār*, November 8, 1962, 9; *al-Ahrām*, November 8, 1962, 9. In the obituaries, Waqqād's rank is listed as major (*rā'id*). He was notable for having served as supervisor of the Egyptian-run NCO College in Yemen in 1959. Maḥrizī, *al-Ṣamt al-ḥā'ir*, 97, 106; Ḥamrūsh, *Qiṣṣat thawrat 23 yūliyū*, 3:229.

[43] This may reflect illiteracy and/or the high cost of publication. As Leonard Binder has written, the very inclusion of an obituary notice in a leading paper was an indication of social status (*In a Moment of Enthusiasm*, 156).

[44] This stricture held true only for recent deaths. Announcements of annual memorials for soldiers killed in action employed the term *shahīd* freely, although the place of death went unmentioned.

tional celebrity, that it became permissible to publish something more about his death in combat. Even so, there was hardly a word about the battle itself, and mostly praise for a martyred true believer in Arab nationalism and the revolution in Yemen. The papers lauded Waqqād's father for declaring to Marshal 'Āmir that he would gladly offer all four of his sons as "sacrifices to Arabism and the homeland."[45]

Another martyr Nasser singled out in his speech at Port Sa'īd was the celebrated commando, Major 'Abd al-Mun'im Sanad, who fell at al-Wataddah, east of Ṣan'ā', at the end of November. The original announcement of his death in the papers on December 11 featured a handsome portrait of the man in uniform but otherwise shed no light on the circumstances of his demise.[46]

The notice did not relate the tragic tale of tribal perfidy that led an inexperienced commander and his men into a deadly trap on a cold mountaintop east of Ṣan'ā', nor did it provide a hint as to the decapitated state of Sanad's mutilated body—although the fact that a prayer session, not a funeral, took place, was perhaps indicative.[47] Sanad was referred to simply as "*al-marḥūm*," yet it was clear from the extraordinary tribute paid to him by various comrades in arms, and by the future commander of Egyptian forces in Yemen, Major General Ṭal'at Ḥasan 'Alī, that Sanad had been an exceptional man who had died in combat. Eventually, even the indirect tribute paid to select Yemen martyrs in the obituary columns of the major Egyptian dailies tapered off, presumably under pressure from the censor.

With time, the gap between the official narrative of a heroic mission performed brilliantly at minuscule cost and the reality of an adventure gone badly wrong grew ever wider. The government took pains to hide the casualties from the Egyptian people. Wounded servicemen, for example, were warned not to speak of their experiences upon discharge from the hospital.[48] Still, it was impossible to conceal the truth completely. As early as January 1963, an American consular report from Alexandria reported widespread anger at the government for sending

[45] *Al-Akhbār*, December 24, 1962, 2.

[46] *Al-Akhbār*, December 11, 1962, 11; *al-Ahrām*, December 11, 1962, 13.

[47] *Time*, December 21, 1962, 28–29; Bayḍānī, *Azmat al-ummah*, 496–98; idem, *Miṣr wa-thawrat al-Yaman*, 116. Waqqād too was betrayed by his Yemeni companions (Maḥrizī, *al-Ṣamt al-ḥā'ir*, 120).

[48] As the reliable Canadian Ambassador put it, "those seriously wounded are discharged after recovery with threats of retaliation if they talk of their experiences." Ford (Cairo) to Ext. 428, September 19, 1963, in FO 371/172864, PRO.

Figure 5.6 The Egyptian military graveyard in Ṣan'ā'. Photo from the collection of Ṣalāḥ al-Dīn al-Maḥrizī. Courtesy of Ahmed El-Mehrezy.

boys off to die for Nasser's injured pride.[49] Families of wounded servicemen often received no word of the incident, of their relatives' repatriation, or of their hospitalization until after they had died in hospital. Even relatives of men killed in action complained that news of the incident was withheld for weeks on end. But postponing bad news did not blunt the impact of information that eventually leaked.

That Nasser felt uncomfortable with the circulating rumors about the human and financial toll of the war is evident from his speech before the National Assembly on November 12, 1964, which he devoted primarily to the economy: "A great deal has been said about Yemen, and the time has not yet come to speak to you openly [about it]; it has been said that we have spent $1 billion on Yemen, and it has been said that we have losses of 10,000 dead.... I will not discuss the numbers in an

[49] "Memorandum of Conversation" [with "Mr. Carl Leonard Burckhardt, prominent Alexandria cotton merchant, and Mrs. Burckhardt"], 4–5, in Clark (Alexandria) to Dept. of State, Airgram no. A-122, January 29, 1963, "Local Opinion on U.A.R. Economic and Political Conditions and U.A.R. Involvement in Yemen," RG 59, CDF 1960–63, Box 2072, NARA.

open session, but brother 'Abd al-Ḥakīm 'Āmir will meet you in a secret session and will speak with you on these subjects and answer all the questions you want to know concerning Yemen, and the casualties, and the costs and the forces, and thus we will put an end to all the talk."[50]

More than three months after Nasser publicly pledged an accounting, he dispatched his deputy to the National Assembly to report on the conduct of the war. When 'Āmir told the legislators (in the portion of his statement that was subsequently publicized) that a total of 1,607 men had died in Yemen, it was clear to all that the real numbers were much higher.[51] The question "How much higher?" has been the subject of considerable speculation—hardly any of it based on hard data. The apologists who populate the low end of the spectrum tend to converge around a figure of 5,000 Egyptian fatalities over the course of the war.[52] The long tail at the sensationalist end of the curve extends from 20,000 combat deaths to more than three times that number.[53] Without access to classified Egyptian data, and given the unreliability of most non-Egyptian sources, it is difficult to state anything with confidence on this subject. The truth probably lies somewhere in between these two extremes.[54]

If so, the war was not as big a military catastrophe as Nasser's detractors would have it. Yemen did not quite amount to the infamous "graveyard of the Turks" (*maqbarat al-atrāk*), who, it is reported, lost 30,000 men in 1905 alone.[55] By comparison, the Soviet Union lost about 15,000

[50] UAR, *Majmū'at khuṭab*, 5:77.

[51] *Al-Ahrām*, February 27, 1965; Aḥmad, *al-Dawr*, 256–63. The US embassy in Cairo, for instance, estimated 15,000–20,000 Egyptian casualties up to this point. Battle (Cairo) to SecState, no. 2994, February 27, 1965, RG 59, CF 1964–66, Box 3027, POL 27 Yemen, NARA.

[52] Haykal, *Sanawāt al-ghalayān*, 20n.; Anwar al-Qāḍī, quoted in Aḥmad, *Dhikrayāt*, 597; Sharaf, *Sanawāt*, 2:650–65; Aḥmad, *Dhikrayāt*, 591–97; and 'Abd al-Muḥsin Kāmil Murtagī, quoted in Aḥmad, *Dhikrayāt*, 597—although Murtagī provided Ṭāriq Ḥabīb with a much higher estimate of 10,000–15,000 dead. Ḥabīb, *Milaffāt*, 243. See also Imām, *Muḥammad Fawzī*, 37.

[53] Abū Dhikrī, *al-Zuhūr*, 5; Schmidt, *Yemen*, 234; Saeed Badeeb, *The Saudi-Egyptian Conflict over North Yemen, 1962–1970* (Boulder, CO: Westview Press, 1986), 105.

[54] Ḥamrūsh, *Qiṣṣat thawrat 23 yūliyū*, 3:261; Micheal Clodfelter, *Warfare and Armed Conflicts: A Statistical Reference to Casualty and Other Figures, 1500–2000* (Jefferson, NC: McFarland, 2002), 635; Ḥadīdī, *Shāhid 'alā ḥarb al-Yaman*, 73, 121. For a similar estimate based on Soviet and American intelligence, see Jesse Ferris, "Egypt, the Cold War, and the Civil War in Yemen, 1962–1966" (PhD thesis, Princeton University, 2008), 258–61.

[55] John Baldry, "Al-Yaman and the Turkish Occupation, 1849–1914," *Arabica* 23, no. 2 (1976): 176.

men in Afghanistan over double the time frame.[56] And the United States lost almost 60,000 men in Vietnam, the war to which Egypt's intervention in Yemen is most often compared. Nevertheless, Egypt lost more troops in the Yemeni civil war than in any of the wars with Israel, with the possible exception of the Six-Day War.[57] The cumulative impact on national morale of 150 to 200 deaths per month, sustained over five years of grueling counterinsurgency, was significant. Although ordinary Egyptians were officially shielded from the truth about Yemen, it was impossible to stifle entirely the stories of more than 150,000 men who rotated in and out of service in Yemen over the course of five years, and of whom at least 10 percent returned dead, maimed, or not at all.[58] The bodies of a great number of those who died in captivity or in remote locations were never recovered; many others were buried in Yemen, where they remain to this day.[59]

Cost

Without access to official data, estimating the costs of the Egyptian war effort is an all but futile undertaking.[60] It is always difficult to isolate additional war-related expenses from defense outlays that would have been incurred in peacetime. It is next to impossible to do so when several of the key cost components remain secret. Estimates by Egyptian historians range from a low of $415 million over the course of five years to as high as $690 million, excluding Soviet aid.[61] Estimates by the So-

[56] Mark Galeotti, *Afghanistan: The Soviet Union's Last War* (London: Frank Cass, 1995), 27.

[57] Clodfelter, *Warfare and Armed Conflicts*, 635; Michael Oren, *Six Days of War: June 1967 and the Making of the Modern Middle East* (Oxford: Oxford University Press, 2002), 305; Muḥammad Fawzī, *Ḥarb al-thalāth sanawāt*, 160–61.

[58] Aḥmad, *Dhikrayāt*, 587.

[59] For accounts and photos of burial on the battlefield or in military cemeteries in Yemen, see Airgram, Blalock (Ta'izz) to Department of State, no. A-81, March 2, 1963, "Observations from Sanaa," p. 2, RG 59, Box 4147A, POL 26–27 Yemen, NARA; Khalīl, *Ḥurūb Miṣr*, 62, 74; Maḥrizī, *al-Ṣamt al-ḥā'ir*, 6, 122, 132; Witty, "Egypt in North Yemen," 431n., 436.

[60] For a fuller discussion, see Ferris, "Egypt," 262–71.

[61] All dollar figures are historical values based on an exchange rate of E£1 = $2.3. Low: Aḥmad, *al-Dawr*, 252–57, 396–99, 481–84. High: Aḥmad, *Dhikrayāt*, 601–13. Nasser aide Sāmī Sharaf has written (in *defense* of the war) that the cost did not exceed E£500 million ($1.15 billion), which is approximately equivalent to Maḥmūd Aḥmad's estimate, if Soviet aid is factored in (*Sanawāt*, 2:287, 655). P. J. Vatikiotis estimated a staggering E£4 bil-

viet, American, and British governments suggest that an average annual outlay of $70 to $100 million is not far off the mark, yielding a total price tag of $350 to $500 million.[62] However, given Egypt's chronic shortage of foreign exchange, the vital statistic is not total spending, but expenditure in hard currency.[63] Unfortunately, this is precisely where most of the uncertainty lies. The first obstacle concerns relations with the principal purveyor of war materiel, the Soviet Union. The secrecy surrounding the nature of Soviet financial commitments to the campaign renders accurate estimates about consumption of equipment, spare parts, and fuel impossible. If most or all of the debt forgiven by the Soviets in the summer of 1965 did in fact represent total Egyptian liabilities to the USSR arising from the intervention in Yemen, then as much as $500 million may be removed from the equation—though not from the political balance book of Soviet-Egyptian relations.[64]

Two budgetary items account for much of the rest of the hard currency expended in the course of the campaign: campaign bonuses and tribal subsidies. Starting in 1963, members of the expeditionary force in Yemen received substantial salary bonuses, paid in riyals. It is difficult

lion ($9.2 billion) for the total cost of the war, and Kirk Beattie cites a figure of $1 million per day. Vatikiotis, *Nasser and His Generation*, 162; Beattie, *Egypt*, 193. See also Baghdādī, *Mudhakkirāt*, 2:191.

[62] V. Kornev (Dep. Dir. OBV MID), "Polozhenie v Iemenskoi Arabskoi Respublike i Iemeno-OARovskie otnoshenia (spravka)," March 13, 1964, f. 5, op. 30, d. 451, p. 40, RGANI; CIA, NIE no. 36.7-63, "The Situation and Prospects in Yemen," November 6, 1963, p. 6, in NSF, NIEs, Box 6, File 36.7 Yemen, LBJL; Battle (Cairo) to SecState no. 4521, June 24, 1965, RG 59, CF 1964–66, Box 589, NARA; American Embassy, Cairo, to Department of State, July 3, 1965, "The Economic Cost to the UARG of Its Involvement in the Yemen," in FO 371/179864, PRO; Note by R. T. Higgins, July 15, 1965, "U.A.R. Cost of the Yemen Campaign," BM 1071/84/G, in ibid.; CIA, "Problems and Prospects for the United Arab Republic," p. 6. These estimates gain some credence from remarks made by Nasser to 'Abd al-Laṭīf al-Baghdādī in late November 1962, according to which 'Āmir's requests for appropriations to cover the first six months of operations amounted to approximately $50 million, and from a statement by Nasser to the East German representative in Cairo in April 1965 that the additional costs imposed by the war in 1965 would amount to about $70 million. Baghdādī, *Mudhakkirāt*, 2:191–92; Telegram, Kiesewetter to Berlin, no. 234, April 20, 1965, p. 1, NY 4182/1336, Nachlass Walter Ulbricht, SAPMO. Marshal Sa'd al-Shādhilī recalls an extra annual military expenditure of $40 million. But he also contends that Egypt suffered a mere one thousand dead and one thousand wounded. Ḥabīb, *Milaffāt*, 245.

[63] For some figures, see Waterbury, *Egypt*, 94; H. B. Walker (Cairo) to R. M. Posnett, June 25, 1965, FO 371/179864, PRO; H. B. Walker (Cairo) to M. J. Weir (Arabian Department), May 19, 1965, ibid.

[64] See chapter four; Aḥmad, *Dhikrayāt*, 509, 609, 649; and Safran, *Saudi Arabia*, 120.

to assess the cost of these bonuses to the Egyptian government because the amounts paid fluctuated with time, and there were multiple exchange rates at any given moment. One source reports that enlisted men received 10 Yemeni riyals a month, while officers got 30 riyals.[65] In theory, these bonuses were worth as much as $23 and $70, respectively. In practice, however, they may have been worth less than a third of that amount. This is both because the Egyptians imposed an artificially low rate on Yemeni banks, which was at odds with the official and black-market rates based on the coin's bullion content, and because the riyals produced in Cairo were debased over time. According to one estimate, this harsh monetary policy forced Yemeni banks to subsidize the cost of Egyptian operations by close to 50 percent.[66] In any event, the additional annual expenditure on salary bonuses for a task force of 60,000, according to these figures, would be on the order of 8.7 million riyals, equivalent to $9 million at official exchange rates and as little as $6 million at the imposed rate. While not enormous, these numbers are not insignificant.[67]

A source of much greater hard currency expenditure in Yemen was the payment of subsidies to the tribes. Unfortunately, there is even less certainty about these figures, since the funds came from a special account in the presidency and do not appear in official budgetary tables. Because of the absence of hard data and the potential for enormous hidden outlays in hard currency, tribal subsidies represent the Achilles heel of any study of the economic side of the Egyptian war effort in Yemen. Chief of Military Intelligence Ṣalāḥ al-Dīn al-Ḥadīdī writes that

[65] Aḥmad, *Dhikrayāt*, 584–85. See also Somerville-Large, *Tribes and Tribulations*, 105; Ḥamrūsh, *Qiṣṣat thawrat 23 yūliyū*, 3:232; Abū Dhikrī, *al-Zuhūr*, 43. While defending Egypt's expenditure in Yemen to the Canadian ambassador in the fall of 1963, 'Abd al-Laṭīf al-Baghdādī claimed that two-thirds of soldier's salaries were paid in Egypt, and much of the rest went unspent because there was nothing to buy in Yemen. Ford (Cairo) to Ext. 491, October 28, 1963, in FO 371/172864, PRO. Aḥmad Ḥamrūsh cites an average of 1 pound spent per soldier per day, which (assuming pounds sterling) would amount to £30 (approximately $85) per month per soldier (*Qiṣṣat thawrat 23 yūliyū*, 3:262).

[66] Report, [Department of State], "Yemen: Financial and Economic Situation," January 1964, pp. 25, 36, in NSF, Files of Robert W. Komer, Box 54, File Yemen: December 1963–March 1966, Part 3, LBJL; Blalock, "Observations from Sanaa," 5; "The Economic Cost to the UARG of Its Involvement in the Yemen," 2.

[67] To cut costs, travel stipends were apparently reduced at some point in 1966–67 by anywhere from 25% to 90%. Fletcher (Cairo) to Weir (Arabian Department), 26 May 1966, FO 371/190230, PRO; Fletcher (Cairo) to Weir (Arabian Department), 5 May 1966, FO 371/185455, PRO.

the initial budget for tribal pacification was £20,000 per month, but climbed rapidly thereafter.[68] Aḥmad Nu'mān, prime minister of the YAR in mid-1965, hinted that at least some of these subsidies were being passed on as debt to the Republican government.[69] Other than that, we know little.

Where does this brief discussion leave us? Even the minimalist figures derived from official Egyptian data indicate a substantial burden on the Egyptian budget at a time of deepening economic crisis.[70] The additional drain of approximately $100 million per year in the mid-1960s cannot be dismissed at a time when Egypt was running a current account deficit in the neighborhood of $250 million.[71] Annual expenditure on the war equaled at least 2 percent of GDP and consumed more than 20 percent of the entire budget for national security. Anwar Sadat, who had good reason to minimize the cost of the intervention, nevertheless conceded that the war "used up a large portion of our hard currency reserves."[72] 'Alī Ṣabrī, who oversaw the implementation of the first five-year-plan, acknowledges that the war affected the execution of the plan.[73] So too did Nasser.[74] Both neglect to mention that the second five-year plan was aborted due to a shortage of resources. These estimates also underscore the magnitude of the Soviet factor. If, as some Egyptians officials contend, the price tag for the war was in the vicinity

[68] Ḥadīdī, *Shāhid 'alā ḥarb al-Yaman*, 72–73n. Some sources estimated the special budget to be as high as £100 million ($280 million) per year at its peak (ibid., 73n). See also Ḥamrūsh, *Qiṣṣat thawrat 23 yūliyū*, 3:261.

[69] Memcon, Aḥmad Nu'mān and Harlan Clark, May 15, 1965, pp. 4–5, in Airgram, Ta'izz to Dept. of State, no. A-410, June 12, 1965, RG 59, CF, 1964–66, Box 3024, POL 15 YEMEN, NARA.

[70] Aḥmad, *al-Dawr*, 256. Such was certainly the impression of the East German minister of foreign trade, who visited Egypt in February 1963. "Bericht über die Reise des Ministers ... J. Balkow," February 15, 1963, p. 2, NY 4182/1337, Nachlass Walter Ulbricht, SAPMO. See also Baker, *Egypt's Uncertain Revolution*, 56–57.

[71] Khalid Ikram, *The Egyptian Economy, 1995–2000: Performance, Policies, and Issues* (New York: Routledge, 2006), 121.

[72] Sādāt, *al-Baḥth*, 212. In conversation with AP journalist George MacArthur, Muḥammad Haykal attributed much of the economic crisis afflicting Egypt in 1964 to the costs of the Yemen campaign. However, as Badeau notes, Haykal was prone to exaggeration, and his estimate of the war's cost on this occasion (E£30 million in hard currency per year) diverged sharply from what he had said on previous occasions. Badeau (Cairo) to Sec. State, no. 1522, November 2, 1964, RG 59 CF, 1964–66, Box 3026, NARA.

[73] Imām, *'Alī Ṣabrī yatadhakkar*, 107. For scholarly remarks in a similar vein, see Efrat, "The Ten-Year Program and Its Results," 66–68, 71.

[74] Baghdādī, *Mudhakkirāt*, 2:191–92.

of $1 billion, of which at least $500 million constituted debt to the USSR, the cancellation of this debt in the summer of 1965 transferred approximately half of the burden of the Egyptian enterprise in Yemen to the Soviet economy.

As various authors have argued, the root cause of Egypt's economic nosedive in the mid-1960s was the failure to grow exports at a rate commensurate with the rapid increase of the population.[75] But it would be a mistake to conclude from this that the war's impact on the economy was marginal. For one, doubts concerning the true magnitude of the war's impact on Egypt's economy need not obscure the historical perception of such an impact. Whether or not guns for Yemen actually came at the expense of butter for the Egyptian peasant, it was significant that the average citizen thought they did. More importantly, the burden Yemen imposed on Egypt's economy derived less from the *direct* costs of the war in local and foreign currency, but rather from the far greater *indirect* costs Egypt incurred in its financial and political relations with the great powers. The availability of foreign resources for development depended on Egypt's international behavior. As we have seen, the intervention generated hundreds of millions of dollars worth of debt to the USSR. Even if much of that debt was subsequently erased, debt forgiveness came at a political price. Just as significant was the fact that, after 1965, the halt to American aid forced the government to shell out more than $100 million annually in scarce and increasingly expensive foreign exchange to purchase food abroad—while continuing to spend a roughly equal amount directly on Yemen.[76] As we shall see, this combination of economic and political pressures, stemming from the intractable conflict in Yemen, precipitated the final blow to Egypt's economy in June 1967.

Corruption

The concerted attempt to shore up support for the war among combatants and their families produced discriminatory practices in many areas of life. The privileges bestowed upon veterans and their associates went beyond the sort of normal compensatory measures appropriate for combatants deployed in the line of fire far from home.[77] The corruption

[75] Aḥmad, *Dhikrayāt*, 643–49; Waterbury, *Egypt*, 94–95.

[76] Cf. Aḥmad, who argues the opposite (*al-Dawr*, 483–84).

[77] For an opposing view, see Aḥmad, *Dhikrayāt*, 581–87.

that often attended the abuse of these privileges maximized their effect. Taken together, these phenomena created a privileged class of soldiers and civilians, linked together in a network of nepotism and patronage, which benefited materially from the prolongation of the war. In effect, the war accelerated the consolidation of the armed forces as a discrete social division, as implied by the inclusion of the "soldiers" among the five allied popular forces invoked in the National Charter of 1962. The emergence of this class, precisely at a time when the Egyptian economy was heading steadily southward, could not fail to provoke widespread resentment in the population at large.[78]

The most basic privilege associated with service in Yemen was the aforementioned travel bonus (*badal al-safar*). A private, for example, received 10 Yemeni riyals a month. Although its value in Egyptian currency fluctuated with the exchange rate, this bonus was at least equal to a peasant draftee's base salary and was roughly equivalent to the average monthly wage in agriculture.[79] Even the modest savings afforded by years of raised pay were sufficient to boost entire families out of poverty and into small business and commerce.[80] Still more substantial was the compensation paid out to wounded servicemen or to the families of those killed or missing in action. One wounded private, for instance, reported receiving E£1,500 in compensation, which sufficed to pay the bride price of a new wife and to purchase a share in a taxi.[81]

Veterans and their relatives received preferential treatment from state bureaucracies in matters ranging from job placement to hospital care. Officers' wives typically received desirable housing in the new urban apartment complexes constructed by the state, priority in the installation of telephone lines, a car for personal use, and a generous stipend. Their children benefited from precedence in admission to schools and universities, while sick relatives received priority in the waiting list for medical procedures or travel for treatment overseas. Veterans also received precedence in the grant of land, vehicles, and country club mem-

[78] Rahmy, *Egyptian Policy*, 246; Vatikiotis, *Nasser and His Generation*, 162; 'Awaḍ, *Aqni'at al-nāṣiriyyah*, 170; Abū Dhikrī, *al-Zuhūr*, 57, 66.

[79] Baghdādī in Ford (Cairo) to Ext. 491, October 28, 1963, in FO 371/172864, PRO; Imām, *Nāṣir wa-'Āmir*, 84; Mabro, *The Egyptian Economy*, 219.

[80] Rahmy, *Egyptian Policy*, 246; Aḥmad, *al-Dawr*, 494–95.

[81] Fletcher (Cairo) to Weir (Arabian Department), May 5, 1966, FO 371/185455, PRO. Abū Dhikrī tells of a wounded veteran murdered by policemen upon leaving the hospital in 1963 for the 500 pounds in compensation he carried on him. The authorities apparently executed the officers but hushed up the story. *Al-Zuhūr*, 64.

berships.[82] Much of this was done completely above board as part of the campaign to drum up support for the war.[83] For example, a notice by the Ministry of Industry on the front page of the daily *al-Gumhūriyyah* in the spring of 1963 announced that Yemen veterans would receive "absolute priority" in the receipt of the latest models of the state-produced Naṣr cars.[84]

In the summer of 1966, the press announced that volunteers for service in Yemen would receive first dibs on land confiscated in the brutal campaign against "feudalism" underway in the Egyptian countryside at the time.[85] The appointment of ʿĀmir, deputy supreme commander of the armed forces, as chairman of the Higher Committee for the Liquidation of Feudalism exemplified the blurring of boundaries between the army's role in defending the nation against external threats and its growing involvement in the revolutionary struggle against internal enemies. Under ʿĀmir's supervision, the military police played a central role in the execution of massive land appropriations from Egyptian citizens—and the transfer of those assets to veterans of the war in Yemen.[86]

The journal of the armed forces exposed the extraordinary effort on the part of the regime to better the lot of the soldiers fighting in Yemen and their families. In one semiregular corner of the magazine, titled "*Akhī fī al-Yaman sanuḥaqqiqu jamīʿ raghbatak*" ("My brother in Yemen, we shall make all your wishes come true"), the staff mediated requests from soldiers serving at the front. A typical series of entries from July 1964 ran as follows:[87]

> **To the fighter Aḥmad al-Sayyid Ṭāhā**: Your request was fulfilled and the operation on your father was carried out; we have received word from Qalyūbiyyah Governorate that the operation was successful, and that your father has recovered and his health has improved.

[82] Ḥadīdī, *Shāhid ʿalā ḥarb 67*, 48; Abū Dhikrī, *al-Zuhūr*, 43, 96; Maḥrizī, *al-Ṣamt al-ḥāʾir*, 113; Rahmy, *Egyptian Policy*, 247; Vered, *Revolution*, 168.

[83] *Pace* Aḥmad (*Dhikrayāt*, 577, 581), there was nothing exceptional or conspiratorial about the way this was done. It was only later, under the impact of popular discontent, that such practices lost official favor.

[84] *Al-Gumhūriyyah*, April 26, 1963; Abū Dhikrī, *al-Zuhūr*, 43. This policy apparently persisted until 1964 (Aḥmad, *Dhikrayāt*, 585). A familiar sight on the streets of Cairo in the war years and after was that of the soldier-turned-taxi-driver, invariably driving his own cab.

[85] Fletcher (Cairo) to Unwin (NEAD), July 28, 1966, FO 371/190187, PRO.

[86] Ḥamrūsh, *Qiṣṣat thawrat 23 yūliyū*, 2:261–62; Fletcher (Cairo) to Unwin (NEAD), June 30, 1966, FO 371/190187, PRO.

[87] *Al-Quwwāt al-Musallāḥah* (hereafter *QM*), no. 416 (July 1, 1964), 40.

To the fighter Muḥammad al-Sayyid Ramaḍān: We have received word from the Governor of Qalyūbiyyah that he has fulfilled your request and directed that your brother be appointed [to a position in] the vegetable oil presses ...

To the fighter 'Abd al-Ghaffār al-Tūnisī al-Sayyid Abū al-Khayr: Your request will be fulfilled when you return from the Yemen Arab Republic. The Governor of Qalyūbiyyah has promised us to appoint you immediately upon your release from the armed service ...

To the fighter Muḥammad Aḥmad Maẓlūm: Your wish has been granted and your brother, 'Aṭiyyah Aḥmad 'Abd al-Hādī, has been transferred from the police at Miṣr al-Gadīdah to the security police of Daqahliyyah so that he may be next to his family.

The governor of Buḥayrah reported in May 1964 that all companies and state institutions within his province now reserved 40 percent of their open positions for Yemen veterans and their families.[88] Some provinces created a special Yemen Affairs Division dedicated to the handling of such matters. According to officials in the Governorate of Alexandria, for example, by the spring of 1964 the division had processed hundreds of requests for jobs, special medical treatment, housing, transfers, and the like. They also boasted of a special medical team dedicated to the treatment of families of soldiers serving in Yemen.[89]

Such institutionalized discrimination could not fail to arouse feelings of superiority and entitlement among the veterans and their families. At the same time, it inevitably provoked resentment among those who felt the war was an unnecessary burden on the country's economy, and those, even in the military, who did not stand to benefit from the food chain stretching out from Ṣan'ā'.[90] Feelings of resentment were compounded by widespread corruption associated with the war effort. At the heart of this lay the tax-free import of luxury goods into Egypt from Yemen, which broadened the scope of the black market at a time of increasingly severe shortages, inflation, and restrictions on imports.[91] In

[88] *QM*, no. 414 (June 1, 1964), 33. It was no coincidence that by the end of 1964, twenty-two of Egypt's twenty-six provinces were governed by ex-officers. Dekmejian, *Egypt under Nasir*, 222.

[89] *QM*, no. 411 (April 16, 1964), 33–34.

[90] Rahmy, *Egyptian Policy*, 247–48; Ḥadīdī, *Shāhid 'alā ḥarb 67*, 48; Aḥmad, *Dhikrayāt*, 538, 585.

[91] Vatikiotis, *Nasser and His Generation*, 162; Rahmy, *Egyptian Policy*, 246–47; Battle (Cairo) to Dept. of State, "Ramadan 1966—Winter of Discontents," December 23, 1966, pp. 4–5, in FCO 39/233, PRO. Perhaps it was no coincidence that the daily *al-Akhbār* of April 23,

one notorious case in 1966, Colonel ʿAlī Shafīq, Marshal ʿĀmir's military secretary, was arrested along with several other officers on charges of fraud, large-scale smuggling, and black-market trade.[92] Inter alia, these men were charged with conspiring to resell Naṣr cars obtained by submitting false names of widows of Yemen martyrs.[93] Around the same time, thirty other officers and noncommissioned officers stood trial for embezzling pension funds due to wounded veterans.

From a broad social perspective, the problem was not so much the isolated, high profile cases of corruption; it was the ubiquity of small-scale abuses by thousands of individuals that mattered. The lifting of customs regulations for returning soldiers created a system tantamount to state-sanctioned smuggling, complete with special port facilities for the handling of duty-free goods brought home aboard military transports at government expense. Especially prized items were Japanese radio transistors, Swiss watches, televisions, cameras, refrigerators, washing machines, and gas stoves.[94] Although the scale of the phenomenon is disputed, it was undoubtedly sufficient to arouse discontent in a population subjected to stringent currency and customs controls and regularly asked to curb consumption so as to sustain Egypt's socialist transformation in an era of shortages.

The increasingly close association of material benefits with service in Yemen tinged a supposedly selfless war of liberation on behalf of a just

---

1966, featured a notice on "Decisive Measures to Defeat the Black Market" on a front page otherwise dedicated to the story of troop contingents returning from Yemen.

[92] Fletcher (Cairo) to Unwin (NEAD), April 21, 1966, FO 371/190186. ʿAlī Shafīq's fall from favor should also be seen in the context of his struggle with Shams Badrān for influence in ʿĀmir's inner circle, and perhaps also in the context of an attempt to cover up ʿĀmir's secret love affair with the singer Berlentī ʿAbd al-Ḥamīd. According to this view, the Yemen-related charges were intended to cover up a personal vendetta and an illicit relationship and should not be taken at face value. For juicy details, see Ḥamrūsh, *Qiṣṣat thawrat 23 yūliyū*, 2:232–33; and especially Imām, *Nāṣir wa-ʿĀmir*, 108–21, 122–23.

[93] Apparently, a lesser offense was much more common: women with connections would pose as mothers of dead soldiers in order to bypass the long waiting list for the purchase of these vehicles. Imām, *Nāṣir wa-ʿĀmir*, 123. Abū Dhikrī reports black-market trade of government cars by ʿĀmir associates linked with the Yemen campaign as early as the summer of 1963 (*al-Zuhūr*, 65). See also Naṣr, *Mudhakkirāt*, 3:43–44; Beattie, *Egypt*, 161n.

[94] Ḥadīdī, *Shāhid ʿalā ḥarb 67*, 47–48; Rahmy, *Egyptian Policy*, 246–47; Abū Dhikrī, *al-Zuhūr*, 43, 60, 80; Somerville-Large, *Tribes and Tribulations*, 105; Patrick Seale, "Rumours of Unrest in Nasser's Army," *The Scotsman*, May 5, 1966; Blalock, "Observations from Sanaa," 5; Aḥmad, *Dhikrayāt*, 585. Aḥmad disputes the scale of these phenomena and finds them justified.

cause with the stain of corruption. Unofficially, Egyptian servicemen started to refer to the campaign as a "war of status improvement" (*ḥarb taḥsīn ḥālah*).[95] The extraordinary privileges and opportunities associated with service in Yemen tended to trump misgivings about the hazards of the mission, creating tremendous pressure from volunteers who used every means at their disposal to get sent to Yemen.[96] In mid-1965, Major General 'Alī 'Abd al-Khabīr sent several hundred troops home after an investigation revealed that noncombat units were bloated with opportunists who had arranged to get sent to Yemen in order to benefit from the special travel allowance.[97] Former Chief of Staff Muḥammad Fawzī recalls his driver approaching him six months into the war, begging to be sent to Yemen to earn some extra money for his children. Fawzī laments that when the Sixth Division returned to Egypt to take part in the war with Israel in 1967, the officers refused to entrust their personal equipment to storage and ended up deploying in Sinai with their duty-free refrigerators.[98] General Ḥadīdī claims that the corrupting influence of material benefits and unjustified honors warped the Egyptians' sense of purpose. For many, victory ceased to be assessed in terms of battlefield progress and was measured instead by the yardsticks of individual achievement and material gain.[99]

Many officers benefited from extraordinary promotions on the battlefield, not always on the basis of merit, and sometimes on the basis of exaggerated or invented tales of heroism.[100] In general, a sort of battlefield equivalent to grade inflation seems to have taken hold of the Egyptian command as medals proliferated and promotions accelerated beyond reason. The reverse also occurred. Samīr Fāḍil, legal council to the Egyptian forces in Yemen in the early stages of the campaign, recalls an instance where 'Āmir's private secretary, the notorious 'Ali Shafīq, ordered a lieutenant colonel demoted to private as punishment for poor battlefield performance. When Fāḍil insisted on a fair trial, 'Āmir

[95] Abū Dhikrī, *al-Zuhūr*, 72.

[96] Vatikiotis, *Nasser and His Generation*, 62; Abū Dhikrī, *al-Zuhūr*, 64.

[97] Aḥmad, *Dhikrayāt*, 587. See also Ḥamrūsh, *Qiṣṣat thawrat 23 yūliyū*, 3:241; Ḥadīdī, *Shāhid 'alā ḥarb 67*, 47.

[98] Imām, *Muḥammad Fawzī*, 35–36.

[99] Ḥadīdī, *Shāhid 'alā ḥarb 67*, 48; idem, *Shāhid 'alā ḥarb al-Yaman*, 155; Abū Dhikrī, *al-Zuhūr*, 53, 57, 62. For an indignant refutation of these charges, see Aḥmad, *Dhikrayāt*, 577–78, 581–83.

[100] Imām, *Nāṣir wa-'Āmir*, 26–27; Ḥadīdī, *Shāhid 'alā ḥarb 67*, 48; Vatikiotis, *Nasser and His Generation*, 162. Again, Aḥmad disputes this (*Dhikrayāt*, 585–86). For an account of apparently merited promotion on the battlefield, see Khalīl, *Ḥurūb Miṣr*, 63.

changed the law, empowering himself to demote an officer of any rank to private without due process.[101] A more positive phenomenon was the decision to broaden the base of the Egyptian officer corps in order to address the needs of the expanding army. In 1963, first sergeants and then privates who had served considerable terms in Yemen were decreed eligible for entry into officer training courses, regardless of whether or not they had completed their secondary education.[102]

These phenomena were not unconnected with the power struggle at the top. ʿĀmir's dependents, ever fearful of another attempt by the president to remove him, exploited the war to consolidate their independent power base. Aside from turning a blind eye on the lucrative illegal activities associated with the war, they appointed loyal men to key positions within the military and civilian establishment. Under the orchestration of his powerful director of human resources, Shams al-Dīn Badrān, ʿĀmir not only oversaw the total restructuring of the officer corps within the military, but also appointed great numbers of protégés as senior bureaucrats, chairmen of the boards of large state corporations, mayors, governors and diplomats, commanders in the National Guard, and leaders in the ASU Youth Organization. He thereby built up a vast network of patronage through which he exercised enormous influence outside the boundaries of the armed forces.[103] Many of these trends began well before the intervention in Yemen.[104] But the war provided an opportunity for deepening and expanding the network of beneficiaries dependent on ʿĀmir and his underlings by providing a legitimate vehicle for perpetuating official discrimination in favor of anyone associated with the campaign.[105]

[101] Samīr Fāḍil, *Kuntu qāḍiyan li-ḥādith al-minaṣṣah: Mudhakkirāt qāḍin ʿaskarī min ḥarb al-Yaman ilā ightiyāl al-Sādāt* (Cairo: Dār Sfinks, 1993), 36.

[102] Be'eri, *Army Officers*, 324.

[103] *Pace* ʿAlī Ṣabrī, who insists that the influence of the military establishment outside the armed forces was limited. Imām, *ʿAlī Ṣabrī yatadhakkar*, 99–101. On ʿĀmir's (and Badrān's) growing responsibilities and influence in the civilian sector in 1966–67, see Battle (Cairo) to Department of State, Airgram A-636, "The Rise of Abdul Hakim AMER," January 27, 1967, RG 59, 1967–69, Box 2554, POL 15-1 UAR, NARA; Munīr Ḥāfiẓ, "al-Tārīkh al-sirrī li-ḥukm Gamāl ʿAbd al-Nāṣir," *Rūz al-Yūsuf*, May 31, 1976; Sādāt, *al-Baḥth*, 220; Beattie, *Egypt*, 195–96; ʿUkāshah, *Mudhakkirātī*, 2:398–99; Imām, *Muḥammad Fawzī*, 126.

[104] See, for instance, Vatikiotis, *The Egyptian Army in Politics*, 224 and passim; Be'eri, *Army Officers*, 324. For the evolving place of officers within the ruling elite from 1952 to 1967, see Dekmejian, *Egypt under Nasir*, 167–224.

[105] Sādāt, *al-Baḥth*, 209–10; Vatikiotis, *Nasser and His Generation*, 163; Ḥadīdī, *Shāhid ʿalā ḥarb 67*, 26–30; idem, *Shāhid ʿalā ḥarb al-Yaman*, 155; Imām, *Nāṣir wa-ʿĀmir*, 12, 50, 84–89;

The Spread of Popular Discontent

A joke circulating in Cairo in the spring of 1963 went something like this: A ship was damaged at sea. The captain suggested that one man of each nationality jump ship, so as to reduce the vessel's load. The first victim selected was an Egyptian. The man, having resigned himself to his fate, stepped forward and threw himself overboard with the cry "For Egypt!" The second man was British, and he too jumped into the ocean, crying out "For Great Britain!" The third man up was a Yemeni. He readied himself, bellowed "For the Yemen Arab Republic!" and promptly pushed the man standing next to him, an Egyptian, headfirst into the sea.[106] Around the same time, a pun poked fun at the ongoing unity talks among Egypt, Iraq, and Syria: Nasser, seeing that the war in Yemen was becoming protracted, decided, in view of the warm revolutionary relations between Egypt and Cuba, to establish a tripartite union among the three states. The name chosen for the new state was "Miṣr-Yaman-Kūbā" ("Egypt-Yemen-Cuba," but also: "Oh, Egypt, you fate-stricken one!").[107]

Humor, however, could only go so far toward alleviating the seriousness of incipient opposition to the war. How strong opposition to the war became, how broadly it was shared, and how deeply it affected decision making at the top, is unfortunately impossible to assess with any confidence based on the available evidence.[108] The key factors at work were the ones discussed above—namely, the rising death toll, the perceived connection between wartime expenditure and the economic crisis, and corruption associated with the campaign—in addition to the tightening of state control over society as the war progressed. Around the intervention's first anniversary, the governor of Cairo conceded in private conversation that the war was no longer popular among the people, who did not understand why it had been necessary.[109] The CIA

Baghdādī, *Mudhakkirāt*, 2:168, 172; Ḥamrūsh, *Qiṣṣat thawrat 23 yūliyū*, 2:214–20, 232–33; Rahmy, *Egyptian Policy*, 249; Canadian Ambassador Ford (Cairo) to External 533, November 16, 1963, "UAR Internal Affairs," p. 3, in FO 371/172862, PRO. For opposing views, see ʿAlī Ṣabrī's comments in Imām, *ʿAlī Ṣabrī yatadhakkar*, 99; and Aḥmad, *Dhikrayāt*, 577–79.

[106] Abū Dhikrī, *al-Zuhūr*, 54.

[107] Ibid. For the importance of jokes as a barometer of Egyptian public opinion, see Sharaf, *Sanawāt*, 2:98.

[108] Cf. Aḥmad, *al-Dawr*, 250–51.

[109] Ford (Cairo) to External 540, November 20, 1963, RG25, vol. 8995, File 20-UAR-1-4, LAC. For Ford's assessment of a drop in Nasser's popularity due to the waning of popu-

concluded in November 1963 that "the Yemen war, with its heavy toll of casualties, is becoming increasingly unpopular in Egypt and, apparently, with its military commanders."[110] At about the same time, pamphlets appeared on the streets of Cairo, Alexandria, and Port Saʿīd, which criticized the regime for intervening in Yemen and Algeria at the expense of Egypt's own welfare.[111] In Abū Dhikrī's fictionalized account, thousands of Egyptians were already in prison by this point due to the expression of sentiments opposed to the war.[112]

US Ambassador John Badeau recalls that by the time he left Egypt in the summer of 1964, "there wasn't much war spirit in the Egyptians." "I do not think," he continued, "they were ever deeply impressed by this adventure.... Whatever Nasser's plans may have been, the average Egyptian has not, in general, been an expansionist, and there were aspects of the Yemen war that chilled the public. I remember ... the funeral of one of the first officers killed in Yemen, a Copt ... the coffin, against popular custom, was closed ... because the corpse was headless; the Yemenis cut off heads. This sort of information began to get back to Cairo, painting an increasingly bloody picture."[113] Some of this criticism was directed at the president, who read letters from citizens complaining about the intervention in Yemen.[114]

Disgruntlement at home was most evident in the economic sphere. While we have no statistical data on Egyptian public opinion at the time, especially on this sensitive matter, there is considerable circumstantial evidence indicating that the Egyptian middle class viewed the regime's embroilment in Yemen as the primary cause of its worsening economic difficulties in the mid-1960s.[115] By contrast, the privileges military officers enjoyed effectively sheltered them from the twin scourges

---

lar enthusiasm for the war and the rise in cost of living, see Ford (Cairo) to External 533, November 16, 1963, in VG 1015/33, FO 371/172862, PRO.

[110] "The Situation and Prospects in Yemen," 6–7.

[111] Haykal blamed them on the Syrian Baʿth. *Al-Ahrām*, November 22, 1963; Maitland (Cairo) to Scrivener (Foreign Office), December 11, 1963, VG 1015/36, FO 371/172862, PRO.

[112] Abū Dhikrī, *al-Zuhūr*, 35. Sāmī Gawhar also attributes the mass imprisonments to the fact that "people [began] to talk about our losses and huge expenditure [in Yemen]" (*al-Mawtā yatakallamūn*, 62).

[113] Badeau, *Reminiscences*, 215.

[114] Sharaf, *Sanawāt*, 2:99, 104.

[115] See, for instance, Parker (Cairo) to Dept. of State, Airgram A-351, October 27, 1965, "The UAR in 1965: Revolutionary Malaise," pp. 4–6, RG 59, CF, 1964–66, Box 2765, NARA.

of shortages and inflation that descended upon Egypt in 1964.[116] As Nasser's biographer Robert Stephens puts it: "The war was not unpopular with all of the Egyptian army, because of the bonuses for service in the Yemen and the chance it gave to buy and bring home foreign goods unobtainable in Egypt. But it was felt as an onerous burden by the Egyptian public. Lives and money, it was believed, were being squandered in a remote and ungrateful country in which Egypt had no real interest, at a time when Egypt herself was running into ever heavier debt to try and finance her own five-year development plans."[117] At the same time, there was only so far monetary and other privileges could go toward assuaging the wounded pride of an impotent army. And it was impossible to buffer the officer corps, constantly rotating in and out of service in Yemen, from discontent at home. As a CIA report concluded in the spring of 1966, "the Egyptian people are unhappy about the costs and casualties, and among the military there is widespread anger and humiliation over the failure to win." "The stalemate in Yemen and the country's economic problems," the report concluded, "have led to political unrest."[118]

A supply crisis unprecedented in postrevolutionary history struck Egypt in 1964. By early January, shortages were beginning to affect the ability of the average citizen to obtain basic foodstuffs and other commodities. At the end of February, the US ambassador reported that "a common sight throughout Cairo during the last two month has been the long lines of people waiting outside cooperative stores."[119] By the time fall arrived, the crisis could no longer be ignored, and it increasingly occupied the front pages of the major newspapers as well as the attention of the government. Nasser exhorted the people to save more and buy less, but otherwise suggested little else that might ease the problem of rising consumption.[120] In early December, *Time* reported

[116] The general point is made in R. Daniell (Cairo) to D. Speares (NEAD), June 30, 1966, VG 1015/31, FO 371/190187, PRO. Canadian Ambassador Ford makes an important distinction between conscripts, who were generally unhappy about the war, and officers, who benefited from it. Ford (Cairo) to Ext. 428, September 19, 1963, in FO 371/172864, PRO.

[117] Stephens, *Nasser*, 417. See also Rahmy, *Egyptian Policy*, 202.

[118] CIA, NIE no. 36.1-66, "The Outlook for the United Arab Republic," May 19, 1966, p. 6, in NSF, National Intelligence Estimates, Box 6, File 36.1 UAR, LBJL.

[119] Badeau (Cairo) to Dept. of State, Airgram A-642, February 28, 1964, "Political Successes and Economic Woes—the UAR in mid-Winter 1964," p. 3, RG 59, CF, 1964–66, Box 2759, NARA; Vered, "Without Decision," 229–31.

[120] Nasser's speech before the National Assembly on November 12, 1964, in UAR, *Majmū'at khuṭab*, 5:61–91, and 83–84 in particular.

that the government, "faced with the unpleasant fact that a measure of austerity is the inescapable price of a crash development scheme ... took the drastic step of banning the slaughter and sale of meat three days out of each week. It's back to corn and beans for the Egyptians on Sundays, Tuesdays and Wednesdays.... Violators could get up to one year in jail."[121] The British ambassador in Cairo reported that "more general discontent is being expressed in the U.A.R. than at any time since the [1952] revolution."[122] The CIA concurred, listing food shortages, black markets, high prices, restrictions on free speech, and the war in Yemen as the primary sources of discontent.[123] Yet this was only the beginning of the supply crunch of 1964–67. Although some of the products missing from the shelves of local stores would vary over time—in early 1964 meat, fats, sugar, and tea topped the list, while by the end of 1966 the items of primary concern were soap, fluorescent light bulbs, sandals, and cooking oils—the fundamental complaints remained the same: low stocks, long lines, poor quality, and soaring prices on a booming black market.[124] The government could not ignore these problems for long. Indeed, from 1964 onward, the deepening economic crisis dominated the domestic agenda of the regime.[125]

On several occasions, Nasser expressed concerns about the negative impact of the war on the economy and on public opinion. As early as November 1962, he acknowledged in private that the special appropriations ʻĀmir demanded for the conduct of operations in Yemen would have to come at the expense of the development plan.[126] In Sep-

[121] "Too Much and Too Little," *Time*, December 18, 1964.

[122] Middleton (Cairo) to Stewart, no. 49, December 18, 1964, "Internal Discontent in the United Arab Republic," FO 371/178580, PRO. See also Maitland (Cairo) to Scrivener (FO), October 30, 1964, VG 1015/38, FO 371/178580, PRO.

[123] "Problems and Prospects for the United Arab Republic," 5, 8.

[124] Ibid.; Battle (Cairo) to Dept. of State, Airgram A-559, December 23, 1966, "Ramadan 1966—Winter of Discontents," p. 4, RG 59, CF, 1964–66, Box 2763, NARA. In March 1967, it was onions. A joke circulating at the time went like this: Nasser was attending the long and dreary sessions of a government conference on production when he was suddenly and mysteriously called out, as was ʻĀmir moments later. When they returned after ten minutes, some of the attendees expressed the hope that nothing serious had happened. Nasser responded: "Oh, no. But onions have just been put on sale at the nearby cooperative." Fletcher (Cairo) to Unwin (NEAD), March 30, 1967, FCO 39/233, PRO.

[125] Sāmī Sharaf reports that Nasser used to read a daily report on the fluctuating stock of key goods such as wheat, flour, and sugar. His most critical concern was to maintain a three-month's supply of wheat. Sharaf, *Sanawāt*, 2:93.

[126] Baghdādī, *Mudhakkirāt*, 2:191–92. See also Ford (Cairo) to External 533, November 16, 1963, "UAR Internal Affairs," pp. 4–5, in FO 371/172862, PRO.

Figure 5.7 Prime Minister Muḥyī al-Dīn clobbers the beast of consumption with the club of price controls: "This is the only way to kill the beast!" *Akhbār al-Yawm,* December 11, 1965. Cartoon by Alexander Ṣārūkhān.

tember 1963, in the course of a conversation with the Canadian ambassador, Nasser drew a connection between the fate of the war effort in Yemen and the position of his regime, cited the deleterious effect of combat casualties upon the morale of the fighting forces, and pointed to the economic burden the war imposed.[127] The president also spoke defensively about the cost of the war in his aforementioned speech of December 23, 1964. And his decision to dispatch 'Āmir to the National Assembly in February 1965 to deliver the first public accounting of the campaign stemmed directly from the regime's perception of the need to respond to mounting criticism.[128]

To a certain extent, popular opposition to the war seems to have been shared by key members of the Egyptian leadership. The two men most

[127] Ford (Cairo) to Ext. 428, September 19, 1963, in FO 371/172864, PRO.

[128] Middleton (Cairo) to Stewart (London), no. 1, January 7, 1966, "UAR: Annual Review for 1965," p. 3, FO 371/190185, PRO.

often cited in this regard are Vice Presidents Kamāl al-Dīn Ḥusayn and ʻAbd al-Laṭīf al-Baghdādī.[129] According to Ḥasan Ibrāhīm, the former "opposed [Nasser's determination] to continue the war and said that it was contrary to Islam, which does not sanction war unless it is in the path of God, and that it did not make sense for a Muslim to fight his fellow Muslim."[130] Ḥusayn confirms that he advised Nasser at the time to withdraw Egypt's forces as soon as possible from a quagmire that had come to resemble Vietnam.[131] Baghdādī too apparently thought it unwise to prolong the war and reports telling Nasser so in July 1963. He warned the president of an impending disaster and drew an analogy between Nasser's predicament in Yemen and Napoleon's in Spain during the Peninsular War (1808–14).[132] Another individual associated with insider opposition to the regime's Yemen policy is Vice President Zakariyyā Muḥyī al-Dīn, whom Nasser appointed prime minister in September 1965 to deal with the worsening economic crisis. Muḥyī al-Dīn sought to rein in reckless government spending in order to rescue Egypt's development plan, and he was known to favor liquidation or substantial contraction of the war effort as one means to this end.[133] In fact, differences with Nasser over the failure to implement the Jiddah peace agreement seem to have been at least partially to blame for his dismissal one year later.[134] Muḥyī al-Dīn's fall from favor paralleled that of the UAR's most respected economic expert, ʻAbd al-Munʻim al-Qaysūnī, who was also known to have argued for substantial cuts in spending on Yemen.[135]

[129] See chapter one.

[130] Quoted by Gawhar, *al-Mawtā yatakallamūn*, 61. See also Abū Dhikrī, *al-Zuhūr*, 19–20; Ḥamrūsh, *Qiṣṣat thawrat 23 yūliyū*, 2:220–21.

[131] Ḥabīb, *Milaffāt*, 243.

[132] Quoted by Gawhar, *al-Mawtā yatakallamūn*, 62; Ḥabīb, *Milaffāt*, 242.

[133] Aḥmad, *al-Dawr*, 400; Ḥamrūsh, *Qiṣṣat thawrat 23 yūliyū*, 3:262–63; Nutting, *Nasser*, 378; Stephens, *Nasser*, 426; CIA, "The Outlook for the United Arab Republic," 7; ʻUmar al-Saqqāf, cited in Telegram, Eilts (Jiddah) to Sec. State, no. 685, February 15, 1966, p. 2, RG 59, CF, 1964–66, Box 3028, POL 27 YEMEN, NARA.

[134] Nutting, *Nasser*, 381; Waterbury, *Egypt*, 96–97. But Nasser spoke only of differences on economic policy. ʻUkāshah, *Mudhakkirātī*, 2:195. And East German intelligence assessed that Muḥyī al-Dīn's attempt to wrest direct control over the organs of internal security constituted the most serious difference between the two. "Einzel information über die Lage in der VAR," October 18, 1966, p. 2, MfS—Hauptverwaltung Aufklärung, Nr. 219, BStU.

[135] Minute by P. M. Unwin (NEAD), June 6, 1966, "U.A.R.: Internal Situation," FO 371/190187, PRO.

However, one should not exaggerate the extent of opposition to Nasser's Yemen policy within the higher echelons of the regime. The fact that several of Nasser's colleagues expressed misgivings about the war does not necessarily mean that Yemen constituted their primary disagreement with Nasser or that a coordinated opposition ever formed within the ruling clique to challenge him on this issue.[136]

By the summer of 1965, as Haykal reports, Nasser understood that the funds being diverted for the war were sufficient to cover Egypt's wheat deficit at a time when the continuation of US food aid was no longer certain.[137] Accordingly, there can be no doubt that economic pressures were significant in Nasser's decision to seek peace in the summer of 1965.[138] To what extent the pressure of public opinion—let alone the threat of a coup—played a role in that decision is another question altogether. American diplomat Richard Parker dismissed the matter at the time, reporting from Cairo that "foreign policy is not an issue. There is grumbling over expenditures in the Yemen or other unprofitable ventures, but the foreign policy of the UAR is not seriously opposed. Foreign affairs is an area of operations for prestige rather than necessity. Nasser can do pretty much as he likes in the foreign field, as far as the Egyptian public is concerned."[139] This is almost certainly an overstatement. As Parker himself conceded, Nasser's new post-Jiddah image as "*baṭal al-salām*" (Hero of Peace) was popular. In other words, the peace process produced immediate political dividends in some corners, at least. Indeed, the average street view of Egypt's predicament in Yemen cannot have been all that different from Nasser's; it was a very costly error. Whether or not an immediate halt to the constant compounding of that error was worth the price in lost prestige was a question upon which reasonable men could disagree. Moreover, as Parker conceded, the important question was not so much the attitude of the man on the street, but that of the man in uniform. And this was much more difficult to discern.[140]

[136] Aḥmad, *al-Dawr*, 259.

[137] Haykal, *al-Infijār*, 182; Telegram, Battle (Cairo) to Sec. State, no. 2571, April 8, 1966, p. 2, RG 59, CF, 1964–66, Box 3028, POL 27 YEMEN, NARA. The CIA estimated in the spring of 1965 that a cessation of PL 480 aid would force Egypt to shell out approximately $75 million per year to buy food on the world market. "Problems and Prospects for the United Arab Republic," 17.

[138] See chapter six.

[139] Parker (Cairo) to Dept. of State, Airgram A-351, October 27, 1965, "The UAR in 1965: Revolutionary Malaise," p. 8, RG 59, CF, 1964–66, Box 2765, NARA.

[140] Ibid. See also Aḥmad, *al-Dawr*, 251, 263–64.

In September 1965, shortly after Nasser returned from Jiddah and Moscow, the Egyptian government launched an unprecedented operation against the Muslim Brotherhood, rounding up hundreds in a highly publicized campaign that captured the headlines for months. Was it a mere coincidence that Nasser's peace initiative in August 1965 preceded the massive crackdown on the Muslim Brotherhood by less than a month?[141] Robert Dekmejian took the foiled conspiracy against the regime as evidence of widespread discontent with the bungled war and concluded that Nasser's trip to Jiddah represented a grudging surrender to public opinion.[142] But the fact that the mass detentions, accompanied as they were by sensational headlines and close coverage of the arrests, allegations, and subsequent trials, came immediately *after* Nasser's return from the summit with Faysal, suggests that they were deliberately staged.[143] If so, why? The most convincing explanation is that Nasser chose to inflate the threat from the Muslim Brotherhood at this time in order to justify coming to terms with Faysal at the probable expense of the Yemeni Republic. The regime, in other words, deflected attention from the external setback by turning inward to meet the enemy from within. While popular discontent over the war may have helped drive Nasser to the negotiating table, it was anticipated oppositionto the terms of peace that precipitated his crackdown on the Muslim Brotherhood. Quite sensibly, Nasser's concerns lay primarily with the military elite, whose reaction to defeat in Yemen troubled him most. That the average Egyptian wanted peace mattered less than that the officer was liable to oppose it.

*

From mid-1963 onward, a number of mutually reinforcing factors impressed upon Nasser the need to come to terms with Saudi Arabia in order to end the conflict in Yemen. Whether it was the intractable situation on the battlefield, the brewing crisis with the United States, the

[141] See also Rahmy, *Egyptian Policy*, 248–49.

[142] Dekmejian, *Egypt under Nasir*, 228, 233. Ali Rahmy essentially concurs: "by the end of 1965, it became obvious that both public opinion and the political institutions were of the view that the intervention in Yemen should be ended by all means." *Egyptian Policy*, 203.

[143] On possible exaggeration of the "Brotherhood menace" by the security services, see Beattie, *Egypt*, 193; Ezra Ben David, "The Confrontation with the Muslim Brotherhood in 1965–1966" (Hebrew), in Shamir, *Decline of Nasserism*, 135–36. Ṣalāḥ Naṣr notes the suspicious origins of the charges against the Muslim Brotherhood in Shams Badrān's office, and Nasser's unnatural decision to task military intelligence with this civilian investigation. Naṣr, *Mudhakkirāt*, 3:115–18.

worsening economic crisis, the mounting casualties, or the grumblings of discontent in Egypt—all factors pointed to the need for a settlement. Against all these arguments for withdrawal stood one intangible but hugely important consideration: prestige. The Free Officers had staked all on Yemen. They had invested the intervention with all the trappings of a holy war. To lose in Yemen would be to concede defeat in the Arab Cold War, forcing Egypt to surrender its claim to Arab primacy. That was unthinkable.

Withdrawal without victory threatened more than Egypt's image abroad; the return of tens of thousands of disgruntled veterans from Yemen might conceivably have imperiled the regime itself.[144] Indeed, defeat in Yemen on the heels of the humiliation of the *infiṣāl* might well have produced a revolutionary situation in the armed services not unlike that which emerged from the defeat in Palestine in 1948.[145] In this respect, Nasser's dilemma after 1963 resembled De Gaulle's a decade before.[146] What Nasser needed was a settlement in Yemen that guaranteed the survival of the republic in the absence of Egyptian troops. This, as we shall see, was easier said than done.

[144] Walker (Cairo) to Posnett (Arabian Department), May 15, 1965, FO 371/179864, PRO; Wilton (Cairo) to Higgins (NEAD), January 31, 1966, FO 371/190186, PRO; Agaf Modi'in/Maḥleket Meḥkar MD (28/586.130.1/M), February 18, 1966, "Special Survey No. 9/66: Egypt's Position on the Question of Yemen" (Hebrew), ISA; CIA, "The Outlook for the United Arab Republic," 7; Dekmejian, *Egypt under Nasir*, 239; Rahmy, *Egyptian Policy*, 248. Nasser acknowledged as much in private on at least two occasions. The first was in conversation with Canadian Ambassador Ford on September 9, 1963. The second occasion was in the spring of 1966, when Nasser confided to US Ambassador Battle that the return of a defeated army from Yemen to Egypt "would present real problems for me." His ambassador in Washington went even further. In conversation with a US official on April 5, 1965, Kāmil stated that Nasser simply could not survive the humiliation of the collapse of the YAR, much as he might want to disengage. It is impossible to dismiss the possibility that such remarks were intended primarily to deflect American pressure for withdrawal. Ford (Cairo) to Ext. 428, September 19, 1962, in FO 371/172864, PRO; Battle (Cairo) to Sec. State, March 20, 1966, RG 59, 1964–66, Box 2768, Pol UAR-US, NARA; Dept. of State, Memorandum of Conversation [between Mostafa Kamel and Curtis Jones], April 5, 1965, "Viet-Nam and Yemen," in NSF, Country File, United Arab Republic, Box 159/1, Folder: UAR, Vol. 3, Memos [2 of 2], 11/64–6/65, LBJL.

[145] E.g., Saudi Ambassador to the UAR 'Alī Riḍā, qtd. in Telegram, Ta'izz to Sec. State, no. 644, March 3, 1965, Section 2, RG 59, CF, 1964–66, Box 3027, POL 27 YEMEN, NARA.

[146] Ford (Cairo) to Ext. 428, September 19, 1962, p. 2, FO 371/172864, PRO; Beattie, *Egypt*, 161.

✷ CHAPTER SIX ✷

The Fruitless Quest for Peace

SAUDI-EGYPTIAN NEGOTIATIONS, 1964–66

SINCE 1948 THE PALESTINE PROBLEM has often served as a "Shirt of 'Uthmān" to cover inter-Arab differences while advancing state interests that have little or nothing to do with the Arab-Israeli conflict.[1] In the 1950s and 1960s, it was, for instance, the tool of choice for Arab governments seeking to apply pressure on the Hashemites of Jordan, whose domestic position and aspirations west of the Jordan River hinged on the suppression of Palestinian nationalism. Palestine has rarely, if ever, been invoked by Arab leaders out of a sincere intention to go to war on behalf of the Palestinians. More often, "Palestine" has served as the highest trump card[2]—in a suit with Reaction and Imperialism—that may be deployed in the inter-Arab contest for legitimacy. Up until his final bluff in 1967, Nasser was the undisputed master of this game. With the launch of the Arab summits, he brought it to its highest perfection. Ostensibly convened to confront the threat posed by Israel's plans to divert water from the Jordan River, the first Conference of the Arab Heads of State, held in Cairo, January 13–16, 1964, was in fact an elaborate mise-en-scène for the launch of negotiations between Egypt and Saudi Arabia over Yemen.[3]

[1] The term invokes Mu'āwiyah's attempt to use the blood-soaked shirt of the martyred Caliph in AD 657 in order to substantiate his own claim to the Caliphate. Avraham Sela, *Unity within Conflict in the Inter-Arab System: The Arab Summit Conferences, 1964–1982* (Hebrew) (Jerusalem: Magnes Press, 1982), 22.

[2] I owe the metaphor to Michael Doran.

[3] My own view accords with Ḥadīdī, *Shāhid 'alā ḥarb al-Yaman*, 97–101; Gause, *Saudi-Yemeni Relations*, 63–64; and Jordanian Prime Minister Waṣfī al-Tall, Remarks at Press Conference, January 7, 1967, in BBC, *Summary of World Broadcasts* (hereafter *SWB*), ME 2361/A/4. For an opposing view, see Moshe Shemesh, *From the Nakbah to the Naksah: The Arab-Israeli Conflict and the Palestinian National Problem, 1957–1967: Nasser's Road to the Six Day War* (Hebrew) (Sdeh Boker: Machon Ben Gurion, 2004), a, 132–42, and passim. Even observers appreciative of the nuances of Nasser's Palestine policy have misinterpreted its relationship to the introduction of summitry. Sela, *Unity*, 27–28; idem, "Nasser's Regional Politics," 194–95; James, *Nasser at War*, 78; Aburish, *Nasser*, 222–23; Kerr, *Arab Cold War*, 96–102; Nutting, *Nasser*, 346.

Nasser's resort to the Palestine card in December 1963 attested to the depth of his predicament in Yemen. The republic, far from approaching stable self-sufficiency, was losing cohesion and legitimacy by the day. More than a year after the revolution, it still required the protection of nearly one-third of the Egyptian armed forces, who were mired in guerilla war with no end in sight. With the disengagement process in shambles and war with Saudi Arabia rendered unthinkable by US opposition, Nasser had little choice but to reach out to Faysal and try to cut a deal. The question was: How could he, the prince of Arab revolution, capitulate to the prince of reaction without massive loss of face? To preserve his honor, and Egypt's, an admission of defeat could only take place under the guise of an urgent call to arms against a greater external foe. As the Arab adage goes, "I and my brother against my cousin; I and my cousin against the stranger." There was no single cause that commanded wider legitimacy in the extended Arab family than the fight against Zionism.

The Egyptians had invoked the image of Palestine from the beginning of the intervention in Yemen in order to illuminate the glum reality of hopeless fratricide with the light of a higher cause. As Egyptian troops poured into the Arabian Peninsula in late 1962, the propaganda machine in Cairo assured them that the road to Palestine ran through Ṣan'ā'.[4] When some began to return home on leave a year later, Nasser exhorted them: "Sailing [home] from the honorable battle in Yemen, you were crying 'Palestine!'"[5] Now, and not for the last time, he marshaled the Palestine cause to provide cover for prospective retreat in Yemen. "For the sake of Palestine," as the president put it in a speech at Port Sa'īd on Victory Day, December 23, 1963, he was willing to sit and talk with his antagonists. By grounding the invitation on the one issue that cut across the battle lines of the Arab Cold War, Nasser assured himself a positive response from the invitees and the enthusiastic support of their peoples. Not even the Saudis could afford to ignore such an appeal.[6]

4 See, e.g., Muḥammad Haykal, "As'ilah 'an al-ma'rakah fī al-Yaman," *al-Ahrām*, November 16, 1962, 9; Abū Dhikrī, *al-Zuhūr*, 16.

5 Speech, Suez, October 22, 1963, in UAR, *Majmū'at khuṭab*, 4:471.

6 Imām, *Ṣalāḥ Naṣr yatadhakkar*, 191; Hart, *Saudi Arabia*, 235; Vered, *Revolution*, 170–71; Dawisha, *Egypt*, 43. Intelligence Information Cable, CIA, Distr. January 9, 1964, "Nasir's Comments on the Arab Summit Conference," 2, NSF Country File, Box 158, UAR, Cables, vol. 1, 11/63–5/64, LBJL. Nasser's quote is from a speech at Port Sa'īd, December 23, 1963, in UAR, *Majmū'at khuṭab*, 4:492.

The First Arab Summit

The Palestine pretext could not conceal the crux of official Egypt's concerns: were the Saudis prepared to talk peace? In the weeks leading up to the conference, the papers obsessed over whether or not Crown Prince Faysal—whom they mistakenly expected to be more pliable than the king—would represent Saudi Arabia at the conference.[7] Given that Faysal had essentially won the internal struggle for power with his elder brother, the ailing Sa'ūd's decision to lead his country's delegation to Cairo all but assured the failure of bilateral talks on Yemen.[8]

The summit did enable Nasser to recoup some of the prestige lost over the course of the previous two years and reassert his position as preeminent leader of the Arab world. Several weeks before the summit, Nasser offered an olive branch to King Hussein, hoping to detach Jordan from the alliance of monarchies and isolate the axis of opposition to Egypt stretching from Damascus to Riyadh.[9] Hussein's acceptance paved the way for the reestablishment of diplomatic relations between the two countries in the course of the summit. Nasser also succeeded in improving relations with the kingdom of Morocco, which he had alienated by providing military aid to Algeria in the border war of 1963. However, despite the flattering portrayal of Sa'ūd in the Egyptian press, and the hopeful images of Nasser, Sallāl, Sa'ūd, and Hussein engaged in animated discussion, there was little progress on Yemen.[10]

Nevertheless, the summit set in motion a dynamic of détente that, abetted by the conciliatory winds blowing from Cairo, produced a Saudi-Egyptian rapprochement within weeks. On March 1, seizing the

[7] See, e.g., the headline of *al-Ahrām* on December 28 and 31, and January 2, 3, and 10. The Americans shared Egyptian preferences in this regard. As NSC staffer Bob Komer noted with characteristic bluntness: "The biggest risk may be if that fool Saud wins out over Faysal. Then we'd be in the soup." Memo, Komer to Bundy, December 17, 1963, National Security File, Country File, Yemen, Box 161, vol. 1, Memos, 11/63–6/64, LBJL. For evidence of Nasser's mistaken assumptions about Faysal, see his letter to 'Āmir of March 7, 1963, in Haykal, *Sanawāt al-ghalayān*, 939.

[8] Sela, *Unity*, 28, 31–32; Vered, *Revolution*, 134, 178–79; Ḥadīdī, *Shāhid 'alā ḥarb al-Yaman*, 99–101. For a useful summary of the power struggle between Sa'ūd and Faysal, see Safran, *Saudi Arabia*, 86–103, or Vassiliev, *History of Saudi Arabia*, 354–68.

[9] Imām, *Ṣalāh Naṣr yatadhakkar*, 192; Naṣr, *Mudhakkirāt*, 3:74; also Nutting, *Nasser*, 347.

[10] *Al-Ahrām*, January 17, 1964, 1, 12; Naṣr, *Mudhakkirāt*, 3:76; Aḥmad, *al-Dawr*, 343–45; Saudi Permanent Undersecretary for Foreign Affairs 'Umar al-Saqqāf, quoted in Telegram, Badeau (Cairo) to Sec. State, no. 1583, January 16, 1964, RG 59, CF, 1964–66, Box 3025, POL 27 YEMEN, NARA.

opportunity afforded by an Iraqi-Algerian mediation effort, Nasser sent ʿĀmir to Saudi Arabia at the head of a high-level delegation including Anwar Sadat and Major General ʿAlī ʿAbd al-Khabīr. The Egyptians conducted three days of talks with a Saudi delegation headed by Undersecretary for Foreign Affairs ʿUmar al-Saqqāf, whose modest title belied his influence over the crown prince. In a triumphant communiqué released at the conclusion of the talks, the two parties renounced any ambitions in Yemen and declared their commitment to the complete independence of Yemen, free of any imperialist influence. While acknowledging that areas of difference remained, they agreed to pursue negotiations in order to resolve them. It was also decided to restore diplomatic relations, which had been severed at the beginning of the war, and to prepare the ground for a summit between Nasser and Faysal at the end of April.[11]

This accord represented a procedural breakthrough in relations between the two countries and marked the beginning of a new phase in the war. The initiation of public, high-level contacts between the two governments put a stop to the vicious propaganda war that had been going on for more than two years. More importantly, the renewal of bilateral ties in earnest eliminated both countries' crippling dependence on the US middleman. The commencement of direct Saudi-Egyptian contacts in early 1964 marked the end of the phase of intensive US mediation between the two countries, which had characterized the disengagement process from the beginning of the war to the end of 1963. Perceptions of American power and influence continued to shape the negotiating process and limit the scope of military action. But the keys to a solution in Yemen no longer lay in Washington.[12]

Nevertheless, the celebratory atmosphere in Riyadh concealed the fact that little of substance had been agreed. The Saudis remained adamant in their refusal to recognize the YAR, while the Egyptians declined to withdraw unless the survival of the republic was guaranteed. Little progress was made in the weeks following the Riyadh talks, in part because the Egyptians' eagerness to restore relations regardless of progress on Yemen revealed weakness, which Faysal was inclined to exploit. Faysal's proposed visit to Cairo never materialized and despite the agreement on immediate restoration of diplomatic ties the crown prince

[11] Sharaf, *Sanawāt*, 2:631–33; Jiddah to FO, no. 144, March 4, 1964, FO 371/178588, PRO; Aḥmad, *al-Dawr*, 346.

[12] Hart, *Saudi Arabia*, 232.

Figure 6.1 ʻĀmir in Saudi Arabia, March 1964. Top: "Marshal ʻĀmir signs the joint communiqué next to Prince Faysal [with Anwar Sadat in the background]." Bottom: "Marshal ʻĀmir in conversation with King Saʻūd after the meeting's conclusion." *Al-Quwwāt al-Musallaḥah*, March 16, 1964.

took four months to send trusted associate Muḥammad ʿAlī Riḍā as ambassador to Cairo. These delays were partly the result of Faysal's continuing preoccupation with the internal power struggle with his brother. Nevertheless, they revealed the limits of Egyptian leverage.[13] It was in the context of this impasse in the negotiations with Saudi Arabia that Nasser made his first and only trip to the battlefield.

Although the president's visit to Yemen in late April 1964 had multiple objectives not directly related to the diplomatic process—raising morale among the troops, forging a Republican consensus, and observing local realities at close hand, to name three—its main purpose was to increase the pressure on Riyadh.[14] Nasser's first bid to force Faysal to the bargaining table had centered on the common threat from Israel; the leitmotif of the second attempt was his other bête noire: British imperialism. The president had already set the tone for the coming campaign in his speech at Port Saʿīd on December 23, 1963: "We declare our full support for the nationalists of Aden and the nationalists of the occupied southern territory, and declare that all the force and capabilities of the U.A.R. will be used to drive out British imperialism from that area because Britain has no right whatsoever to remain in Aden.... We cannot accept at all that Britain continues to colonize a part of the Arab nation ... when she has abandoned her other colonies."[15] In late March 1964, when British warplanes bombed a fort inside Republican territory in retaliation for raids against the federation by the EAF, the Egyptian and Yemeni governments seized on this pretext to whip up an international campaign against the United Kingdom. But it was only upon his arrival in Yemen the following month that Nasser placed the full force of his rhetorical capacity behind the new anti-British campaign.

The reintroduction of the old imperialist punching bag into the ring was designed to expose—and, if possible, sunder—the treacherous alliance between Arab reaction (the Saudi monarchy) and Western imperialism (the British bugaboo). By opening a new front, which could be expected to garner broad popular support throughout the Arab world, Nasser in effect created two wars out of one. To the original war between Egypt and Saudi Arabia over the political fate of northern Yemen

[13] Jiddah to FO, no. 9 Saving, March 11, 1964, FO 371/178588, PRO; Letter, Maitland (Cairo) to Crawford (FO), VG 1051/27, July 9, 1964, 2, FO 371/178595, PRO; Vered, *Revolution*, 180–83.

[14] Cf. O'Ballance, *War in the Yemen*, 123–24; James, *Nasser at War*, 76–78. See also Vered, *Revolution*, 190, 192–93; Rabinovich, "The Embroilment," 222; Nutting, *Nasser*, 350.

[15] Telegram, Beeley (Cairo) to FO, no. 994, December 24, 1963, p. 2, FO 371/172862.

he now added a war between Egypt and Great Britain over the future of southern Yemen and, by extension, the peninsula as a whole. The strategic ramifications of this new war were enormous; the immediate tactical implications were no less significant.

In theory, the division of the war into two wars enabled Egypt to deal separately with its two peninsular adversaries, threatening each with the prospect of a separate deal with the other. An Egyptian-British deal over Aden threatened to leave Saudi Arabia isolated in its fight with Egypt.[16] Similarly, an agreement between Nasser and Faysal over the north would free the Egyptians to focus their energies on fueling the insurgency in the south. The sharp decrescendo in attacks on Faysal betrayed Nasser's priorities in this regard. As Adeed Dawisha has observed, in the six speeches Nasser delivered in Yemen, he referred to British imperialism ninety-six times, to reaction nineteen times, and to Saudi Arabia only once.[17] Nasser did not wish to antagonize the Saudis at this juncture; the new campaign was designed to strengthen his hand in the upcoming negotiations with Faysal by shifting the framework of the debate from the Egyptian intervention in northern Yemen to the British occupation of southern Yemen—a cause from which the Saudis could not safely disassociate themselves.[18] No doubt Nasser also sought to inject fresh legitimacy into the foundering military campaign at a time when criticism at home and abroad was increasingly focused on the disturbing contradictions of a fratricidal conflict pitting Muslim against Muslim, Arab against Arab, carried out under the banner of fraternal Arabism.[19] The assault on the British served to recast the Egyptian occupation of a fellow Arab country as a patriotic duty. War on reaction had been a good bugle call; war on colonialism was even better.[20]

[16] The effectiveness of this strategy is evidenced by King Faysal's subsequent concerns over a separate British-Egyptian deal. Telegram, Man (Jiddah) to FO, no. 337, July 18, 1965, FO 371/179880, PRO.

[17] Dawisha, *Egypt*, 149n.

[18] Aḥmad, *al-Dawr*, 337–39; Imām, *Ṣalāḥ Naṣr yatadhakkar*, 197; Vered, *Revolution*, 187, 191. Faysal, evidently, had similar ideas in mind when he ordered an escalation of Royalist military activity in March 1964. Smiley, *Arabian Assignment*, 167.

[19] Nasser's Islamic references also bespeak of a quest for new legitimacy. See, for instance, UAR, *Majmūʿat khuṭab*, 4:550–51, 556–61.

[20] Telegram, Riddell (Cairo) to External, no. 251, April 27, 1964, RG 25, vol. 8885, 20-UAR-1-3, vol. 2, LAC; Telegram, Cortada (Taʿizz) Sec. State, no. 602, April 28, 1964, RG 59, CF, 1964–66, Box 3024, POL 15 YEMEN, NARA; Telegram, Badeau (Cairo) to Sec. State, no. 2514, April 27, 1964, RG 59, CF, 1964–66, Box 3026, POL 27 YEMEN, NARA; Wenner,

From June to August the Egyptians followed up this ideological offensive with a series of large-scale military operations in the northwest, culminating in a two-pronged strike on the headquarters of the Imam at Jabal Rāziḥ. The offensive aspired to crush the leadership of the resistance, seal off the northwestern border, and persuade the Saudis that time was not on their side. But the Imam managed to slip away into Saudi territory, and the offensive, though initially successful, swiftly petered out.[21] Within weeks the Royalist forces regrouped and mounted a sizeable counteroffensive, in the course of which the Republican chief of staff lost his life, and the minister of defense came under protracted siege along with a handful of Egyptian officers.[22] By January 1965, the Royalists had regained practically all the ground they had lost over the fall. Once again, the Egyptians confronted the inadequacy of military action.

The Second Arab Summit

On the eleventh anniversary of the Egyptian Revolution in July, King Hussein, once the most zealous supporter of restoration in Yemen, paid the price of rapprochement with Nasser and recognized the YAR. But aside from Jordanian recognition, Nasser had little to show in Yemen for six months of conciliation.[23] On August 17, in a letter to President Johnson, Prince Faysal formally renounced the disengagement agreement Ellsworth Bunker brokered in the spring of 1963, thereby effectively terminating the United Nations observers' mission, which had been renewed at bimonthly intervals since November 1963.[24] This set the peace process back more than a year. Faysal explained to the US

Yemen Arab Republic, 213–14; Badeau, *American Approach*, 148–49. Cf. O'Ballance, *War in the Yemen*, 123–24. Egyptians typically cite the liberation of the south as one of the primary achievements of intervention in the north. See, for instance, Sādāt, *al-Baḥth*, 211.

[21] Schmidt, *Unknown War*, 178–80; Vered, *Revolution*, 198–99; O'Ballance, *War in the Yemen*, 125–28; Rahmy, *Egyptian Policy*, 152; Gause, *Saudi-Yemeni Relations*, 64. Egyptian General Fatḥī 'Abd al-Ghānī denies that the capture of Badr was a major objective of the operation (Aḥmad, *Dhikrayāt*, 315–16).

[22] Both Soviet and Yemeni officials insinuated that the Egyptians had assassinated COS Ḥusayn al-Dafa'ī for political reasons. Airgram, Ta'izz to Dept. of State, no. A-80, September 5, 1964, p. 1, RG 59, CF, 1964–66, Box 3026, POL 27 YEMEN, NARA; Airgram, Ta'izz to Dept. of State, no. A-86, September 5, 1964, p. 5, in ibid.; Schmidt, *Unknown War*, 210.

[23] Vered, *Revolution*, 197.

[24] Letter, Faysal to Johnson, August 17, 1964, in RG 59, CF, 1964–66, Box 3026, POL 27 YEMEN, NARA.

ambassador that his decision stemmed from the failure of Egyptian forces to withdraw from Yemen, their offensive posture, and his fear of encirclement by an Egyptian-Jordanian-Iraqi alliance. The prince exhorted his American friends to halt the counterproductive supply of food to Egypt and demanded to know what the US government would do to protect Saudi Arabia in the likely event of a renewal of border clashes.[25] Finally, he divulged his own intention to renew suspended military aid to the Royalists. The exasperated Egyptians likewise reverted to US diplomatic channels, threatening war unless Faysal came to Egypt to negotiate an end to Saudi support for the Royalists.[26]

It was a second summit of Arab leaders in Alexandria that provided the political cover for Faysal's eventual arrival in Egypt on September 4.[27] Once again, the Palestine cause was used to foster the illusion of Arab solidarity and serve as a camouflage for the private discussion of differences.[28] Although the talks revolved around the need to do something about Israel, these were, as the Saudi regent confessed to a US diplomat, of little practical consequence. "Let the Arabs enjoy their show, just as children enjoy their new toys," was Faysal's advice to the US government.[29] Although the crown prince refused to include Yemen on the official agenda, he opened up to Nasser in a series of private discussions held on the sidelines of the conference and in two days of secret talks after the delegates had dispersed on September 11.[30] Faysal provided this colorful account of the summit in a heart-to-heart talk with US diplomat Isa Sabbagh on September 22, 1964:[31]

[25] Telegram, Hart (Jiddah) to Sec. State, no. 133, August 18, 1964, in ibid.; Airgram, Jiddah to Dept. of State, no. A-73, September 8, 1964, "Ambassador Hart's Conversation with Prince Faysal, August 29, 1964," in ibid.

[26] Telegram, Cairo to Sec. State, no. 437, August 6, 1964, RG 59, CF, 1964–66, Box 3026, POL SAUD-UAR, NARA; Boswell (Cairo) to Sec. State, no. 3155, June 24, 1964, RG 59, CF, 1964–66, Box 3026, POL 27 YEMEN, NARA. See also Vered, *Revolution*, 200.

[27] Rabinovich, "The Embroilment," 224.

[28] See Saqqāf's characterization of the PLO as a Nasserist tool designed to undermine Arab security. Telegram, Hart (Jiddah) to Sec. State, no. 171, August 26, 1964, p. 2, RG 59, CF, 1964–66, Box 3026, POL 27 YEMEN, NARA. The Saudi-Egyptian agenda at the summit seems to have been lost on the Soviets. Telegram, Erofeev (Cairo) to MID, September 13, 1964, *BVK*, 2:438–41.

[29] Although he did warn against excessive retaliatory measures by Israel that might drive the Arabs into a corner. Memcon, Crown Prince Faysal and [US diplomat] Isa Sabbagh, Jiddah, September 22, 1964, 6–7, in RG 59, CF, 1964–66, Box 2761, POL 7 UAR, NARA.

[30] Cf. Sela, *Unity*, 40–42; Aḥmad, *al-Dawr*, 348–49.

[31] Memcon, Crown Prince Faysal and [US diplomat] Isa Sabbagh, Jiddah, September 22, 1964, in RG 59, CF, 1964–66, Box 2761, POL 7 UAR, NARA.

> It is no secret that at one time Nasser and I were the best of friends. We used to exchange views on the most delicate subjects. Then this period of bitterness set in. The face-to-face encounter has been very helpful. We had frank exchanges. I told Nasir he had been the victim of his own men, giving him false reports on Saudi Arabia and Yemen. At one private meeting between the two of us with his men and mine present, I pointed an accusing finger at Anwar al-Sadat and described him as the person who did the most harm between the two countries, especially on Yemen about which he was the most ignorant of the UAR group. Nasir replied "You should have taken him to Saudi Arabia and tried him, then!" I said "What's the use, what's done is done. Besides, he is your man, not ours." Sadat admitted he had had many misconceptions on Yemen . . .
>
> Nasir and Amer repeated this naïve contention (which Amer and Sadat had expressed to me in Riyadh) that [the] UAR went to Yemen with no ulterior motives, no ambitions, just to help an oppressed people who wanted a Republic. I told them not to think me so gullible . . .
>
> [Faysal:] "What have you gained from your venture in the Yemen? We know full well that you've had many difficulties and losses. To what avail? Where has it taken you?"

Here it was Faysal's turn to stretch credulity:

> I admit that the Yemeni preoccupation has cost us a lot of anguish and intruded [*sic*] a great deal of bitterness towards you. We did nothing against you (UAR). It was we who had no ulterior motive in the Yemen. We know the Yemen, the Yemenis and Badr more than you will ever know them. We've dealt with the Yemenis for 40 years. We marched into the Yemen and finally left it alone realizing it was a bundle of trouble, a hive of wasps. But they are our neighbors. I never had much respect for Badr. The way Ahmad was ruling his people was very often criticized by us in our private conversations with him and his men. These neighbors came to us asking for help, appealing to our traditional Arab sense of "*nakhwah*" (chivalrous help in adversity). What did you expect us to do in the circumstances?
>
> . . . Where do you want to go from here? I don't think you delude yourself into believing that you actually have the Yemenis' love or the genuine support of the Arab world for your policy in the Yemen. Let's face it, it is a sore point which would have caused a lot of wrangling had we allowed it to be openly discussed at our Summit meetings, and we would have gotten nowhere . . .

> We feel you want to end this problem as well as anyone. We too want peace and tranquility in order to get on with our task in our country.... Why don't you pull your forces out of Yemen?

Nasser, according to Faysal, responded that he would like to withdraw, but how could he do it with *karāmah* (dignity)?

> [NASSER:] "What could I tell my forces whom we've pumped to saturation with their lofty mission in Yemen?"
>
> [FAYSAL:] "That's your own fault, the result of your rash jumping into a dark cavern."
>
> [NASSER:] "Why don't you recognize the Republic since you yourself said you didn't like or respect Badr?"
>
> [FAYSAL:] "Our stand on the Yemen is one of principle and not for the sake of Badr. We firmly believe in the principle of self-determination of peoples. You've tried your hand, used your own methods and we all know the results so far. Why don't you agree to something you cannot in all honesty disagree with, i.e., self-determination? Why don't we both try our best to facilitate for the Yemeni people the chance to make their wishes known, freely.... *Surely you are as disillusioned in Sallal as much as we are with Badr. Let's agree to let the Yemenis have a popular plebiscite* [emphases added]. If they opt for a Republic we'd be the first to recognize such a choice, if they want a monarchy then you should recognize it similarly."

At this, Nasser allegedly balked. But Faysal stressed that if the Egyptians stuck to their guns and insisted on Saudi recognition of the republic, no deal was possible and it was best to "let time take care of events."[32] Although the two leaders failed to compromise on the form of the postwar regime, they agreed to refrain from prejudging the issue while the Yemenis worked out an acceptable political arrangement among themselves.[33] When added to the old disengagement tradeoff between Saudi cessation of aid and Egyptian withdrawal, the makings of a bargain began to take shape.

[32] Ibid., 4.

[33] This point was subsequently confirmed by Saqqāf, Fir'awn, and Sulṭān. Telegram, Ta'izz to Sec. State, no. 644, March 3, 1965, p. 2, RG 59, CF, 1964–66, Box 3027, POL 27 YEMEN, NARA; Airgram, Jiddah to State, no. A-246, March 9, 1965, p. 4, RG 59, CF, 1964–66, Box 3027, POL 27 YEMEN, NARA; Enclosure, Airgram, Jiddah to State, no. A-292, March 28(?), 1965, p. 1, RG 59, CF, 1964–66, Box 3027, POL 27 YEMEN, NARA.

The talks concluded with a secret agreement between the two leaders, which has never been published. Fortunately for posterity, the Saudis provided a copy of one of the two originals to US Ambassador Parker Hart.[34] A translation of the text, reproduced below, closely accords with Sāmī Sharaf's citation from the copy apparently preserved in the Egyptian presidential archives.[35]

> Made between His Excellency President Jamal 'Abd al-Nasir, President of the United Arab Republic, and His Royal Highness, Deputy King and Prime Minister of Saudi Arabia, on the following matters:
>
> 1. First, the two countries will work for an immediate cease-fire between the parties concerned in the Yemen.
> 2. The Kingdom of Saudi Arabia will continue stoppage of [Sharaf has: *tuwaqqif*, will stop] its military and financial aid which is of a nature to perpetuate the fighting; there will be complete withdrawal of all forces of the United Arab Republic from the Yemen territory by stages, provided that agreement is reached on ways to guarantee maintenance of security and stability.
> 3. Execution of the points mentioned in the two foregoing paragraphs shall begin after liaison with the parties concerned in the Yemen and after agreement on the stages, manner and time limit for withdrawal [Sharaf has also: *wa-takwīn lajnah taḥḍīriyyah tumaththilu al-fi'āt al-mukhtalifah*, and the establishment of a preparatory committee representative of the various groups].
>
> [Signed] Faysal Jamal 'Abd al-Nasir
> Alexandria, 8 Jumādā al-ūla, 1382
> 14 September 1964

This terse document left a considerable amount undetermined. As such, it reflected a combination of poor preparation for the summit on the part of the Saudi and Egyptian negotiating teams and the breadth of the differences separating their two governments. The deal's striking lack of specificity set it up for distortion and misrepresentation at the hands of Saudis and Egyptians alike, causing considerable confusion in the months that followed.[36] But the biggest potential for trouble lay in

[34] Telegram, Jiddah to State, no. 862, May 4, 1965, p. 2, RG 59, CF, 1964–66, Box 3027, POL 27 YEMEN, NARA. The translation is the embassy's.

[35] Sharaf, *Sanawāt*, 2:633–34.

[36] In his presentation to US envoy Phillips Talbot six months later, Nasser conveniently forgot the Egyptian commitment to withdraw and added an imaginary clause pertaining to the exclusion of the Ḥamīd al-Dīns from the political future of Yemen. Likewise, in

the highly contingent nature of the two key commitments embodied in the accord: the Saudi commitment to suspend aid to the Royalists and the Egyptian commitment to withdraw. By making execution of the main body of the deal contingent on the vagaries of local politics, Nasser and Faysal planted the seed of its eventual demise.

Nevertheless, the mutual recognition of the fact that any solution entailed a compromise that took into account Yemeni realities, not merely Saudi and Egyptian interests, represented a step forward. At Alexandria, the Saudi pretense of ignoring the republic was dropped in exchange for an equivalent Egyptian agreement to cease dismissing the Royalists as a party for dialogue.[37] Significantly, this point was reiterated in the public communiqué released at the conclusion of the talks on September 14, which stated the two leaders' resolve to negotiate a peaceful settlement, their decision "to cooperate fully in solving existing differences *between the various parties in Yemen* [emphasis added], and their determination to prevent armed clashes."[38]

The first practical outcome of the Alexandria talks was the convocation of ten Republican and eight Royalist representatives in Sudan from October 29 to November 3. With Faysal's tacit agreement, the Ḥamīd al-Dīn family stayed away from the conference.[39] This important compromise, which presaged Saudi preparedness to ditch Badr in exchange for an Egyptian withdrawal, did not, however, entail an abandonment of the conservative cause as a whole; still less did it signify a willingness to recognize the republic.[40] In fact, Faysal may well have calculated that

conversation with the American ambassador five months later, the Saudi undersecretary for foreign affairs, 'Umar al-Saqqāf, neglected to mention the conditional aspect of Egyptian undertakings or the Saudi commitment to cease aid to the Royalists. Telegram, Battle (Cairo) to SecState, no. 3653, April 8, 1965, section 3, p. 1, NSF, Country File, UAR, Box 159, United Arab Republic, vol. 3, Cables 11/64–6/65, LBJL; Telegram, Jiddah to Sec. State, no. 637, March 2, 1965, section 1, p. 2, RG 59, CF, 1964–66, Box 3027, POL 27 YEMEN, NARA.

[37] See Gause, *Saudi-Yemeni Relations*, 65; Saudi adviser Rashād Fir'awn, cited in Airgram, Jiddah to State, no. A-246, March 9, 1965, p. 1, RG 59, CF, 1964–66, Box 3027, POL 27 YEMEN, NARA.

[38] Telegram, Cairo to Sec. State, no. 905, September 15, 1964, RG 59, CF, 1964–66, Box 3026, POL 27 YEMEN, NARA; Aḥmad, *al-Dawr*, 349–51.

[39] Telegram, Boswell (Cairo) to Sec. State, no. 877, September 15, 1964, RG 59, CF, 1964–66, Box 3026, POL 27 YEMEN, NARA.

[40] Faysal made sure his position was not misunderstood in a telegram of congratulations to Badr on the second anniversary of his accession to the throne. Although the crown prince published both his letter and Badr's effusive response in the Saudi press, he struck one particularly offensive passage, shown below in italics, from Badr's reply—an

he need not insist on such details, since any political arrangement sufficient to secure Egyptian withdrawal would eventually succumb to the historical reality of Zaydī power.[41] In any event, the delegates, with Saudi and Egyptian prodding, declared a cease-fire in Yemen, to begin November 8, and agreed to convene a peace conference in Yemen on November 23 that would hammer out a political compromise to end the war. They could not, however, reach agreement on the location of the conference or on the proportion of representation for each of the two parties, referring both matters to Faysal and Nasser. Given the support of both leaders, the cease-fire went into effect and held for several weeks. Meanwhile, negotiations continued in Riyadh and in Cairo between Faysal adviser Rashād Fir'awn and a number of Egyptian officials, including UAR ambassador to Yemen Aḥmad Shukrī, tribal affairs expert Maḥmūd Qāsim, Sadat, and 'Āmir.[42]

These visible signs of progress, compounded by the secrecy surrounding the Alexandria talks, sounded the alarm bells among those in Yemen who had most to lose from a Saudi-Egyptian settlement. Unfortunately for the cause of peace, two of the individuals most strongly opposed to compromise were the leaders of the rival causes, President Sallāl and Imam Badr, neither of whom had any interest in a process that would result in their marginalization and probable exile. Compounding these inclinations was the fact that neither Nasser nor Faysal was prepared to break openly with his local figurehead. The vocal opposition to an agreement by influential Yemenis hamstrung progress toward compromise, delegitimized the concessions needed to bring it about, and corroded the nascent Saudi-Egyptian willingness to cooperate.

Unfortunately for the Egyptians, who faced the unenviable task of squaring two years of bombastic statements and extravagant promises

---

editorial feat about which he boasted to American diplomat Isa Sabbagh: "To His Royal Highness, the friendly, faithful brother Prince Faysal, the Regent, may God keep him. I acknowledge with utmost gratitude receipt of Your Highness' congratulation for which I thank you, and entreat Allah . . . to lead the Yemeni people and help them and us *in order to cleanse the homeland of the intruding imperialist and* move towards building up our country, hoping that God would give you victory and success. . . . God bless and keep you. Your Brother Muhammad al-Badr." Memcon, Crown Prince Faysal and Isa Sabbagh, Jiddah, September 22, 1964, p. 5, in RG 59, CF, 1964–66, Box 2761, POL 7 UAR, NARA.

[41] Vered, *Revolution*, 201.

[42] Telegram, Battle (Cairo) to Sec. State, no. 1569, November 5, 1964, RG 59, CF, 1964–66, Box 3026, POL 27 YEMEN, NARA; Airgram, Jiddah to State, no. A-246, March 9, 1965, RG 59, CF, 1964–66, Box 3027, POL 27 YEMEN, NARA; Sharaf, *Sanawāt*, 2:634–35; Aḥmad, *al-Dawr*, 351–52.

with the unattractive requisites of compromise, the Republicans proved to be particularly intransigent. The principal accommodations required of the Zaydī core of the Republican leadership were these: first, a comprehensive deal with the Zaydī Royalists; and second, the meaningful inclusion of the historically disenfranchised Shāfi'ī majority of central and southern Yemen in power. Neither of these was easy to achieve without significant Egyptian prodding. The principle stick the Egyptians held over recalcitrant Republicans was the threat of withdrawal. But since the consequence of a precipitous evacuation was as clear to the Yemenis as it was to the Egyptians—"they know that if our troops leave, Badr will come to Ṣan'ā' by helicopter within two hours" explained one Egyptian officer—that threat was essentially empty. The bigger stick in Egypt's arsenal was to threaten obdurate influentials with removal from power. As one well-connected commander in the Egyptian headquarters in Ṣan'ā' put it: "Whenever [Vice President Ḥasan] al-'Amrī, or anyone else, decides he has [had] enough of Yemeni politics, he is welcome to go to Cairo for 'medical treatment.'"[43]

'Āmir went to Yemen soon after the Alexandria summit to warn radical Republicans that they had only months to put their house in order before they were left on their own to face the consequences. But he ended up assuaging feelings injured by the recognition of the Royalist cause implicit in the Alexandria communiqué's reference to various "parties" (*aṭrāf*). 'Āmir's dubious explanation, according to which the parties in question were the tribes, not the Royalists, exemplified the sort of twisted formulations to which the Egyptians would increasingly resort in the march to compromise.[44] But such dubious rhetorical devices, once employed, took on a life of their own, trapping Egyptian negotiators in equivocal positions and inevitably seeping back into the negotiating chambers in Cairo and Riyadh. Because this dynamic took place almost exclusively on the Republican side, one must accord the Egyptians a greater share of the responsibility for deviating from the Alexandria agreement and derailing the peace process in late 1964.[45]

[43] Lieutenant Colonel Muḥammad Shawqāt, quoted in Airgram, Ta'izz to Dept. of State, no. A-103, October 3, 1964, pp. 1, 2, RG 59, CF, 1964–66, Box 3024, POL 15 YEMEN, NARA. The Arabic verb "*ta'antafa*"—from the Russian "*Antonov*"—was coined to describe the departure of disgruntled Yemenis for Cairo.

[44] Ibid., 4.

[45] Nasser adviser Ṣabrī al-Khūlī confessed as much. Presidential adviser Ḥasan Ṣabrī al-Khūlī, quoted in Telegram, Battle (Cairo) to Sec. State, no. 1932, December 3, 1964, RG 59, CF, 1964–66, Box 3026, POL 27 YEMEN, NARA. See also the comments of a senior

Despite ʿĀmir's admonitions, the inevitable differences between the Republicans and Royalists, and among different factions within each camp, over details ranging from the proportion of rival delegates to the nature of the interim government, could not fail to confound the ill-defined understandings Nasser and Faysal reached at Alexandria. Many Republicans, for instance, expected a Republican-majority conference to place a rubber stamp on the fait accompli of the republic and leave the Egyptian protective force in place. Most Royalists, by contrast, expected equal representation at a conference that would not prejudge the type of the resultant regime and would focus on ending the Egyptian occupation of Yemen. Such fundamental disagreements over the format and agenda of the peace conference postponed its convocation indefinitely and poisoned the partnership between Egypt and Saudi Arabia. Thus it was that despite the genuine good will that seems to have informed the September agreement between Nasser and Faysal, the irresolvable differences between their respective allies in Yemen required further high-level negotiations to resolve problems that both justice and expedience demanded the Yemenis themselves decide.[46]

By early December two principal obstacles had emerged that would continue to undermine successive Saudi-Egyptian understandings over the next two years. The first revolved around the definition of the Yemeni regime. The Saudis, with reluctant Royalist approval, agreed to the neutral designation "State (*dawlah*) of Yemen," while the Egyptians, under pressure from their clients in Ṣanʿāʾ, held out for a "Republic" (*jumhūriyyah*). Although largely semantic, the difference illustrated the qualitative divergence of goals: to the Saudis, who merely sought to deny the Egyptians an enduring triumph in Yemen, the ultimate restoration of the Imamate was not necessary. They would not go so far as to recognize the republic, as the Egyptians demanded, but neither were they wedded to the Imamate. For the Egyptians, by contrast, both the

---

Egyptian political affairs officer in Yemen shortly after the summit. Lieutenant Colonel Muḥammad Shawqāt, quoted in Airgram, Taʿizz to Dept. of State, no. A-103, October 3, 1964, p. 2, RG 59, CF, 1964–66, Box 3024, POL 15 YEMEN, NARA. But ʿĀmir blamed the Saudis for suddenly demanding that the transitional regime be labeled a "State." Telegram, Taʿizz to Sec. State, no. 304, February 1, 1965, RG 59, CF, 1964–66, Box 3027, POL 27 YEMEN, NARA; Telegram, Taʿizz to Sec. State, no. 644, March 3, 1965, RG 59, CF, 1964–66, Box 3027, POL 27 YEMEN, NARA.

[46] Telegram, Taʿizz to Sec. State, no. 200, November 14, 1964, RG 59, CF, 1964–66, Box 3024, POL 15 YEMEN, NARA; Airgram, Jiddah to State, no. A-246, March 9, 1965, RG 59, CF, 1964–66, Box 3027, POL 27 YEMEN, NARA; Vered, *Revolution*, 202–4; Dawisha, *Egypt*, 45; Rabinovich, "The Embroilment," 225.

enormous stock of prestige invested in the campaign and the huge risks of withdrawal dictated the pursuit of a demonstrable victory encapsulated by the preservation of the republican form of government.

The second major disagreement to emerge in the aftermath of the second Arab summit had to do with the place of the Ḥamīd al-Dīn family in Yemen's political order. The Saudis, seeking to hold on to a shred of credibility with domestic hardliners and local allies, insisted that a member of the royal family sit on the Presidency Council envisioned to succeed both Badr and Sallāl. The Egyptians, on the other hand, gave voice to Republican fears of an eventual restoration of the Imamate by insisting on the complete exclusion of the Ḥamīd al-Dīns from Yemeni political life. Behind these two issues lurked the tangible matter of Egyptian withdrawal from Yemen. The Saudis sought a full and expeditious evacuation of the Egyptian task force, regardless of political conditions in Yemen—it did not matter who governed Yemen as long as no Egyptians remained, was how Prince Faysal put it to the British ambassador—while the Egyptians insisted on a phased, possibly partial, withdrawal tied to concrete political milestones.[47]

These stumbling blocks exposed the fundamental issue at stake in the war once initial Egyptian hopes for a Saudi collapse had evaporated: the future orientation of Yemen. As we have seen, the geographic asymmetry of the conflict dealt Nasser a much weaker hand. Since in the long run Yemeni political culture could be relied on to reestablish some form of conservative government, while geographic proximity could be depended upon to restore Saudi influence, Faysal could afford to downplay the complexities of Yemeni politics and focus on ending the Egyptian presence in Yemen. Precisely for these reasons, Nasser was wary of withdrawal without an agreement that locked Yemen into a course of Republican government and pro-Egyptian policy. But this was fantasy. As long as Egypt remained committed to the survival of the republic beyond what became known in the Vietnam context as a "decent interval" following withdrawal, it was virtually impossible to

[47] Presidential adviser Ḥasan Ṣabrī al-Khūlī, quoted in Telegram, Battle (Cairo) to Sec. State, no. 1932, December 3, 1964, RG 59, CF, 1964–66, Box 3026, POL 27 YEMEN, NARA; Saudi adviser Rashād Fir'awn, quoted in Telegram, Jiddah to Sec. State, no. 420, December 2, 1964, RG 59, CF, 1964–66, Box 3026, POL 27 YEMEN, NARA; Prince Faysal, quoted in Telegram, Jiddah to FO, no. 19, January 9, 1965, FO 371/183907; Muḥammad Haykal, in conversation with Colin Crowe, in Letter, Crowe (Oxford) to Roger Allen (FO), July 15, 1965, p. 2, FO 371/183912, PRO; 'Umar al-Saqqāf, cited in Telegram, Jiddah to Sec. State, no. 637, March 2, 1965, RG 59, CF, 1964–66, Box 3027, POL 27 YEMEN, NARA.

proceed with a substantial evacuation of forces, because no agreement could guarantee the survival of the republic even absent Saudi interference. Since the Saudis were in any case disinclined to abandon their allies entirely or embrace the Republican form of government, deadlock ensued. The fact that Saudi-Egyptian negotiations remained hostage to the perennial spoiling effect of Yemeni politics, in which many profited from the prolongation of the conflict, rendered any breakthrough unsustainable.

The Jiddah Agreement

The unraveling, over the winter of 1964/65, of the vague agreement reached at Alexandria placed the Egyptians and the Saudis back in the same position they had occupied prior to the second summit: the political and military stalemate required intervention by the two leaders, neither of whom wished to appear too eager for peace.[48] With a third Arab summit only scheduled for September in Morocco, the pan-Arab setting that had hitherto provided political cover for the Saudi-Egyptian summits in Cairo could not be relied upon to do so again. But with Faysal (who, in the meantime, had finally become king) refusing to honor Nasser with another visit to Egypt, and Nasser reluctant to show up as a supplicant at Faysal's doorstep, the stage was set for a protracted diplomatic tango that culminated in "Nasser's Canossa" at Jiddah.

In Cairo, the urgency of reaching an agreement that would permit a substantial drawdown of troops grew over the course of the year with the deepening economic crisis in Egypt, the rise of domestic discontent, and the darkening clouds on the horizon of relations with the great powers. The bleakness of the military picture underscored the necessity of peace. The failure of the fall offensive in northwestern Yemen demonstrated the futility of conventional military operations, at least so long as the Royalist sanctuaries on Saudi territory remained inviolate. In the early months of 1965, several Royalist successes drove this lesson home. In the northwest, the siege of Jabal Rāziḥ continued, Egyptian attempts to break it notwithstanding. In the northeast, Royalist forces managed to sever the main supply line into the Jawf, cutting off Egyp-

[48] See, for instance, Nasser's comments to Phillips Talbot in Telegram, Battle (Cairo) to SecState, no. 3653, April 8, 1965, section 3, p. 1, NSF, Country File, UAR, Box 159, United Arab Republic, vol. 3, Cables 11/64–6/65, LBJL. Cf. Haykal, *al-Infijār*, 187–88.

tian forces in the region for several weeks. Royalist forces then staged a series of successful operations in eastern Yemen, culminating in the reconquest of Ḥarīb, Ma'rib, Ṣirwāḥ, and Jīḥānah.[49] Frustrated by the strategic straitjacket imposed on operations at the border, senior Egyptian military commanders began to dust off old plans to carry the battle into Saudi territory.[50]

At least as troubling as the military situation was Egypt's inability to overcome the political divisions within the Republican camp. These divisions deepened as the possibility of an Egyptian departure took shape. On December 2, 1964, three of the most influential members of the Republican government—Muḥammad al-Zubayrī, 'Abd al-Raḥmān al-Iryānī, and Aḥmad Nu'mān—resigned in protest at the concentration of power under Sallāl and, by implication, the overbearing nature of the Egyptian occupation. Rather than accede to their demands, the Egyptians made the Republican strongman and Sallāl loyalist, Ḥasan al-'Amrī, prime minister on January 6. In response, Zubayrī, the most popular of the Republican dissidents, formed the independent Party of God (*Ḥizb Allāh*), which threatened to undermine the credibility of the regime among the tribes still further. The new party was neither Royalist nor Republican, but called for reform of the government and the withdrawal of Egyptian forces. When, on April 1, Zubayrī fell to an assassin's bullet in northern Yemen, the swell of discontent, nurtured by allegations that the Egyptians were behind the deed, threatened to wipe out the regime's residue of tribal support entirely.[51] Giving expression to his frustration in a conversation with the East German representative in Cairo, Nasser confessed that what had happened in 1962 had not been a revolution but rather a "putsch."[52]

[49] Schmidt, *Unknown War*, 214–23; O'Ballance, *War in the Yemen*, 138–39; Aḥmad, *al-Dawr*, 271–73; Aḥmad, *Dhikrayāt*, 316.

[50] See, e.g., 'Āmir's combative comments to the Soviet ambassador in Telegram, Erofeev (Cairo) to MID, February 23, 1965, *BVK*, 2:458–62. Telegram, Maitland (Cairo) to Weir (FO), March 23, 1965, FO 371/179864, PRO; Memo, Brenchley (FO), May 19, 1965, "Level of U.A.R. Forces in the Yemen," in ibid.

[51] Airgram, Ta'izz to Dept. of State, no. A-247, January 23, 1965, RG 59, CF, 1964–66, Box 3024, POL 15-1 YEMEN, NARA; Airgram, Ta'izz to Dept. of State, no. A-262, January 30, 1965, RG 59, CF, 1964–66, Box 3024, POL 12 YEMEN, NARA; Naṣr, *Mudhakkirāt*, 3:81–82; Aḥmad, *Dhikrayāt*, 364–66; Aḥmad, *al-Dawr*, 285–91; Gause, *Saudi-Yemeni Relations*, 65–66; Rahmy, *Egyptian Policy*, 166–68; Schmidt, *Unknown War*, 224–27; O'Ballance, *War in the Yemen*, 142–43.

[52] Telegram, Kiesewetter to Berlin, no. 234, April 20, 1965, p. 1, NY 4182/1336, Nachlass Walter Ulbricht, SAPMO.

Realizing that the narrow base of Sallāl's regime had to be broadened if compromise were ever to become possible, the Egyptians boldly decided to allow an influential Shāfiʿī associate of Zubayrī, Aḥmad Nuʿmān, to form a new government on April 20. The new prime minister wasted no time in sending feelers to Faysal and convened a peace conference in the town of Khamir in the first week of May. The attendees, who included several prominent sheikhs occasionally affiliated with the Royalist cause—the most important being Amīn Abū al-Rās, one of the two most important sheikhs of the Bakīl tribal confederation (the fickle Nājī al-Ghādir of the Khawlān being the other)—expressed criticism of Sallāl and ʿAmrī and spoke out in favor of a restriction of presidential powers and peace with Saudi Arabia.[53]

Not surprisingly, the ascendance of Nuʿmān, who promised national reconciliation, effective government, direct talks with Saudi Arabia, and increasing Yemeni independence from Egypt, produced euphoria in Western diplomatic circles. But the elation was short-lived. The Egyptians had anointed Nuʿmān largely to assuage tribal anger. However, his prompt assertion of independence from Cairo and efforts to dilute the power of President Sallāl soon proved intolerable. Nuʿmān believed that by replacing Egyptians "stooges" with strong-minded patriots like himself he would be able to convince the Saudis to recognize the YAR and abandon the Ḥamīd al-Dīns, thereby removing the pretext for the Egyptian occupation and ending the war. The Egyptians had other ideas.[54] Opting to reinforce Sallāl, they soon made it impossible for Nuʿmān to govern. On July 1, scarcely two months after taking office, he resigned and was soon replaced by Republican strongman Ḥasan al-ʿAmrī. Foreign diplomats puzzled over Nasser's decision to revert to rule by stooge, but the fact was that the emergence of an independent Yemeni line under Nuʿmān, however promising for the cause of peace, threatened Egypt's ability to control the pace and direction of Yemeni politics. Once again Nasser resolved the dilemma between assured con-

[53] Telegram, Taʿizz to Sec. State, no. 490, May 13, 1965, RG 59, CF, 1964–66, Box 3027, POL 27 YEMEN, NARA; Telegram, Jiddah to FO, no. 227, May 12, 1965, FO 371/179864, PRO; Letter, Everett (Washington) to Posnett (FO), May 18, 1965, FO 371/179855, PRO; Aḥmad, *Dhikrayāt*, 367; Aḥmad, *al-Dawr*, 292–95.

[54] Memcon, PM Aḥmad Nuʿmān and US Chargé Harlan Clark, May 15, 1965, p. 3, in Airgram, Taʿizz to Dept. of State, no. A-410, June 12, 1965, RG 59, CF, 1964–66, Box 3024, POL 15 YEMEN, NARA; Airgram, Taʿizz to Dept. of State, no. A-380, May 8, 1965, RG 59, CF, 1964–66, Box 3024, POL 15-1 YEMEN, NARA; Naṣr, *Mudhakkirāt*, 3:82–86, 90; Schmidt, *Unknown War*, 228–31; O'Ballance, *War in the Yemen*, 145–47.

trol over an unpopular government and weak influence over a popular one by perpetuating the rule of Sallāl. The political fallout from this decision was immediate: near the end of July, thirty-seven Republican leaders, led by Sheikh ʿAbd Allāh al-Aḥmar, paramount sheikh of the Ḥāshid tribal confederation and the former mainstay of tribal support for the regime, defected along with two hundred followers to British-controlled territory in the federation, whence some proceeded to Saudi Arabia to meet with Faysal.[55] The thorough discrediting of the republic in the aftermath of Zubayrī's assassination formed a crucial component of the political backdrop for Nasser's decision to go to Jiddah.

Saudi-Egyptian negotiations continued throughout the spring, primarily between Saudi Ambassador Muḥammad ʿAlī Riḍā and Egyptian officials in Cairo. In late March, ʿĀmir reiterated Egyptian willingness to convene a national peace conference under the precondition that the resultant state be called a republic. He also continued to insist on the exclusion of the Ḥamīd al-Dīn family from Yemeni politics, but implied Egypt might be willing to exclude prominent Republicans like Sallāl and ʿAmrī from a future political settlement as well. ʿĀmir prevaricated on the question of withdrawal, maintaining that the presence of Egyptian forces in Yemen was necessary to assist in the liberation of occupied southern Yemen. The Saudis rejected all three arguments, but negotiations continued nonetheless.[56]

By June the Egyptians conceded the need to include a representative of the Ḥamīd al-Dīns in the peace conference, but continued to insist on prejudging the form of government, and pushed discussion of a withdrawal plan until after the conference convened and a satisfactory political settlement had been attained.[57] In conversation with Morgan Man, the British ambassador to Saudi Arabia, on July 17, Faysal vented his frustration with Nasser, raging about the impossibility of coming to terms with this "repository of evil and deceit." Nasser, said the king,

[55] Letter, Fyjis-Walker (Cairo) to Posnett (FO), July 16, 1965, BM 1015/53, FO 371/179855, PRO; Airgram, Taʿizz to Dept. of State, no. A-26, July 24, 1965, RG 59, CF, 1964–66, Box 3023, POL 1 YEMEN, NARA; Aḥmad, *Dhikrayāt*, 368; Aḥmad, *al-Dawr*, 296–97; Naṣr, *Mudhakkirāt*, 3:86–88; O'Ballance, *War in the Yemen*, 148; Gause, *Saudi-Yemeni Relations*, 67. Sheikh al-Aḥmar returned to government service in Yemen following the Jiddah Agreement.

[56] Saudi ambassador to the UAR, ʿAlī Riḍā, cited in Telegram, Maitland (Cairo) to Weir (FO), March 23, 1965, FO 371/179864, PRO; and in Telegram, Battle (Cairo) to Sec. State, no. 3360, March 25, 1965, RG 59, CF, 1964–66, Box 3027, POL 27 YEMEN, NARA.

[57] Riḍā, quoted in Telegram, Carden (Cairo) to Weir (FO), June 25, 1965, FO 371/179864, PRO.

would never withdraw his troops, because if he did, it would be the end of him. The return of 50,000 disgruntled troops from Yemen would pose such a threat to Nasser's position that he would not risk it.[58] A week later, Faysal told Ambassador Man that Nasser had recently conveyed his earnest desire to restart negotiations with the aim of reaching an agreement that would permit Egyptian forces to withdraw over the course of six months. But the appeal for peace had been accompanied by a warning: if no solution were found, a clash between Egypt and Saudi Arabia was unavoidable. The Saudi monarch confessed that he had not yet decided how to respond to the Egyptian probes. Although he did not intend to reject the offer, which he considered sincere, an agreement was unrealistic because Nasser was politically unable to follow through on any commitment to withdraw.[59]

Several weeks later Nasser attempted to force a response to these overtures by repeating them in public. He ignited his summer peace offensive with a fiery speech on the twelfth anniversary of the Egyptian revolution, proclaiming his government's determination to break the deadlock in talks with Saudi Arabia.[60] To demonstrate his sincerity, the president dangled a plan to withdraw Egyptian forces from Yemen within six months of the conclusion of an accord. To underscore his seriousness, he warned that failure to reach agreement soon would precipitate an Egyptian attack on the insurgents' bases of supply inside Saudi Arabia. This was an ultimatum to Faysal. As such, it raised the risk of conflict by locking Egypt into a course of confrontation if peace talks failed. At the same time, by upping the ante in such a public manner, Nasser increased the pressure on Faysal to come to terms, not least because the latter could not safely assume he was bluffing.[61]

While negotiations proceeded in secret between Nasser adviser Ḥasan Ṣabrī al-Khūlī and Saudi ambassador to Egypt ʻAlī Riḍā, the Egyptian press swung into action.[62] The main thrust of the media campaign was to shape public perception of any peace accord by emphasizing that while Nasser had approached Faysal with an olive branch in one hand,

[58] Telegram, Man (Jiddah) to FO, no. 337, July 18, 1965, FO 371/179880, PRO.

[59] Telegram, Man (Jiddah) to FO, no. 355, July 25, 1965, FO 371/179880, PRO.

[60] Speech, July 22, 1965, in UAR, *Majmūʻat khuṭab*, 5:367; Telegram, Middleton (Cairo) to FO, no. 46 Saving, July 23, 1965, p. 2, FO 371/183889, PRO.

[61] Maḥmūd Aḥmad presents Nasser's threat as a straightforward response to recent Royalist battlefield successes (Aḥmad, *Dhikrayāt*, 316).

[62] Letter, Wilton (Cairo) to Scrivener (FO), VG 1022/69, August 13, 1965, p. 1, FO 371/183889, PRO; Aḥmad, *al-Dawr*, 368–69.

he had done so with a sword brandished in the other. To reinforce this perception and preserve presidential dignity, the press strove to rationalize the decision for peace by placing it in the context of Egyptian victory in Yemen and the Arab obligation to focus on the common threat from Israel.[63] All the while, a second propaganda vector threatened Saudi Arabia with war.[64] This war of nerves served to maximize the pressure on the Saudis to come to the table or face consequences. It was understandably hard to interpret the threat of bullets as an invitation to dialogue. But such was the idiom of Egyptian foreign policy at the time.

While the attempt to craft a stance of negotiation from strength was transparent, it was backed by just enough steel to render it credible. In late March there were reports of heavy concentrations of Egyptian ground forces on the coastal plane in northern Yemen. In early August, the EAF resumed sorties over Saudi territory.[65] Though skeptical, US diplomats both in Jiddah and Cairo could not rule out a lightning attack on Jīzān.[66] The threat or use of force immediately prior to a major diplomatic initiative was characteristic of Nasser's diplomacy. In this respect, the maneuvers of the spring and summer of 1965 echoed the Egyptian offensives that preceded the disengagement agreement in the spring of 1963 and the Alexandria summit in the fall of 1964.[67]

General 'Abd al-Muḥsin Kāmil Murtagī, commander of Egyptian land forces at the time, has insisted that the military presented Nasser with serious plans for an attack on Saudi Arabia in the summer of 1965. 'Āmir and other senior commanders were apparently convinced that the only way to win the war was to force Saudi Arabia to desist from supporting the Royalists. To do so, they suggested a division-size land invasion of southern Saudi Arabia under the questionable assumption that the United States, deeply engaged in Vietnam, would not respond with force. The idea was to assault Jīzān and annex it, along with the

[63] See, e.g., the lead story in *al-Ahrām*, August 15, 1965.

[64] This was most evident in the prominent coverage given to 'Āmir's trip to Yemen at the end of July, which carried the unmistakable subtext that planning for a major offensive was underway. See the headline of *al-Ahrām* on July 30 and 31, and on August 1 and 5.

[65] Letter, Trench (Washington) to Brenchley (FO), August 4, 1965, FO 371/179881, PRO.

[66] Telegram, Hart (Jiddah) to Sec. State, no. 739, March 31, 1965, RG 59, CF, 1964–66, Box 3027, POL 27 YEMEN, NARA; Telegram, Battle (Cairo) to Sec. State, no. 3448, April 2, 1965, RG 59, CF, 1964–66, Box 3027, POL 27 YEMEN, NARA.

[67] Cf. Schmidt, *Unknown War*, 206. Gause sees Jiddah as the sole exception in this pattern: an admission of defeat (*Saudi-Yemeni Relations*, 63, 64, 68).

surrounding territory, to Yemen, which had historical claims to the land. As Murtagī tells it, his own misgivings concerning requisite force levels and the anticipated US reaction won the day. Nasser ordered his generals to delay execution until after his return from peace talks with Faysal and insisted on introducing three escalatory phases into the plan, at each of which an operational pause would be inserted to gauge the Saudi/American reaction.[68] Without access to Egyptian documents, it is hard to dispute this account. However, it seems unlikely that Nasser would have been willing to test American resolve to uphold Saudi territorial integrity with such a blatant violation of state sovereignty. It is more plausible that he ordered the attack plans drawn up to add credibility to his political pressure on the Saudis and perhaps also to assuage frustration within the Egyptian high command.[69]

In any event, the Saudis appeared to take Egypt's threats seriously and wasted no time in sending out distress signals. At the end of March the king instructed his minister of defense to convey to President Johnson an urgent request for a squadron of F-104s for the defense of Saudi territory from an apparently imminent invasion aimed at occupying Jīzān and Najrān.[70] On August 11, Prince Sulṭān appealed to the British for protection, entreating the British ambassador to send a warship to the Saudi coast and put a squadron of fighter aircraft on alert for deployment at short notice.[71] The British, wary of getting too deeply involved and crossing the Americans, acceded promptly to the former request but stalled on the second.[72] So did the US government.

Despite these affectations of panic, the king stood his ground and was soon rewarded for his steadfastness. On August 18, the Saudi ambassador to Egypt, ʻAlī Riḍā, revealed to his British counterpart that Nasser had agreed to come to Jiddah to meet Faysal. Moreover, he had accepted the Saudi precondition that talks revolve around the mecha-

[68] First, aerial bombardment. Second, a small incursion ending in return to Yemeni soil. Third, the occupation of a slice of Saudi territory. Cited in Aḥmad, *Dhikrayāt*, 317–18; Ḥabīb, *Milaffāt*, 241.

[69] For a similar view, see James, *Nasser at War*, 80.

[70] Telegram, Jiddah to State, no. 726, March 29, 1965, RG 59, CF, 1964–66, Box 3027, POL 27 YEMEN, NARA. However, the obvious linkage between the specific request for a squadron and the ongoing competition between the American and British governments over a major arms deal with the Saudi government suggests that it was in part a negotiating tactic. See also Saqqāf's earlier concerns in Telegram, Jiddah to Sec. State, no. 637, March 2, 1965, RG 59, CF, 1964–66, Box 3027, POL 27 YEMEN, NARA.

[71] Telegram, Brown (Jiddah) to FO, no. 383, August 11, 1965, FO 371/179881, PRO.

[72] Telegram, FO to Jiddah, no. 836, August 13, 1965, FO 371/179881, PRO.

nism of transition to a "State of Yemen," entailing an all-Yemeni peace conference and Egyptian withdrawal within six months. The fact that Sallāl was apparently being detained in Alexandria until the conclusion of the talks further attested to Nasser's earnestness. In public, the Egyptians portrayed the visit as a last-ditch bid for peace. To highlight the consequences of failure, the armed forces went on high alert.[73]

Faysal's own preparations for the summit were both more subtle and more effective. Two weeks before the summit, he arranged a meeting between Royalists and renegade Republicans at al-Ṭā'if. The talks resulted in a remarkable appeal to the Saudi monarch to help secure a period of peace that would enable a transitional government to lead the Yemenis to a national referendum in which they would determine their own destiny free of foreign influence. The agreement called for a transitional "Islamic State of Yemen" to be headed by a Supreme National Council (which would replace the presidency), a cabinet of ministers, and a consultative council. This formula, reminiscent of one of Faysal's proposals at Alexandria, was soon to reappear in the Jiddah accords, and it added fresh evidence of Egypt's loss of control over the course of Yemeni politics. Faysal's engineering of the conference at this juncture proved to be an astute tactical ploy that set the tone for the settlement he hammered out with Nasser several days later.[74]

Nasser set sail from the Red Sea port of Berenice on the evening of August 21, arriving in Jiddah the next afternoon, accompanied by Vice Presidents Muḥyī al-Dīn and Sadat. For the next two days the two leaders and their advisers thrashed out the key elements of a settlement in Yemen. Unfortunately for historians, the proceedings at Jiddah suffer from a lack of transparency reminiscent of the negotiations at Alexandria the year before. Sāmī Sharaf quotes widely from the Egyptian minutes of the summit, but his selection privileges mutual professions of

[73] Telegram, Middleton (Cairo) to FO, no. 675, August 18, 1965, FO 371/179881, PRO; BBC, *SWB*, August 19, 1965, ME/1940. Cf. Sharaf's implausible contention, according to which it was Nasser who insisted on going to Jiddah, even when Faysal proposed to come once again to Alexandria (*Sanawāt*, 2:635). Nasser gave the following explanation to an Indian journalist: "As I did not want to waste time on questions of prestige, neutral ground and all such nonsense, I expressed my willingness to meet Feisal in Jeddah itself." *Blitz*, May 7, 1966, 14.

[74] Muḥammad al-Shu'aybī, *Mu'tamar Ḥaraḍ wa muḥāwalāt al-salām bi-l-Yaman* (Damascus: Dār al-Kitāb, 1990), 65–70; Aḥmad Nu'mān, cited in enclosure to Airgram, Ta'izz to State, no. A-120, October 16, 1965, p. 2, RG 59, CF, 1964–66, Box 3027, POL 27 YEMEN, NARA; Aḥmad, *Dhikrayāt*, 371; Aḥmad, *al-Dawr*, 297–98; Gause, *Saudi-Yemeni Relations*, 67–68; Rahmy, *Egyptian Policy*, 182; O'Ballance, *War in the Yemen*, 148–49.

friendship over matters of substance.[75] Luckily, the public announcement that followed this summit contained considerable detail. The text released to the media upon conclusion of the talks featured the following operative points:[76]

> First: The Yemeni people shall have their say and shall determine the system of government they want for themselves in *a popular plebiscite* [*istiftā' sha'bī*] to be held not later than 23rd November 1966.
>
> Second: The period remaining until the date of the plebiscite shall be considered *a transitional period* [*fatrah intiqāliyyah*] during which preparations and arrangements shall be made for the said plebiscite.
>
> Third: The Kingdom of Saudi Arabia and the United Arab Republic shall cooperate in the setting up of *an interim congress* [*mu'tamar intiqālī*] *composed of 50 members representing all national forces and decision-making elements of the Yemeni people* [*jamī' al-qiwā al-waṭaniyyah wa-ahl al-ḥall wa-l-'aqd li-l-sha'b al-yamanī*] after consultation and agreement between the various Yemeni groups. The said conference shall convene at the city of Harad on 23rd November 1965.
>
> This congress shall undertake the following tasks:
>
> A. *Determining the system of government* [*ṭarīqat al-ḥukm*] *during the transitional period* and until the popular plebiscite is held.
>
> B. *Forming a provisional cabinet* [*wizārah mu'aqqatah*] which shall exercise the powers of government during the transitional period.
>
> C. Determining the form and procedure of the plebiscite which shall be held not later than 23rd November 1966.
>
> Fourth: *The two governments shall sponsor and back up the decisions of the said interim Yemeni congress* and shall cooperate in making their implementation successful. They hereby declare their acceptance of the existence of a joint neutral committee from the two countries for follow-up and for supervising the plebiscite in the event the congress decides that such a neutral committee is necessary.
>
> Fifth: The Kingdom of *Saudi Arabia shall immediately cease all operations involving the supply of military assistance* in any form or the use of Saudi territory for action against Yemen.

[75] Sharaf, *Sanawāt*, 2:636–39. Likewise, Muḥammad Haykal, who attended the talks, provides a colorful account lacking in substance (*al-Infijār*, 188–96).

[76] Telegram, Cairo to Sec. State, no. 562, August 24, 1965, RG 59, CF, 1964–66, Box 3027, POL 27 YEMEN, NARA. The document quotes the official Egyptian English version of the treaty. For the Arabic version, see Sharaf, *Sanawāt*, 2:639–41; Aḥmad, *al-Dawr*, 370–72.

Sixth: *The United Arab Republic shall withdraw its military forces* [Ar. all of its forces, *kāffat quwwātihā al-'askariyyah*] *from Yemen with[in] ten months starting on 23rd November, 1965.*

Seventh: *Armed clashes in Yemen shall be halted forthwith* and a joint peace committee from the two sides shall be formed to undertake the following:

A. *Observing the cease-fire* through special observation committees.

B. *Observing borders and ports* and ceasing military assistance in all its forms. As for food aid, it shall be extended under its [the peace committee's] supervision. The said observation committees may use the necessary means of transport and can freely use Yemeni territory. If necessary, they can also use Saudi territory enabling them to reach the observations posts to be agreed on.

Eight[h]: The Kingdom of Saudi Arabia and the United Arab Republic shall cooperate and work positively for the safeguarding and implementation of this agreement and the establishment of stability on Yemeni territory until the result of the plebiscite is announced. They shall do so by earmarking a force from the two countries which the committee shall use when the necessity arises to *crush any deviation from this agreement or any action to obstruct it* or any troubles standing in the way of its successful implementation.

Ninth: For the purpose of promoting cooperation between the United Arab Republic and the Kingdom of Saudi Arabia and of effecting the transition from the present phase to the state of normalcy and of establishing the relations between the two countries on the footing where they once stood and where they should stand, direct contact shall be established between President Gamal Abdel-Nasser and His Majesty King Feisal to avoid any difficulties hampering the implementation of this agreement. (Emphases added)

The agreement's most noteworthy aspect is the extent of Nasser's concessions. First, the word "Republic"—hitherto a key sticking point in the negotiations—is nowhere to be found. The accord left the eventual form of government to the Yemeni populace, with the interim regime to be determined by a representative council. Second, the stipulation of unconditional Egyptian withdrawal within a strict time frame stands in marked contrast to the multiple conditions attached to the evacuation clause in the Alexandria agreement. Third, the notion of a neutrally designated transitional government followed by a referendum strongly resembles the proposals Royalists and dissident Republicans

Figure 6.2 Lifeguard Nasser saving the damsel of Arab peace from the stormy sea of Yemen. "Imperialism and Zionism are in trouble following the peace agreement." *Akhbār al-Yawm,* August 28, 1965.

Figure 6.3 Nasser and Faysal stride confidently down the road to peace. "No obstacles stand in our way." *Akhbār al-Yawm,* August 21, 1965. Cartoon by Alexander Ṣārūkhān.

submitted at Ṭā'if several weeks before. Taken together, these concessions pointed to a willingness to relinquish control over the Yemeni political process in order to execute an orderly withdrawal, come what may. In key respects the agreement represented a Saudi victory.[77]

Despite the reported abundance of goodwill at Jiddah, the fundamental problem remained one of trust. Faysal, in particular, feared Nasser's reputation for ill-timed publication of secret agreements.[78] The king was also wary of Egypt's poor track record in upholding previous private understandings concerning Yemen. It was almost certainly for fear of Egyptian legerdemain—and not, as Faysal told both Nasser and Ambassador Badeau, because he wanted to leave as much

[77] My view accords in large measure with that of Aḥmad, *al-Dawr*, 373.

[78] Kamāl Adham, cited in Telegram, Jiddah to Sec. State, no. 790, March 12, 1966, pp. 2–3, RG 59, CF, 1964–66, Box 3028, POL 27 YEMEN, NARA.

as possible for the Yemenis to decide[79]—that the king insisted on publishing the accord in its entirety.[80] This was a bad decision, for it necessarily limited the substance that could be included in the agreement. Since there would be no secret appendix, some of the most sensitive components of a political settlement—those pertaining to the exclusion of certain individuals or parties from the political future of Yemen, for example—had to remain unwritten, and to a large extent undetermined. A series of oral "gentlemen's agreements," which were hardly known, if at all, outside of the leaders' closest circle of advisers, doomed the Jiddah accord to the same fate as its predecessors—dissolution amid misunderstanding, misinterpretation, and misrepresentation to allies.

Although the oral understandings that surround the Jiddah accord are not preserved in a single reliable source, scrutiny of the confidences of a number of Egyptian, Yemeni, and Saudi officials reveals the following key elements:

1. Egypt and Saudi Arabia would each select half of the fifty-man congress.
2. The Royalist and Republican delegations would each consist of fifteen Zaydīs and ten Shāfi'īs.
3. President Sallāl, his close supporters, and all members of the Ḥamīd al-Dīn family would be excluded from the peace conference.
4. Both Sallāl and Badr would be barred from participation in the interim government and would eventually be exiled from Yemen.[81]

[79] Nasser, cited in Telegram, Battle (Cairo) to Sec. State, no. 2139, February 21, 1966, p. 1, RG 59, CF, 1964–66, Box 3028, POL 27 YEMEN, NARA; Faysal, cited in Telegram, Jiddah to Sec. State, no. 728, February 24, 1966, p. 2, RG 59, CF, 1964–66, Box 3028, POL 27 YEMEN, NARA.

[80] Letter, Walker (Cairo) to Weir (FO), BS 1022/61, September 1, 1965, FO 371/179881, PRO. But Egyptian Vice President Muḥyī al-Dīn claimed *both* Nasser and Faysal desired to make as much of the agreement public as possible. Telegram, Battle (Cairo) to Sec. State, no. 585, August 26, 1965, RG 59, CF, 1964–66, Box 3027, POL 27 YEMEN, NARA. Arguably, the two leaders could have drafted a secret accord in such a way that its publication would cause equal damage to both signatories.

[81] It is possible that a further understanding was reached, according to which the interim government would be neither a republic nor a monarchy. Intercepted Telegram, Faysal to 'Alī Riḍā (Cairo), undated, quoted in Haykal, *al-Infijār*, 237; Battle (Cairo) to Sec. State, no. 585, August 26, 1965, RG 59, CF, 1964–66, Box 3027, POL 27 YEMEN, NARA; Telegram, Seelye (Jiddah) to Sec. State, no. 149, August 29, 1965, p. 2, RG 59, CF, 1964–66, Box 3027, POL 27 YEMEN, NARA; Telegram, Battle (Cairo) to Sec. State, no. 661, September 7, 1965, RG 59, CF, 1964–66, Box 3027, POL 27 YEMEN, NARA; Airgram, Jiddah to State, no. A-110, September 27, 1965, RG 59, CF, 1964–66, Box 3027, POL 27 YEMEN,

The unfortunate combination of detail in public and obscurity in private was not the only weakness inherent in the agreement. The decision to hold a popular referendum only partly concealed the arrogant disrespect for Yemeni opinion embodied in the accord and most evident in the ferocious tone of article eight. As the British ambassador to Egypt, George Middleton, indicated: "I would expect that this quite extraordinary agreement, in which two states purport to decide the future of a third after no more than a parenthetical reference to their having consulted representatives of it, will keep U.A.R.-Saudi relations on an even keel until well after this Arab summit. However, it is clear that in the longer term the agreement provides wide scope for disputes."[82] Thus despite the laudable clarity of the agreement and comparative level of detail, problems were likely to surface at a still finer level of granularity.

The deficiencies of the approach adopted at Jiddah were not immediately apparent. The Saudis, pleased with the agreement, attributed the breakthrough to Nasser's flexibility.[83] Egyptian officials, similarly pleased, launched enthusiastically into the hard work of implementation.[84] Most Yemeni Republicans, by contrast, were dismayed by the accords, which spelled out, for the first time, what an imposed settlement would look like. The appalling ease with which Nasser had apparently abandoned the Republicans at Jiddah drove together such former rivals as Aḥmad Nuʿmān and Ḥasan al-ʿAmrī in a common cause to save the republic.[85] Their complaints centered on the equal status accorded the Royalists, the omission of any reference to Yemen as a republic, and the apparent

NARA; Airgram, Taʿizz to State, no. A-110, October 2, 1965, RG 59, CF, 1964–66, Box 3027, POL 27 YEMEN, NARA; Airgram, Taʿizz to State, no. A-157, November 20, 1965, RG 59, CF, 1964–66, Box 3028, POL 27 YEMEN, NARA; Khūlī, cited in Telegram, Battle (Cairo) to Sec. State, no. 2033, February 10, 1966, p. 2, RG 59, CF, 1964–66, Box 3028, POL 27 YEMEN, NARA; Gause, *Saudi-Yemeni Relations*, 68; Schmidt, *Unknown War*, 238–39; Aḥmad, *al-Dawr*, 380.

[82] Telegram, Middleton (Cairo) to FO, no. 694, August 25, 1965, FO 371/179881, PRO. See also Aḥmad, *al-Dawr*, 372–73.

[83] Telegram, Seelye (Jiddah) to Sec. State, no. 149, August 29, 1965, p. 2, RG 59, CF, 1964–66, Box 3027, POL 27 YEMEN, NARA.

[84] Telegram, Battle (Cairo) to Sec. State, no. 661, September 7, 1965, RG 59, CF, 1964–66, Box 3027, POL 27 YEMEN, NARA.

[85] Telegram, Clark (Taʿizz) to Sec. State, no. 60, August 30, 1965, RG 59, CF, 1964–66, Box 3027, POL 27 YEMEN, NARA; Airgram, Taʿizz to State, no. A-110, October 2, 1965, RG 59, CF, 1964–66, Box 3027, POL 27 YEMEN, NARA; Airgram, Taʿizz to State, no. A-120, October 16, 1965, RG 59, CF, 1964–66, Box 3027, POL 27 YEMEN, NARA; Despatch, Brenchley (AD) to Stewart (FO), January 25, 1966, "Yemen: Annual Review for 1965," p. 3, FO 371/185445, PRO.

failure to secure the exile of the Ḥamīd al-Dīns from Yemen. Although some conceded in private that "they [Nasser and Faysal] had no choice but to decide for us," others were furious at the Saudi-Egyptian presumption to dictate the Yemenis' own future. The top brass of the YAR military command feared it would be left to face the wrath of the Royalists alone in the aftermath of an Egyptian withdrawal and would play no role in a non-Republican government. And intense speculation began about the proportion of Republican and Royalist delegates to the peace conference and the future of Sallāl and Badr—both matters covered by private Saudi-Egyptian understandings. The rumblings of discontent coming out of wide swaths of the Republican camp in the weeks leading up to the Ḥaraḍ conference did not augur well for the prospects of peace.[86]

The all-Yemeni peace conference convened at Ḥaraḍ on November 23.[87] Originally scheduled to last five days, it dragged on for more than four weeks of inconclusive wrangling, punctuated by nightly reconciliation feasts requiring the slaughter of sheep at a rate of forty-five per day.[88] The Republicans bore a large measure of responsibility for the failure of the conference.[89] On November 28, the Republican delegation appealed to Nasser and Faysal to intervene, complaining in a bitter letter about the unfairly high proportion of Royalists at the conference, the "abolition" of the republic implicit in the Jiddah accord, and the failure to exclude the Ḥamīd al-Dīn family from Yemen.[90] Nasser's response left it up to the Yemenis to overcome the impasse.[91] The delegates finally adjourned on December 24, after failing to reach agreement on such basics as the title of the transitional state or voting procedures.[92] A

[86] Airgram, Ta'izz to State, no. A-157, November 20, 1965, RG 59, CF, 1964–66, Box 3028, POL 27 YEMEN, NARA; Shu'aybī, *Mu'tamar Ḥaraḍ*, 75–91; Aḥmad, *al-Dawr*, 375–79.

[87] For documentation, see 'Abd Allāh al-Ḥusaynī, ed., *Mu'tamar Ḥaraḍ: Wathā'iq wa-maḥāḍir* (Beirut: Dār al-Kitāb al-Jadīd, 1966).

[88] Telegram, Battle (Cairo) to Sec. State, no. 1441, December 10, 1965, RG 59, CF, 1964–66, Box 3028, POL 27 YEMEN, NARA.

[89] Nasser later admitted as much in conversation with John Badeau. Telegram, Battle (Cairo) to Sec. State, no. 2139, February 21, 1966, RG 59, CF, 1964–66, Box 3028, POL 27 YEMEN, NARA. See also Guldescu, "Yemen: The War and the Haradh Conference," 324, 327–30; Vered, "Without Decision," 244–45.

[90] For an unofficial translation, see Airgram, Ta'izz to State, no. A-170, December 4, 1965, RG 59, CF, 1964–66, Box 3028, POL 27 YEMEN, NARA.

[91] Telegram, Battle (Cairo) to Sec. State, no. 1397, December 6, 1965, RG 59, CF, 1964–66, Box 3028, POL 27 YEMEN, NARA.

[92] Telegram, Clark (Ta'izz) to Sec. State, no. 178, November 27, 1965, RG 59, CF, 1964–66, Box 3028, POL 27 YEMEN, NARA; Telegram, Clark (Ta'izz) to Sec. State, no. 186, De-

fundamental problem was that no one—not Nasser, not Faysal, neither moderate Republicans nor temperate Royalists—wished to commit themselves publicly to the most drastic measures necessitated by compromise, in particular the abandonment of the republic (by the Egyptians and Republicans) and of the Ḥamīd al-Dīns (by the Saudis and Royalists). This accounted both for critical gaps in the Jiddah Agreement and the failure to compromise at Ḥaraḍ. In any event, the Yemenis' inability to take the risks necessary for peace, despite apparently earnest prodding from both Cairo and Riyadh, dealt the first serious blow to the Jiddah Agreement.[93]

The Yemenis, at Ḥaraḍ, essentially threw the problem back at Nasser and Faysal. In so doing they forced the two leaders, who had hitherto avoided detailed understandings concerning the political future of Yemen, to roll up their sleeves and delve into the minutiae of an acceptable political settlement. But as mistrust crept back into the relationship between Egypt and Saudi Arabia over the winter of 1965/66, the practical discussion of how to implement the Jiddah Agreement dissolved into a fresh round of negotiations that questioned the accord's basic assumptions.

On January 5, 1966, Faysal sent Nasser a confidential letter calling attention to the fact that execution of the two main clauses—Saudi cessation of aid and the beginning of Egyptian withdrawal—was not contingent on the status of intra-Yemeni negotiations.[94] The Saudis, wrote Faysal, had lived up to their side of the bargain, while the Egyptians had not. Strictly speaking, he continued, the Egyptians were to have begun withdrawing on November 23, the very day the conference

cember 1, 1965, RG 59, CF, 1964–66, Box 3028, POL 27 YEMEN, NARA; Shu'aybī, *Mu'tamar Ḥaraḍ*, 93–121.

[93] Telegram, Clark (Ta'izz) to Sec. State, no. 180, November 28, 1965, RG 59, CF, 1964–66, Box 3028, POL 27 YEMEN, NARA; Telegram, Jiddah to Sec. State, no. 441, December 1, 1965, RG 59, CF, 1964–66, Box 3028, POL 27 YEMEN, NARA; Shu'aybī, *Mu'tamar Ḥaraḍ*, 101, 111; Aḥmad, *al-Dawr*, 386–91; Gause, *Saudi-Yemeni Relations*, 68–69. Aḥmad Nu'mān accused Nasser of publicly professing his desire for peace while applying massive pressure on the Republican delegation behind the scenes not to compromise. But Nu'mān himself may have been attempting to shift the blame for avoiding a politically risky compromise. See Airgram, Ta'izz to State, no. 207, undated [ca. December 28, 1965], pp. 3–6, RG 59, CF, 1964–66, Box 3028, POL 27 YEMEN, NARA; Rashād Fir'awn, cited in Memcon, Fir'awn, Dinsmore, and Seelye, Riyadh, January 7, 1966, pp. 2–3, in Airgram, Jiddah to State, no. A-209, January 10, 19656, pp. 3–6, RG 59, CF, 1964–66, Box 3028, POL 27 YEMEN, NARA; and 'Abd al-Raḥmān al-Iryānī, cited in Telegram, Clark (Ta'izz) to Sec. State, no. 254, January 26, 1966, RG 59, CF, 1964–66, Box 3028, POL 27 YEMEN, NARA.

[94] For the full text, see Sharaf, *Sanawāt*, 2:644–47.

convened at Ḥaraḍ and before it could possibly have issued even a single decision.[95] Thus the claim that the dissolution of the conference precluded withdrawal was baseless. Moreover, the Saudis could not be held responsible for its failure. They had used the three months between Jiddah and Ḥaraḍ to influence their local allies in the direction of compromise, while the Egyptians had let their clients act and speak as they wished. As a result, the question of the form of the transitional government had become conflated with the form of the postplebiscite regime, and the conference had dissolved in disarray. Despite all this, Faysal professed to accept that evidence of Egyptian disinclination to enforce the agreement did not reflect Nasser's commitment to its execution, and proposed to send a trusted emissary to Cairo to iron out these differences.

On January 11, Nasser responded with a short note assuring Faysal of Egypt's enduring commitment to the Jiddah accords and to the preservation of good relations with Saudi Arabia.[96] This nonresponse would have been offensive had not Nasser—in a testimony to his own fear of untimely publication—opted to convey a more substantial reply orally.[97] Even so, Nasser's proposals bordered on the insulting. These called for an Egyptian withdrawal on schedule; the establishment of an interim government, made up of one-third Royalists and two-thirds Republicans, which would be named "*ḥukūmat al-Yaman al-intiqāliyyah*" (transitional government of Yemen); and the exile of the Ḥamīd al-Dīn family during the transitional period, that is, prior to completion of the Egyptian evacuation. Faysal was incensed. Not only had Nasser casually introduced a conditional aspect to Egyptian withdrawal by including these points together in a single proposal, he also had brazenly eroded the egalitarian principle enshrined in the secret understandings that accompanied the Jiddah Agreement. To add insult to injury, Nasser had added a politically impossible provision concerning the royal family. "How long," the king asked, "should we continue to permit the UAR to delay by raising new conditions?"[98]

[95] Ibid., 645.

[96] Ibid., 648–49.

[97] For the contents, see Fir'awn, cited in Telegram, Eilts (Jiddah) to Sec. State, no. 595, January 18, 1965, RG 59, CF, 1964–66, Box 3028, POL 27 YEMEN, NARA. See also, Haykal, *al-Infijār*, 235–36.

[98] Quoted in Telegram, Eilts (Ẓahrān) to Sec. State, no. 236, February 20, 1966, p. 2, RG 59, CF, 1964–66, Box 3028, POL 27 YEMEN, NARA.

But it was Faysal who took almost six weeks to respond, a delay that annoyed the Egyptians to no end. His reply, when it came, indicated the breadth of the chasm that had opened up between the Saudi and Egyptian positions. Voicing agreement with Nasser's unobjectionable proposals concerning the timetable for withdrawal and the title of the transitional government, Faysal refused to budge from the 50:50 precedent set in the Jiddah accords. At the same time, he expressed his willingness to have the Yemeni government consider the exile of the Ḥamīd al-Dīns once the Egyptian evacuation was complete. Nasser responded sharply, digging in on the 2:1 ratio and insisting that the exile of the royal family take place before the completion of the Egyptian withdrawal. Although he offered to commence the pullout immediately and carry it out over the possible objections of a (Republican-dominated) interim government, the president added an ominous take-it-or-leave-it clause, stating that were his offer to be rejected, he would keep his troops in Yemen indefinitely. The diplomatic tit for tat continued, but this sequence of slight and counterslight boded ill for the future of the Jiddah Agreement.[99]

From the Islamic Pact to the Long Breath Strategy

The apparent failure of diplomacy set the Egyptians on a unilateralist course. Within weeks of the effective collapse of the Jiddah Agreement at Ḥaraḍ, Egyptian policy makers were hard at work planning a military

[99] Khūlī, cited in Telegram, Battle (Cairo) to Sec. State, no. 1855, January 21, 1966, RG 59, CF, 1964–66, Box 3028, POL 27 YEMEN, NARA; Saqqāf, cited in Telegram, Eilts (Jiddah) to Sec. State, no. 610, January 25, 1966, RG 59, CF, 1964–66, Box 3028, POL 27 YEMEN, NARA; Faysal, cited in Telegram, Allen (Jiddah) to Sec. State, no. 236, February 20, 1966, p. 2, RG 59, CF, 1964–66, Box 3028, POL 27 YEMEN, NARA; Nasser, cited in Telegram, Battle (Cairo) to Sec. State, no. 2139, February 21, 1966, pp. 1–3, RG 59, CF, 1964–66, Box 3028, POL 27 YEMEN, NARA; Sadat, cited in Dept. of State, Memcon, Sadat, Rusk et al., February 23, 1966, pp. 1–2, RG 59, CF, 1964–66, Box 3028, POL 27 YEMEN, NARA; Faysal, cited in Telegram, Weathersby (Khartoum) to Sec. State, no. 636, March 13, 1966, RG 59, CF, 1964–66, Box 3028, POL 27 YEMEN, NARA; Faysal, cited in Telegram, Eilts (Jiddah) to Sec. State, no. 728, February 24, 1966, RG 59, CF, 1964–66, Box 3028, POL 27 YEMEN, NARA; Telegram, Eilts (Jiddah) to Sec. State, no. 776, March 8, 1966, RG 59, CF, 1964–66, Box 3028, POL 27 YEMEN, NARA; Adham, cited in Telegram, Eilts (Jiddah) to Sec. State, no. 809, March 15, 1966, RG 59, CF, 1964–66, Box 3028, POL 27 YEMEN; Khūlī, cited in Telegram, Battle (Cairo) to Sec. State, no. 2267, March 7, 1966, RG 59, CF, 1964–66, Box 3028, POL 27 YEMEN, NARA.

alternative. The so-called Strategy of the Long Breath (*siyāsat al-nafas al-ṭawīl*) aimed to provide long-term security for the republic at a reduced cost to Egypt. The idea was to withdraw a sizable portion of the Egyptian task force from the country and redeploy the remainder in the tight triangle of territory formed by the three main towns of the Republican heartland: Ḥudaydah, Ṣan'ā', and Ta'izz. To avert recapture of the evacuated areas, the Egyptians counted on a combination of deals with tribal leaders, deployment of newly trained Yemeni forces, and the threat of massive retaliation. From an economic perspective, the evacuation of the frontier would reduce manpower and cut transportation costs. From a military perspective, the plan would eliminate numerous isolated outposts and create short, more easily defensible interior lines of communication. Finally, from a regional perspective, the reduced presence in Yemen would preserve the Republican wedge between the Saudis and the British at Aden, enabling Nasser to influence the political fate of the peninsula.[100]

On February 22, 1966, in a speech at Cairo University on the eighth anniversary of the union with Syria, Nasser hinted at the change in strategy. For the first time he made explicit the contingent nature of the commitment Egypt had undertaken at Jiddah: Egyptian forces would not pull out of Yemen until an acceptable transitional government had been formed. Striking a defiant tone, he declared that the Egyptians were not, *pace* Faysal, tired of the war or consumed with internal problems. On the contrary, they were prepared to remain in Yemen five years, if necessary, and would in any case wait out the British in Aden.[101] Exactly one month later, in a speech before the Arab Socialist Union at Suez, the president spelled out how this would be done. Nasser unveiled Egypt's new plan for military retrenchment in Yemen, which would enable Egyptian forces to remain there until the revolution was capable of standing on its own two feet. "Should we surrender to Faysal or should we sit ten years in Yemen? I say, we shall sit for twenty!" But "sitting" on the peninsula did not mean that Egyptian forces would henceforth assume a purely defensive posture: "I say today that whoever shall intervene in Yemen, we shall strike him.... I say these words clearly ... we shall strike at the bases of aggression."[102]

[100] Telegram, Clark (Ta'izz) to Sec. State, no. 367, March 28, 1966, RG 59, CF, 1964–66, Box 3028, POL 27 YEMEN, NARA; Aḥmad, *al-Dawr*, 436–39; Vered, "Without Decision," 247.

[101] UAR, *Majmū'at khuṭab*, 5:502, 504. See also Schmidt, *Unknown War*, 238.

[102] UAR, *Majmū'at khuṭab*, 5:537.

By the time Nasser gave his "Long Breath" speech on March 22, the operation was already underway. Within a month the internal redeployment was complete and as many as 20,000 troops—approximately one-third of the entire task force—set sail for home. On April 22, the first shipload of returning soldiers arrived in Egypt.[103] By the summer of 1966, only 40,000 troops remained in Yemen.

On April 7 Nasser announced to the US ambassador that the Jiddah Agreement was "finished."[104] "We have given up," he explained. "King Feisal believed when I entered into the Jidda agreement that it was a move from weakness, but it was not. It was a move to avoid a clash between the United Arab Republic and Saudi Arabia. That clash is now before us." Muḥammad Haykal reinforced the warning in less presidential language the following day, telling Ambassador Battle that "no force in the world" could prevent Egypt from assaulting Jīzān and Najrān in the event the Saudis permitted the Royalists to occupy the areas being evacuated by Egyptian forces.[105] In part this was no doubt bluster intended to resurrect the mechanism of indirect pressure on Riyadh via Washington, which Nasser had employed to great effect in the winter of 1962/63. In another conversation with Battle two weeks earlier, Nasser had urged the United States to stay involved: "If shooting resumes, you will be a party at interest immediately.... You must therefore follow this issue closely."[106]

Through the chest thumping, it was possible to perceive an almost reassuring aspect to Nasser's message: the Egyptians were proceeding unilaterally with a substantial withdrawal and were understandably eager to convince others that they were doing so from a position of strength. "We are consolidating our troops and will withdraw in large numbers, perhaps even up to half of them, but we can stay in Yemen for ten years. We are not weak. This does not cost as much as Feisal thinks it does."[107] But it was Haykal's formulation that exposed the real purpose

[103] Khūlī, cited in Telegram, Battle (Cairo) to Sec. State, no. 2673, April 18, 1966, p. 1, RG 59, CF, 1964–66, Box 3028, POL 27 YEMEN, NARA; Aḥmad, *al-Dawr*, 438; Rahmy, *Egyptian Policy*, 155.

[104] Telegram, Battle (Cairo) to Sec. State, no. 2571, April 8, 1966, p. 2, RG 59, CF, 1964–66, Box 3028, POL 27 YEMEN, NARA; James, *Nasser at War*, 84.

[105] Telegram, Battle (Cairo) to Sec. State, no. 2581, April 9, 1966, RG 59, CF, 1964–66, Box 3028, POL 27 YEMEN, NARA.

[106] Telegram, Battle (Cairo) to Sec. State, no. 2388, March 20, 1966, p. 3, RG 59, 1964–66, Box 2768, Pol UAR-US, NARA.

[107] Telegram, Battle (Cairo) to Sec. State, no. 2571, April 8, 1966, p. 2, RG 59, CF, 1964–66, Box 3028, POL 27 YEMEN, NARA.

behind Nasser's representation: to deter the Saudis from taking advantage of the Egyptian redeployment in order to make territorial gains in northern Yemen. On May Day, Nasser issued a still starker warning to Faysal in public. He promised that future attacks originating in Saudi Arabia would be answered not only with retaliation against the "bases of aggression" but also with their *occupation,* hinting darkly that ancient Yemeni claims to the southern Saudi provinces of Jīzān and Najrān would be revived.[108] Whether or not a storm would break out, there could be no doubt: clouds were gathering over Yemen.

The Egyptian position had undergone a dramatic transformation over the course of the winter. As late as November 1965, the Egyptian government seems to have fully intended to implement the Jiddah Agreement. Yet by March 1966 this was no longer the case. The question is: Why? Besides the familiar hurdle of Yemeni politics, which had tripped up the peacemakers at Ḥaraḍ, what had transpired to overturn Nasser's resolve to rid Egypt of its Yemeni burden?

A momentous development in British policy provides part of the answer. On February 22, 1966, the very same day Nasser gave his speech at Cairo University, the British government announced its decision not to maintain defense obligations toward, or military facilities or forces in, South Arabia after the grant of independence in the course of 1967 or 1968. In practice, this meant the closure of the huge air and sea base at Aden, thereby removing the principle pillar of British military might east of Suez. This statement, the most explicit yet concerning British plans for South Arabia, had serious regional implications. To conservative friends like Iran and Saudi Arabia, the imminence of British abandonment raised fears of a wave of nationalism that would sweep through the peninsula, filling the vacuum left by British forces and leaving toppled sheikhdoms in its wake. To revolutionary foes, Britain's declaration signaled the imminence of victory for the revolutionary cause in southern Yemen—and for Nasser as its primary regional sponsor. Within as little as two years, Nasser would be in a position to declare the final victory over British imperialism in the Middle East. But in order to gain the most propaganda mileage out of the British withdrawal, and be in an advantageous position to influence the future political course of the Arabian Peninsula, it was necessary to maintain Egyptian troops on the ground.

[108] UAR, *Majmūʿat khuṭab,* 5:554.

There is no argument that the shift in British policy in early 1966 created a new rationale for the perpetuation of the Egyptian occupation of Yemen.[109] It is even probable that this logic had some effect on policy. But from here to the claim—voiced most consistently by British and Saudi hawks—that the inopportune British announcement was to blame for Nasser's abandonment of the Jiddah Agreement is a bit of a stretch.[110] For one, the overall trajectory of British policy in the region had been known for some time. In particular, the intent to grant independence to South Arabia by 1968 had been official policy since July 1965, one month prior to the Saudi-Egyptian peace agreement. Had British policy been the primary factor affecting Egyptian calculations, Nasser would never have gone to Jiddah. To be sure, the revelation of the imminent liquidation of British *military* power in Yemen within the time frame for independence added strategic rationale and rhetorical justification for the Egyptian decision not to withdraw, but the surprising conclusions of the British defense review almost certainly came too late to affect a policy already adopted in Cairo.[111] Not only had the failure of the Ḥaraḍ conference in December doomed the Jiddah Agreement well before any inkling of Britain's new defensive posture had leaked beyond a tight circle of British officials,[112] but also any chances of its resurrection were

[109] The British were not unaware of the negative effects of this announcement on Egypt's commitment to withdraw from Yemen. But for a number of reasons, they deemed it important to couple the announcement with the publication of the Annual Defense Review, which placed the withdrawal from Aden in a much broader context of cost-saving measures and redeployments throughout the world. See Cabinet, Defence and Oversea Policy Committee, OPD (66) 16, January 19, 1966, "Outcome of Defence Review: Aden Base," in CAB 148/27, PRO. See also Gause, *Saudi-Yemeni Relations*, 70; Schmidt, *Unknown War*, 278.

[110] Their sentiments are echoed by O'Ballance, *War in the Yemen*, 156; and to a lesser extent by Stephens, *Nasser*, 422–44. See also James, *Nasser at War*, 83–87.

[111] Nasser had already shared the outline of the Long Breath Strategy with the US ambassador the day before the surprise announcement in London. Telegram, Battle (Cairo) to Sec. State, no. 2139, February 21, 1966, p. 2, RG 59, CF, 1964–66, Box 3028, POL 27 YEMEN, NARA. For the argument that the British declaration changed Nasser's calculations fundamentally, see Letter, McCarthy (Aden) to Goulding (FO), April 27, 1966, BM 1015/85, FO 371/185447, PRO.

[112] That said, a full month before the announcement, the US ambassador to Egypt speculated that the Egyptians had reevaluated their peninsular policy as a result of an anticipated British decision to abandon Aden, "creating [a] vacuum and precipitating [a] struggle to fill it." Telegram, Battle (Cairo) to Sec. State, no. 1856, January 21, 1966, p. 2, RG 59, CF, 1964–66, Box 3028, POL 27 YEMEN, NARA. See also Aḥmad, *Dhikrayāt*, 395–97.

doomed before the end of the year by the accumulation of evidence concerning the challenge to Egyptian hegemony a newly assertive Saudi Arabia posed.

On December 8, 1965, in the midst of the tumultuous proceedings at Ḥaraḍ, Faysal departed on a singularly ill-timed visit to Iran.[113] This weeklong visit—the first by a Saudi monarch in a decade—signified rapprochement with Egypt's principal geopolitical rival in the region. In Tehran, Faysal was warmly received by the Shah, a vehement opponent of Nasser and active supporter of the Royalist cause in Yemen, whose "interest in expelling the Egyptians from the Peninsula [was] second only to Feisal's," as journalist Patrick Seale put it.[114] By embarking on the journey at such a critical juncture in Saudi-Egyptian negotiations over Yemen, Faysal signaled his intent to challenge Nasser precisely at a point where restraint was most needed. There is no reason to doubt that the king was fully conscious of the likely repercussions of the trip. Why, then, did he decide to go? Part of the answer may lie in procedural considerations. The visit had been postponed several times over the previous months, and the date may have been set before Nasser exposed his willingness to compromise at Jiddah. Nevertheless, Faysal's agenda in Iran suggests that he was mounting a deliberate challenge to Nasser, and that he was doing so either out of despair at the prospects of peace or out of confidence in the changing balance of power reflected in the Jiddah Agreement.

Although the most tangible outcome of the Tehran summit was the demarcation of a medial line between the two countries in the Persian Gulf, there were greater issues afoot. One was certainly the common threat from Egypt. Another was the policy of the British government. Although the British decision to evacuate Aden was not yet known, it was generally anticipated that British forces would exit the Persian Gulf over the next decade. Accordingly, the question of who would inherit the British position of dominance in the region acquired increasing urgency at this time. In theory, Saudi Arabia and Iran were the only powers capable of fulfilling that role, and they could either compete for the mantle or shoulder it jointly. From Egypt's perspective, the former scenario was by far the preferable one. Any sign of strategic cooperation between the two countries, to the probable exclusion of Egyptian

[113] For a decent third-party summary, see Telegram, Wright (Teheran) to Stewart, no. 52, December 30, 1965, FO 371/185478, PRO. See also Vered, "Without Decision," 246–47.

[114] "King Faisal Looks to the Gulf," *The Observer*, December 12, 1965.

influence, was liable to furrow eyebrows in Cairo. That this cooperation might take place under the auspices of a proposed new alignment of Muslim states made matters worse.

The summit ended with a joint call to convoke a conference of the heads of the Muslim states in order to promote Islamic solidarity. The idea was not new. Faysal himself had voiced an appeal for such a conference in April 1965, while King Sa‘ūd had toyed with the idea back in 1957.[115] The proposal could even be seen as a reincarnation of the turn-of-the-century Ottoman policy of pan-Islamism. Faysal probably came to power in late 1964 with the idea already firmly planted in the back of his head. To a man who had spent the last decade as a subordinate participant in the Arab Cold War, patiently awaiting his turn to rule, the kingdom's abysmal deficit of legitimacy in the face of the Nasserist onslaught of the late 1950s and early '60s must have cried out for a remedy. What better antidote could the guardian of Islam's holy sites devise for the secular poison of Arab nationalism than an alternative affiliation that was transnational and religious in focus?

Although the proposal was neither novel nor particularly menacing, its vigorous revival by Faysal at the end of 1965 set off alarm bells in Cairo. The Free Officers firmly believed that Egypt possessed the inalienable birthright to Arab leadership. Consequently, any challenge to the supremacy of pan-Arabism as the organizing principle of regional politics represented a challenge to the very legitimacy of their regime. Ferocious opposition was de rigueur. From Nasser's perspective, Faysal's proposed "Islamic Conference"—in which Iran would figure prominently—was an obvious attempt to supplant Arab summitry and transplant the nervous center of Middle East politics from Cairo to Riyadh. Faysal's initiative amounted to a front for a new strategic alliance on the model of the Baghdad Pact, directed primarily against Cairo and the pan-Arab underpinnings of Egyptian leadership. And it resonated with continuing worries about the strength of the Muslim Brotherhood in Egypt. Although these concerns were not entirely unfounded,[116] what made Faysal's unremarkable stroke in the game of

[115] As early as June 1965, British diplomats were reporting a new plan on the drawing tables in Riyadh, evidently designed to foster Islamic solidarity as a countermagnet to Nasserist pan-Arabism. Letter, Man (Jiddah) to Brenchley (FO), BS 1022/27, June 23, 1965, FO 371/179880, PRO.

[116] Faysal adviser Kamāl Adham admitted as much in conversation with Roy Atherton. Telegram, Eilts (Jiddah) to Sec. State, no. 669, February 13, 1966, p. 2, RG 59, CF, 1964–66, Box 3028, POL 27 YEMEN, NARA.

Figure 6.4 Faysal singing from the playbook of "Imperialism," surrounded by the broken instruments of previous military pacts. "It doesn't matter whether you change your instrument, the important thing is that you change your tune!" *Akhbār al-Yawm*, November 5, 1966. Cartoon by Alexander Ṣārūkhān.

geopolitics so devastating was the hypersensitivity of the Egyptian leadership to any slight to national prestige. From Nūrī Sa'īd to King Sa'ūd, no Arab leader had challenged Nasser's leadership with impunity.

Although the Egyptian press reacted to the visit with uncharacteristic restraint, the effect on official Cairo could only be caustic. On January 27, Faysal followed up on his Tehran trip with a weeklong visit to Jordan, another traditional base of conservative opposition to Nasser, and repeated the theme of Islamic solidarity. Still the press hounds held back. Finally the president himself exploded. Exposing just how sore the subject had become, Nasser devoted fully two-thirds of his famous speech of February 22 to the theme, attempting to taint Faysal's ploy as the last link in a long chain of failed imperialist-sponsored defense pacts stretching back into the 1950s.[117] The "Islamic Pact," as it became known in Egypt, shredded the fragile fabric of trust Nasser and Faysal wove at Jiddah and made implementation of the agreement almost impossible.[118] More broadly, it reignited the Arab Cold War.

The new assertiveness of Saudi Arabia under Faysal's stewardship, in conjunction with Britain's imminent bow out from the Middle East, heightened the likelihood that radical nationalist movements supported and inspired by Egypt would lose out to traditionalist forces in the struggle to shape the political future of the Persian Gulf. The theoretical threat from an Anglo-Saudi conspiracy to perpetuate the conservative, pro-Western orientation of the peninsular states gained concreteness when, in January 1966, news of a $400 million Anglo-Saudi-American arms deal leaked out.[119] Although the deal had been under negotiation for the better part of three years, and was clearly defensive in orientation, its thrust was anti-Egyptian. The deal's main contribution to Saudi security was to improve the kingdom's vulnerable air defenses, which had been tested at the outset of the Yemen War and found wanting. More importantly, the massive equipping of the Saudi air force indicated an Anglo-American decision to anoint King Faysal as the heir to the British imperial position east of Suez and the guarantor of Persian Gulf security in the coming decades. The arms deal, much maligned in the Egyptian press, heightened Egyptian anxieties over the future of the Arabian Peninsula. It strengthened the case for an extended armed presence on the ground, which would be in position to influence the course of events at the moment of transition.

Although local and regional factors predominated in the Egyptian change of course, great power attitudes also played an important role. Soviet policy, in particular, weakened Egyptian resolve to liquidate the problem of Yemen. The dramatic act of debt forgiveness in Moscow, coming so soon after the summit in Jiddah, cannot have strengthened

[117] UAR, *Majmū'at khuṭab*, 5:504–14; *al-Ahrām*, February 23, 1966, 1. The clamor against the "Islamic Pact" soon spread to the Soviet press. See, e.g., "Naser: Islamskii Pakt—imperialisticheskii pakt," *Pravda*, February 27, 1966, 5; Evgenii Primakov, "So spyschennym zabralom," *Pravda*, March 14, 1966.

[118] Haykal, *al-Infijār*, 239; Gause, *Saudi-Yemeni Relations*, 69–70; Telegram, Battle (Cairo) to Sec. State, no. 1441, December 10, 1965, RG 59, CF, 1964–66, Box 3028, POL 27 YEMEN, NARA; Khūlī, cited in Telegram, Battle (Cairo) to Sec. State, no. 1712, January 8, 1965, RG 59, CF, 1964–66, Box 3028, POL 27 YEMEN, NARA. Cf. James, *Nasser at War*, 84.

[119] Haykal, *al-Infijār*, 239–40.

Nasser's determination to consummate his reluctant bid for peace.[120] Moreover, though the Soviets, with an eye on Washington, may have pressed for the attenuation of Saudi-Egyptian tensions, they did not wish for peace in Yemen to come at the expense of the ongoing battle for Aden. Thus Soviet endorsement of the peace reached at Jiddah was considerably more ambivalent than the public announcements would lead one to believe. The "Long Breath Strategy," which reduced friction with the Saudis in northern Yemen while maintaining the pressure on the British in the south, suited these contradictory preferences perfectly. To the extent that Soviet aid continued to underwrite the costly Egyptian presence in Yemen at a time of increasing economic hardship, the Kremlin's attitude almost certainly contributed to the decision to hunker down for the long haul.

The dimming prospects of a renewal of large-scale US food aid over the course of 1965–66 also weakened Egypt's susceptibility to pressure from Washington for a total withdrawal from Yemen. Although the Americans, unlike the Soviets, sought to end Egyptian support for the liberation movement in south Arabia, they were more concerned with the possibility that a collision between Egypt and Saudi Arabia might draw US armed forces into an inter-Arab war. Thus Egypt's new strategy, though hardly optimal from Washington's perspective, was more in line with American priorities than any previous line taken by Nasser. The new policy, in other words, approximated the interests of the superpowers while preserving Egypt's nuisance value.[121]

The Kuwaiti Mediation and the Return of Sallāl

As the Saudi-Egyptian rift widened and became public in the spring of 1966, the Emir of Kuwait launched an intensive mediation effort that would last until the end of the year. The details of this process need not concern us here.[122] Essentially, it was a mediated extension of Saudi-Egyptian negotiations over the implementation of the Jiddah accords. The talks degenerated quickly into protracted squabbling over the pre-

[120] See chapter four.

[121] Cf. Telegram, Battle (Cairo) to Sec. State, no. 1856, January 21, 1966, RG 59, CF, 1964–66, Box 3028, POL 27 YEMEN, NARA; Guldescu, "Yemen," 325–27. See also Dawisha, *Egypt*, 47–49.

[122] The most comprehensive account is to be found in US diplomatic reports, in particular RG 59, CF, 1964–66, Boxes 3028–29, NARA. See also Aḥmad, *al-Dawr*, 463–66.

cise ratio of Republicans, Royalists, and neutrals in a prospective Yemeni government, and the exact stage in the Egyptian evacuation at which the Yemeni government, on cue from Cairo and Riyadh, would order the Ḥamīd al-Dīns into exile. As before, these seemingly mundane details stood as tokens for the issues most critical to each side. The composition of the transitional government bespoke Egypt's preoccupation with the nature of the future regime, while the preservation of the Ḥamīd al-Dīns as an alternative source of legitimacy represented the most valuable card in the Saudis' arsenal for ensuring what mattered most to them: a full withdrawal of Egyptian forces. Nonetheless, the historian looking back on these drawn-out deliberations cannot help but wonder, along with Faysal, whether the prolongation of the process was not in fact Nasser's paramount goal at this point.[123]

Meanwhile, in Yemen, former Sallāl ally Ḥasan al-ʿAmrī was beginning to strike an independent stance reflective of the mood of the Yemeni political elite. ʿAmrī, who was suspicious of the Kuwait-mediated negotiations going on behind his back, grew increasingly resentful of Egyptian imperiousness. In one particularly humiliating instance in May, Nasser, in a bid to head off a Soviet-Yemeni arms deal that would circumvent the Egyptian middleman, attempted to block the prime minister's access to Kosygin in Cairo. When, on August 11, the Egyptian government sent the deeply unpopular Yemeni president back to Yemen, ending more than nine months of imposed exile, the country erupted. The unwelcome news of Sallāl's arrival on the twelfth provoked ʿAmrī to hatch plans for an armed insurrection of the Yemeni army—an eventuality averted only by the preponderance of Egyptian force in the capital. The prime minister marshaled the support of Republican notables behind a denunciation of the "Egyptian occupation of Yemen," while his chief of staff rallied the Republican army to the cry "the Pharaohs must go!" This was too much for the Egyptians. When ʿAmrī, accompanied by his chief of staff and a sizable delegation of Republican leaders, flew to Cairo to protest the imposition of Sallāl, the Egyptian authorities threw the Yemeni prime minister and his entire entourage into prison, where they remained until the summer of 1967.[124]

[123] See, e.g., Telegram, Cranston (Jiddah) to FO, no. 403, July 12, 1966, FO 371/185447, PRO; Telegram, Eilts (Ẓahrān) to Sec. State, no. 236, February 20, 1966, p. 2, RG 59, CF, 1964–66, Box 3028, POL 27 YEMEN, NARA.

[124] The Egyptian intention may have been to use Sallāl as a bargaining chip for the Ḥamīd al-Dīns in the ongoing negotiations in Kuwait. Airgram, Taʿizz, to State, no. A-63, August 24, 1966, "The Return of Sallal: Story of a UAR Putsch," RG 59, CF, 1964–66, Box

This shocking incident exposed just how low Egypt's influence had sunk. No allegations of imperialist conspiracy could cover the fact that the Egyptian occupation of Yemen was now bereft of any political base and relied almost entirely on a blend of bribes and coercion. Back in Ṣan'ā', Sallāl presided over a series of violent crackdowns, in the course of which hundreds of Yemenis were arrested and several put to death. By year's end, the bankruptcy of the Egyptian position in Yemen was complete. The republic had degenerated into an Egyptian puppet regime, which, within the contracted boundaries of its jurisdiction, scripted political life down to the minutest detail. A mixture of monetary incentives and brute force held hostile forces throughout the rest of the country at bay. In particular, an aerial bombing campaign of extraordinary ferocity served as the principle bulwark of peace in the evacuated north. Although the Egyptians had experimented with chemical warfare earlier in the war, their frustration from late 1966 onward generated some of the most horrific gas bombings of the entire campaign.[125]

With Faysal on the ascendant, the Jiddah accord in tatters, and the republic thoroughly discredited, Nasser opted to terminate his truce with reaction and revert to the policy of overt confrontation that had characterized the early phases of the war. Muḥammad Haykal helped prepare the ideological groundwork for the policy change by lifting the veil on the pretense of Arab unity at the summits in a sharply worded article on June 10. In a remarkable argument that could easily have been turned on its head, Haykal accused the Saudis of cynically exploiting Arab solidarity against Israel in order to gain legitimacy at home and abroad: "Arab reaction hates Israel, but it hates Arab revolution more!" was Haykal's refrain.[126] Nasser hinted at the abandonment of summitry in a speech five days later.[127] Then on July 22 he called for the "indefinite postponement" of the fourth Arab summit, scheduled for September 5 in Algiers, declaring, "we cannot sit side by side with

3025, POL 15-1 YEMEN, NARA; Telegram, Turnbull (Aden) to FO, no. 232, August 15, 1966, FO 371/185447, PRO; Telegram, Cranston (Jiddah) to FO, no. 458, August 18, 1966, FO 371/185447, PRO; Schmidt, *Unknown War*, 282–84; O'Ballance, *War in the Yemen*, 158–60; Vered, "Without Decision," 248–49.

[125] Airgram, Dinsmore (Ṣan'ā') to State, no. A-7, December 20, 1966, "Situation Report—December 1966," RG 59, CF, 1964–66, Box 3023, POL 2 YEMEN, NARA; Schmidt, *Unknown War*, 260–69, 281–85; O'Ballance, *War in the Yemen*, 165–66; Aḥmad, *al-Dawr*, 440, 456–60.

[126] "Dārajāt fī al-karāhiyyah!" *al-Ahrām*, June 10, 1966.

[127] UAR, *Majmū'at khuṭab*, 5:599. Sela, *Unity*, 64–65.

reactionaries."[128] The resumption of bombing against Najrān and Jīzān on October 14 and 15 shattered any remaining pretenses of a peace process.[129] With that, the inter-Arab thaw of 1964–66 came to an end.

*

In mid-December 1966, Nasser welcomed his old nemesis, former King Sa'ūd of Saudi Arabia, to Cairo and promptly enlisted him in a vigorous propaganda campaign to delegitimize the reign of his brother, Faysal.[130] The employment of Sa'ūd against Faysal recalled the recruitment of the renegade Prince Ṭallāl against Sa'ūd at the outset of the struggle in Yemen. With the resurrection of regime change as Egypt's official policy toward Saudi Arabia in late 1966, relations between the two countries came full circle. It was Egypt's deep hostility toward the kingdom that had precipitated the intervention in Yemen and fueled the ensuing proxy war with Saudi Arabia. It was only Egypt's manifest inability to win the war in Yemen, in large part due to the effectiveness of Saudi resistance, that had convinced Nasser to sue for peace in 1964–65. But the failure to find a workable formula for honorable withdrawal, exacerbated by the emergence of Saudi Arabia as a potential challenge to Egypt's preeminence in a post-British era, destroyed Nasser's inclination to mend his fences with Faysal.

As the intervention in the Yemeni civil war entered its fifth year, Saudi-Egyptian relations returned to the acrimonious standoff that had characterized the aftermath of the *infiṣāl*. But there was one critical difference. Egypt had begun its proxy war in Yemen in 1962 as the dominant power in the Arab world, up against an obsolete kingdom teetering on the verge of collapse. Four years later, the balance of power in the Arab world was beginning to shift. Although Egypt's formal centrality remained undisputed, its strength and reputation had suffered greatly. A new power, flush with wealth and confidence, had emerged strengthened from its encounter with Egyptian power in Yemen, to begin a long journey that would end with the displacement of Cairo at the heart of the Arab political system. The Saudis were about to receive help from a completely unexpected direction.

[128] *Al-Ahrām*, July 23, 1966, p. 1; Sela, *Unity*, 64–65.

[129] Telegrams, Man (Jiddah) to FO, Nos. 576, 581, October 14 and 16, 1966, FO 371/185479, PRO.

[130] Aḥmad, *al-Dawr*, 445–48.

✷ CHAPTER SEVEN ✷

The Six-Day War and the End of the Intervention in Yemen

Sailing from Yemen you were crying "Palestine"!
—*Nasser in a speech to soldiers returning from Yemen, October 22, 1963*

AS 1966 DREW TO A CLOSE, an atmosphere of deep crisis descended upon Egypt. The crackdown against the Muslim Brotherhood had spread to the countryside, where a ruthless campaign against the Egyptian "kulaks" was underway. A massive purge of the public sector began to take shape. Thousands of suspected dissidents languished in prison. The corrupt *chef de cabinet* of the commander of the armed forces was appointed minister of war. Such basics as soap, fluorescent bulbs, rice, and cooking oil began to disappear from the shelves. There were no foreign currency reserves to speak of. And the national stockpile of wheat held barely enough reserves to last through January.

Nor were things any better on the international front. A rash of coups had afflicted Nasser's nonaligned peers, raising concerns that he might be next: Ben Bella of Algeria, Nkrumah of Ghana, and Sukarno of Indonesia had all been swept from power by mid-1966. The pan-Arab honeymoon of 1964–65 had ended in divorce, with the Arab states divided once more between "revolutionaries" and "reactionaries," and the Arab Cold War raging in full force. Egypt's relations with Jordan were awful. Relations with Saudi Arabia hovered on the brink of war. Although ties with Syria had greatly improved, a radical and unpredictable regime held sway in Damascus. And 40,000 of the army's best troops remained mired in Yemen.

Graver still, Egypt's vital relationships with the great powers were beginning to show the strains of a decade of hyperactivity on the international scene. The rupture of diplomatic relations with West Germany and the United Kingdom in 1965 was symptomatic of the general deterioration of Egypt's relations with the West. Unfortunately for Nasser, he could not look to the East for compensation. Egypt's crushing debt obligation to the USSR did not make for easy relations with Moscow in any case. However, the Soviet decision to exploit Egypt's plight in the pursuit of strategic gains placed a serious strain on the relationship. To make matters worse, the Soviet government was in the process of diversifying its Mideast portfolio to include such historic Cairo antagonists as Syria and Iran.

But the biggest international problem facing Egypt's leadership at the beginning of 1967 was the crisis in relations with the United States of America. As Vice President Muḥyī al-Dīn acknowledged in conversation with American diplomats in February, US-Egyptian relations had reached their lowest ebb since 1952.[1] The primary theater of confrontation was in Yemen where, the vice president alleged, the Johnson administration had allowed itself to be dragged by Faysal to the threshold of confrontation with Egypt. The United States countered Muḥyī al-Dīn's concerns with a fresh offer to mediate an end to the conflict between Egypt and Saudi Arabia.[2] But the Egyptians never responded. For, as seen from Cairo, the main bone of contention was no longer Yemen but the originally derivative question of US aid.

By the beginning of 1967, the Johnson administration had kept the Egyptian government on hold for more than eight months, providing no answer to its formal request for a new one-year PL 480 aid package. President Johnson, tired of Nasser's tirades and increasingly preoccupied with Vietnam, dragged his feet throughout the spring.[3] In the meantime, Nasser, torn between the conflicting dictates of necessity and pride, dimmed chances of a rapprochement by launching regular attacks on the United States.[4] This was Nasser's way of asking for help—by appearing to reject it.

On March 4, in a farewell interview described by departing US Ambassador Lucius Battle as "of [the] most emotional character yet displayed in my meetings with him," Nasser declared that the UAR would

[1] Telegram, Battle (Cairo) to Sec. State, no. 4279, February 1, 1967, RG 59, SNF 1967–69, Box 2556, POL UAR-US, NARA.

[2] Telegram, Battle (Cairo) to Sec. State, March 1, 1967, in *FRUS*, 1964–68, vol. 18, doc. 393.

[3] E.g., Memorandum, Walt Rostow to President Johnson, February 14, 1967, *FRUS*, 1964–68, vol. 18, doc. 390; Jeremy Suri, "American Perceptions of the Soviet Threat before and during the Six Day War," in *The Soviet Union and the June 1967 Six Day War*, ed. Yaacov Ro'i and Boris Morozov (Washington, DC: Woodrow Wilson Center Press; Stanford, CA: Stanford University Press, 2008), 104–6.

[4] Burns, *Economic Aid*, 166–69.

not buckle under pressure. More ominously, he warned of the damage he was capable of doing to any country that attempted to hurt Egypt.[5] Then, on March 13, Nasser publicly retracted Egypt's application for aid. In a weekly column for *al-Ahrām*, Muḥammad Haykal provided an embellished version of Nasser's message to Johnson, conveyed via Ambassador Battle the week before: "Please tell him that while appreciating and thanking you for all the facilities accorded to us in the wheat question, we want nothing now. In February 1966 we requested you to supply us with wheat. Since then we have neither renewed [our request] nor reminded you of it. Now we beg you not to consider it valid anymore. When we want American wheat in the future we shall buy it at market prices and conditions. We have been very patient with all the pressure you have applied to us because of the wheat, but our patience has run out."[6] In his conversation with the American ambassador, Nasser had, in fact, left the door open for a resumption of US aid. But his audience in Washington could be excused for hearing it slam shut.

The Egyptian ambassador to Washington, Muṣṭafā Kāmil, pleaded with Secretary of State Dean Rusk to reopen the aid pipeline and so avoid a major confrontation. "If wheat did not flow, the Cold War will flare up," he was paraphrased predicting under instructions from Cairo. Or was it a threat? Kāmil continued: "*Egypt must have wheat*. Failure to get it would have the greatest repercussions on all [US] relations and interests in the Near East and even on US relations with the Soviet Union. This was a more important matter than the Soviet arms to Egypt or the Aswan Dam. It was indeed the most important decision the US had faced with respect to the Near East since World War II."[7] Even after a hefty discount for hyperbole, could there be any doubt an explosion was at hand?

In an extraordinary series of articles, titled "We and America" and published in *al-Ahrām* between February and May 1967, Muḥammad Haykal analyzed the deterioration of US-Egyptian relations from the revolution to the present impasse. Haykal depicted four phases of decline, beginning with the unsuccessful attempt by Eisenhower and Dulles to tame the Egyptian revolution (1952–55), followed by their attempts

[5] Telegram, Battle (Cairo) to Sec. State, no. 5030, March 1, 1967, *FRUS*, 1964–68, vol. 18, doc. 393.

[6] *Al-Ahrām*, March 13, 1967, as translated in BBC, *SWB*, 1967, ME/2420/A/4.

[7] Memcon, Dr. Muṣṭafā Kāmil, Sec. Dean Rusk et al., December 29, 1966, in RG 59, SNF 1967–69, Box 2556, POL UAR-US, 2–4; Memcon, Dr. Muṣṭafā Kāmil, Sec. Dean Rusk et al., January 12, 1967, in RG 59, SNF 1967–69, Box 2556, POL UAR-US, 2–4, 2.

to punish Egypt for choosing the neutralist path (1956–58), and then to contain Egyptian power in the aftermath of the Iraqi revolution (1959–62). The final stage, in Haykal's telling, was that of "violence" (1963–67), waged by the Kennedy and Johnson administrations in response to Nasser's foray into their "stronghold" on the Arabian Peninsula. Egypt's most senior journalist left his readers in no doubt: relations between the United States and Egypt hung by a thread. An early example of op-ed diplomacy, these remarkable pieces were composed for foreign as much as domestic consumption. Perhaps their primary purpose was to serve the Johnson administration a stark warning of the consequences of further delay on the aid front. Read nearly half a century later, Haykal's weekly installments illuminate the crux of the matter in real time, eerily tracing the downward spiral toward war.[8]

The bellicosity with which the Egyptian media assailed America in the early months of 1967 underscored how fundamentally Egyptian attitudes toward the great powers had changed over the preceding five years. The root of that transformation, as we have seen, lay in Yemen. The intervention had been, in the first instance, an offshoot of inter-Arab tensions, in which great power considerations were secondary and derivative. In the early days of the war, Egypt had harnessed the resources and influence of the great powers to wage an Arab civil war in Yemen. By the beginning of 1967, the situation was nearly reversed. It was not that inter-Arab stresses had subsided. Far from it. But great power calculations had taken center stage. Back in 1962 Washington had functioned primarily as a benevolent provider of economic aid and an instrument of pressure on the source of evil in Riyadh. By 1967 it had become the focal point of Egyptian anxiety. A similar, though far less obvious, transformation had occurred in Egypt's relationship with the USSR. Back in 1962 Moscow had served as a beneficent purveyor of military hardware. By 1967 it had been transformed into a bullying loan shark, pressing hard for strategic advantage. Egypt was now threatening an international crisis—in Yemen, Tunisia, or perhaps Sinai?—in a panicked attempt to grab Washington's fading attention and escape Moscow's tightening bear hug.

David Nes, chargé d'affaires at the US embassy in Cairo, took issue with his government's policy and warned of its possible consequences

[8] See, in particular, *al-Ahrām*, February 24, March 3, April 28, and May 5, 1967. See also C. Ernest Dawn, "The Egyptian Remilitarization of Sinai, May 1967," *Journal of Contemporary History* 3, no. 3 (1968): 207.

in a disgruntled letter to a sympathetic superior in October 1966: "I believe we are moving inexorably toward a showdown in the area . . . even if we do no more than stand by and watch we shall be inextricably involved. The attempt [to bring Nasser down] will not, in my opinion, succeed, nor will our continued withholding of Egypt's life's blood, i.e., food, have any greater success in bending Nasser to our will than our maladroit handling of arms and the High Dam a decade ago."[9]

At the end of April, Nes heard the opening shot of the coming US-Egyptian confrontation ring out more than 2,000 kilometers away in Ta'izz, where the Yemeni government, almost certainly acting at Egyptian instigation, had accused US aid officials of launching a lethal bazooka attack on a military base. The authorities sent a mob to ransack the local US AID building, then arrested the resident diplomats, threatening to evict two of them from the country.[10] On May 11, Nes wrote with an uncanny premonition of disaster: "In my view the current Yemen imbroglio is just the first of a series of attacks to be mounted through the next six months in a final effort to destroy our friends in the area and eliminate all remaining US-UK political and economic presence and influence. We seem to have driven Nasser to a degree of irrationality bordering on madness, fed by the frustrations and fears generated by his failures both domestic and foreign. Our debate here revolves around where he will strike next."[11] Surveying the Middle Eastern morass from the vantage point afforded by the US Embassy in Cairo, Nes tended to exaggerate his own government's responsibility for the crisis. Yet his criticism reflects a keen awareness of the nub of the problem. Within days, the situation would deteriorate beyond his darkest fears.

The Sinai Option

The Six-Day War has attracted more than its fair share of conspiracy theories.[12] The Israelis, the Soviets, the Americans, and the Egyptians have all taken their turn in the dock of history, standing accused of con-

[9] Letter, David Nes to Roger Davies, October 17, 1966, AC 84-37, "Papers of David G. Nes," LBJL.

[10] *FRUS*, 1964–68, vol. 21, doc. 441. For Egypt's perspective, ibid., doc. 443.

[11] Letter, David Nes to Roger Davies, May 11, 1967, AC 84-37, "Papers of David G. Nes," LBJL.

[12] Richard Parker, "The June War: Whose Conspiracy?" *Journal of Palestine Studies* 21, no. 4 (1992): 5–21.

spiring, each for their own reasons, to produce the war that transformed the Middle East.[13] On the opposite end of the agency-contingency spectrum, Michael Oren, in his definitive account of the war, presents its origins as a chain of accidents in a combustible context.[14] This is not the place for a detailed reevaluation of the war's causes. What follows is a fresh perspective on Egypt's role based on the cumulative evidence amassed in the preceding six chapters.

The key to the enigma of Egypt's surprising decision to send troops into the Sinai Peninsula on May 14, 1967, lies not in Damascus, Jerusalem, or even Moscow, as many accounts have it, but between Cairo, Riyadh, and Washington.[15] The crisis that produced the Six-Day War grew out of mounting border tensions between Israel and Syria. But the obvious centrality of Damascus in the crisis masks a more important but hidden dynamic in Cairo, without which it is impossible to understand how the war came about. Simply put, it was the existential crisis in Egypt, precipitated by five years of conflict with Saudi Arabia in Yemen, that set the stage for the grand conflagration of 1967. And it was the deadlock in US-Egyptian relations that formed the crucial ingredient in the convulsion that produced the Six-Day War—the coup de grâce to Nasser's hegemonic ambitions and the proximate cause of Egypt's withdrawal from Yemen.

It is, of course, impossible to reconstruct Nasser's thinking with any certainty. However, it is hard to resist the conclusion that in moving to flood the demilitarized Sinai Peninsula with military forces in broad daylight, Nasser, far from reacting to a threat, was exploiting an opportunity. Faced with a worsening economic crisis at home and a deteriorating political situation abroad, the Egyptian president seized upon the pretext afforded by Syrian-Israeli tensions to launch a bold public relations gambit designed to transform Egypt's international position. For Nasser, the remilitarization of the Sinai offered a silver bullet with

[13] Representatives of this genre include Isabella Ginor, "The Cold War's Longest Cover-Up: How and Why the USSR Instigated the 1967 War," *MERIA* 7, no. 3 (2003) (Soviets); Haykal, *al-Infijār* (Americans); Patrick Seale, *Asad of Syria: The Struggle for the Middle East* (Berkeley: University of California Press, 1989), 117–41 (Israelis); Moshe Gat, "Nasser and the Six Day War, 5 June 1967: A Premeditated Strategy or an Inexorable Drift to War," *Israel Affairs* 11, no. 4 (2005): 608–35 (Egyptians).

[14] Michael Oren, *Six Days of War: June 1967 and the Making of the Modern Middle East* (New York: Oxford University Press, 2002), 2, 32, and passim.

[15] The classic account remains that of Charles Yost, "The Arab-Israeli War: How It Began," *Foreign Affairs* 46 (January 1968): 304–20.

which to kill several acute problems at once: first, by going on the offensive against Israel, he would restore Egypt's battered prestige in the Arab arena at a minimal risk of war; second, by withdrawing combat troops unilaterally from Yemen so as to confront a greater enemy, he would mitigate the potentially fatal acknowledgment of failure that compromise through the peace process entailed; and third, by taking "Palestine" out of the icebox, he would grab the slackening attention of the United States and extort the resumption of aid so desperately needed to avoid economic collapse and vassalage to an increasingly aggressive Soviet Union. When the Soviets, for their own reasons, supplied Nasser with what seemed like actionable intelligence, he seized on it as a pretext to roll his armies into Sinai. Then events spun out of control.

A number of Egyptians have gone further, arguing that Nasser manufactured the crisis with Israel in order to craft an honorable exit from Yemen.[16] The Egyptian president, the argument goes, saw the writing on the wall and fearing that what he had done to King Farouk would soon be done to him, devised a strategy that would enable his troops to return home from Yemen via a face-saving pitstop in Sinai.[17] This thesis is an appealing one, and no doubt it contains a grain of truth. To Nasser, the situation on the eve of the Six-Day War must have resembled the prerevolutionary situation he and his comrades had exploited in the aftermath of the 1948 Palestine war. A disgruntled army, frustrated with failure on the battlefield, stood poised to return home to a humiliated nation on the verge of starvation.[18] However, the documentary record—such as it is—indicates that in the spring of 1967 Nasser, far from throwing in the towel, was determined to hold out until the British completed their planned evacuation of Aden in 1968, allowing him to claim victory and withdraw.

[16] Rahmy, *Egyptian Policy*, 248–50; Rā'id 'Aṭṭār in *al-Ahrām*, December 17, 1977; Abū Dhikrī, *al-Zuhūr*, 161, 174. Aḥmad Yūsuf Aḥmad rejects this hypothesis on similar grounds but replaces it with an equally implausible theory, according to which it was the *Israelis* who manufactured the crisis in order to force the Egyptians out of Yemen (*al-Dawr*, 433–35). See also Aḥmad, *Dhikrayāt*, 637–38; Gamasī, *Mudhakkirāt*, 30; Gawhar, *al-Ṣamitūn*, 175–76; Gluska, *Eshkol*, 208.

[17] The intention may not have been physically to withdraw the troops via Sinai but to set the stage for their honorable extraction in the aftermath of a major propaganda victory over Israel.

[18] Some units returning from Yemen were apparently subject to intense scrutiny by the security services and a cooling-off period before reunification with their families (Maḥrizī, *al-Ṣamt al-ḥā'ir*, 132–40).

Egypt withdrew less than a third of the troops remaining in Yemen in the buildup to June 5.[19] In practice, therefore, the crisis did not function as a subterfuge for withdrawal. Moreover, even after the war, when all had been lost and a continued presence in Yemen appears scarcely conceivable, Nasser seems to have been unable to accept that defeat against Israel meant the end of the campaign in Yemen. In a revealing, if apocryphal, remark to his estranged comrade Kamāl al-Dīn Ḥusayn in the immediate aftermath of the defeat, Nasser betrayed no awareness of the depth of his predicament. When Ḥusayn conditioned his acceptance of a command position at the front in Suez on a complete withdrawal from Yemen, Nasser, incredulous, interrupted him: "And relinquish [the country] to Badr?"[20] If such were Nasser's thoughts *after* the debacle in Sinai, a fortiori this must have been his position in the months preceding it.

To the end, Nasser appears to have resisted the need to cut his losses on the Arabian Peninsula. He insisted on maintaining a token force in Yemen at least until the anticipated British departure from Aden.[21] This would ensure the establishment of a pro-Egyptian government in southern Arabia. Here is Nasser speaking to Egyptian leaders on the eve of the Khartoum summit in late August: "The disagreement between us and Saudi Arabia has been going on for several years. The Yemeni revolution is now established and it is difficult for the monarchy to return to Sanaa. When the June War broke out we had eight military brigades in Yemen and we desperately needed those forces here to take part in the fighting. However, I refused to bring all of them back and I removed only two brigades and some artillery units, the reason being that I was afraid that Britain would delay its withdrawal from Aden. *Even if* [emphasis added] our troops withdraw from Yemen, we have prepared a special military force to go to Aden on 9 January 1968 to protect and uphold Aden's independence."[22] In short, there is no indication that Nasser contemplated the withdrawal of Egyptian combat forces from the YAR until the Saudis compelled him to do so at Khartoum.

The Sinai option was tempting on several levels. Domestically, it appeared to fulfill the prophecy Egyptian leaders had been making over

[19] See Ḥadīdī, *Shāhid 'alā ḥarb al-Yaman*, 139.

[20] *Rūz al-Yūsuf*, August 4, 1975, 97; Gawhar, *al-Ṣāmitūn*, 225.

[21] According Sāmī Sharaf, this was Nasser's position as far back as August 1965 (*Sanawāt*, 2:641). Such also was the US assessment (*FRUS*, 1964–68, vol. 21, doc. 455).

[22] Quoted in Abdel Magid Farid, *Nasser: The Final Years* (Reading: Ithaca Press, 1994), 48.

Figure 7.1 Soldiers returning from Yemen, 1963. *Al-Quwwāt al-Musallaḥah*, November 16, 1963.

the past four years—that the arduous campaign in Yemen was in fact a necessary way station on the road to the liberation of Palestine. Internationally, as in the dark days of December 1963, playing the Palestine trump card guaranteed an instant turning of the tables: it would silence Cairo's Arab critics and rally the entire Arab world around Egypt's leadership of the arch-legitimate struggle against Israel. By evicting the UN peacekeepers behind whom Egypt was accused of hiding from confrontation with Israel, and flooding the Sinai Peninsula with Egyptian troops, Nasser would achieve a grand propaganda victory against his Arab rivals; he would remind the United States forcefully of his capacity for troublemaking; and, in all likelihood, he would gain early delivery of advanced weapons being held back on various pretenses by the Soviet Union. In the words of David Nes, Nasser stood to achieve "his biggest political victory since Suez."[23]

Success of this gambit hinged on Israel's acceptance of the new status quo on its southern borders and on the readiness of the great powers to

[23] Telegram no. 7760, Cairo to State, May 21, 1967, RG 59, CF, 1967–69, POL Arab-Isr, NARA.

intervene and forestall war. Both the precedent of 1956, in which the superpowers had rushed in to halt the war once it had gotten underway, and the experience of 1960, in which Israel had tolerated a brief—though quiet—remilitarization of the peninsula by substantial Egyptian forces without resort to military action, suggested things could be kept under control.[24] The tacit assurance of Soviet support, coming in the form of urgent intelligence transmitted directly from the Kremlin, provided the final impetus to action, not least because it entangled the Soviet government in a web of commitment for all that might ensue.

That the remilitarization of Sinai constituted more than a spontaneous reaction to new intelligence does not necessarily mean that premeditation on the subject ever crystallized into an operational plan in the months prior to May 1967. At this point, absent official documentation, there is no conclusive proof of Egyptian planning. But the available evidence strongly suggests that the idea of remilitarizing the Sinai existed in the minds of senior Egyptian officials more than six months before the war. Muḥammad Haykal, for one, claims it had been floated as early as 1965. He describes the establishment, in December 1966, of a special policy task force charged with formulating a plan to terminate the United Nations Emergency Force's (UNEF) presence on Egypt's borders with Israel. Tellingly, the plan envisioned giving the UN forces no less than *six months* to comply with Cairo's demand that they withdraw.[25] Plan or no plan, Egypt was not bent on war.

Another anecdote points in the same direction. At the end of November 1966, following his disastrous trip to Moscow, ʻĀmir proceeded to Pakistan with the primary objective of convincing President Ayub Khan to desist from supplying weapons to the Saudis and from supporting their effort to establish an anti-Egyptian alliance of Muslim states. From Rawalpindi, ʻĀmir reportedly sent Nasser a telegram proposing the eviction of UN peacekeeping forces from parts of Sinai in response to the humiliating propaganda war being waged against Egypt by its opponents in the Arab world. Although the telegram itself has not come to light, enough independent sources corroborate the story that we may

[24] On the significance of these precedents, see Naṣr, *Mudhakkirāt*, 3:221–26; Fawzī, *Ḥarb*, 71; Aḥmad, *Dhikrayāt*, 629; Uri Bar-Joseph, "Rotem: The Forgotten Crisis on the Road to the 1967 War," *Journal of Contemporary History* 31, no. 3 (1996): 547–66; Yigal Sheffy, *Hatraʻah be-mivḥan: Parashat "Rotem" u-tefisat ha-biṭaḥon shel Yisraʼel, 1957–1960* (Tel Aviv: Maʻarakhot, 2008), 264 and passim.

[25] Haykal, *al-Infijār*, 368–70. See also Parker, *Politics of Miscalculation*, 89–96, 242; Fawzī, *Ḥarb*, 69–73.

reasonably assume it to be true. However, it is unclear who initiated the telegram and why.[26] Those most eager to exonerate Nasser of responsibility for the debacle of 1967 have painted the cable as the product of 'Āmir's reckless initiative.[27] But Nasser's detractors, most notably Egyptian intelligence chief Ṣalāḥ Naṣr, who accompanied 'Āmir to Pakistan, have argued that it was a calculated ruse designed to draw the attention of Western governments to Egypt's plans.[28] According to this interpretation, it was Nasser who requested that 'Āmir send the telegram from abroad in the hope that Western intelligence agencies—presumably the US National Security Agency—would intercept it.[29] Why might Nasser have wanted the US government to know that Egypt was considering the expulsion of UNEF? Perhaps this was his subtle way of warning Washington that if aid were not forthcoming, he was serious about taking Palestine out of the icebox to thaw in the desert heat.[30]

The Syrian Connection

On February 23, 1966, a military coup in Damascus produced a revolutionary regime so insecure that its legitimacy became immediately bound up in the pursuit of armed conflict with Israel and subversion of the neighboring monarchy in Jordan. In order to minimize the chances of Israeli retaliation, the Syrian method of choice was to encourage Palestinian saboteurs to launch attacks on targets inside Israel from bases in Jordan.[31] This method carried the added benefit of provoking Israeli counterattacks against the Hashemite Kingdom, thereby reviving an

[26] Muḥammad Fawzī, *al-Ahrām*, Weekly Supplement, June 5–11, 1997; *al-Ahrām*, February 25, 1968; Aḥmad, *Dhikrayāt*, 628; Haykal, *al-Infijār*, 368; Gamasī, *Mudhakkirāt*, 43; Sharaf, *Sanawāt*, 1:293; Avraham Ben-Tzur, *Gormim Sovietiyim u-Milḥemet sheshet-hayamim* (Tel Aviv: Sifriyat po'alim, 1975), 165–68, 173–75.

[27] Fawzī, *Ḥarb al-thalāth sanawāt*, 72–73; Haykal, *al-Infijār*, 368–69; Sharaf, *Sanawāt*, 1:293.

[28] Naṣr, *Mudhakkirāt*, 3:189.

[29] Following the war, KGB Chief Yuri Andropov asked his Egyptian counterpart to change his transmission system because the Americans had allegedly cracked the cipher used to encode it and were reading Egypt's diplomatic communications (Huwaydī, *Khamsūn 'āman*, 494–95).

[30] The deliberate leak may also have been intended to reduce the risk of war by alerting the Americans and the Israelis to Egypt's limited intentions.

[31] Walter Laqueur, *The Road to War 1967: The Origins of the Arab-Israeli Conflict* (London: Weidenfeld and Nicolson, 1969), 44–47.

old Egyptian practice of deploying the Israeli army as a hot weapon in the Arab Cold War.[32] But as border clashes escalated, Israel's patience began to run out. Weak and isolated, the new leaders in Damascus turned for support to the two revolutionary powers that mattered: the Soviet Union and Egypt.

The Soviets, eager to beef up the "progressive" forces aligned against the Saudi-led Islamic Pact, responded positively to the consolidation of the radical regime in Damascus and urged their Egyptian allies to do the same.[33] The Egyptians, on the other hand, who were still smarting from the Syrian secession and loath to imply recognition of the status quo through an exchange of ambassadors, were somewhat less enthusiastic.[34] In April, Prime Minister Yūsuf Zu'ayyin went to Moscow at the head of a high-profile delegation that included Foreign Minister Ibrāhīm Mākhūs and Defense Minister Hafez al-Assad—all closely allied to the regime's de facto leader, General Ṣalāḥ Jadīd. The visit resulted in a $133 million loan to finance the construction of a hydroelectric dam on the Euphrates and a pledge of political support. In a sign of things to come, the Soviet press followed up on Zu'ayyin's visit with a barrage of articles warning that Israeli forces stood poised for war on the border with Syria. Time and again over the course of the following year, the Syrian government, fearing internal subversion and foreign aggression, would appeal to the Soviets for protection. Time and again the Soviets would respond by playing up the crisis in public while issuing stern warnings in private to the two targets of Syrian grievance: Israel and Jordan.[35]

On September 27, 1966, following a failed coup d'état in Damascus on September 8 and warlike remarks by Israeli Chief of Staff Yitzhak Rabin on September 9, Syrian President Nūr al-Dīn al-Atāsī wrote a letter to Nasser, expressing fears of an Israeli assault and seeking closer

[32] The most devastating of these counterstrikes took place on November 13 against the West Bank town of al-Samū' following a series of deadly guerilla attacks launched from Jordanian territory. Israel's armored incursion, conducted in broad daylight and resulting in dozens of casualties, shook the foundations of Hussein's regime and drew censure from the US government for undermining the common interest in Jordan's stability.

[33] "Pamiatka k besede v TsK KPSS s glavoi siriiskoi pravitel'stvennoi delegatsii . . . Iusefom Zueinom," April 20, 1967, F. 5, Op. 30, D. 489, pp. 214–15, RGANI; Rami Ginat, "The Soviet Union and the Syrian Ba'th Regime: From Hesitation to Rapprochement," *Middle Eastern Studies* 36, no. 2 (2000): 150–71; Ghālib, *Mudhakkirāt*, 113; Oren, *Six Days of War*, 28.

[34] See, e.g., the remarks of Aḥmad Ḥasan al-Faqqī, Under Secretary of the Egyptian Foreign Ministry, to Gromyko on July 22, 1966 (*BVK*, 2:514).

[35] A blow-by-blow account of the first of these cycles is preserved in *BVK*, 2:503–13.

cooperation with Egypt. The depth of Nasser's concern may be gauged from the fact that more than a month went by before he agreed to receive a Syrian delegation. In two days of talks at the beginning of November, Prime Minister Zu'ayyin, Foreign Minister Mākhūs, and Chief of Staff Aḥmad al-Suwaydānī unsettled their hosts with a mad proposal to launch a popular war of liberation against Israel.[36] Contemptuous of the folly of waiting for the balance of conventional forces to shift in favor of the Arabs, the Syrians spoke passionately of throwing the Arab masses into an epic battle against the outnumbered Zionists. Nasser and 'Āmir hastened to throw cold water on these ideas and with a view to calming the nervous Atāsī—and restraining his hotheaded lieutenants—agreed to closer cooperation. The talks resulted in renewed diplomatic relations between the two governments and a pledge to come to each other's defense if necessary.[37]

The Syrians made a similar appeal to the Soviets, who responded by warning the Israeli and Jordanian governments against escalation, pledging to continue exposing "imperialist intrigues" against Syria in the press, and moving to block UN Security Council resolutions that would have singled out the Syrian government for opprobrium.[38]

On April 7, 1967, a border incident on the Golan Heights escalated into a major aerial battle, in the course of which Israeli fighters felled six Syrian MiGs and then took a victory lap over Damascus. The exchange humiliated the Jadīd regime and exacerbated its internal crisis of legitimacy. On May 7, following an unprecedented wave of domestic protest, the Syrian press launched a campaign blaming the nation's troubles on

[36] The first two had served, along with President Atāsī, as volunteers in the Algerian Civil War while the third had soaked up Maoist doctrine as military attaché in Peking (Seale, *Asad*, 106–7).

[37] *BVK*, 2:521–22; Haykal, *al-Infijār*, 362–67; Muḥammad Fawzī, quoted in Sulaymān Maẓhar, *I'tirāfāt qādat ḥarb yūniyū: Nuṣūṣ shahādātihim amāma lajnat tasjīl tārīkh al-thawrah* (Cairo: Dār al-Ḥurriyyah, 1990), 36; Shemesh, *Naksah*, 570–72. Cf. Oren, *Six Days of War*, 31. What Zu'ayyin said in public matched what he uttered in private. In a speech delivered on May 1, the Syrian PM declared: "The day the liberation war breaks out and the masses throw all their might into the battlefield, boundaries will vanish and Arab division on which Israel has thrived will end. On that day neither fleets nor aircraft will be able to stand in the way of the advancing masses." However, he added, "the Arab march to Palestine must first pass through Amman, Riyadh and Tunis to overthrow the puppet regimes in Jordan, Saudi Arabia and Tunisia." Speech of Prime Minister Zu'ayyin, BBC, *SWB*, May 1, 1967.

[38] Telegram, Foreign Ministry to the Ambassador in Cairo, October 11, 1966, *BVK*, 2:518–19.

a Zionist-imperialist conspiracy.[39] On May 9 the Soviet press joined the campaign. On the fourteenth, the Egyptian army marched into Sinai.

The Soviet Spark

As is well known, the Egyptian decision to send forces into the demilitarized Sinai Peninsula in mid-May followed the receipt of intelligence from the Soviet government, according to which an Israeli attack on Syria was imminent. However, the mode of transmission, the precise nature of the intelligence transmitted, and its source remain unclear. In part because the facts are still in dispute, scholars have struggled to come up with a convincing explanation for Soviet actions. Recent studies of the war's causes have concluded either that Soviet motivations remain obscure; that the Soviet government acted to deter Israel from launching an attack on Syria or to shore up the Syrian regime's legitimacy; that alleged divisions within the Kremlin produced a schizophrenic policy geared simultaneously to raise regional tensions and avoid war; or that the Soviet leadership, acting in probable collusion with Egypt, sought to thwart Israel's nuclear ambitions.[40]

The keys to understanding Soviet policy in the lead-up to the war lie in two primary locations: first, a mysterious visit to Cairo by Soviet Foreign Minister Andrei Gromyko shortly before the crisis erupted; and second, the pattern of false alarms set off in Moscow over the course of the entire year preceding the war.

On March 29, 1967, Gromyko arrived in Cairo for a three-day visit announced the day before. Diplomats at the time—and historians ever since—have struggled to explain the Soviet foreign minister's sudden arrival so soon before the advent of the crisis that led to war. As the British representative in Cairo put it at the time, "there are nearly as many

[39] Dawn, "The Egyptian Remilitarization of Sinai," 205–6, 212; Fred H. Lawson, *Why Syria Goes to War: Thirty Years of Confrontation* (Ithaca, NY: Cornell University Press, 1996), 42–51; Seale, *Asad*, 115.

[40] Richard Parker, *The Politics of Miscalculation in the Middle East* (Bloomington: Indiana University Press, 1993), 20; Galia Golan, "The Soviet Union and the Outbreak of the June 1967 Six-Day War," *Journal of Cold War Studies* 8, no. 1 (2006): 7; Oren, *Six Days of War*, 43, 54–55; Boris Morozov, "The Outbreak of the June 1967 War in Light of Soviet Documentation," in Ro'i and Morozov, *The Soviet Union*, 52–53; Isabella Ginor and Gideon Remez, *Foxbats over Dimona: The Soviets' Nuclear Gamble in the Six Day War* (New Haven, CT: Yale University Press, 2007).

theories as to why he has come at the present juncture as there are diplomatic missions in Cairo."[41] Inevitably based on scant evidence, most theories assume that the Soviets anticipated Nasser's actions in May and that Gromyko's purpose was either to coordinate or to prevent (depending on the interpretation) the launch of the crisis with Israel.[42]

A particularly intriguing interpretation ties Gromyko's visit to the Egyptian presence in Yemen. According to this theory, the Soviets, anticipating the British withdrawal, sought to usurp the Egyptian position on the Arabian Peninsula and take charge of the revolutionary movement. To achieve this, they had thought up a scheme that would enable the Egyptians to leave Yemen without losing prestige. The plan centered on demonstrating the need for a large Egyptian force in Sinai. This interpretation adds a twist to the Egyptian "withdrawal-with-honor" thesis, portraying the Soviets as helping the Egyptians out of Yemen with a view to saving their face—and taking their place. The notion that the Kremlin sought to dislodge the Egyptians from Yemen suggests an explanation for the spark that ignited the crisis of May 1967: the transmission of false intelligence to the Egyptians may have been "designed to provide the *mise-en-scène* for the evacuation of Yemen by compelling the Egyptians to come to the defense of the Syrians, or . . . to provide a cover for their doing so."[43] Notwithstanding the elegance of this theory, the evidence for a Soviet change in policy toward Yemen in early 1967 is flimsy at best.[44] It seems to anticipate the end of this story

[41] W.H.G. Fletcher, "Visit of Mr. Gromyko to Cairo," March 30, 1967, FCO 39/263, PRO.

[42] See, e.g., Ganor and Remez, *Foxbats over Dimona*, 77; Ben-Tzur, *Gormim Sovietiyim*, 178–79.

[43] Yaacov Ro'i, *From Encroachment to Involvement: A Documentary Study of Soviet Policy in the Middle East, 1945–1973* (Jerusalem: Israel Universities Press, 1974), 437, 496–97. See also *al-Gumhūriyyah*, March 29, 1967, cited in Ben-Tzur, *Gormim Sovietiyim*, 177–78. Some of the Free Officers speculated at the time that it was *Israel* that was attempting to tie down Egyptian forces in Sinai so as to prevent the dispatch of reinforcements to Yemen. Sāmī Gawhar, *al-Ṣāmitūn yatakallamūn* (Cairo: al-Maktab al-Miṣrī al-Ḥadīth, 1976), 166.

[44] Ro'i relies on a quote from the Yugoslav news agency *Tanyug*, according to which Nasser and Gromyko had discussed UNEF. He also points to the conclusion of a Soviet-Yemeni treaty the week before, which allegedly solidified direct bilateral relations between the two countries and circumvented the hitherto omnipresent Egyptian middleman. Both elements are dubious: the press reference is speculative, while the treaty of March 21, 1967, is a mirage born of confusion with the treaty signed during Sallāl's visit to Moscow precisely three years earlier: on March 21, 1964. The origins of this error apparently lie in a speech by the Soviet ambassador to the YAR, Mirzo Rakhmatov, broadcast by Radio Ṣan'ā' on October 31, 1968. For the text of the 1964 treaty, see United Nations, *Treaty Series*, vol. 553, 1966, 267–74. Guy Laron makes a similar argument but appears to

in December 1967 when the Soviet air force rushed in to fill the void the departing Egyptians left. Although absence of evidence is not evidence of absence, the lack of any indications to the contrary strongly suggests that the Soviet position toward the Egyptian presence in Yemen on the eve of the Six-Day War remained essentially the same as it had been over the last three years: cautiously supportive of Egypt's posture but averse to direct involvement.

A more convincing explanation for Gromyko's mystery visit should be sought in an important development in Soviet policy toward the broader Middle East. As we have seen, Soviet-Egyptian relations hit a nadir in the winter of 1966 as a result of Egypt's deepening economic dependence on the USSR and the Soviets' new determination to exploit Egypt's weakness in order to obtain military base rights. The beginning of 1967 witnessed the injection of a new source of tension into the relationship: On January 4, 1967, following four months of negotiations, a Soviet trade mission signed a 100-million-ruble arms deal with the Shah's representatives in Tehran.[45]

The Soviet-Iranian arms deal broke the Anglo-American monopoly on weapons supplies to Iran, a linchpin of the anti-Soviet Central Treaty Organization (CENTO). As such, the deal was a huge coup for the Kremlin. It was also a slap in the face to Nasser. For years, the Shah had been complaining to all who would listen—to the Americans, the Israelis, and the British in particular—about Nasser's growing power in the gulf and the threat he posed to Iranian interests. And now, the Shah seemed to have found a receptive ear—in Moscow, of all places. From Cairo's perspective, the Iranians had just presented the Soviets with a viable alternative to their troubled alliance with Egypt.[46] Although the agreement restricted supplies to nonoffensive weaponry that was of limited use against Egypt, there was no getting around the fact that the Soviets had elected to support one of Nasser's most vocal antagonists and a central pillar of the Islamic Pact. Even more ominous, from Egypt's

---

conflate Egyptian concerns about Soviet intentions in South Arabia with actual Soviet policy ("Stepping Back from the Third World: Soviet Policy toward the United Arab Republic, 1965–1967," *Journal of Cold War Studies* 12, no. 4 [2010]: 108–10). For Nasser's concerns, see Haykal, *al-Infijār*, 418.

[45] Research Department Memorandum, "Irano-Soviet Relations, 1962–67," p. 8, FCO 51-50 RD, PRO; Krakhmalov, *Zapiski*, 143; Ro'i, *Encroachment*, 435–36.

[46] This is how the Shah depicted the development to visiting Israeli Chief of Staff Yitzhak Rabin in April. "Conversation of the Chief of Staff with the Shah," April 16, 1967, p. 3, HZ 3998/7, ISA.

perspective, was the fact that the two governments agreed to keep the deal under wraps—until UPI leaked the story five weeks later.[47]

The Kremlin's failure to alert the Egyptian government about this critical development in its relations with Iran was a serious lapse of judgment. In the context of rising tensions over the base issue, the Soviets' less-than-forthcoming attitude to Egypt's own arms requests, and the acute crisis in Egyptian relations with the other superpower, the disclosure of a secret arms deal between Moscow and Tehran could not fail to arouse suspicions of conspiracy in Cairo.[48]

This then was the background for the decision to dispatch Andrei Gromyko to Egypt at the end of March. While a Machiavellian interpretation of Soviet motives may be tempting, the truth is almost certainly more prosaic: Gromyko went to Cairo to reassure Nasser that the deal with the Shah did not diminish Soviet support for Egypt.[49]

Why, then, did the Soviets furnish false information to the Egyptian and Syrian governments six weeks later, thereby precipitating Egypt's fateful move into Sinai? We may never find the archival smoking gun in the form of a document from the presidential archives spelling out Soviet calculations. But the most likely explanation is also the simplest: the Soviets, acting in good faith on bad but plausible intelligence, made a reasonable decision to share it with the two allies most likely to be affected.

This is how Brezhnev presented the origins of the crisis to his comrades on the Central Committee on June 20, 1967:

> Over the last several months, we have followed the development of the situation in the Near East with special attention. There were solid grounds for doing so. It was not just that military incidents markedly increased on the Israeli-Jordanian and Israeli-Syrian borders. Many signs pointed to the conclusion that a serious international crisis was brewing and that Israel, leaning on the support of the Western powers, was preparing an [act of] aggression. In the middle of May—I call attention [to this point]—we received information that Israel was pre-

[47] Ro'i, *Encroachment*, 435–36.

[48] The postponement of Brezhnev's planned visit to Cairo could not have helped, and it even led some to suspect collusion between Moscow and Washington. Haykal, *Sphinx and Commissar*, 168–70; idem, *al-Infijār*, 416–17.

[49] For a partial report of Nasser's exchange with Gromyko, see Haykal, *Sphinx and Commissar*, 169, 174; idem, *al-Infijār*, 416–18; and Haykal's remarks to the British representative in Cairo, Telegram no. 273, Cairo to Foreign Office, April 17, 1967, FCO 39/263, PRO. Cf. Gluska, *Eshkol*, 210–11.

paring to land a military strike against Syria and other Arab countries. The Politburo decided to bring that information to the attention of the governments of the UAR and Syria. They, in turn, informed us that they were taking appropriate military measures and that their armed forces had been brought to full combat readiness. UAR Foreign Minister [Maḥmūd] Riad told the Soviet Ambassador on the 16th of May that an attack on Syria would be considered by the United Arab Republic as an attack on itself and that "all precautionary measures are being taken to prevent a recurrence of the events of 1956."[50]

US intercepts of the Egyptian cable that conveyed the intelligence report from Moscow to Cairo largely confirm Brezhnev's version and emphasize the restraining purpose of the Soviet message. According to a CIA report of the intercept, "Soviet Deputy Foreign Minister Semenov had told the Egyptians that Israel was preparing a ground and air attack on Syria—to be carried out between 17 and 21 May. It stated that the Soviets had advised the UAR to be prepared, to stay calm, and not to be drawn into fighting with Israel, and that they had advised the Syrians to remain calm and not give Israel the opportunity for military operations. The message also said that the USSR favored informing the Security Council before Israel took military action against Syria."[51] Similarly, instructions sent from the Soviet Ministry of Foreign Affairs to Ambassador Anatolii Barkovskii in Damascus on May 12, asking him to relay sensitive information to Syrian Foreign Minister Ibrāhīm Makhūs, referred merely to the possibility of an Israeli attack—not to

[50] "Doklad tov. Brezhneva L. I. na Iun'skom (1967 g.) plenyme TsK KPSS 'o politike sovetskogo soiuza v sviazi s agressiei izrailia na Blizhnem Vostoke,'" June 20, 1967, F. 2, Op. 3, D. 59, pp. 7–8, RGANI.

[51] http://www.foia.cia.gov/cpe/caesar/caesar-50.pdf, 5, cited in Guy Laron, "Playing with Fire: The Soviet-Syrian-Israeli Triangle, 1965–1967," *Cold War History* 10, no. 2 (2010): 177. See also Roland Popp, "Stumbling Decidedly into the Six-Day War," *Middle East Journal* 6, no. 2 (2006): 288. Cf. Ghālib, *Mudhakkirāt*, 121; Sadat, *In Search of Identity*, 171–72. Contrary to what most scholars have assumed, the specifics concerning Israeli troop dispositions were apparently of Syrian, not Soviet, provenance. See, e.g., the remarks of Shams Badrān to the Soviet ambassador on May 16, in *BVK*, 2:554; Oren, *Six Days of War*, 55. Cf. Richard Parker, "The June 1967 War: Some Mysteries Explored," *Middle East Journal* 46, no. 2 (1992): 181–82; idem, *Politics of Miscalculation*, 5–11. Nasser himself did not claim more than this in his resignation speech. He spoke of a "plan of the enemy to attack Syria" and of a Soviet warning to Sadat's delegation concerning "a plot being hatched against Syria" [*qaṣdan mubayyatan*]—without a word about "troop concentrations." Speech, June 9, 1967, in Gamal Abdel Nasser, *Wathā'iq 'Abd al-Nāṣir: Khuṭab, aḥādith, taṣrīḥāt* (Cairo: Markaz al-Dirāsāt al-Siyāsiyyah wa-l-Istrātijiyyah bi-l-Ahrām, 1973-), vol. 1, 226.

hard data concerning mobilization of forces—and stressed that the accuracy of the intelligence could not be guaranteed.[52]

In fact, throughout the spring of 1967 the high command of the Israel Defense Forces (IDF) was almost unanimous in its support of an operation directed at Syria and designed to bring an end to the attacks of Syrian-sponsored Fataḥ.[53] Although Israeli Prime Minister Levi Eshkol was known to oppose such action and had been resisting the pressure of his generals for several months, who was to say he would not change his mind in response to the next Syrian provocation—as he had on the eve of the assault on the West Bank town of al-Samū‘ six months earlier? In fact, no "troop concentrations" existed on Israel's border with Syria on May 13, 1967. But it would have been irresponsible, given what we now know, for Soviet intelligence at the time *not* to have assumed an attack on Syria was possible if not likely in the near future. We have, in short, little reason to doubt the essentials of Brezhnev's account.

However, the Soviet leader's explanation fails to account for the series of similar warnings stretching back to Kosygin's visit to Cairo the previous May—and to Zu‘ayyin's visit to Moscow several weeks before that—all accompanied by a loud clamor in the Soviet press about alleged concentrations of Israeli forces.[54] A complicated dynamic was at work here. To understand it, one must factor in the tensions between the Kremlin's various objectives at the global and regional levels.

By early 1967 the fault lines of the Cold War and the major rifts within the Arab world lay superimposed more neatly than ever before. On the one hand stood the Soviet-supported republics of Egypt, Syria, Algeria, Yemen, and Iraq; on the other stood the US-backed monarchies of Saudi Arabia, Jordan, Libya, and Morocco. (The odd man out in this arrangement was Habib Bourgiba, independent-minded president of the Republic of Tunisia.) Notwithstanding the differences between the Soviet Union and Egypt at this time, the convergence of global and regional patterns of competition and the extreme polarization of regional politics crystallized an alignment of interests concerning the biggest question on their common agenda. Policy makers in Moscow and Cairo reacted with

[52] Cited in Morozov, "The Outbreak of the June 1967 War," 46. Another directive, dated May 14 and intended for Prime Minister Zu‘ayyin, similarly refers to Israeli military preparations without specifics.

[53] Gluska, *Eshkol*, 143–90, 213. By early May, Eshkol seems to have come around to the conclusion of his generals (ibid., 198–99).

[54] Laqueur, *Road to War*, 73–74.

similar horror to the prospect of a consolidation of the pro-American powers under the auspices of the Saudi-led Islamic Pact. Both resolved to block its emergence.

Lacking a robust military presence in the region, the Soviets responded mostly with rhetoric. To verbal assaults on the reactionary axis they added optimistic visions of a progressive alternative. Soviet communications of this period are suffused with wishful thinking about the alleged ascendance of a progressive bloc that would counter the reactionary pact. Without Syria, the ideal of a progressive counterbloc was fantasy. This explains why protecting the vulnerable regime in Damascus—by defending it vocally whether right or wrong—and fostering cooperation among pro-Soviet states—mostly by asserting that such cooperation existed even when it did not—were such important pieces in Moscow's policy puzzle.[55]

The demands of national defense reinforced the dictates of ideology and geopolitics. As we have seen, Soviet strategists in early 1967 were bent on the acquisition of air and sea bases on the eastern shores of the Mediterranean. The attainment of this sensitive objective depended on crafting political legitimacy for the stationing of Soviet forces on Arab soil. In this context the repeated allegations of Israeli troop concentrations on the borders with Syria did more than intimidate the Israelis, reassure the Syrians, and drive progressives everywhere closer together; they provided just the sort of legitimacy required for the realization of Soviet strategic aims. The claims of a Zionist-Imperialist conspiracy underscored the necessity of deploying Soviet naval contingents in the eastern Mediterranean, utilizing air and sea facilities on Egyptian and Syrian territory in order to defend them against Israel's auxiliary, the US Sixth Fleet.

In passing along information of dubious authenticity underscoring Syria's vulnerability to attack, Brezhnev and his Kremlin colleagues were, no doubt, acting out of sincere concern for the fate of the regime in Damascus. But they were also acting in a manner broadly consistent with the preoccupations of their generals. By stoking the embers of regional conflict while drawing attention to the threat the Sixth Fleet posed, they were highlighting Soviet indispensability, softening local resistance to a naval counterpresence, and applying subtle pressure on Nasser to

[55] See, e.g., the remarks of Soviet Deputy Foreign Minister Vladimir Semenov to Egyptian Ambassador Murād Ghālib, May 30, 1966, in *BVK*, 2:513; and those of Shimon Shamir in Parker, *Six Day War*, 63–64.

give way on the base issue. In all likelihood the Soviets did not know the intelligence they had given their allies was false, did not anticipate that Egypt would remilitarize the Sinai Peninsula in reaction, and almost certainly did not foresee that war would result from the ensuing crisis. They did, however, seek to emerge from the situation with an enhanced capacity to meet the threat to Soviet cities posed by American submarines lurking in the eastern Mediterranean.

In practice, the crisis of the spring of 1967 provided the Soviet government with the opportunity to resubmit to the government of Egypt the same demands rejected scarcely six months before—this time under the guise of aid to an embattled ally. On April 24, Brezhnev issued an extraordinary statement attacking the US naval presence in the Mediterranean and implicitly justifying the need for a temporary Soviet counterweight: "There is no justification for the permanent presence of the Sixth Fleet of the USA in southern Europe's coastal waters ... the US Sixth Fleet cruises the Mediterranean, utilizing army bases, ports and early warning stations in a row of Mediterranean countries. Obviously, this represents a serious threat to the independence of all littoral countries. The time has come to demand in a loud voice that the US Sixth Fleet leave the Mediterranean."[56] Exactly one month later, as Israeli-Egyptian tensions escalated to the brink of war, the Soviet naval command drafted a letter from Brezhnev to Nasser proposing the temporary stationing of Soviet aircraft on Egyptian soil.[57] On the same day, the Soviet ambassadors in Cairo and Damascus received instructions to meet their respective heads of state and propose a visit of Soviet warships.[58] The deployment, presented to the two Arab governments as a

[56] *Konferentsia evropeīskikh kommunisticheskikh i rabochikh partiī po voprosam bezopasnosti v evrope, Karlovy Vary, 24–26 aprelia, 1967 g.* (Moscow: Izdatel'stvo politicheskoi literatury, 1967), 36.

[57] Letter, Brezhnev to Nasser, May 24, 1967, TsVMA, f.2, op. 307ss, d. 139, 34, reproduced in Ro'i and Morozov, *The Soviet Union*, 286–87. Shams Badrān reports succumbing to the old Soviet demand for a naval air base at Alexandria during his trip to Moscow two days later. "U'linu mas'ūliyyatī al-kāmilah 'ammā yusammā ... bi-l-ta'dhīb!" *al-Ḥawādith*, September 2, 1977.

[58] Memorandum, Semenov to the Soviet Ambassadors in Cairo and Damascus, May 24, 1967, TsVMA, f. 2, op. 307ss, d. 139, 35, in Ro'i and Morozov, *The Soviet Union*, 285–86. This was the context of Grechko's infamous parting remarks to Shams Badrān at the airport in Moscow on May 28: "If America enters the war we will enter it on your side.... Our fleet is in the Mediterranean, near your shores. We have destroyers and submarines with missiles and arms unknown to you ... if something happens and you need us, just send us a signal. We will come to your aid immediately in Port Said or elsewhere." Parker, *Politics of Miscalculation*, 32.

deterrent measure designed to forestall war, also constituted the incipient realization of a long-standing Soviet ambition.

But if the attainment of Soviet naval objectives required the elevation of tensions between Israel and its neighbors—or at least the exploitation of their existence for public relations—the need to avoid conflict with the United States militated in favor of restraint. For the Soviet Union stood to lose from confrontation with the United States—and superpower conflict would almost certainly ensue from war in the Middle East. This explains what Michael Oren refers to as the schizophrenic character of Soviet policy in the buildup to the war.[59] Indeed, the need to prevent elevated tensions from escalating to war produced a peculiar exercise in deterrence. The Kremlin would respond to each flare-up on the border with an attempt to intimidate Israel—in private by issuing stern démarches via diplomatic channels and in public by stirring up a tempest on the pages of *Pravda* and *Izvestia*. This behavior, designed to force the Israeli leadership to think carefully about Moscow's potential response before launching an attack on Syria, made perfect sense as one piece of a deterrent strategy. Curiously missing, however, was any serious attempt to restrain the Syrians from provoking Israel.

Ultimately, the Soviet fixation on phantom Israeli troop concentrations is comprehensible only if seen as a manifestation of weakness. Ironically, Damascus profited from a handicap common to Moscow and Jerusalem. Just as the Israeli government found it safer to retaliate against Jordan even when Fataḥ actions were clearly being directed from Damascus, the Soviets found it easier to lash out at Israel and Jordan when Syrian bellicosity was the root cause of the escalatory dynamic. Soviet officials well understood that restraining terrorist groups operating from Syrian territory was indispensible for the preservation of peace. But they were reluctant to call Syria's leaders to task for their inflammatory statements and actions. Not without reason did King Hussein erupt when the Soviet ambassador showed up in May 1966—at the behest of the Syrian government—to deliver a sharply worded démarche protesting alleged Israeli-Jordanian intrigues in Syria. The Soviets, Hussein retorted, would do well to resist attempts to drag them into the internal disputes of the Arabs.[60]

A key reason for Soviet defensiveness seems to have been Chinese criticism of détente. In a revealing assessment sent to the Central Com-

[59] Oren, *Six Days of War*, 43.

[60] Telegram, Ambassador in Jordan to the Foreign Office, May 28, 1966, *BVK*, 2:510. Cf. the comments of Israeli Ambassador in Washington Avraham Harman to Assistant Secretary of State Raymond Hare on October 11, 1966, *FRUS*, 1964–68, vol. 18, doc. 327.

mittee in November 1966, Gromyko started out by blaming Israeli aggression for the escalation of regional tensions, but then he proceeded to acknowledge the inflammatory effect of Fataḥ attacks on Israel. Singling out the troubling influence of the Chinese government, he warned that the Chinese were encouraging PLO activists to provoke a "second Vietnam" in the Middle East. From this analysis, the Soviet foreign minister derived two recommendations for action: first, to serve a stern warning to the government of Israel, holding it accountable for the repercussions of its aggressive policies; and second, to inform the Arab governments about the warning to Israel and convey Soviet concerns regarding Chinese intrigues. This dynamic—vocal condemnation of Israel coupled with (somewhat tortuous) private appeals for Arab restraint—betrayed remarkable deference to the leadership in Damascus. Paradoxically, the conjuring up of nonexistent armies in the press served to camouflage anemic appeals for restraint made in confidence, presenting Soviet timidity as bravado—to the Soviet people, the citizens of Communist countries, and Third World elites. Like Nasser's reaction to the taunting of his Arab rivals, the Soviets responded to the challenge of Chinese extremism by smothering their calls for moderation in a blanket of feigned radicalism. Not surprisingly, the message got lost in the process.[61]

The Egyptian Initiative

Nasser's behavior in 1967 was as bewildering to his generals at the time as it has been to historians since. After all, Nasser could have reacted to the threat of an Israeli assault on Syria—or even to an actual attack—by doing nothing, which is precisely what Israeli intelligence expected him to do.[62] Several senior Egyptian commanders attest to the confusion surrounding their government's motivations for the remilitarization of Sinai and hint that Syria had little to do with it. Amīn Huwaydī, who inherited both Shams Badrān's and Ṣalaḥ Naṣr's portfolios as min-

[61] "Note from the Foreign Minister ... to the Central Committee," *BVK*, 2:529–30. This despite the Soviet ambassador to Israel's repeated requests for more vigorous action to restrain the Syrians, e.g., Telegrams, Chuvakhin to the Foreign Ministry, October 11 and 12, 1966, *BVK*, 2:517, 519–21. See also Laron, "Playing with Fire" 167. On the nature and effects of Chinese criticism, see Jeremy Friedman, "Soviet Policy in the Developing World and the Chinese Challenge in the 1960s," *Cold War History* 10, no. 2 (2010): 247–72.

[62] Gluska, *Eshkol*, 156–58, 174, 197.

ister of war and chief of intelligence in the aftermath of the war, puzzles over Nasser and 'Āmir's leap to action on the basis of unverified intelligence that was swiftly proven false.[63] Neither Chief of Staff Muḥammad Fawzī nor General Muḥammad 'Abd al-Ghanī al-Gamasī accepts the official explanation that Egypt was mounting a credible threat on Israel's southern borders in order to deter an imminent strike against Syria. Both hint that Nasser's true aim must have been to restore the pre-1956 status quo through the eviction of UNEF under pretext of preparations for a defensive war against Israel.[64] Chief of Land Forces 'Abd al-Muḥsin Kāmil Murtagī implies much the same in his memoirs, blaming the political leadership for choosing a bad moment to try and recoup the Suez losses by staging a show of force in the Sinai desert.[65] So too does the Egyptian chief of operations, Lieutenant General Anwar al-Qāḍī: "Egypt's political leaders sought to escalate the situation—we knew not why—while continuous and contradictory orders sent entire divisions into Sinai without planning or strategic objectives."[66] The Syrians were similarly shocked by Egypt's overreaction.[67] Indeed, the alacrity with which the Egyptian media seized on the impending Israeli attack on Syria suggests that the story met more than the needs of international legitimacy; the myth of a Zionist assault served the important *internal* purpose of mobilizing the Egyptian public.[68]

In short, there seems to have been little justification for Egypt's response to the warning from Moscow. But this is precisely the point: *Nasser was not reacting* to Soviet intelligence when he decided to send seven divisions into Sinai. Rather, the Egyptian president was *seizing the opportunity* Soviet intelligence afforded in order to implicate the Kremlin in a gambit that had little to do with Syrian security or Soviet intentions. Nasser knew the cautious inhabitants of the Kremlin were hardly likely to condone actions that might lead to confrontation with the United States. For this reason he could not consult them in advance. By forcing the Soviets to assume responsibility for the alleged consequences of their candor, Nasser hoped to trap one superpower in a web

[63] Huwaydī, *Khamsūn 'āman*, 198.

[64] Fawzī, *Ḥarb*, 70–72; al-Gamasī, *Mudhakkirāt*, 40–43, 69. See also al-Ḥadīdī, *Shāhid 'alā ḥarb 67*, 150; idem, *Shāhid 'alā ḥarb al-yaman*, 139; Fawzī, quoted in Maẓhar, *I'tirāfāt*, 51, 58–59; Ṣidqī Maḥmūd, quoted in Maẓhar, *I'tirāfāt*, 109–10.

[65] Murtagī, *al-Farīq*, 13, 23–24, 42, 47–48, 57–58.

[66] Quoted in Oren, *Six Days of War*, 58.

[67] Ibid., 55; Huwaydī, *Khamsūn 'Āman*, 198. See also Naṣr, *Mudhakkirāt*, 3:209.

[68] Dawn, "The Egyptian Remilitarization of Sinai," 212.

of commitment to a high-stakes maneuver directed primarily against the other.

This dynamic became more evident with time. As the crisis escalated, Nasser strove to deepen Soviet commitment in private while erecting a deterrent facade of collusion between Cairo and Moscow in public. Both the decision to demand the removal of UNEF from Sinai and the decision to close the Gulf of Aqaba to Israeli shipping—commonly accepted as the point where war became inevitable—were taken without consulting the Soviet government. Here is Brezhnev again, explaining the train of events that issued from the transmission of the intelligence to Cairo and Damascus:

> I must say that the government of the UAR [then] took a row of rash [*neprodumannykh*] steps. In what was a complete surprise for us, on the 19th [sic] of May the leadership of the UAR demanded the removal of the UN forces from the armistice lines. In taking such a critical decision which, under the existing conditions, could also be interpreted as a step toward aggravation of the situation, the government of the UAR did not consult us. The goal of this measure, as then First Vice President of the UAR Marshal Amer explained, was that by confronting Israel face-to-face with the armed forces of the UAR on its southern borders, Israel would be deprived of the possibility of concentrating her forces on the Syrian border, and unable to undertake massive military action against Syria.
>
> On May 22, President Nasser announced to us by means of the Soviet Ambassador that as a result of the decisive actions taken by the leadership of the UAR, the situation in the Middle East was swiftly changing in a positive direction. He repeated his readiness to come swiftly to the aid of Syria if she were subject to attack. At the same time, he informed the Ambassador, as if of an accomplished fact, that the government of the UAR was closing the Gulf of Aqaba to Israeli ships and to the ships of third countries supplying strategic materiel to Israel. The Soviet government was not informed in advance about this important action, which brought in its train serious consequences, either.[69]

The Soviet archives capture Nasser trying to explain this fait accompli to Dmitrii Pozhidaev, the Soviet ambassador in Cairo, on May 22.

[69] "Doklad," 8.

The Israeli threats against Syria in early May had been intolerable, Nasser began. Israel and its supporters evidently supposed that the UAR, mired in Yemen, was powerless to intervene on Syria's behalf. The UAR, he continued, had been compelled to disprove this thesis through action. This, Nasser concluded, they had now done. The Egyptian president's review of the origins of the crisis reads almost like an apology. As the protocol betrays, Nasser felt it necessary to justify his actions to Pozhidaev—without once mentioning the provenance of the intelligence that allegedly sparked them. His posture is thoroughly inconsistent with that of a man tricked into action by false information. Rather, Nasser comes across as rash leader out on a limb meekly seeking retroactive endorsement from his great power ally.[70]

Yet Nasser's apologetic stance on May 22 did not prevent him from shifting responsibility onto the Soviets once it became clear that his decision to close the straits could well lead to war. In a conversation with Pozhidaev two days later, Haykal quotes the Egyptian leader as saying: "I want you to understand that everything that is happening now follows from the information and advice which we have received from your government. You are responsible to me for all this. Your people in Moscow must understand that politically, and on the military plane, I want this to be translated into material aid as quickly as possible. We need an airlift. I propose sending our Defense Minister, Shamseddin Badran, to Moscow to discuss deliveries."[71]

Badrān himself expressed a similar combination of sentiments to Kosygin when the two met on the May 26. The Egyptian minister of war opened his presentation by reminding Kosygin that the intelligence on which Egypt's decision to remilitarize the Sinai was based had come from the Egyptian embassy in Moscow and from the Syrian chief of staff. He went on to explain how mounting a credible defense of Syria and the continuation of Arab propaganda attacks had first "compelled" the Egyptian government to call for the removal of UNEF and then "made it necessary" for Egyptian forces to occupy Sharm el-Sheikh.

[70] *BVK*, 2:561–63. Nasser also seized the opportunity to thank the Soviet government for responding to Shams Badrān's request for more specific intelligence on Israeli troop dispositions, hinting that Egypt's initial move into Sinai had been based on intelligence of lesser quality (ibid., 561). Note Vitalii Naumkin's confusion on this and Gerogii Kornienko's clarification in Richard Parker, ed., *The Six Day War: A Retrospective* (Gainesville: University Press of Florida, 1996), 38, 51–53, 71–72.

[71] Haykal, *Sphinx and Commissar*, 178.

When Kosygin then launched into his own lengthy justification of Soviet behavior in the crisis, Badrān interrupted the Soviet premier to stress Soviet responsibility for the crisis and underscore the Kremlin's present obligations toward Egypt:

> KOSYGIN: When Israel concentrated forces against Syria we informed you about it.
> BADRĀN: And this is what impelled us to mobilize our forces.
> KOSYGIN: The intelligence was unequivocal [*ṣarīḥah*]. We informed you and you acted.[72]

Much of the rest of the two men's meetings on May 26 and 27 was devoted to tentative efforts by the Soviet premier to get the Egyptians to consolidate their gains and pull back from the brink.[73]

The idea of sending his minister of war to Moscow at the height of the crisis was vintage Nasser. As no one but Badrān himself seems to have recognized, the point of his trip was not so much the procurement of arms or the furtherance of joint planning; it was the trip itself. To be sure, urgent arms requests formed a part of Badrān's mission (at several points in the conversation the Egyptian minister of war and the Soviet premier trade jokes about the former facing court-martial should he return to Cairo empty-handed). So too did the coordination of policy. But these were afterthoughts. Nasser's primary objective in sending Badrān to Moscow was to create the *impression* in Jerusalem and Washington that the UAR and the USSR were operating in close cooperation, thereby increasing the pressure on Israel to stay put. Although Nasser ultimately failed to frighten Israel into inaction, his efforts to fool diplomats at the time and historians since must be judged successful.[74]

[72] Memcon, Shams Badrān and Aleksei Kosygin, May 26, 1967, in Huwaydī, *Khamsūn ʿāman*, 419. Badrān later added this commentary on the exchange: "I did not answer out of respect [for Kosygin]." *Al-Ḥawādith*, September 2, 1977. For a similarly emphatic affirmation of the veracity of Soviet intelligence by Marshal Grechko, see Ghālib, *Mudhakkirāt*, 121.

[73] See also Haykal, *Sphinx and Commissar*, 178–80.

[74] Galāl Kishk mocks ʿĀmir's last-minute effort to compile a wish list for Badrān to take with him to Moscow, finding it much like the Egyptian who, upon hearing his friend is going on a trip to Europe, leaps at the opportunity to jot down the details of a spare part for the washing machine he needs (*Al-Ḥawādith*, September 2, 1977). The plan to send Zakariyyā Muḥyī al-Dīn to Washington complemented the dispatch of Badrān to Moscow.

The Impact of the Yemen War on Egyptian Military Performance in the Six-Day War

Virtually all of Egypt's senior generals concur that the Yemeni experience had a negative impact on the army's performance in June 1967.[75] A number of them have gone so far as to suggest that had it not been for the intervention in Yemen, the outcome in the Sinai could have been different. The attempt to blame the Yemen War for the Sinai debacle has obvious exculpatory value for the disaster's military architects and must be taken with a grain of salt. While it may be impossible to disprove this negative hypothesis entirely, the question remains: to what extent did the war in Yemen affect Egyptian military performance in the Six-Day War?

Critics of the Yemen War argue that the Egyptian military atrophied during five years of conventional warfare against an unconventional opponent. That five years of low-intensity conflict in Yemen had an adverse impact on the army's capacity to fight a conventional, combined-arms desert war is not in question; nor is it in doubt that the habituation to air supremacy, superiority in firepower, and small unit action impaired Egypt's capabilities when faced with the IDF. But it is a leap from this to the conclusion that the outcome in 1967 could have been much different absent the intervention in Yemen. This is not only because Israel's preemptive air strike on June 5 checkmated the Egyptian military in the very first hours of the war. It is because Nasser's fundamental decision to sacrifice Egypt's battle readiness in order to preserve the domestic security of his regime, taken long before the spring of 1967, rendered war against any competent foe virtually unwinnable.[76]

An army that decided to go without large-formation exercises so as to spare its generals potential embarrassment in front of their troops was in trouble whether or not it was being harassed by insurgents in a distant land.[77] If anything, the insurgency in Yemen provided an opportunity for the practice of complex logistics, communications, and

[75] Fawzī, *Ḥarb al-thalāth sanawāt*, 9, 26–28, 60–61, 67; Murtagī, *al-Farīq*, 12–13, 23–27, 31–32; idem, quoted in Maẓhar, *I'tirāfāt*, 171–72; Ḥadīdī, *Shāhid 'alā ḥarb 67*, 37–38, 48–50, 84; Gamasī, *Mudhakkirāt*, 62–67. See also Rahmy, *Egyptian Policy*, 250–52. Ṣidqī Maḥmūd, on the other hand, stresses the beneficial aspects of the prolonged "exercise with live ammunition" in Yemen for the Egyptian air force (Maẓhar, *I'tirāfāt*, 128–29).

[76] Ernest Dawn makes this point succinctly in Parker, *Six Day War*, 57.

[77] Fawzī, *Ḥarb al-thalāth sanawāt*, 60.

maneuver under difficult battlefield circumstances that, while vastly different from the conventional face-off with Israel, constituted better preparation for large-scale war than life in the barracks. Amīn Huwaydī has a point when he discounts claims that the presence in Yemen of forces desperately needed for the war effort in Sinai caused the disaster. On the contrary, he argues, those forces could have done nothing to avert the catastrophe produced by the appalling lack of preparation, and were in fact spared annihilation on the battlefield with Israel.[78]

This is not to deny that a war in two theaters is always more difficult than a single-front war, or that Egypt's resources had been strained severely by five years of counterinsurgency in Yemen. But then a more convincing argument would be this: by avoiding the temptation to intervene in Yemen in 1962, and launching instead a concerted effort to prepare the Egyptian armed forces for combat—along the lines Sadat pursued in the three years preceding the war of 1973—the Egyptian leadership might well have achieved different results in 1967. We shall return to the question of Egypt's grand-strategic alternatives in the afterword.[79]

In the course of six days, Israel defeated the armed forces of Egypt, Syria, and Jordan, tripling its size in one of the most decisive military victories of modern times. But time would tell that the true victor of the third Arab-Israeli war was not Israel—which ended up fighting a bloody war over the same territory six years later—but a country that had not placed a single soldier in harm's way: The Kingdom of Saudi Arabia.

The Khartoum Conference and the Withdrawal of the Egyptians from Yemen

On August 29, 1967, the leaders of the Arab states convened in the Sudanese capital of Khartoum to discuss the consequences of the third Arab-Israeli war. As had been the case in all previous summits, the public agenda dominated by Palestine obscured the back-stage dynamic of inter-Arab jostling. Behind the scenes at the Khartoum confer-

[78] Amīn Huwaydī, *Ḥurūb 'Abd al-Nāsir* (Beirut: Dār al-Ṭalī'ah, 1977), 138–47; idem, *Khamsūn 'āman*, 190–92, 283, 287–88. For related arguments, see Aḥmad, *Dhikrayāt*, 614–49; Sharaf, *Sanawāt*, 2:650–51.

[79] For an analysis of Egypt's military performance in 1967, see Pollack, *Arabs at War*, 58–88.

ence—famous for its three "no's" concerning Israel—a more consequential series of discussions took place between Nasser and Faysal about Saudi-Egyptian relations and the future of Yemen. The outcome of these negotiations cemented the change in the Arab balance of power that had taken place in the wake of Israel's victory over Egypt.

At Khartoum, for the first time, Nasser confronted the necessity of unilaterally withdrawing his forces from the Arabian Peninsula. The key bargain struck in the course of these deliberations traded an end to the Egyptian military presence in Yemen for Saudi financial aid to the crippled Egyptian economy.[80] The Egyptians initially proposed to resurrect the Jiddah Agreement, which would have meant rehashing the vexing question of the future regime in Yemen. The Saudis, strengthened immeasurably by Israel's victory, rejected this. They insisted on finalizing plans for Egyptian withdrawal before any further discussion of Yemen's political future could take place.[81] As compensation for trimming Egypt's ambitions, Saudi Arabia, Kuwait, and Libya offered Egypt (and Jordan) a package of desperately needed financial aid. Henceforth, Egypt would receive £95 million in annual support—roughly equivalent to the revenues lost due to the closure of the Suez Canal.[82]

The unofficial text of the agreement reached between Nasser and Faysal at Khartoum reads as follows:[83]

> Being anxious to clear the Arab atmosphere, implement the bonds of fraternity between the Arab brothers and reach a final solution to the Yemen problem, it was agreed on the following:
>
> 1. The formation of a three man committee to tackle the Yemen problem. The committee was formed by Saudi Arabia selecting one country, the UAR another, while the third is to be selected by

[80] See, e.g., Telegrams, Khartoum to Foreign Office, Nos. 423, 441, and 480, July 31, August 5, and August 28, 1967, FCO 8/697, PRO; Telegram, Jiddah to FO, no. 577, September 4, 1967, in FCO 8/697, PRO; Letter, King Faysal to President Johnson, September 7, 1967, *FRUS*, 1964–68, vol. 21, doc. 301; Claude Deffarge and Gordian Troeller, *Yemen 62–69: De la révolution sauvage à la trêvedes guerriers* (Paris: Robert Laffont, 1969), 215–16; Farid, *Nasser*, 55; Ḥadīdī, *Shāhid 'alā ḥarb al-Yaman*, 140; Primakov, *Russia and the Arabs*, 98–99; Schmidt, *Yemen*, 290; Waterbury, *Egypt*, 415.

[81] Telegrams, Jiddah to Foreign Office, nos. 530 and 567, August 2 and 28, 1967, FCO 8/697, PRO.

[82] Sela, *Unity*, 79; *FRUS*, 1964–68, vol. 21, doc. 458. Sāmī Sharaf finds this something to boast about (*Sanawāt*, 2:655).

[83] Telegram, Reddaway (Khartoum) to FO, no. 486, August 31, 1967, FCO 8/697, PRO. See also Sela, *Unity*, 72–73.

> the Arab Foreign Ministers Conference or agreed upon by the two countries.
>
> 2. The responsibility of this committee will be to formulate a plan that would ensure the withdrawal of UAR troops from Yemen and ensure the stoppage of Saudi military assistance from [*sic*] all Yemenis.
>
> 3. This Committee is to exert efforts that would enable Yemen to achieve stability in accordance with the genuine desires of its citizens and in harmony with the rights of Yemen's sovereignty and complete independence.
>
> 4. The committee is to consult with both Saudi Arabia and the UAR, on all issues that might cause obstacles, with a view to facilitating such difficulties, and reach a settlement acceptable to all parties concerned, so as to remove causes of dispute, preserve Arab blood and ensure Arab unity.

But this was just for show. Behind closed doors, Nasser undertook to withdraw Egyptian forces from Yemen within three months in exchange for the retention of Sallāl as president until a plebiscite could be held—three to six months after the departure of the Egyptian army.[84] Without any means of guaranteeing the results of the plebiscite, this was tantamount to surrender. Tellingly, Nasser apparently volunteered at one point that he did not care what happened in Yemen after the evacuation so long as no offensive was allowed to develop while Egyptian troops were still on the ground.[85]

The evacuation plan had two phases. The preparatory phase, lasting from mid-September to mid-October, entailed concentration of heavy equipment and the bulk of Egyptian forces at Ḥudaydah and the transfer of various military and civilian installations to Yemeni hands. The second phase, which lasted from mid-October to mid-December, consisted of the seaborne evacuation of troops and equipment to Egyptian soil. To help the Egyptians out of Yemen, the Saudis agreed to provide five ships for the evacuation of materiel. The Egyptians initially refused to submit to the humiliation of evacuating their men on Saudi boats, but later relented. However, the Yemeni authorities would not permit the Saudi ships to dock unless they flew the flag of the YAR. When the Saudis failed to comply, Egypt had no choice but to deploy its own ships for this purposes, out of concern that further delays would

[84] Telegram, Khartoum to FO, no. 489, September 1, 1967, FCO 8/697, PRO.

[85] Telegram, Jiddah to FO, no. 580, September 4, 1967, FCO 8/697, PRO.

expose the dwindling forces concentrated around Ḥudaydah to tribal predations.[86]

The Egyptian withdrawal began on September 10. By this point, only six Egyptian infantry brigades remained in Yemen, which, along with supporting forces, totaled about 25,000 troops. Execution of the withdrawal plan was complicated not only by the vulnerability of retreating convoys to tribal attack but also by the wrath of pro-Republican forces, who feared the consequences of Egypt's abandonment and were outraged by what they perceived to be the Egyptian sellout at Khartoum. On at least one occasion, Yemeni frustration translated into violence. On October 3, several dozen Egyptians were massacred in the streets of Ṣan'ā' after Egyptian soldiers opened fire on an angry mob protesting the arrival of the three-member peace commission agreed upon at Khartoum.[87]

During the final stages of the withdrawal, emboldened tribal forces hostile to the republic began to close in on Ṣan'ā'. The besieged Yemeni government had no choice but to appeal to the Kremlin for assistance. On November 3, President Sallāl left Ṣan'ā' on a plane bound for Moscow. Abandoned by his Egyptian sponsors, Sallāl probably knew what was coming.[88] The next night, a group of officers launched a coup d'état and handed power to a triumvirate headed by 'Abd al-Raḥmān al-Iryānī.

Iryānī picked up where Sallāl had left off. In a desperate bid to win Soviet support, the new Yemeni leader met with the Soviet ambassador four times in the space of seven days.[89] The Soviets were eager to prevent the collapse of the republic but not at the cost of repeating Egypt's mistakes. Concerned about the incipient vacuum on the peninsula due to the near-simultaneous departure of the British and the Egyptians, they decided there was no time to lose. On November 17, the Soviet government initiated an airlift of arms and personnel to Yemen. They

[86] Huwaydī, *Khamsūn 'āman*, 284–85; Telegrams, Jiddah to FO, nos. 577 and 612, September 4 and 13, 1967, FCO 8/697, PRO.

[87] Huwaydī, *Khamsūn 'āman*, 285; Maḥrizī, *al-Ṣamt al-ḥā'ir*, 182; Aḥmad, *Dhikrayāt*, 596–97; O'Ballance, *War in the Yemen*, 187; Deffarge and Troeller, *Yemen 62–69*, 217; Faraj, *Rijāl fī khanādiq*, 224–25; Ḥamrūsh, *Qiṣṣat thawrat 23 yūliyū*, 3:258; Rahmy, *Egyptian Policy*, 238; Schmidt, *Yemen*, 291–92.

[88] Sallāl never made it to Moscow. After an unfruitful stop in Cairo, he alighted in Baghdad, where he spent the next 14 years in exile.

[89] "Khronika po sobytii po YAR" (January 24, 1967–November 21, 1967), F. 88, op. 19, p. 14, d. 10, AVPRF; Primakov, *Russia and the Arabs*, 99.

also dispatched a small contingent of combat aircraft to take over the air defense of Ṣanʻā'. One of these, a MiG-17, was shot down over northern Yemen while strafing a Saudi supply column in December.[90]

At one point in mid-December, Ṣanʻā' stood on the verge of collapse. But a combination of tenacious resistance led by Ḥasan al-ʻAmrī, the advantages afforded by Soviet air cover, and disarray among the besieging forces eventually turned the tide in the republic's favor. It was perhaps fitting that a botched intervention made possible at the outset by unprecedented Soviet air support for Egypt's force-projection efforts should end with Soviet aerial intervention to save the remnants of Yemen's revolutionary experiment. Although fighting continued, the republic survived, and Soviet attention soon turned southward.

*

On November 29, 1967, two ceremonies took place at different ports on the Arabian Peninsula. In Aden, following the conclusion in Zurich of a transfer-of-power agreement between British Minister Lord Edward Shackleton and NLF leader Qaḥṭān al-Shaʻbī, the last contingent of British commandos on the peninsula flew out aboard twelve helicopters to the carrier *Albion*. Meanwhile, at al-Ḥudaydah, some 300 kilometers to the north, General Ḥasan al-ʻAmrī and a host of dignitaries bid farewell to the last of the Egyptian soldiers in Yemen.[91] The decolonization of Yemen was complete.

[90] "Report by the Bulgarian Foreign Minister on the Ministerial Meeting in Warsaw regarding the situation in the Middle East, 19-21 December, 1967," *Cold War International History Project (CWIHP)*, www.cwihp.org; *FRUS*, 1964–68, vol. 21, docs. 464, 468, 470; Bissell, "Soviet Use of Proxies," 98; Page, *The USSR and Arabia*, 108; idem, *The Soviet Union and the Yemens*, 6; Schmidt, *Yemen*, 294–97; personal interview, Vladimir Shubin, Moscow, October 25, 2005.

[91] *New York Times*, November 30, 1967; *al-Ahrām*, November 30, 1967. The last Egyptian soldier apparently departed Yemen one week later. *Al-Ahrām*, December 9, 1967.

✷ AFTERWORD ✷

The Twilight of Egyptian Power

THE SIX-DAY WAR ENDED a decade and a half of Egyptian ascendancy. Having lost Sudan in 1956 and Syria in 1961, Egypt in 1967 conceded the Arabian and Sinai Peninsulas as well. Not since Muhammad Ali's defeat at the hands of Great Britain in 1840 had a rising local power suffered such an imperial contraction.

Egypt's misfortune was more than the shattering of an imperial dream. It was the end of an era. The age of Arab revolution began with the seizure of power in Cairo by the Free Officers in the summer of 1952. Thereafter, Arab nationalists from Algeria in the West to Iraq in the East looked to Nasser for inspiration and support. When his star waned, theirs lost its shine. By 1967 the glory days of Arab revolution lay in the past. Ahead lay four decades of stagnation, repression, and fading legitimacy. The twilight of Egyptian power and the sunset of Arab revolution were one.

Egypt's defeat in six days shook the faith of millions in the champion of Arab revolution. In retrospect, one can see that Nasser's revolutionary project was crumbling well before Israel delivered the coup de grâce in Sinai. The decline of Nasserism began with the dissolution of the UAR in 1961 and culminated in the defeat of 1967. But much of the process of decline—the end of the Egyptian bid for regional domination—took place in Yemen.

Nasser's ill-starred decision to pursue a proxy war with Saudi Arabia in Yemen eroded the foundations of his power by destabilizing Egypt's relations with the great powers. The intervention in Yemen brought Egypt into direct conflict with two key American allies on the Arabian Peninsula. The clash with Saudi Arabia and Great Britain destroyed the US-Egyptian relationship, ending the food program upon which the Egyptian economy depended. The suspension of American aid drove Egypt deeper into debt to the Soviet Union. The uneasy dependence on Moscow, in conjunction with the rupture in relations with Washington, shattered Egypt's neutrality and precipitated the disaster of 1967. The story of Egypt's intervention in Yemen is thus the tale of an ambitious local power's failed attempt to multiply the limited forces at its disposal by harnessing the great powers to its bid for regional hegemony. Egypt's quest failed because the very resources shrewd diplomacy generated in Washington and Moscow were contingent on its continued subservience.

Egypt's decline has had a profound influence on the international politics of the Middle East. Most obvious, perhaps, was its effect on the Arab-Israeli conflict. Before 1967 the conflict with Israel had been a derivative of Egypt's Arab policy. Palestine, Nasser once quipped, was the "peg upon which Arab unity hangs."[1] That Nasser was more concerned about leadership of the Arabs than victory over the Jews was most obviously demonstrated in his dogged pursuit of Arab civil war in Yemen at the supposed peak of the Arab-Israeli conflict. For a brief period after 1967, Israel became a direct preoccupation for Egyptian policy makers bent on the recovery of lost territory and prestige. But this exceptional period, which included the War of Attrition and the Yom Kippur War, ended with the conclusion of the Camp David Accords. Once they had quit the inter-Arab playing field, the Egyptians lost interest in the Palestine cause. Their withdrawal greatly diminished the chances of interstate war in the Levant.

But even Egypt's preoccupation with the Palestine cause after the Six-Day War had less to do with hostility toward Israel and more to do with attracting America. Indeed, after wrecking Egypt's neutralist policy in Yemen, both Nasser and Sadat worked hard to win back American favor. This was not surprising. After all, Egypt had "lost America" more than the United States had "lost Egypt." The threat Nasser posed to US interests from 1963 onward had convinced policy makers in Washington that support for Egypt in the vain hope that the hero of Arab nationalism would cool his revolutionary ardor was bad policy. But the Soviets were in no position to make up for the loss of US aid. Nor was the Kremlin able to return territory held by Israel. This is why, immediately after 1967, Nasser plunged his country back into a protracted war with Israel, intentionally embroiling the Soviet Union in another attempt to grab the attention of officials in Washington. From the War of Attrition to the Camp David Accords, Egypt's pursuit of war and peace with Israel served the ultimate goal of recapturing American favor. Once that goal was achieved, foreign policy under Sadat and Mubarak fell into the quiescent mold envisioned by Eisenhower and Kennedy.

[1] Telegram, Kiselev (Cairo) to the Foreign Office, January 1, 1957, in *BVK*, 2:7.

Moscow ultimately failed to profit from the angry divorce between Cairo and Washington. In the immediate aftermath of the defeat, Nasser gave the Soviets everything they had been asking for and more. He provided the Soviet air force and navy with bases on Egyptian soil and invited Soviet air defense units to take the lead in warding off Israeli attacks. However, in doing so, Nasser was not only harnessing Soviet armed might against Israel but also making sure his neighborhood brawl became a global contest, which the United States could not afford to ignore. After Nasser's death in 1970, Sadat took these efforts one step further, using Soviet weaponry to try and eke out a small victory against Israel in 1973—only to dump the Kremlin for the White House in the war's aftermath. Tellingly, the entire Cold War relationship between the Soviet Union and Egypt, from 1955 to 1975, is framed by one American president refusing Egypt aid and another succumbing to Egyptian advances. For Egypt, relations with Washington had always mattered more than relations with Moscow.

Viewed in retrospect, the launch of the joint revolutionary project in Yemen defines the high-water mark of Soviet-Egyptian relations and the peak of Soviet influence in the region. To be sure, the peak of military cooperation between the two countries still lay half a decade in the future, when the Soviet Union would send some twenty thousand men to resurrect the beaten Egyptian army and defend the Nile Valley from attack. But by then, the effusive Khrushchev had departed the scene, the grand revolutionary project in Yemen had soured, and the Egyptian army lay in ruins. Gone were the confidence in Egypt's total independence and the anticipation of imminent revolutionary triumph that had characterized the construction of the air bridge to Ṣan'ā' in the fall of 1962.

Paradoxically, Soviet support for the intervention in Yemen carried with it the seeds of future discord. The Soviets' eventual dislodgment from Egypt, their most important ally in the Arab Middle East, can be traced back to the injection of strategic desiderata into a relationship previously maintained by the appearance of selfless aid and mutually beneficial trade. It was the Soviets' quasi-colonial military presence in Egypt in the years 1967–72, combined with their inability to erase the consequences of the 1967 war by diplomatic or military means, that contributed most to the poisoning of relations between the two countries and hastened Sadat's turn to Washington in the wake of the 1973 war. Sadat gave expression to his countrymen's growing disenchantment with their Communist allies in his decision to evict Soviet combat forces from Egypt in the summer of 1972. But the disillusionment of Egypt's ruling circles with Soviet policy began much earlier, as the product of Egypt's growing dependence on Soviet aid, and of the parallel escalation of Soviet strategic demands in the latter stages of the Yemen war.

Egypt's retreat from Yemen also heralded a fundamental shift in the regional balance of power in the late twentieth century: the decline of Egypt and the rise of Saudi Arabia. The transformation of Nasser at the Khartoum summit from arch-nemesis to supplicant was a sign of things to come. The new Middle East was to be built with Saudi capital—and Egyptian labor. Ostracized under Sadat, lackluster under Mubarak, Egypt—increasingly preoccupied with internal challenges—lost its prominence after Nasser's death. The prosperous Saudis, by contrast, became the kingmakers of Arab politics. To be sure, the Saudi ascendance in the decades after 1967 had much to do with the rise of oil as a factor in the global economy. But it owed as much to the removal of the Egyptian menace. The withdrawal of Egypt's armies from Yemen ended the existential threat to Saudi Arabia for a generation—until Iraq's Saddam Hussein repeated Nasser's mistake in 1991, invading Kuwait and bringing the wrath of America upon him.

More broadly, Egypt's setback signaled the decline of the resource-poor Levant—hitherto the central axis of Arab politics—and the rise of the oil-rich gulf as the primary arena of geostrategic competition in the Middle East. Not surprisingly, two of Nasser's most prominent would-be heirs, Saddam Hussein and Mahmud Ahmadinejad, arose in the gulf to contest Saudi primacy. The Sunni dictator of Iraq and the Shiite president of Iran each borrowed pages from Nasser's playbook in their quest for regional supremacy. Both spoke directly to the Arabs over their governments, employed terrorism and subversion as methods of choice, used the Palestine problem to legitimize their claim for regional leadership, exploited their adversaries' reliance on Western support to question their legitimacy, and attempted to harness Russian military and diplomatic might in order to multiply the limited force at their disposal and balance US power in the international arena. This last point is especially significant. Since the end of the Cold War, the absence of a rival superpower has been perhaps the most important factor inhibiting the rise of a regional hegemon in the mold of Nasser's Egypt. What the rise of China portends for the Middle East is thus one of the bigger questions hanging over the future of regional geopolitics in the twenty-first century.

Although the Saudi-Egyptian conflict of the 1960s was primarily a struggle for political influence, like the global Cold War it was ultimately a competition for legitimacy between contending political orders. In general terms, the Arab Cold War, in its mature phase, pitted the secular-socialist model of nationalist republicanism, which although hostile to the West ultimately rested on ideas imported from Europe, against a model of monarchic conservatism that was, for all its external reliance on Western power, grounded in the Islamic tradition of government. Neither system benefited from an excess of legitimacy. In fact, it was precisely the weakness common to Egyptian republicanism and Saudi monarchism that generated the conflict between them. The physical battlefield on which they chose to wage their struggle happened to be Yemen.

Lacking natural resources, Egypt's claim to Arab leadership rested ultimately on the appeal of its ruler and the force of his call. In revolutionary pan-Arabism, Nasser hit upon a formula that played on the contradictions between illegitimate governments and restless populations in the Arab Middle East. His powerful message resonated with the Arab masses and placed him on the right side of the ruler-people divide. The persistent call of "Voice of the Arabs" to overthrow the imperialist puppets and replace them with progressive republics was highly attractive in theory. But the translation of theory into practice exposed the hollowness of the proffered alternative.

As long as Egypt's involvement was restricted to propaganda—as was the case in Iraq in 1958—the typically horrible results of regime change could be dismissed as an aberration beyond Cairo's control. But once Nasser assumed responsibility over the course of events, the consequences became his. As it turned out, the export of Egypt's revolution produced not liberty, prosperity, and unity but repression, expropriation, and considerable bloodshed. It was already hard to keep this a secret after the dissolution of the UAR in 1961. But Yemen was the ultimate test case.

However unintended the consequences, Egypt's decision to intervene on behalf of Yemen's revolutionaries was the culmination of a decade of support for revolutionary movements. Egyptian propaganda portrayed the war as a Manichaean battle between the forces of progress and the forces of reaction. For both the United Arab Republic and the Saudi Arabian Kingdom, therefore, the intervention became a winner-take-all contest. The Arab Cold War had turned hot; losing was no longer an option. For Nasser in particular, as the Arab east's would-be Bismarck, winning this blood-and-iron contest was essential. In that context, the inability of his modern armies to overcome a host of tribesmen constituted a political disaster of the first order.

The awkward attempt to export Egypt's revolutionary experience to Yemen played a major role in the diminution of Egyptian soft power and the decline of pan-Arabism. Nasser's inability to make the republic stick without massive application of force betrayed the emptiness of his revolutionary promise. The Egyptians went to Yemen with the honest intention of establishing an enlightened republic. But they ended up creating a police state. Protesting that the goal of freeing the Yemenis from obscurantist tyranny justified the means, the Egyptians in Yemen could not avoid sounding like the European colonizers against whose domination Egypt's own revolution was premised. For all the rhetoric of selfless sacrifice, it was hard to believe that Egypt's efforts were directed at bettering the lot of the Yemeni people rather than enhancing the prestige of the Egyptian leadership. As it turned out, the liberation of their Arab brethren in Yemen came at the expense of the freedom and prosperity of the Egyptians themselves. The export of revolution to Yemen thus exposed the shortcomings of the Egyptian revolution while simultaneously accelerating its most negative trends. And by disproving the theory underlying Nasser's claim to Arab leadership, the Yemen experience rendered that claim illegitimate.

In Egypt itself the intervention hastened the consolidation of the officer corps as a privileged elite. Under Marshal 'Abd al-Ḥakīm 'Āmir, the army dramatically extended its influence into society, economy, and government. The creation of a "socialist Mamluk" order of society—in which army officers not only monopolized power but also appropriated national wealth—was naturally resented by those to whom it brought no benefit.[2] After 'Āmir's death against the backdrop of a rumored coup attempt in the aftermath of the 1967 war, Nasser and his successors responded to this resentment by reducing the armed forces' visible role in politics.[3] At the same time, Sadat and Mubarak enabled the army to expand its special role in the economy. It was this mixed legacy that al-

[2] Muḥammad Galāl Kishk, *al-Naksah wa-l-ghazw al-fikrī* (Beirut, 1969), 67.

[3] Mark Cooper, "The Demilitarization of the Egyptian Cabinet," *International Journal of Middle Eastern Studies* 14, no. 2 (1982): 203–25. See also Robert Springborg, *Mubarak's Egypt: Fragmentation of the Political Order* (Boulder, CO: Westview Press, 1989). Cf. Robert Satloff, *Army and Politics in Mubarak's Egypt* (Washington, DC: Washington Institute, 1988).

lowed the commanders of the Egyptian armed forces to pose as honest brokers between Mubarak and the people in the upheaval of February 2011 and perpetuate their control in its immediate aftermath.

In Yemen, to be sure, Egypt's balance sheet was not all bleak. After all, the Royalist cause did not survive the war. Yet the revolutionary cause can scarcely be said to have triumphed. For one, it has been Saudi influence—not Egyptian—that has predominated in Yemen ever since 1967. Second, notwithstanding the tremendous growth of the state, tribal politics continue to play a major role in its affairs—and may yet prove its undoing. Third, the republic did not deliver on the transformational promises of the revolution. Like Egypt, Yemen has not escaped many of the ills common to the Arab republics, including a bloated bureaucracy, an enormous security apparatus, runaway population growth, huge gaps between rich and poor, rampant corruption, and heavy dependence on foreign aid. Ironically, in following the example set by the Free Officers in Egypt, the Yemeni revolutionaries of 1962 destined their descendants to march on Ṣan'ā' 's Tahrir Square in similar emulation of Cairo. Nasser sowed the wind of Egyptian republicanism in Yemen in the 1960s. A half-century later, Hosni Mubarak and Ali Abdullah Saleh reaped the whirlwind.

The jury is still out on the unity of Republican Yemen. In the short run, the political division between North and South Yemen only deepened after the departure of the Egyptians. The end of Egyptian support for FLOSY made it easier for the more radical NLF to seize control of the south after the British withdrawal and proclaim the independence of the People's Republic of South Yemen. Within a few years, the NLF had established a Marxist police state, renamed the People's Democratic Republic of Yemen (PDRY), and struck an alliance with the Soviet Union. For two decades, the Yemen Arab Republic in the north and the PDRY in the south maintained a hostile standoff (interrupted by occasional border wars), before unifying in 1990. Despite another bout of civil war in 1994, the Republic of Yemen held together. So far, at least, the Egyptian intervention seems to have hastened the political consolidation of Yemen into a single state. Whether it will survive in the face of dimming economic prospects, waning legitimacy, and a host of challenges to central authority remains to be seen.

The threat of nationalist revolution by military officers acting under the inspiration and often direct support of the Egyptian government was the most potent one facing Saudi Arabia and the other conservative monarchies of the Middle East in the 1950s and 1960s. After 1967 that threat swiftly receded. Ultimately, the conservative monarchies came out ahead in the contest for legitimacy—and longevity—with Egyptian republicanism. The triumph of the Arab monarchs was not so much that they had staved off the physical threat Nasser's armies posed, but that they had withstood the powerful ideological challenge to their legitimacy Egyptian-sponsored pan-Arabism presented. Although there could be no knockout victory in this battle of illegitimates, it was the Egyptians who came up short. In Yemen, the Saudis successfully broke the brunt of the nationalist assault, exposing the republican model as a sham and providing conservative monarchies from Morocco to Bahrain an extended lease on life. Nasser and Faysal, both perched in glass towers, were equally foolish to be pelting each other. But it was Nasser who was running low on stones.

The demise of Nasserism—as a powerful propaganda tool if not as a basis for domestic policy—spelled the end of the Arab Cold War and the beginning of what P. J. Vatikiotis has called the de-ideologization of inter-Arab relations.[4] Although the inter-Arab contest for power and legitimacy continues, the axis of controversy has shifted. The stark ideological divide between socialist nationalists and conservative royalists has given way to a debate over the role of Islam. In this debate, the state-to-state struggle for power has been upstaged by an assault on state legitimacy by nonstate actors acting initially in the name of nationalism (such as the PLO) but increasingly in the name of religion (such as Hamas, Hizbullah, and al-Qaeda).

The failure of the Arab socialist alternative Nasser proffered from 1962 onward paved the way for the ascendance of political Islam. In 1952 the liberal elites that had led the struggle against the British in the interwar period were succeeded by military officers who, while hostile to liberalism, continued the resistance to European domination based on ideas similarly borrowed from the West. But all along, Islam presented a bubbling undercurrent of alternative legitimacy. When Arab nationalism ran aground in the mid-1960s, that current rose to the surface. To a certain degree, the revival of Islam in Egypt since 1967 reflected a turn away from the foreign ideas that had underlain both Egyptian liberalism and Arab socialism and a return to the perceived authenticity of the Islamic heritage. As Fouad Ajami has argued, the tendency to fall back on tradition was a natural response to the disaster of 1967. For conser-

[4] P. J. Vatikiotis, "Conflict in the Middle East Reconsidered," in *Arab and Regional Politics in the Middle East* (New York: St. Martin's Press, 1984), 161.

vative rulers, the catastrophe that befell Egypt provided a useful vindication of the traditional order. For ordinary Arab Muslims whose world had just fallen apart, religion offered comforting answers to questions about an otherwise incomprehensible reality. And for resentful citizens inclined to oppose the dominant order, Islam suggested a legitimate mode of resistance to those in power and a vehicle for expressing frustration with an unjust world. With the decline of pan-Arabism, Islam—in its conservative and millenarian guises—became an argument both for upholding the status quo and for upending it.[5]

The return to the perceived authenticity of the Islamic tradition has not, thus far, resulted in a reconstituted model of Arab government. Instead, in Egypt and elsewhere, it degenerated into a bloody struggle between dictators bent on preserving their monopoly of power and violent extremists bent on overthrowing them in the name of religion. In this too, the pattern had been set in the Nasser years. Those who refuse to acknowledge the continuity between the populist republic of the 1950s and its caricature fifty years later—the infamous *jumlūkiyyah* ("republarchy"), in Sa'd al-Dīn Ibrāhīm's memorable formulation—are nostalgic for a golden era that never was.[6]

Although Nasser never waged the sort of general assault on Islam that Ataturk led in Turkey, his war on its more radical proponents was every bit as determined. Ultimately, Nasser's crackdown on the Muslim Brotherhood did not succeed in squelching the voices of the most militant proponents of Islam in Egypt. If anything, Nasser's persecution of the Muslim Brothers may have strengthened radical Islam in the long run. In particular, the execution of the brotherhood's leading intellectual, Sayyid Quṭb, in 1966, transformed him into a martyr whose influence over the evolution of violent Sunni Islamist movements in Egypt and Saudi Arabia was considerable.[7] This was partly because Nasser's successor, unlike Ataturk's, did not perpetuate his legacy. On

[5] Fouad Ajami, *The Arab Predicament: Arab Political Thought and Practice since 1967*, updated ed. (Cambridge: Cambridge University Press, 1993), 170–252; Paul Salem, *Bitter Legacy: Ideology and Politics in the Arab World* (Syracuse, NY: Syracuse University Press, 1994), 26–27, 260.

[6] See, e.g., Burhan Ghalioun, "The Persistence of Arab Authoritarianism," *Journal of Democracy* 15, no. 4 (2004): 126–27. On the origins of *jumlūkiyyah*, see *al-Majallah*, July 2–8, 2000.

[7] In 1974, Quṭb's brother, Muḥammad, also imprisoned under Nasser, went into exile in Saudi Arabia, where he became a professor of Islamic studies, disseminated the work of his brother, and probably taught both Ayman al-Zawahiri and Osama bin Laden.

the contrary, Sadat took the lead in repudiating key aspects of Nasserism, rehabilitating the brotherhood, and emphasizing Islamic values in a tragic bid to burnish his own legitimacy. Although Mubarak resumed Nasser's uncompromising struggle against the brotherhood in the aftermath of Sadat's assassination, the movement remained the obvious alternative to his rule after thirty years in power. Indeed, in Egypt and elsewhere the "Arab Awakening" has opened up an unprecedented opportunity for Islamists to fashion a new political order on the ruins of Arab republicanism.

Faysal's turn to Islam as a weapon against the threat of Arab nationalism was natural. Viewed from within the crucible of the Arab Cold War, Faysal's effort to undermine Nasser's rule at home by means of the Muslim Brotherhood, and to counter his influence abroad by means of the Islamic Pact, must have seemed like the last resort of a reactionary has-been. In the space of a few short years, however, those same efforts would appear avant-garde. Nonetheless, the Saudi triumph in 1967 was temporary, and it may yet turn out to be pyrrhic. It was temporary because within little more than a decade the Saudis were already being outflanked by another charismatic revolutionary: Ayatollah Khomeini of Iran hoisted not the banner of nationalism but the banner of Islam, and he succeeded in shaking the foundations of the Arab political order from the Persian Gulf to the Mediterranean. The Saudis' victory may turn out to have been pyrrhic because the genie they ushered out of the bottle to contend with the allegedly godless socialists in Egypt soon returned to haunt them. When zealots took over the Grand Mosque of Mecca in 1979, they exposed how frail Saudi legitimacy really was, invoking as they did the very values upon which the existing order was based in denouncing its leaders as apostates. The House of Saʻūd's subsequent attempts to deflect the Islamist challenge from within have had major repercussions for world history—from the attacks of September 11, 2001, in the West to the two Afghan wars in the East.[8]

The republican model established in Egypt and tested in Yemen survived for decades after Nasser's death. But its vitality had been sapped in the struggles of the 1950s and '60s. The demise of Nasser and the softening of interstate rivalry did not erase the legitimacy deficit that had fueled the Arab Cold War. After an interlude of soul-searching in the

[8] Yaroslav Trofimov, *The Siege of Mecca: The Forgotten Uprising in Islam's Holiest Shrine and the Birth of al Qaeda* (New York: Anchor Books, 2008).

immediate aftermath of the Six-Day War, the legitimacy problem disappeared beneath the calmer surface of Arab political discourse, festering for four decades before exploding on the streets of Tunisia, Egypt, Yemen, Syria, and Bahrain.

The popular uprisings of 2011 were astonishing in many ways. Yet it should not have come as a surprise that the protests made their first and deepest inroads in the Arab republics. To be sure, the absence of oil was a significant factor in most cases. The monarchies—with the important exceptions of Jordan and Morocco—possess the advantage of being able to buy off opposition as long as oil and gas supplies last. But the uprisings succeeded most where the legitimacy problem was gravest. No Arab country received a stellar report card from the United Nations when it began to issue its Arab Human Development Reports in 2002. But the monarchies, with few exceptions, came out ahead of the republics on most of the indexes pertaining to governance and civil liberties.

Nasser invented the modern Arab security state; his successors and imitators perfected it. Lacking Nasser's charisma, a viable ideology, tribal roots, or religious sanction, Egypt and the other Arab republics turned to increasingly repressive measures in an effort to keep the lid on resentful, restless, and burgeoning populations. Severe repression, rampant corruption, rigged elections, huge gaps between the profligate and the destitute and incipient family rule—these were some of the nasty phenomena that gnawed away at the vestiges of legitimacy in the Arab republics between 1967 and 2011.[9]

Alternatives to Egypt's Grand Strategy under Nasser

This critique of Nasser's foreign policy raises the question: what could he—or another ruler of Egypt at midcentury—have done differently? Given the cards dealt the Free Officers in 1952, was there a viable alternative strategy that would have produced dramatically improved results for Egypt?

All Egyptian governments in the second half of the twentieth century faced the same basic predicament: how to contend with rapid population

[9] See, e.g., United Nations Development Programme, *Arab Human Development Report 2002* (New York: United Nations Publications, 2002), 112, 165; *Arab Human Development Report 2004*, 136, 214; *Arab Human Development Report 2009*, 262; World Bank, *World Governance Indicators* [1996–2009], available at http://info.worldbank.org/governance/wgi/index.asp. See also Ajami, *The Arab Predicament*, 26–27.

growth unmatched by a commensurate increase of available resources. In theory, there were two ways out of this bind: to curb the expansion of the population or to expand the stock of available resources. In fact, an optimal policy might have combined elements of both.

Global efforts to control population growth in the twentieth century have been a practical and moral disaster.[10] But in the 1960s, population control was fashionable—and it was particularly popular in India, a model for Egypt in other policy areas. Therefore, the historian cannot avoid asking whether or not, moral questions aside, a determined Egypt leadership could have pursued an effective policy to curb birth rates in the face of popular and clerical opposition. What would such a policy have looked like? Would it have focused on education and contraception, on compulsion and sterilization, on economic incentives or on legal penalties? And, most importantly, could it have contributed meaningfully, in conjunction with other measures, to the transformation of Egypt's economic prospects? We do not know. The one-child policy of China in the 1980s and 1990s provides some indication of how effective a strong regime can be in defusing a population explosion in a traditional agrarian society.[11] In Egypt, by contrast, the birth control program announced in 1966 was implemented half-heartedly and had little lasting effect on long-term trends.[12] The country's fertility rate stayed above five through the 1980s, creating the bulging cohort of young Egyptians who played such a key role in the ouster of Mubarak.

A realistic assessment of the potential for growing Egypt's resources would have concluded that foreign expansion was unlikely to prove rewarding in a world dominated by two superpowers, each determined to deny the other advantage in any corner of the globe. For Egypt, the most promising direction for expansion was eastward, toward the oil-rich Persian Gulf. But the gulf was not only remote and inaccessible; it was dominated by Anglo-American might. After the discovery in 1959 of significant oil reserves in Libya, westward expansion became feasible as well. But in Libya the potential clash with the United States, which had an important stake in continued access to Wheelus Air Base, was even more direct. By midcentury it was no longer conceivable that the

[10] Matthew Connelly, *Fatal Misconception: The Struggle to Control World Population* (Cambridge, MA: Belknap Press of Harvard University Press, 2008).

[11] Of course, it is virtually impossible to isolate cause from effect. Since China's fertility rates were dropping precipitously in any case, the marginal impact of government intervention is hard to gauge. Egypt's own fertility rate had dropped to around three by 2010.

[12] Baker, *Egypt's Uncertain Revolution*, 77–79.

United States would acquiesce in the forceful acquisition of any significant portion of the region's oil reserves—although this fact would not find concrete expression in policy until the Iranian revolution and the invasion of Afghanistan elicited the Carter Doctrine in 1979.

If the acquisition of oil wealth by force was not in the cards, might it perhaps have been acquired by peaceful means? As demonstrated by Egypt's brief union with Syria, it was not inconceivable in the climate of the time for an Arab state to enter into some form of confederation with Egypt in return for protection from neighboring predators. But which oil-rich state would have acquiesced and for how long in such a geographically perverse arrangement? Pan-Arab ideologues waxed poetic over the fundamental unity of the Arabs across the artificial boundaries of the post-Ottoman Middle East. But wishful thinking is no basis for grand strategy. To practitioners of power politics, the "United" Arab Republic proved that the Arabs were in fact divided. If such were the case when two "progressive" republics opted to merge, a fortiori it would have been so had Egypt sought a merger with one of the tribal monarchies of Arabia. As the experience in Yemen demonstrated, the export of revolution was a risky and expensive proposition with diminishing returns over time. Viewed in this light, the theoretical appeal of federation with a better-endowed state seems like fools' gold. The quest for an alternative grand strategy begins with the recognition that there were no shortcuts, no get-rich-quick schemes that could have gotten Egypt out of its predicament at midcentury. There were only two potential sources for funding Egypt's development: domestic growth and foreign aid.

In retrospect, Nasser placed a bad bet on socialism. Egypt at midcentury was a cosmopolitan entrepôt, a vibrant trading hub and a bridge between East and West. Instead of building on this legacy, Nasser squandered it. Instead of cultivating Egypt's prosperous minorities, with their mercantile dynamism, economic expertise, and access to international capital, he expropriated their wealth and drove them out of the country. Instead of nurturing the private sector, he created a massive bureaucracy, nationalized the economy, and delivered it into the hands of the army. Some degree of socialism was probably unavoidable at a time when leaders throughout the Third World were bent on emulating the Soviet model. But the excesses of Nasser's "Arab Socialism" proved disastrous for Egypt's growth prospects.

If Nasser's choice of the socialist path led Egypt into an avoidable domestic trap, his mishandling of Egypt's foreign policy led him into a similarly evitable predicament on the international front. When Nasser gambled on Soviet aid, he compounded his domestic wager on socialism. In retrospect, the winning cards in Egypt's foreign aid deck were the two states Nasser chose to antagonize the most. Instead of courting the well-heeled Saudis and the prosperous Americans, he launched an unnecessary war that landed him squarely in the hard-up Soviet camp. Neutralism was a brilliant strategy for maximizing aid in a bipolar world. But when Nasser conflated neutralism with anti-Westernism, he threw away the keys to Egypt's economic future.

It does not appear feasible for Egypt to have opted out of the inter-Arab struggle for power and legitimacy at midcentury. But in order to avoid the risks and costs associated with foreign adventures, Egypt's leaders would have had to espouse disciplined moderation in the pursuit of their foreign policy objectives. Above all, this meant avoiding wars of choice. It also entailed the restriction of aid to foreign revolutionaries and the curtailment of hostile propaganda. The pursuit of such a course might have come at the expense of some foreign aid, from the Eastern bloc in particular. It might also have brought about some diminution of Egypt's regional stature. But a more cautious policy, still oriented to securing foreign aid from both sides in the Cold War, but less bent on sowing regional havoc, could have proved more profitable for Egypt in the long run. Nasser's own balancing act of the 1950s, though it proved difficult to sustain, demonstrates that it could be done.

The intervention in Yemen was symptomatic of Nasser's tendency to overreach after 1956. A sounder approach to overcoming Egypt's structural constraints would almost certainly have entailed the abandonment of foreign adventures at least until such time as they could be afforded. Empowered by their success in terminating the British occupation and the political victory of Suez, the Free Officers might have told the Egyptian people frankly that while foreign challenges abounded—Israel, the remnants of British imperialism, and Arab reactionaries, to name three—overcoming them was not in Egypt's power in the foreseeable future. The amassing of Egyptian power would take time—decades, perhaps—in the course of which Egyptians would have to focus on building domestic capacity.

To abandon guns for butter would not have been rational for a military regime reliant on the support of its officer class. However, a realistic approach to the challenges of Egyptian national security after 1956 would have concluded that showering the army with hardware and perquisites could not lead to military strength. The trauma of Suez should have led to a massive purge of the Egyptian armed forces followed by a dedicated effort to build up an effective fighting force, with the help of foreign advisors, over the course of a decade or more of hard work. We need not accept Ṣādiq al-ʻAẓm's radical contention that Nasser's Arab socialism did not go far enough.[13] But merely going through the motions of change was inadequate—for the creation of an effective fighting force as for the transformation of a traditional society into a socialist utopia.

There may well have been no alternative to a state-led effort to transform Egypt's agrarian economy into an industrial powerhouse reliant on abundant cheap labor. The remedy that suggests itself in the twenty-first century—capitalizing on Egypt's human resources to promote the emergence of a liberal, knowledge-based economy—appears hopelessly anachronistic in the context of the 1960s. At the same time, the expropriations and nationalizations of the 1960s destroyed Egypt's entrepreneurial class and damaged its productive capacity. A more fruitful approach might have combined state-led investment in infrastructure with incentives to big business, underwritten by guarantees for the protection of private property.

People were both Egypt's asset and its liability. A country of 30 million lacking natural resources had to invest in its citizens. Nasser did much to expand educational opportunities to all Egyptians, but not enough. Coupled with a concerted effort to halt population growth, investment in preparing young Egyptians—men *and* women—for life in the modern world presented the best path to future prosperity. As the example of India in the 1990s illustrates, the combination of market reforms that foster entrepreneurship and educational reforms that expand opportunity can produce results in a poor agricultural economy despite substantial outlays on national security. In Egypt, the attainment of higher levels of education, also associated with lower birth rates, might have carried the added benefit of obviating the more draconian components of a population control policy.

Did the unleashing of the Egyptian people's economic potential in the 1960s depend on political liberalization? Does it today? The example of India suggests the answer is yes. The experience of China, for the moment, suggests otherwise. The compatibility of market economics with dictatorship is, of course, one of the biggest questions confronting political scientists in the twenty-first century. We will not settle it here.

[13] Ṣādiq al-ʻAẓm, *al-Naqd al-dhātī baʻda al-hazīmah* (Beirut: Dār al-Ṭalīʻah, 1968).

Yet even if we set economic considerations aside, Nasser's greatest failing may well have been his failure to open up space for political participation. It was not just a question of creating a popular base for his rule (as Nasser repeatedly sought to do, from the Liberation Rally to the Arab Socialist Union), but of enabling genuinely participatory politics that would ensure the future of the regime and guide Egypt forward once the great leader left the stage. As Henry Kissinger has written, "statesmen who build lastingly transform the personal art of creation into institutions that can be maintained by an average standard of performance." Although his failures became apparent in his lifetime, Nasser's tragedy, like Bismarck's "was that he left a heritage of unassimilated greatness."[14] This was certainly true of Egypt's inefficient bureaucracy and armed services, which demanded reform whether or not Nasser's successors took the path of representative government. But it probably held true for the attainment of broader political participation as well. Would not the introduction of even a modicum of accountability—not to mention a representative parliament, an independent judiciary, and rule of law—have guided Egypt's rulers onto a course more conducive to the advancement of the national interest? The example of Turkey after 1950 demonstrates that it is possible—for a time, at least—to allow multiparty politics without forfeiting military control. In any event, from the vantage point of 2012, the continued exclusion of Egypt's population from the political process seems like a grave mistake.

Could a flesh-and-blood leader in Egypt of the 1960s have transformed this rough sketch into reality? If Nasser survived Egypt's humiliating defeat in 1967, there is little reason to doubt he would have survived the inauguration of a phase of moderation following the perceived triumph of 1956. A leader of Nasser's stature, in other words, had options after Suez. To be sure, the pursuit of such an inward-focused policy would have meant that the legitimacy of the regime came to rest on domestic performance, not foreign pyrotechnics. But as Stalin demonstrated in the 1920s and 1930s, "socialism in one country," in the hands of a determined and charismatic leadership, was a surprisingly viable approach even for the vanguard of international socialism.

How dramatically would such an inward turn have altered Egypt's destiny? Was there *any* way to forestall perhaps inevitable decline without oil? None of the structural factors at work in this story was wholly

[14] Henry Kissinger, "The White Revolutionary: Reflections on Bismarck," *Daedalus* 97, no. 3 (1968): 890.

immune to human agency. But they seem so difficult to surmount. One reason why it may be particularly difficult to imagine an alternative history for Egypt is the larger-than-life character of Gamal Abdel Nasser. Another leader might have chosen to step back from dreams of regional hegemony to focus on incremental development at home. But to act thus would have been to stage an improbable retreat from the soaring ambitions inherent in Nasserism.

✷ Bibliographical Note ✷

THE DECLASSIFICATION of non-Arab archival material—especially in the United States and the United Kindom—has produced the greatest rewards for students of Egyptian foreign policy in recent years. Documentation from the Kennedy and Johnson administrations benefits from the privileged position occupied by Washington in Egyptian eyes throughout the period under discussion, and from the singular perspective afforded by diplomatic representation in all three of the capitals most relevant to this study: Cairo, Ṣan'ā', and Riyadh. Yet it contains surprisingly little of interest to the military historian. British documents profit from the accumulated wisdom of more than a century of close involvement in Arab affairs and from the unique vantage point of Aden. However, the utility of British sources is diminished by the eviction of British diplomats from Yemen in the spring of 1963, which put an end to the paper trail streaming out of Republican Yemen, and by the subsequent deterioration of British-Egyptian relations, which led to a marked decline of access and intelligence in Cairo. Canadian sources also provide a valuable perspective, especially in the first year of the war, during which Ambassador Robert Ford ably represented Ottawa in Cairo.

The archives of the Israeli military were still closed for the post-Suez period at the time of writing. Although the Israelis lacked diplomatic representation in any of the Arab capitals relevant to this study, their intense interest in the conflict produced voluminous intelligence, valuable scraps of which have landed among the papers of the Ministry of Foreign Affairs available for consultation at the Israel State Archives in Jerusalem. Of even greater utility is the Arab Press Archive at the Dayan Center at Tel Aviv University, which houses perhaps the largest collection of modern Arab newspapers in the world. Also noteworthy is a collection of Egyptian military documents captured by the Israelis in 1967 and available for consultation at the Intelligence and Terrorism Information Center in Gelilot.

Since the foreign policy of Egypt during the Cold War is all but incomprehensible without equal attention to its Eastern and Western components, a major goal of the research effort underpinning this book has been to counterbalance the tendency to rely on Western diplomatic documents by tapping the enormous potential of sources from Eastern Europe, primarily in Russia and Germany. East German sources proved surprisingly accessible yet ultimately yielded little that was original or relevant to this study—a fact perhaps best explained by the remoteness of the conflict in Yemen from German preoccupations in Europe. Although Soviet sources proved much more valuable, access to Russian archival material remains spotty and is becoming more difficult. Moreover, Russia's declassification process, such as it is, has replicated the State Department's fixation on the Arab-Israeli conflict as the supposed primary fault line in the region. It is telling that the published documents pertaining to US-Egyptian relations during the Johnson administration are to be found in a volume titled "Arab-Israeli Dispute," while the most comprehensive set of declassified documents on Soviet-Egyptian relations is to be found in a two-volume edition titled *Blizhnovostochnyĭ konflikt* (the "Near East Conflict")—a misleading euphemism in Russian that signifies the same as its equivalent in English. In any event, the tremendous effort required to cull source material in Russia's current political environment is an exercise that produces rapidly diminishing returns.

The best scholarly treatment of the intervention in Arabic remains Aḥmad Yūsuf Aḥmad's classic study, *al-Dawr al-miṣrī fī al-Yaman, 1962–1967* (*The Egyptian Role in Yemen, 1962–1967*) (Cairo, 1981). Most Egyptian scholarship since Aḥmad's book appeared has been produced by veterans with a tendency to blur the boundaries between eyewitness testimony and historical analysis. The most important exemplars of this genre are Maḥmūd 'Ādil Aḥmad's *Dhikrayāt ḥarb al-Yaman, 1962–1967* (*Memoirs of the Yemen War*) (Cairo, 1992); *Shāhid 'alā ḥarb al-Yaman* (*Witness to the Yemen War*) (Cairo, 1984), by Egypt's former chief of military intelligence, Ṣalāḥ al-Dīn al-Ḥadīdī; *The Egyptian Policy in the Arab World: Intervention in Yemen, 1962–1967: Case Study* (Washington, DC, 1983), by Major Ali Abdel Rahman Rahmy; and *Azmat al-ummah al-'arabiyyah wa-thawrat al-Yaman* (*The Crisis of the Arab Nation and the Yemen Revolution*) (Cairo, 1983), by 'Abd al-Raḥmān al-Bayḍānī, a colorful Yemeni émigré who spent most of his life in Cairo. Bayḍānī subsequently published a modified version under the title *Miṣr wa-thawrat al-Yaman* (*Egypt and the Yemen Revolution*) (Cairo, 1993). Also noteworthy are *al-Zuhūr tudfanu fī al-Yaman* (*The Flowers Are Buried in Yemen*) (Cairo, 197?), a fictionalized account of the war by Wagīh Abū Dhikrī; and Aḥmad Ḥamrūsh's multivolume study of the Nasser era, *Qiṣṣat thawrat 23 yūliyū* (*The Story of the July 23rd Revolution*) (Cairo, 1974–), which includes an informative chapter on the intervention.

A number of Egyptian officials have addressed the intervention in their memoirs and historical treatises. Although it downplays the significance of the intervention, Muḥammad Ḥasanayn Haykal's massive three-volume study of Egypt's international relations during the Nasser era, *Ḥarb al-thalāthīn sanah* (*The Thirty-Year War*) (Cairo, 1988–90), is nevertheless indispensible for students of this period. So too is the memoir of Nasser's private secretary and close associate, Sāmī Sharaf. *Sanawāt wa-ayyām ma'a Gamāl 'Abd al-Nāṣir: Shahādat Sāmī Sharaf* (*Years and Days with Gamal Abdel Nasser: The Testimony of Sāmī Sharaf*) (Cairo, 2005–6) contains an especially original account of the origins of the intervention. *Mudhakkirāt Ṣalāḥ Naṣr* (*The Memoirs of Ṣalāḥ Naṣr*) (Cairo, 1999), written by Nasser's long-standing chief of intelligence, contains invaluable references to the intelligence aspects of the intervention and the logic of decision making at the pinnacle of the regime. Amīn Huwaydī, Egypt's minister of war in the latter half of 1967, offers insightful discussion of the origins and denouement of the intervention in his *Khamsūn 'āman min al-'awāṣif: Mā ra'aytuhu qultuh* (*Fifty Years of Storms: I Reported What I Saw*) (Cairo, 2002).

Little has been written about the military aspects of the war. One of the most important sources on Egyptian operations is the memoir of Egyptian Major General Ṣalāḥ al-Dīn al-Maḥrizī. *Al-Ṣamt al-ḥā'ir wa-thawrat al-Yaman* (*The Embarrassed Silence and the Yemen Revolution*) (Cairo, 1998) provides a fascinating glimpse into life on the battlefield from the perspective of a battalion commander. The memoirs of General 'Abd al-Mun'im Khalīl, *Ḥurūb Miṣr al-mu'āṣirah fī awrāq qā'id maydānī* (*The Wars of Contemporary Egypt in the Papers of a Field Commander*) (Cairo, 1990), include a valuable chapter on his experience as a field commander in Yemen. Two exceptions to the general lack of scholarly attention to the military dimension of the war are David Witty's "A Regular Army in Counterinsurgency Operations: Egypt in North Yemen, 1962–1967" (*The Journal of Military History*, 2001), which makes the most of the extant Arabic literature on the subject; and Kenneth Pollack's *Arabs at War: Military Effectiveness, 1948–1991* (Lincoln, 2002), which contains a chapter critiquing the Egyptian performance in Yemen. The story of British covert support for the Royalist war effort is told in Clive Jones, *Britain and the Yemen Civil War, 1962–1965: Ministers, Mercenaries, and Mandarins: Foreign Policy and the Limits of Covert Action* (Brighton, 2004);

and Duff Hart-Davis, *The War That Never Was: The True Story of the Men Who Fought Britain's Most Secret Battle* (London, 2011).

Outside Egypt, much of the literature in Arabic has naturally come from Yemen. The extensive Yemeni literature on the revolution and the civil war cannot adequately be discussed here. A superb bibliography is provided by Paul Dresch in *A History of Modern Yemen* (Cambridge, 2000), upon which I have relied more heavily than is apparent from the notes. Although Yemeni works on this period are indispensible sources of local color and flavor, much of the material is unreliable, suffers from the uncritical use of sources, and provides little insight on Egyptian policy. Among the most important Yemeni sources of relevance in the present context are 'Abd Allāh Juzaylān, *Muqaddimāt thawrat al-Yaman* (*Antecedents of the Yemen Revolution*) (Beirut, 1995); idem, *al-Tārīkh al-sirrī li-l-thawrah al-yamaniyyah: Min sanat 1956 ilā sanat 1962* (*The Secret History of the Yemeni Revolution, 1956–1962*) (Beirut, 1977); 'Abd al-Ghanī Muṭahhar, *Yawm wallada al-Yaman majdah: Dhikrayāt 'an thawrat sibtimbir sanat 1962* (*The Day Yemen Delivered Its Glory: Memoirs of the September 1962 Revolution*) (Cairo, 1984); Aḥmad Aḥmad Faraj, *Rijāl fī khanādiq al-difā' 'an al-thawrah* (*Men in the Trenches of Defense of the Revolution*) (Ṣan'ā', 1995); 'Abd Allāh'Abd al-Ilāh, *Naksat al-thawrah fī al-Yaman* (*The Setback of the Revolution in Yemen*) (Beirut, 1964); 'Abd al-Raḥīm 'Abd Allāh, *Mudhakkirāt 'Abd al-Raḥīm 'Abd Allāh* (*Memoirs of 'Abd al-Raḥīm 'Abd Allāh*) (Beirut, 1987); Fatḥī al-Dīb, *'Abd al-Nāṣir wa-ḥarakat al-taḥarrur al-yamanī* (*Abdel Nasser and the Yemeni Liberation Movement*) (Cairo, 1990).

Perhaps the best work on the subject in a language other than Arabic is a virtually unknown work in Hebrew by Yael Vered, an Israeli diplomat who followed the events in Yemen from her post in Paris. *Revolution and War in Yemen* (Tel Aviv, 1967) is a remarkable essay in contemporary history, based largely on rigorous scrutiny of the Arab press, which has stood up well to the test of time. In English, the classic accounts of two journalists remain relevant: Dana Adams Schmidt, *Yemen: The Unknown War* (New York, 1968), and Edgar O'Ballance, *War in the Yemen* (Hamden, 1971). It is a tribute to these two enterprising journalists—and a testimony to the poverty of scholarly understanding of the military aspects of the war—that students of the war continue to rely on their work for the description of battlefield developments. Schmidt's work in particular suffers from a distinct Royalist bias. But it is an invaluable source of fact and insight into reality on the ground in Yemen. Saeed Badeeb's *The Saudi-Egyptian Conflict over North Yemen, 1962–1970* (Boulder, 1986) presents a Saudi perspective on the war that is similarly unsympathetic to Egypt. Laura James's *Nasser at War: Arab Images of the Enemy* (Basingstoke, 2006) contains two insightful chapters on Yemen based on interviews with Egyptian participants and an extensive reading of the literature in Arabic. Also noteworthy is F. Gregory Gause's *Saudi Yemeni Relations: Domestic Structures and Foreign Influences* (New York, 1990), which contains a couple of useful chapters on the subject.

Some classic studies of modern Yemeni history that shed light on the civil war are John E. Peterson, *Yemen: The Search for a Modern State* (Baltimore, 1982); Robert W. Stookey, *Yemen: The Politics of the Yemen Arab Republic* (Boulder, CO, 1978); and Manfred W. Wenner, *Modern Yemen, 1918–1966* (Baltimore, 1967). Nasser's two major English biographers also include insightful chapters on Yemen: Robert Stephens, *Nasser: A Political Biography* (London, 1971); and Anthony Nutting, *Nasser* (New York, 1972). Similarly perceptive are the memoirs of former US ambassador to Egypt, John Badeau: *The Middle East Remembered* (Washington, DC, 1983).

Among the most useful articles on the war are Michael B. Bishku's "The Kennedy Administration, the U.N. and the Yemen Civil War," *Middle East Policy* 1, no. 4 (1992): 116–28; Richard E. Bissell's "Soviet Use of Proxies in the Third World: The Case of Yemen," *Soviet Studies* 30, no. 1 (1978): 87–106; Adeed Dawisha's "Perceptions, Decisions, and Consequences in Foreign Policy: The Egyptian Intervention in Yemen," *Political Studies* 25, no. 2 (1977): 201–26; his "Intervention in the Yemen: An Analysis of Egyptian Perceptions and Policies," *Middle East Journal* 29, no. 1 (1975): 47–63; Christopher Gandy's "A Mission to Yemen: August 1962–January 1963," *British Journal of Middle Eastern Studies* 25, no. 2 (1998): 247–74; Stanko Guldescu's "Yemen: The War and the Haradh Conference," *Review of Politics* 28, no. 3 (1966): 319–31; and Itamar Rabinovich's "The Embroilment," in Shimon Shamir's edited volume from 1978, *The Decline of Nasserism*, 218–28.

✷ Bibliography ✷

Archives

The Agency of the Federal Commissioner for the Stasi Records (BStU). Berlin, Germany.

Al-Ahrām Organization and Information Technology Center (ORITEC). Cairo, Egypt.

The Arab Press Archive of the Moshe Dayan Center (APA). Tel Aviv, Israel.

Archive of the Foreign Policy of the Russian Federation (AVPRF). Moscow, Russia.

Foundation Archives of Parties and Mass Organisations of the GDR (SAPMO). Berlin, Germany.

Government Archive of the Russian Government (GARF). Moscow, Russia.

Intelligence and Terrorism Information Center (ITIC). Gelilot, Israel.

Israel State Archives (ISA). Jerusalem, Israel.

Library and Archives Canada (LARC). Ottawa, Canada.

Lyndon Baines Johnson Presidential Library (LBJL). Austin, Texas, USA.

The National Archives (PRO). Kew, Surrey, United Kingdom.

The National Archives and Records Administration (NARA). College Park, Maryland, USA.

The Political Archive of the Foreign Office (PAAA). Berlin, Germany.

Russian Government Archive of Contemporary History (RGANI). Moscow, Russia.

Published Collections of Documents

British Broadcasting Corporation. *Summary of World Broadcasts* (SWB).

Fursenko, Aleksandr A., ed. *Prezidium TSK KPSS 1954–1964: Chernovye protokol'nye zapisi zasedanii, stenogrammy, postanovleniia: v 3 tomakh*. Moscow: ROSSPEN, 2004.

Al-Ḥusaynī, 'Abd Allāh, ed. *Mu'tamar Ḥaraḍ: Wathā'iq wa-maḥāḍir*. Beirut: Dār al-Kitāb al-Jadīd, 1966.

International Monetary Fund. *Balance of Payments Yearbook, 1962–66*.

Maẓhar, Sulaymān. *I'tirāfāt qādat ḥarb yūniyū: Nuṣūṣ shahādātihim amāma lajnat tasjīl tārīkh al-thawrah*. Cairo: Dār al-Ḥurriyyah, 1990.

Nasser, Gamal Abdel. *Wathā'iq 'Abd al-Nāṣr: Khuṭab, aḥādith, taṣrīḥāt*, 2 vols. Cairo: Markaz al-Dirāsāt al-Siyāsiyyah wa-l-Istrātijiyyah bi-l-Ahrām, 1973–.

Naumkin, Vitalii V., et al., eds. *Blizhno-vostochnyĭ konflikt: Iz dokumentov arkhiva vneshnei politiki Rossiskoi Federatsii*. 2 Vols. Moscow: Mezhdunarodnyi fond "Demokratiya," 2003.

United Arab Republic. *Majmūʻat khuṭab wa-taṣrīḥāt wa-bayānāt al-ra'īs Gamāl ʻAbd al-Nāṣir*. 5 Vols. Cairo: Maṣlaḥat al-Istiʻlāmāt, undated.
United Nations. *Treaty Series*. (New York): United Nations, 1947–.
United Nations Security Council. *Official Records*, 1962–66.
United States Department of State. *Foreign Relations of the United States* (*FRUS*).
USSR Ministry of Foreign Trade. *Vneshniaia Torgovlia SSSR: Statisticheskii sbornik, 1918–1966*. Moscow: Mezhdunarodnye Otnosheniia, 1967.
World Bank. *World Governance Indicators* (1996–2009). http://info.worldbank.org/governance/wgi/index.asp.

Newspapers and Periodicals in Arabic

al-Ahrām
al-Akhbār
Akhbār al-Yawm
Ākhir Sāʻah
al-Ayyām
al-Gumhūriyyah
al-Ḥawādith
al-Majallah
Majallat al-Quwwāt al-Bariyyah
Majallat al-Quwwāt al-Jawwiyyah
al-Muṣawwar
al-Quwwāt al-Musallaḥah
Rūz al-Yūsuf
al-Ṭalīʻah

Newspapers and Periodicals in European Languages

Kommunist
Krasnaia Zvezda
Kryl'ia Rodiny
Le Monde
New York Times
Novoe Vremia
Pravda
Izvestia
Time
The Times of London

Published Sources in Semitic Languages

Aḥmad, Aḥmad Yūsuf. *al-Dawr al-miṣrī fī al-Yaman (1962–1967)*. Cairo: al-Hay'ah al-Miṣriyyah al-ʻĀmmah li-l-Kitāb, 1981.

Aḥmad, Maḥmūd ʻĀdil. *Dhikrayāt ḥarb al-Yaman, 1962–1967*. Cairo: Maṭbaʻt al-Ukhuwwah, 1992.

ʻAlī, ʻAbd al-Munʻim Muḥammad. *Taṭawwur al-khadamāt al-ṣiḥḥiyyah bi-l-Yaman, 1962–1967*. Cairo, 1971.

ʻAwaḍ, Luwīs. *Aqniʻat al-nāṣiriyyah al-sabʻah: Munāqashat Tawfīq al-Ḥakīm wa-Muḥammad Ḥasanayn Haykal*. Beirut: Dār al-Qaḍāyā, [1975?].

Al-ʻAẓm, Ṣādiq. *al-Naqd al-dhātī baʻda al-hazīmah*. Beirut: Dār al-Ṭalīʻah, 1968.

Badrān, Shams al-Dīn. "Uʻlinu mas'ūliyyatī al-kāmilah ʻammā yusammā ... bi-l-taʻdhīb," al-Hawādith, September 2, 1977, 18–23.

Al-Baghdādī, ʻAbd al-Laṭīf. *Mudhakkirāt ʻAbd al-Laṭīf al-Baghdādī*. 2 Vols. Cairo: Al-Maktab al-Ḥadīth, 1977.

Al-Bayḍānī, ʻAbd al-Raḥmān. *Azmat al-ummah al-ʻarabiyyah wa thawrat al-Yaman*. Cairo: Author, 1983.

———. *Miṣr wa-thawrat al-Yaman*. Cairo: Dār al-Maʻārif, 1993.

Ben-Tzur, Avraham. *Soviet Factors and the Six Day War* (Hebrew). Tel-Aviv: Sifriyat poʻalim, 1975.

Abū Dhikrī, Wagīh. *al-Zuhūr tudfanu fī al-Yaman*. Cairo: Dār al-Waṭan al-ʻArabī, 1977.

Fāḍil, Samīr. *Kuntu qāḍiyan li-ḥādith al-minaṣṣah: Mudhakkirāt qāḍin ʻaskarī min ḥarb al-Yaman ilā ightiyāl al-Sādāt*. Cairo: Dār Sfinks, 1993.

Fawzī, Muḥammad. *Ḥarb al-thalāth sanawāt, 1967/1970: Mudhakkirāt al-farīq awwal Muḥammad Fawzī, wazīr al-ḥarbiyyah al-asbaq*. Cairo: Dār al-Mustaqbal al-ʻArabī, 1984–1986.

Faraj, Aḥmad Aḥmad. *Rijāl fī khanādiq al-difāʻ ʻan al-thawrah*. Ṣanʻā', 1995.

Al-Gamasī, Muḥammad ʻAbd al-Ghanī. *Mudhakkirāt al-Gamasī: Ḥarb uktūbir 1973*. Paris: al-Manshūrāt al-Sharqiyyah, 1990.

Gawhar, Sāmī. *al-Mawtā yatakallamūn*. Cairo: al-Maktab al-Miṣrī al-Ḥadīth, 1977.

———. *al-Ṣāmitūn yatakallamūn*. Cairo: al-Maktab al-Miṣrī al-Ḥadīth, 1975.

Ghālib, Murād. *Maʻa ʻAbd al-Nāṣir wa-l-Sādāt: Sanawāt al-intiṣār wa-ayyām al-miḥan: Mudhakkirāt Murād Ghālib*. Cairo: Markaz al-Ahrām li-l-Tarjamah wa-l-Nashr, 2001.

Gluska, Ami. *Eshkol, Give the Order! The IDF and the Government of Israel on the Road to the Six Day War, 1963–1967* (Hebrew). Tel Aviv: Maʻarakhot, 2004.

Ḥabīb, Ṭāriq. *Milaffāt thawrat yūliyū: Shahādāt 122 min ṣunnāʻihā wa-muʻāṣirīhā*. Cairo: Markaz al-Ahrām li-l-Tarjamah wa-l-Nashr, 1997.

Al-Ḥadīdī, Ṣalāḥ al-Dīn. *Shāhid ʻalā ḥarb al-Yaman*. Cairo: Maktabat Madbūlī, 1984.

———. *Shāhid ʻalā ḥarb 67*. Cairo: Dār al-Shurūq, 1974.

Al-Ḥakīm, Tawfīq. *ʻAwdat al-waʻī*. Beirut: Dār al-Shurūq, 1974.

———. *Bank al-qalaq*. Cairo: Dār al-Maʻārif, 1966.

———. *Kull shay' fī maḥallih*. In *5 Egyptian-Arabic One Act Plays*, edited by Karl Prasse, 36–61. Copenhagen: Museum Tusculanum, 2000.

Ḥamrūsh, Aḥmad. *Qiṣṣat thawrat 23 yūliyū*. 5 Vols. Cairo: Maktabat Madbūlī, 1983–84.

Haykal, Muḥammad Ḥasanayn. *Sanawāt al-Ghalayān*. Cairo: al-Ahrām, 1988.

———. *1967: Al-Infijār*. Cairo: al-Ahrām, 1990.

Huwaydī, Amīn. *Khamsūn 'āman min al-'awāṣif: Mā ra'aytuhu qultuh*. Cairo: Markaz al-Ahrām li-l-Tarjamah wa-l-Nashr, 2002.

———. *Ḥurūb 'Abd al-Nāṣir*. Beirut: Dār al-Ṭalī'ah, 1977.

Idrīs, Yūsuf. *al-Mukhaṭṭaṭīn*. al-Fajjālah: Maktabat Miṣr, 196?.

Imām, 'Abd Allāh. *'Alī Ṣabrī yatadhakkar*. Beirut: Dār al-Waḥdah, 1988.

———. *al-Farīq Muḥammad Fawzī: al-Naksah, al-istinzāf, al-sijn*. Dār al-Khayyāl, 2001.

———. *al-Iftirā' 'alā thawrat yūliyū: Hazīmat yūniyū, mu'āmarat al-mushīr 'Āmir wa-intiḥāruh, al-ṣulḥ ma'a Isrā'īl*. Cairo: Dār al-Khayyāl, 2003.

———. *Nāṣir wa-'Āmir*. Cairo: Rūz al-Yūsuf, 1985.

———. *Ṣalāḥ Naṣr yatadhakkar: al-Thawrah, al-mukhābarāt, al-naksah*. Cairo: Dār al-Khayyāl, 1999.

al-Imām, Ṣalāḥ. *Ḥusayn al-Shāfi'ī wa-asrār thawrat yūlīyū wa-ḥukm al-Sādāt*. Cairo: Maktab Ūzīrīs li-l-Kutub wa-l-Majallāt, 1993.

Juzaylān, 'Abdullāh. *Muqaddimāt thawrat al-Yaman 26 sibtimbir 1962*. Beirut: Manshūrāt al-'Aṣr al-Ḥadīth, 1995.

———. *al-Tārīkh al-sirrī li-l-thawrah al-Yamaniyyah: Min sanat 1956 ilā sanat 1962*. Beirut: Dār al-'Awdah, 1977.

Khalīl, 'Abd al-Mun'im. *Ḥurūb Miṣr al-mu'āṣirah fī awrāq qā'id maydānī: 1939–45, 1948–49, 1956, 1962–67, 1967, 1968–70, 1973*. Cairo: Dār al-Mustaqbal al-'Arabī, 1990.

Kishk, Muḥammad Galāl. *Al-Qawmiyyah wa-l-ghazw al-fikrī*. Beirut: Dār al-Irshād, 1970.

Maḥfūẓ, Nagīb. *al-Karnak*. Cairo: Maktabat Miṣr, 1974.

———. *Mīrāmār*. Cairo: Maktabat Miṣr, 1967.

———. *Thartharah fawqa al-Nīl*. al-Fajjālah: Maktabat Miṣr, 1965.

Miṣrī, Aḥmad 'Aṭiyyah. *Tajribat al-Yaman al-dīmuqrāṭiyyah, 1950–1972*. 1974.

Al-Maḥrizī, Ṣalāḥ al-Dīn. *al-Ṣamt al-ḥā'ir wa-thawrat al-Yaman*. Cairo, 1998.

Murtagī, 'Abd al-Muḥsin Kāmil. *al-Farīq Murtagī yarwī al-ḥaqā'iq*. Cairo: Dār al-Waṭan al-'Arabī, 1976.

Muṭahhar, 'Abd al-Ghanī. *Yawm walada al-Yaman majdah: Dhikrayāt 'an thawrat sibtimbir sanat 1962*. Cairo: Dār al-Bāz, 1984.

Nājī, Sulṭān. *al-Tārīkh al-'askarī li-l-Yaman 1839–1967*. Beirut: Dār al-'Awdah, 1988.

Naṣr, Ṣalāḥ. *Mudhakkirāt Ṣalāḥ Naṣr*. 3 Vols. Cairo: Dār al-Khayyāl, 1999.

Peresypkin, Oleg G. *al-Yaman wa-l-yamaniyyūn fī dhikrayāt diblūmāsī Rūsī*. Beirut: Dār wa-Maktabat al-Hilāl, 2005.

Rabinovich, Itamar. "The Embroilment" (Hebrew). In *The Decline of Nasserism*, edited by Shimon Shamir, 218–28.

Riyāḍ, Maḥmūd. *Mudhakkirāt Maḥmūd Riyāḍ, 1948–1978*. 3 Vols. Cairo: Dār al-Mustaqbal al-ʿArabī, 1986.

al-Sādāt, Anwar. *al-Baḥth ʿan al-dhāt: Qiṣṣat ḥayātī*. Cairo: al-Maktab al-Miṣrī al-Ḥadīth, 1978.

Sela, Avraham. *Unity within Conflict in the Inter-Arab System: The Arab Summit Conferences, 1964–1982* (Hebrew). Jerusalem: Magnes Press, 1982.

Al-Shahārī, Muḥammad ʿAlī. *Ṭarīq al-thawrah al-yamaniyyah*. Cairo: Dār al-Hilāl, 1966.

———. *al-Yaman: al-Thawrah fī al-janūb wa-l-intikāsah fī al-shimāl*. Beirut: Dār Ibn Khaldūn, 1972.

Shamir, Shimon, ed. *The Decline of Nasserism, 1965–1970: The Fall of a Messianic Movement* (Hebrew). Tel-Aviv: Mifʿalim universiṭaʾiyim le-hotsaʾah la-or, 1978.

Sharaf, Sāmī. *Sanawāt wa-ayyām maʿ Gamāl ʿAbd al-Nāṣir: Shahādat Sāmī Sharaf*. 2 Vols. Cairo: Dār al-Fursān li-l-Nashr, 2005–6.

Sharaf al-Dīn, Aḥmad Ḥusayn. *al-Yaman ʿabra al-tārīkh: Dirāsah jughrāfiyyah, tārīkhiyyah siyāsiyyah shāmilah*. Cairo: Maṭbaʿat al-Sunnah al-Muḥammadiyyah, 1964.

Sheffy, Yigal. *Early Warning on Trial: The "Rotem" Affair and Israel's National Security Concept, 1957–1960* (Hebrew). Tel Aviv: Maʿarakhot, 2008.

Shemesh, Moshe. *From the Nakbah to the Naksah: The Arab-Israeli Conflict and the Palestinian National Problem, 1957–1967: Nasser's Road to the Six Day War* (Hebrew). Sdeh Boqer: Makhon Ben Gurion, 2004.

ʿUkāshah, Tharwat. *Mudhakkirātī fī al-siyāsah wa-l-thaqāfah*. 2 Vols. Cairo: Dār al-Hilāl, 1990.

Vered, Yael. *Revolution and War in Yemen* (Hebrew). Tel Aviv: ʿAm ʿOved, 1967.

Published Sources in European Languages

Aburish, Saïd. *Nasser: The Last Arab*. London: Duckworth, 2004.

Ahlberg, Kristin. "'Machiavelli with a Heart': The Johnson Administration's Food for Peace Program in India, 1965–1966." *Diplomatic History* 31, no. 4 (2007): 665–701.

Ahmed, Akbar. *Resistance and Control in Pakistan*. London: Routledge, 2004.

Ajami, Fouad. *The Arab Predicament: Arab Political Thought and Practice since 1967*. Cambridge and New York: Cambridge University Press, 1981.

Aliboni, Roberto. *The Red Sea Region: Local Actors and Superpowers*. Syracuse, NY: Syracuse University Press, 1985.

Almaney, A. "Government Control of the Press in the United Arab Republic, 1952–1970." *Journalism Quarterly* 49 (1972): 344–47.

Anderson, Richard D., Jr. *The Mitrokhin Archive II: The KGB and the World*. London: Allen Lane, 2005.

———. *Public Politics in an Authoritarian State: Making Foreign Policy during the Brezhnev Years*. Ithaca, NY: Cornell University Press, 1993.

Arbatov, Georgi A. *The System: An Insider's Life in Soviet Politics*. New York: Times Books, 1992.

El Attar, Mohamed Said. *Le sous-développement économique et social du Yemen: Perspectives de la révolution yéménite*. Algiers: Editions Tiers-Monde, 1964.

Auda, Mohamed. "Nasser: The Revolution Continues." *Arab Papers*, no. 8. London: Arab Research Centre, 1981, 19–32.

Bach, Quintin V. S. *Soviet Aid to the Third World: The Facts and Figures*. Sussex: The Book Guild, 2003.

Bacon, Edwin, and Mark Sandle, eds. *Brezhnev Reconsidered*. New York: Palgrave Macmillan, 2002.

Badeau, John S. *The American Approach to the Arab World*. New York: The Council on Foreign Relations, 1968.

———. *The Middle East Remembered*. Washington, DC: Middle East Institute, 1983.

———. *The Reminiscences of John Badeau*. New York: Oral History Research Office, Columbia University, 1979.

Badeeb, Saeed M. *The Saudi-Egyptian Conflict over North Yemen, 1962–1970*. Boulder, CO: Westview Press, 1986.

Baker, Raymond W. *Egypt's Uncertain Revolution under Nasser and Sadat*. Cambridge, MA: Harvard University Press, 1978.

Baldry, John. "Al-Yaman and the Turkish Occupation, 1849–1914," *Arabica* 23, no. 2 (1976): 156–96.

Balfour-Paul, Glen. *The End of Empire in the Middle East*. Cambridge: Cambridge University Press, 1991.

Bar-Joseph, Uri. "Rotem: The Forgotten Crisis on the Road to the 1967 War." *Journal of Contemporary History* 31, no. 3 (1996): 547–66.

Barnett, Michael N. *Confronting the Costs of War: Military Power, State, and Society in Egypt and Israel*. Princeton, NJ: Princeton University Press, 1992.

———. *Dialogues in Arab Politics: Negotiations in Regional Order*. New York: Columbia University Press, 1998.

Bass, Warren. *Support Any Friend: Kennedy's Middle East and the Making of the U.S.-Israel Alliance*. New York: Oxford University Press, 2003.

Bausin, Lev Alekseevich. *Spetssluzhby mira na Blizhnem Vostoke*. Moscow: Olma-Press, 2001.

Beattie, Kirk. *Egypt during the Nasser Years: Ideology, Politics, and Civil Society*. Boulder, CO: Westview Press, 1994.

Be'eri, Eliezer. *Army Officers in Arab Politics and Society*. New York: Praeger, 1970.

Beinin, Joel. "The Communist Movement and Nationalist Political Discourse in Nasirist Egypt." *Middle East Journal* 41, no. 4 (1987): 568–84.

Beliaev, I. P., and E. M. Primakov. *Egipet: Vremia prezidenta Nasera*. Moscow: Mysl', 1974.

Bidwell, Robin L. *The Two Yemens*. Boulder, CO: Westview Press, 1983.

Binder, Leonard. *In a Moment of Enthusiasm: Political Power and the Second Stratum in Egypt*. Chicago: University of Chicago Press, 1978.

Bishku, Michael B. "The Kennedy Administration, the U.N. and the Yemen Civil War." *Middle East Policy* no. 4 (1992): 116–28.

Bissell, Richard E. "Soviet Use of Proxies in the Third World: The Case of Yemen." *Soviet Studies* 30, no. 1 (January 1978): 87–106.

Blasius, Rainer A. "'Völkerfreundschaft' am Nil: Ägypten und die DDR im Februar 1965." *Vierteljahrshefte für Zeitgeschichte* 46, no. 4 (1998): 747–805.

Bohlen, Charles. *Witness to History, 1929–1969*. New York: Norton, 1973.

Bower, Tom. *The Perfect English Spy: Sir Dick White and the Secret War, 1935–1990*. New York: St. Martin's Press, 1995.

Breslauer, George W. *Khrushchev and Brezhnev as Leaders*. London: Allen and Unwin, 1982.

Brooker, Paul. *Defiant Dictatorships: Communist and Middle-Eastern Dictatorships in a Democratic Age*. Basingstoke: Macmillan, 1997.

———. *Non-Democratic Regimes: Theory, Government, and Politics*. New York: St. Martin's Press, 2000.

Browers, Michaelle L. *Political Ideology in the Arab World: Accommodation and Transformation*. New York: Cambridge University Press, 2009.

Brown, L. Carl, ed. *Diplomacy in the Middle East: The International Relations of Regional and Outside Powers*. New York: I. B. Tauris, 2001.

———. *International Politics and the Middle East: Old Rules, Dangerous Game*. Princeton, NJ: Princeton University Press, 1984.

Brutents, Karen N. *Tridtsat' let na staroi ploshchadi*. Moscow: Mezhdunarodnye Otnoshenia, 1996.

Burlatski Fedor. *Khrushchev and the First Russian Spring*. London: Weidenfeld and Nicolson, 1991.

Burnett, John Howard, Jr. *Soviet Egyptian Relations during the Khrushchev Era: A Study in Soviet Foreign Policy*. Ann Arbor: University Microfilms, 1967.

Burns, William J. *Economic Aid and American Policy toward Egypt, 1955–1981*. Albany: State University of New York Press, 1985.

Burrowes, Robert. *The Yemen Arab Republic: The Politics of Development, 1962–1986*. Boulder, CO: Westview Press, 1987.

Clodfelter, Michael. *Warfare and Armed Conflicts: A Statistical Reference to Casualty and Other Figures, 1500–2000*. Jefferson, NC: McFarland, 2002.

Connelly, Michael. *Fatal Misconception: The Struggle to Control World Population*. Cambridge, MA: Belknap Press of Harvard University Press, 2008.

Cooper, Johnny, with Anthony Kemp. *One of the Originals: The Story of a Founding Member of the SAS*. London: Pan Books, 1991.

Cooper, Mark. "The Demilitarization of the Egyptian Cabinet." *International Journal of Middle Eastern Studies* 14, no. 2 (1982): 203–25.

Copeland, Miles. *The Game of Nations: The Amorality of Power Politics*. London: Weidenfeld and Nicolson, 1969.

Dannehl, Charles R. *Politics, Trade, and Development: Soviet Economic Aid to the Non-Communist Third World, 1955–89*. Aldershot: Dartmouth, 1995.

Davis, Eric. "Ideology, Social Class and Islamic Radicalism in Modern Egypt." In *From Nationalism to Revolutionary Islam*, edited by Said Amir Arjomand, 134–57. Albany: State University of New York Press, 1984.

Dawisha, Adeed. *Arab Nationalism in the Twentieth Century: From Triumph to Despair*. Princeton, NJ: Princeton University Press, 2003.

———. *Egypt in the Arab World: The Elements of Foreign Policy*. London: Macmillan, 1976.

———. "Intervention in the Yemen: An Analysis of Egyptian Perceptions and Policies." *Middle East Journal* 29, no. 1 (1975): 47–63.

———. "Perceptions, Decisions, and Consequences in Foreign Policy: The Egyptian Intervention in Yemen." *Political Studies* 25, no. 2 (1977): 201–26.

Dawisha, Karen. *Soviet Foreign Policy towards Egypt*. London: Macmillan, 1979.

Dawn, C. Ernest. "The Remilitarization of Sinai, May 1967." *Journal of Contemporary History* 3, no. 3 (1968): 201–24.

Deffarge, Claude, and Gordian Troeller. *Yemen 62-69: De la révolution sauvage à la trêve des guerriers*. Paris: Robert Laffont, 1969.

Dekmejian, R. Hrair. *Egypt under Nasir: A Study in Political Dynamics*. London: University of London Press, 1971.

Dobrynin, Anatoly F. *In Confidence: Moscow's Ambassador to America's Six Cold War Presidents (1962–1986)*. New York: Random House, 1995.

Doran, Michael S. "Egypt: Pan-Arabism in Historical Context." In *Diplomacy in the Middle East*, edited by L. Carl Brown, 97–120.

———. *Pan-Arabism before Nasser: Egyptian Power Politics and the Palestine Question*. New York: Oxford University Press, 1999.

Dragnich, George S. *The Soviet Union's Quest for Access to Naval Facilities in Egypt Prior to the June War of 1967*. Arlington, VA: Center for Naval Analysis, [1974].

Dresch, Paul. *A History of Modern Yemen*. Cambridge: Cambridge University Press, 2000.

———. *Tribes, Government, and History in Yemen*. New York: Oxford University Press, 1989.

Eilts, Hermann F. "Saudi Arabia's Foreign Policy." In *Diplomacy in the Middle East*, edited by L. Carl Brown, 219–44.

d'Encausse, Helene Carrere. *La politique sovietique au Moyen-Orient, 1955–1975*. Paris: Presses de la Fondation nationale des sciences politiques, 1975.

Fain, W. Taylor. "Unfortunate Arabia: The United States, Great Britain and Yemen, 1955–1963." *Diplomacy & Statecraft* 12, no. 2 (2001): 125–52.

Farah, Caesar. *The Sultan's Yemen: Nineteenth-Century Challenges to Ottoman Rule*. London: I. B. Tauris, 2002.

Farid, Abdel Magid. *Nasser: The Final Years*. Reading: Ithaca Press, 1994.

Ferris, Jesse. "Egypt, the Cold War, and the Civil War in Yemen, 1962–1966." PhD diss., Princeton University, 2008.

———."Guns for Cotton? Aid, Trade, and the Soviet Quest for Base Rights in Egypt, 1964–1966." *Journal of Cold War Studies* 13, no. 2 (2011): 4–38.

———. "Soviet Support for Egypt's Intervention in Yemen, 1962–1963." *Journal of Cold War Studies* 10, no. 4 (2008): 5–36.

Friedman, Jeremy. "Soviet Policy in the Developing World and the Chinese Challenge in the 1960s." *Cold War History* 10, no. 2 (2010): 247–72.

Fursenko, Aleksandr A., and Timothy Naftali. *Khrushchev's Cold War: The Inside Story of an American Adversary*. New York: Norton, 2006.

———. *One Hell of a Gamble: Khrushchev, Castro, and Kennedy, 1958–1964*. New York: W. W. Norton, 1997.

Gaddis, John Lewis. *We Now Know: Rethinking Cold War History*. New York: Oxford University Press, 1994.

Galeotti, Mark. *Afghanistan: The Soviet Union's Last War*. London: Frank Cass, 1995.

Galula, David. *Counterinsurgency Warfare: Theory and Practice*. New York: Praeger, 1964.

Gandy, Christopher. "A Mission to Yemen: August 1962–January 1963." *British Journal of Middle Eastern Studies* 25, no. 2 (1998): 247–74.

Gat, Moshe. "Nasser and the Six Day War, 5 June 1967: A Premeditated Strategy or an Inexorable Drift to War." *Israel Affairs* 11, no. 4 (2005): 608–35.

Gause, F. Gregory III. *Saudi-Yemeni Relations: Domestic Structures and Foreign Influences*. New York: Columbia University Press, 1990.

Gerges, Fawaz A. *The Superpowers and the Middle East: Regional and International Politics, 1955–1967*. Boulder, CO: Westview Press, 1994.

Gershoni, Israel, and James Jankowski, eds. *Rethinking Nationalism in the Middle East*. New York: Columbia University Press, 1997.

Ghalioun, Burhan. "The Persistence of Arab Authoritarianism." *Journal of Democracy* 15, no. 4 (2004): 126–32.

Ginat, Rami. *Egypt's Incomplete Revolution: Lutfi al-Khuli and Nasser's Socialism in the 1960s*. London: Frank Cass, 1997.

———. *The Soviet Union and Egypt, 1945–1955*. London: Frank Cass, 1993.

———."The Soviet Union and the Syrian Ba'th Regime." *Middle Eastern Studies* 36, no. 2 (2000): 150–71.

Ginor, Isabella. "The Cold War's Longest Cover-Up: How and Why the USSR Instigated the 1967 War." *MERIA* 7, no. 3 (2003): 31–59.

Ginor, Isabella, and Gideon Remez. *Foxbats over Dimona: The Soviets' Nuclear Gamble in the Six Day War*. New Haven, CT: Yale University Press, 2007.

Glassman, Jon D. *Arms for the Arabs: The Soviet Union and War in the Middle East*. Baltimore: Johns Hopkins University Press, 1975.

Golan, Galia. "The Soviet Union and the Outbreak of the June 1967 Six-Day War." *Journal of Cold War Studies* 8, no. 1 (2006): 3–19.

Goldman, Marshall I. *Soviet Foreign Aid*. New York: Praeger, 1967.

Gordon, Joel. *Nasser: Hero of the Arab Nation*. Oxford: Oneworld Publications, 2006.

———. *Nasser's Blessed Movement: Egypt's Free Officers and the July Revolution*. New York: Oxford, 1992.

Gray, William Glenn. *Germany's Cold War: The Global Campaign to Isolate East Germany, 1949-1969*. Chapel Hill: University of North Carolina Press, 2003.

Griffiths, Franklyn. "Forward Deployment and Foreign Policy." In *Soviet Naval Developments: Capability and Context*, edited by Michael MccGwire, 9–15. New York: Praeger, 1973.

Guldescu, Stanko. "Yemen: The War and the Haradh Conference." *Review of Politics* 28, no. 3 (1966): 319–31.

Hansen, Bent, and Karim Nashashibi. *Foreign Trade Regimes and Economic Development: Egypt*. New York: Columbia University Press, 1975.

Hart, Parker T. *Saudi Arabia and the United States: Birth of A Security Partnership*. Bloomington: Indiana University Press, 1998.

Hart-Davis, Duff. *The War That Never Was: The True Story of the Men Who Fought Britain's Most Secret Battle*. London: Century, 2011.

Hassouna, Hussein A. *The League of Arab States and Regional Disputes: A Study of Middle Eastern Conflicts*. Dobbs Ferry, NY: Oceana Publications, 1975.

Haykal, Muḥammad [Mohamed Heikal]. *Sphinx and Commissar: The Rise and Fall of Soviet Influence in the Middle East*. New York: Harper and Row, 1978.

Herrick, Robert W. *Soviet Naval Doctrine and Policy, 1956–1986*. Lewiston, NY: Edwin Mellen Press, 2003.

Higgins, Rosalyn. *United Nations Peacekeeping, 1946–1967: Documents and Commentary*. London: Oxford University Press, 1969.

Hoe, Alan. *David Stirling: The Authorised Biography of the Founder of the SAS*. London: Little, Brown, 1992.

Horn, Carl von. *Soldiering for Peace*. New York: David McKay, 1967.

Hudson, Michael. *Arab Politics: The Search for Legitimacy*. New Haven, CT: Yale University Press, 1977.

Humphreys, R. Stephen. *Between Memory and Desire: The Middle East in a Troubled Age*. Berkeley: University of California Press, 1999.

El Hussini, Mohrez M. *Soviet-Egyptian Relations, 1945–85*. New York: St. Martin's Press, 1987.

Iakubovich, Nicolai. "An-12: Sorok let v stroiu." *Kryl'ia Rodiny*, no. 3, 1997.

Ikram, Khalid. *Egypt: Economic Management in a Period of Transition*. Baltimore: Johns Hopkins University Press, 1980.

———. *The Egyptian Economy, 1952–2000: Performance, Policies, and Issues*. New York: Routledge, 2006.

Iskander, Mohammed A. "Vliyanie Egipta na vnutropoliticheskoe razvitie Iemena v 60-e gody XX veka." Diss., Moscow, 2001.

James, Laura. *Nasser at War: Arab Images of the Enemy*. Basingstoke: Palgrave Macmillan, 2006.

Jankowski, James. *Nasser's Egypt, Arab Nationalism, and the United Arab Republic*. Boulder, CO: Lynne Rienner Publishers, 2001.

Johnson, Lyndon B. *The Vantage Point: Perspectives of the Presidency, 1963–1969*. New York: Holt, Rinehart and Winston, 1971.

Jones, Clive. *Britain and the Yemen Civil War, 1962–1965: Ministers, Mercenaries, and Mandarins: Foreign Policy and the Limits of Covert Action*. Brighton: Sussex Academic Press, 2004.

Kapitanets, Ivan M. *Bitva za mirovoi okean v "kholodnoi" i budushchikh voinakh*. Moscow: Veche, 2002.

———. *Na sluzhbe okeanskomu flotu 1946–1992: Zapiski komanduiuschego dvumia flotami*. Moscow: Andreevskii Flag, 2000.

Karsh, Efraim. *The Cautious Bear: Soviet Military Engagement in Middle East Wars in the post-1967 Era*. Boulder, CO: Westview Press, 1985.

Katz, Mark N. *Russia and Arabia*. Baltimore: Johns Hopkins University Press, 1986.

Katz, Mark N., ed. *The USSR and Marxist Revolutions in the Third World*. Cambridge: Cambridge University Press, 1990.

Kedourie. Elie. *The Chatham House Version and Other Middle Eastern Studies*. New York: Praeger, 1970.

———. *Politics in the Middle East*. New York: Oxford University Press, 1992.

Kerr, Malcolm H. *The Arab Cold War: Gamal 'Abd al-Nasir and His Rivals, 1958–1970*. Oxford: Oxford University Press, 1971.

———. "'Coming to Terms with Nasser': Attempts and Failures." *International Affairs* 43, no. 1 (1967): 65–84.

Khrushchev, Nikita S. *N. S. Khrushchev: Vospominania—vremia, liudi, vlast'*. 4 Vols. Moscow: Moskovskie novosti, 1999.

Kirpichenko, Vadim A. *Iz arkhiva razvedchika*. Moscow: Mezhdunarodnye Otnoshenia, 1993.

Kissinger, Henry. *A World Restored: Metternich, Castlereagh, and the Problems of Peace, 1812–1822*. Boston: Houghton Mifflin, 1957.

———. "The White Revolutionary: Reflections on Bismarck." *Daedalus* 97, no. 3 (1968): 888-924.

Kodyri, Habibulla. *Iemensko-Egipetskie vpechatlenia* (Uzbek). Tashkent, 1967.

Kornienko, Gregorii. *Kholodnaia voina: Svidetel'stvo ee uchastnika*. Moscow: Olma Press, 2001.

Kostiner, Joseph. *The Struggle for South Yemen*. London: Croom Helm, 1984.

Krakhmalov, Sergei Petrovich. *Zapiski voennogo attashe: Iran, Egipet, Iran, Afganistan*. Moscow: Russkaya Razvedka, 2000.

Kramer, Mark. "The Role of the CPSU International Department in Soviet Foreign Relations and National Security Policy." *Soviet Studies* 42, no. 3 (1990): 429–46.

Lacouture, Jean. *Nasser*. Translated by Daniel Hofstadter. New York: Knopf, 1973.

Laqueur, Walter. *The Road to War 1967: The Origins of the Arab-Israeli Conflict*. London: Weidenfeld and Nicolson, 1969.

———. *The Struggle for the Middle East: The Soviet Union and the Middle East, 1958–70*. Harmondsworth: Penguin, 1972.

Laron, Guy. "Playing with Fire: The Soviet-Syrian-Israeli Triangle, 1965–1967." *Cold War History* 10, no. 2 (2010): 163–84.

———. "Stepping Back from the Third World: Soviet Policy toward the United Arab Republic, 1965–1967." *Journal of Cold War Studies* 12, no. 4 (2010): 99–118.

Lavrenov, Sergei I. *Sovetskii Soiuz v lokal'nykh voinakh i konfliktakh*. Moscow: Astrel', 2003.

Lavy, George. *Germany and Israel: Moral Debt and National Interest*. London: Frank Cass, 1996.

Lawson, Fred H. *Why Syria Goes to War: Thirty Years of Confrontation*. Ithaca, NY: Cornell University Press, 1996.

Little, Tom. *South Arabia: Arena of Conflict*. London: Pall Mall, 1968.

Mabro, Robert. *The Egyptian Economy, 1952–1972*. Oxford: Clarendon Press, 1974.

———. "Egypt's Economic Relations with the Socialist Countries." *World Development* 3, no. 5 (1975): 299–313.

Macro, Eric. *Yemen and the Western World, since 1571*. New York: Praeger, 1968.

Mahr, Horst. *Die Rolle Ägyptens in der amerikanischen und sowjetischen Aussenpolitik: Von der Suez-Krise 1956 bis zum Sechs-Tage-Krieg 1967: Exkurs, Sadats Umkehrung derAllianzen 1974*. Baden-Baden: Nomos, 1993.

Mansfield, Peter. *Nasser*. London: Methuen, 1969.

Mastny, Vojtech. *The Cold War and Soviet Insecurity*. New York: Oxford University Press, 1996.

McGwire, Michael, ed. *Soviet Naval Developments: Capability and Context*. New York: Praeger, 1973.

Menon, Rajan. *Soviet Power and the Third World*. New Haven, CT: Yale University Press, 1986.

Montefiore, Simon Sebag. *Stalin: The Court of the Red Tsar*. New York: Vintage Books, 2005.

Morozov, Boris. "The Outbreak of the June 1967 War in Light of Soviet Documentation." In *The Soviet Union and the June 1967 Six Day War*, edited by Yaacov Ro'i and Boris Morozov, 43–64.

Naumkin, Vitalii V. *Natsional'nyi Front v bor'be za nezavisimost' Iuzhnogo Iemena i natsional'nuiu demokratiiu, 1963–1969*. Moscow: Nauka, 1980.

———. *Red Wolves of Yemen: The Struggle for Independence*. London: Oleander, 2004.

Nordeen, Lon O., and David Nicolle. *Phoenix over the Nile: A History of Egyptian Air Power, 1932–1994*. Washington, DC: Smithsonian Institution Press, 1996.

Nutting, Anthony. *Nasser*. New York: Dutton, 1972.

O'Ballance, Edgar. *War in the Yemen*. Hamden: Archon Books, 1971.

Oren, Michael B. *Six Days of War: June 1967 and the Making of the Modern Middle East*. New York: Oxford University Press, 2002.

Page, Stephen. *The Soviet Union and the Yemens: Influence on Asymmetrical Relationships*. New York: Praeger, 1985.

———. *The USSR and Arabia: The Development of Soviet Policies and Attitudes towards the Countries of the Arabian Peninsula, 1955–1970*. London: Central Asian Research Centre, Canadian Institute of International Affairs, 1971.

Parker, Richard B. *The Politics of Miscalculation in the Middle East*. Bloomington: Indiana University Press, 1993.

———. "The Six Day War: Some Mysteries Explored." *Middle East Journal* 46, no. 2 (1992): 177–97.

———. "The Six Day War: Whose Conspiracy?" *Journal of Palestine Studies* 21, no. 4 (1992): 5–21.

Parker, Richard B., ed. *The Six Day War: A Retrospective*. Gainesville: University Press of Florida, 1996.

Peterson, John E. *Yemen: The Search for a Modern State*. Baltimore: Johns Hopkins University Press, 1982.

Podeh, Elie. *The Decline of Arab Unity: The Rise and Fall of the United Arab Republic*. Brighton: Sussex Academic Press, 1999.

———. "Ending an Age-Old Rivalry: The Rapprochement between the Hashemites and the Saudis, 1956–1958." In *The Hashemites in the Modern Arab World: Essays in Honour of the Late Professor Uriel Dann*, edited by Asher Susser and Aryeh Shmuelevitz, 85–110. London: Frank Cass, 1995.

———. "'Suez in Reverse': The Arab Response to the Iraqi Bid for Kuwait, 1961–63." *Diplomacy and Statecraft* 14, no. 1 (2003): 103–30.

Podeh, Elie, and Onn Winckler, eds. *Rethinking Nasserism: Revolution and Historical Memory in Modern Egypt*. Gainesville: University Press of Florida, 2004.

Pollack, Kenneth M. *Arabs at War: Military Effectiveness, 1948–1991*. Lincoln: University of Nebraska Press, 2002.

Popp, Roland. "Stumbling Decidedly into the Six-Day War." *Middle East Journal* 6, no. 2 (2006): 281–309.

Porter, Bruce D. *The USSR in Third World Conflicts: Soviet Arms and Diplomacy in Local Wars, 1945–1980*. Cambridge: Cambridge University Press, 1984.

Prasse, Karl, et al., eds. *5 Egyptian-Arabic One Act Plays: A First Reader*. Copenhagen: Museum Tusculanum, 2000.

Primakov, Evgenii M. *Russia and the Arabs: Behind the Scenes in the Middle East from the Cold War to the Present*. New York: Basic Books, 2009.

———. *Strany Aravii i kolonializm*. Moscow: Gosudarstvennoe Izdatel'stvo Politicheskoi Literatury, 1956.

Quandt, William B. "America and the Middle East: A Fifty-Year Overview." In *Diplomacy in the Middle East*, edited by L. Carl Brown, 59–74.

———. *Decade of Decisions: American Policy toward the Arab-Israeli Conflict, 1967–1976*. Berkeley: University of California Press, 1977.

Rahmy, Ali Abdel Rahman. *The Egyptian Policy in the Arab World: Intervention in Yemen, 1962–1967: Case Study*. Washington, DC: University Press of America, 1983.

Ro'i, Yaacov. *From Encroachment to Involvement: A Documentary Study of Soviet Foreign Policy in the Middle East, 1945–1973*. New York: Wiley, 1974.

Ro'i, Yaacov, and Boris Morozov, eds. *The Soviet Union and the June 1967 Six Day War*. Washington, DC: Woodrow Wilson Center Press; Stanford, CA: Stanford University Press, 2008.

Ro'i, Yaacov, and David Ronel. *The Soviet Economic Presence in Egypt and Its Political Implications*. The Soviet and East European Research Centre, the Hebrew University of Jerusalem, Research Paper no. 9, September 1974.

Rubinstein, Alvin. "The Middle East in Russia's Strategic Prism." In *Diplomacy in the Middle East*, edited by L. Carl Brown, 75–94.

Rusk, Dean, with Richard Rusk and Daniel S. Papp. *As I Saw It*. New York: W. W. Norton, 1990.

El-Sadat, Anwar. *In Search of Identity*. New York: Harper and Row, 1977.

Safran, Nadav. *From War to War: The Arab-Israeli Confrontation*. New York: Pegasus, 1969.

———. *Saudi Arabia: The Ceaseless Quest for Security*. Cambridge, MA: Belknap Press of Harvard University Press, 1985.

Sakharov, Vladimir, and Umberto Tosi. *High Treason*. New York: Ballantine Books, 1980.

Saivetz, Carol R., and Sylvia Woodby. *Soviet-Third World Relations*. Boulder, CO: Westview Press, 1985.

Salem, Paul. *Bitter Legacy: Ideology and Politics in the Arab World*. Syracuse, NY: Syracuse University Press, 1994.

Satloff, Robert. *Army and Politics in Mubarak's Egypt*. Washington, DC: Washington Institute, 1988.

Schmidt, Dana Adams. *Yemen: The Unknown War*. New York: Holt, Rinehart and Winston, 1968.

Seale, Patrick. *Asad of Syria: The Struggle for the Middle East*. Berkeley: University of California Press, 1989.

Semanov, Sergei. *Brezhnev: Pravitel' "zolotogo veka."* Moscow: Veche, 2002.

Shemesh, Moshe. *Arab Politics, Palestinian Nationalism, and the Six Day War: The Crystallization of Arab Strategy and Nasir's Descent to War, 1957–1967*. Brighton: Sussex Academic Press, 2008.

Shevchenko, Arkady N. *Breaking with Moscow*. New York: Alfred A. Knopf, 1985.

Shishchenko, I., and A. P. Glazkov, eds. *Smoliane-Internatsionalisty: Sbornik vospominanii voinov-internatsionalistov Smolenshchiny*. Smolensk: Smiadyn', 2000.

Shrader, Charles R. *The First Helicopter War: Logistics and Mobility in Algeria, 1954–1962*. Westport, CT: Praeger, 1999.

Smiley, David. *Arabian Assignment*. London: Leo Cooper, 1975.

Smolansky, Oles M. *The Soviet Union and the Arab East under Khrushchev*. Lewisburg, PA: Bucknell University Press, 1974.

Somerville-Large, Peter. *Tribes and Tribulations: A Journey in Republican Yemen*. London: Robert Hale, 1967.

Springborg, Robert. *Mubarak's Egypt: Fragmentation of the Political Order*. Boulder, CO: Westview Press, 1989.

Stephens, Robert. *Nasser: A Political Biography*. London: Allen Lane, 1971.

Stone, Randall W. *Satellites and Commissars: Strategy and Conflict in the Politics of Soviet-Bloc Trade*. Princeton, NJ: Princeton University Press, 1996.

Stookey, Robert W. *America and the Arab States: An Uneasy Encounter*. New York: John Wiley and Sons, 1975.

———. *Yemen: The Politics of the Yemen Arab Republic*. Boulder, CO: Westview Press, 1978.

Suri, Jeremy. "American Perceptions of the Soviet Threat before and during the Six Day War." In *The Soviet Union and the June 1967 Six Day War*, edited by Yaacov Ro'i and Boris Morozov, 102–21.

Taubman, William. *Khrushchev: The Man and His Era*. New York: W. W. Norton, 2003.

Taylor, John W. R. *Jane's All the World's Aircraft*. New York: McGraw-Hill, 1964–65.

Tibi, Bassam. *Arab Nationalism: Between Islam and the Nation-State*. New York: St. Martin's Press, 1997.

Trevelyan, Humphrey. *The Middle East in Revolution*. London: Macmillan, 1970.

Trofimov, Yaroslav. *The Siege of Mecca: The Forgotten Uprising in Islam's Holiest Shrine and the Birth of Al Qaeda*. New York: Anchor Books, 2008.

Ulam, Adam B. *Expansion and Coexistence: The History of Soviet Foreign Policy, 1917–67*. New York: Praeger, 1968.

United Nations Development Programme. *Arab Human Development Report 2002*. New York: United Nations Publications, 2002.

———. *Arab Human Development Report 2004*. New York: United Nations Publications, 2005.

———. *Arab Human Development Report 2009*. New York: United Nations Publications, 2009.

Váli, Ferenc A. *The Turkish Straits and NATO*. Stanford, CA: Hoover Institution Press, 1972.

Valkenier, Elizabeth K. *The Soviet Union and the Third World: An Economic Bind*. New York: Praeger, 1983.

Vassiliev, Alexei, M. *The History of Saudi Arabia*. London: Saqi Books, 1998.

———. *Russian Policy in the Middle East: From Messianism to Pragmatism*. Reading: Ithaca Press, 1993.

Vatikiotis, P. J. *Arab and Regional Politics in the Middle East*. New York: St. Martin's Press, 1984.

———. *The Egyptian Army in Politics: Pattern for New Nations?* Bloomington: Indiana University Press, 1961.

———. *Nasser and His Generation*. New York: St. Martin's Press, 1978.

Vatikiotis, P. J., ed. *Egypt since the Revolution*. New York: Praeger, 1968.

Volkogonov, Dmitri A. *Autopsy for an Empire: The Seven Leaders Who Built the Soviet Regime*. New York: Free Press, 1998.

Waterbury, John. *The Egypt of Nasser and Sadat: The Political Economy of Two Regimes*. Princeton, NJ: Princeton University Press, 1983.

Wenner, Manfred W. *Modern Yemen, 1918–1966*. Baltimore: Johns Hopkins University Press, 1967.

———. *The Yemen Arab Republic: Development and Change in an Ancient Land*. Boulder, CO: Westview Press, 1991.

Westad, Odd Arne. *The Global Cold War: Third World Interventions and the Making of Our Times*. Cambridge: Cambridge University Press, 2005.

Witty, David M. "A Regular Army in Counterinsurgency Operations: Egypt in North Yemen, 1962–1967." *Journal of Military History* 65 (April 2001): 401–40.

Woodward, Peter. *Nasser*. London: Longman, 1992.

Yost, Charles. "The Arab-Israeli War: How It Began." *Foreign Affairs* 46 (January 1968): 304–20.

Zolotarev, V. A., ed. *Rossia (SSSR) v' local'nykh voinakh i voennykh konfliktakh vtoroi poloviny XX veka*. Moscow: Kuchkovo Pole, 2000.

Zubok, Vladislav M. "Spy vs. Spy: The KGB vs. the CIA, 1960–1962," Cold War International History Project Bulletin no. 4 (1994), 22–33.

———. *A Failed Empire: The Soviet Union in the Cold War from Stalin to Gorbachev*. Chapel Hill: University of North Carolina Press, 2007.

Zubok, Vladislav M., and Constantine Pleshakov. *Inside the Kremlin's Cold War: From Stalin to Khrushchev*. Cambridge, MA: Harvard University Press, 1996.

✷ Index ✷

Note: Page numbers in italic type indicate illustrations.